Anti-racism in Britain

Manchester University Press

Racism, Resistance and Social Change

Series editors: John Solomos, Satnam Virdee, Aaron Winter

To buy or to find out more about the books currently available in this series, please go to: https://manchesteruniversitypress.co.uk/series/racism-resistance-and-social-change/.

Anti-racism in Britain

Traditions, histories and trajectories, c. 1880–present

Edited by

Saffron East, Grace Redhead and Theo Williams

MANCHESTER UNIVERSITY PRESS

Copyright © Manchester University Press 2024

While copyright in the volume as a whole is vested in Manchester University Press, copyright in individual chapters belongs to their respective authors, and no chapter may be reproduced wholly or in part without the express permission in writing of both author and publisher.

Published by Manchester University Press
Oxford Road, Manchester, M13 9PL

www.manchesteruniversitypress.co.uk

British Library Cataloguing-in-Publication Data
A catalogue record for this book is available from the British Library

ISBN 978 1 5261 7111 5 hardback

First published 2024

The publisher has no responsibility for the persistence or accuracy of URLs for any external or third-party internet websites referred to in this book, and does not guarantee that any content on such websites is, or will remain, accurate or appropriate.

Typeset by Newgen Publishing UK

Contents

Series editors' foreword — vii
List of abbreviations — viii

Introduction: Anti-racism in Britain: Traditions, histories and trajectories – Saffron East, Grace Redhead and Theo Williams — 1

Part I: Domestic, imperial and global anti-racist alliances and encounters

1 Countering racial discrimination in Britain, 1880s–1913 – David Killingray — 25
2 From racist humanitarianism to colonial human rights: The British Congo Reform Movement and the complicated history of (anti-)racism – Felix Lösing — 44
3 George Orwell, pan-Africanism and reconciling anti-imperialism with 'Britishness' – Theo Williams — 64
4 British anti-racism in Australia: Exploring the nexus through the anti-racist activism of Jessie Street, 1950–60 – Alison Holland — 79

Part II: Anti-racism and the making of postimperial Britain

5 Celebrating African culture in the north-east of England, 1930s–40s – Vanessa Mongey — 103
6 British Jews and the Race Relations Acts – Joseph Finlay — 124
7 South Asian political Blackness in Britain: Lessons and limitations of anti-racist solidarity – Saffron East — 143
8 'Unfinished activisms': From Black self-help to mutual aid organising today – Sophia Siddiqui — 164

Part III: Anti-racism, memory and identity

9 Memory, multiculturalism and anti-racism in east London, 1990–2006 – Finn Gleeson 187
10 Tartan inclusivity or workers' internationalism? The St Andrew's Day Anti-Racism March and Rally in Scotland – Talat Ahmed 207
11 'Martin Luther King fought for a colour-blind society': African American civil rights in UK political discourse – Megan Hunt 228

Afterword – Priyamvada Gopal 247
Index 254

Series editors' foreword

The study of race, racism and ethnicity has expanded greatly since the end of the twentieth century. This expansion has coincided with a growing awareness of the continuing role that these issues play in contemporary societies all over the globe. Racism, Resistance and Social Change is a new series of books that seeks to make a substantial contribution to this flourishing field of scholarship and research. We are committed to providing a forum for the publication of the highest-quality scholarship on race, racism, anti-racism and ethnic relations. As editors of this series we would like to publish both theoretically driven books and texts with an empirical frame that seek to develop further our understanding of the origins, development and contemporary forms of racisms, racial inequalities, and racial and ethnic relations. We welcome work from a range of theoretical and political perspectives, and as the series develops we ideally want to encourage a conversation that goes beyond specific national or geopolitical environments. While we are aware that there are important differences between national and regional research traditions, we hope that scholars from a variety of disciplines and multidisciplinary frames will take the opportunity to include their research work in the series.

As the title of the series highlights, we also welcome texts that can address issues about resistance and anti-racism as well as the role of political and policy interventions in this rapidly evolving discipline. The changing forms of racist mobilisation and expression that have come to the fore in recent years have highlighted the need for more reflection and research on the role of political and civil society mobilisations in this field.

We are committed to building on theoretical advances by providing an arena for new and challenging theoretical and empirical studies on the changing morphology of race and racism in contemporary societies.

Abbreviations

ACSHO	African-Caribbean Self-Help Organisation
AGO	Archive of Gilda O'Neill, Bishopsgate, London
APS	Aborigines' Protection Society
ARN	Anti-Raids Network
ASAPS	Anti-Slavery and Aborigines' Protection Society
ASS	Anti-Slavery Society
ATOR	*African Times and Oriental Review*
AYM	Asian Youth Movement
BAME	Black, Asian and Minority Ethnic
BBC	British Broadcasting Corporation
BHM	Black History Month
BIPOC	Black, Indigenous and People of Colour
BLF	Black Liberation Front
BNP	British National Party
BoD	Board of Deputies
BoD DC	Board of Deputies Defence Committee
BPA	Black People's Alliance
BUFP	Black Unity and Freedom Party
BWFYA	Broadwater Farm Youth Association
CAR	Council for Aboriginal Rights
CARD	Campaign against Racial Discrimination
CMEB	Commission for Multi-Ethnic Britain
CPGB	Communist Party of Great Britain
CPSA	Civil and Public Services Association
CRE	Commission for Racial Equality
DCMS	Department for Culture, Media and Sport
EIC	East India Company
EU	European Union
FCAA	Federal Council for Aboriginal Advancement
FN	Front National

List of abbreviations

GCUAC	Glasgow Caledonian University Archive Centre, Records of the Scottish Trades Union Congress
GLC	Greater London Council
IASB	International African Service Bureau
ICMAA	International Coloured Mutual Aid Association
ILP	Independent Labour Party
IWA	Indian Workers' Association
LCP	League of Coloured Peoples
LMA	London Metropolitan Archives
LPGPC	Law, Parliamentary and General Purposes Committee
LUB	League of Universal Brotherhood
MSF	Manufacturing, Science and Finance
NAA	National Archives of Australia
NALGO	National and Local Government Officers' Association
NGO	Non-governmental organisation
NLA	National Library of Australia
NSM	New Social Movement
OWAAD	Organisation of Women of African and Asian Descent
PoC	person/people of colour
RAAS	Radical Action Adjustment Society
SAAC	Scottish Asian Action Committee
SARM	Scottish Anti-Racist Movement
SBS	Southall Black Sisters
SNP	Scottish National Party
SOAS	School of Oriental and African Studies, University of London
SRBM	Society for the Recognition of the Brotherhood of Man
STUC	Scottish Trades Union Congress
SU	Student Union
SYM	Southall Youth Movement
TNA	The National Archives, Kew
TUC	Trades Union Congress
UBWAG	United Black Women's Action Group
UCPA	Universal Coloured People's Association
UN	United Nations
UNIA	Universal Negro Improvement Association
WASU	West African Students' Union
WL	Wiener Library, London

Introduction: Anti-racism in Britain: Traditions, histories and trajectories

Saffron East, Grace Redhead and Theo Williams

The histories of racism and anti-racism in Britain are today a subject of national debate. This volume brings together contributions from a conference that took place in February 2021, when Black Lives Matter protests had, the previous summer, toppled the statue of the slave-trader Edward Colston in Bristol. This protest was the culmination of years of campaigning for its removal by local anti-racist activists, part of what Saima Nasar calls 'an established tradition of social justice campaigning', in a city that has 'historically placed itself at the centre of Britain's anti-racist struggles'. In response, supporters of Colston's statue presented their own triumphalist histories of British anti-racism – in particular its role in the abolitionist movement, so central to national myth-making about traditions of tolerance and liberty.[1] Within these mythologised visions of British anti-racism, used to delegitimise anti-racist action in the present, Britain's elites – and therefore the class and race hierarchies of Britain – are positioned as having handed freedom and equality down. The research presented within this volume interrogates histories of anti-racism in Britain, and argues that if Britain has a long history of anti-racism, then it has been a history made by the 'bitterly fought struggles' of its racialised citizens and colonial subjects.[2]

This introduction falls into five parts. The first considers Britain's histories and traditions of anti-racism, and particularly the struggle between British traditions of anti-racism and the British institutions that have sought to borrow selectively from these traditions in order to remake and defend whiteness and racial hierarchies. The second section considers how anti-racism in Britain emerged within the metropolitan space of imperial and later postcolonial Britain, where encounters between transnational intellectual traditions of pan-Africanism, socialism and Christian idealism challenged imperial orders, and where migrants from the Empire, Commonwealth or wider world met, lived together, and organised together. The third section argues that beyond such encounters, those committed to anti-racism in Britain worked consciously to construct solidarities around a range of causes, identities, political philosophies and activist practices. While some solidarities fragmented, these histories are reanimated and reclaimed by new generations. The fourth section considers how these histories speak to present orientations of anti-racism, and concepts of solidarity and history in contemporary anti-racist movements. The final section outlines the structure of the volume.

A British 'tradition'? Exploring paternalism and solidarity

Is there a 'tradition' of British anti-racism? Britain has historically represented itself as a nation underpinned by values of liberalism, multiculturalism and 'tolerance'. Yet, as Kennetta Hammond Perry has analysed, the British state and media constructed and upheld this 'mystique of British anti-racism' to protect Britain's international reputation.[3] In this way, Britain's history of violent slavery, colonialism and imperialism is denied, and the ways that British statecraft, media and institutions have continued to reproduce racism and inequality, even after racial equality was enshrined in law, are obscured. Indeed, Britain's traditions of intolerance, racism and fascism, and the continuities, remakings and reinventions of these traditions, have been well documented.[4]

Anti-racist movements in Britain have confronted overt racism in Britain's institutions, politics and everyday life, but have also confronted the false and distorted histories of British 'anti-racism' characterised by what Perry has called the 'reveries of abolition construed by a white British imaginary'.[5] This set of historical discourses locates abolition as a completed and past event, rather than as an ongoing project, and seeks to erase Britain's violent history of colonialism, slavery and exclusion by presenting Britain as progressive, tolerant and committed to equality. Many scholars have explored the construction and use of this 'history', the repression of histories that cast light on British atrocities in its Empire, and the legacies of forced labour and extracted wealth in the metropole.[6] This mythologised tradition of British 'tolerance' and abolition is used in the present to justify racist and exclusionary policy – for example in the public discussion of asylum and refugee policy, in which idealised memories of 'generosity' to the refugees of the past are mobilised to absolve Britain of responsibility in the present.[7] The history of 'liberal paternalism' and postwar British humanitarian non-governmental organisations (NGOs) is 'a history of whiteness', seeking to resuscitate 'white moral authority'.[8] Invocations of a British tradition of anti-racism have long been enlisted to ensure the continuation of racialised hierarchies. Its modality is paternalism – in which equality, civil rights and justice can only be granted from above.

Internal divisions in geography, government and identity have shaped multiple mythologies of anti-racism across the nations of Britain, which unsettle notions of a 'British' anti-racism. Recent studies have noted that political narratives of Wales and Scotland as 'tolerant of difference' have emerged in opposition to a chauvinist English identity.[9] Meanwhile, notions of an 'inclusive', newly multicultural British identity, defined against a purportedly ethnocentric Scottish or Welsh nationalism, have been used to argue for the continued existence of the Union.[10] Such dichotomies erase Wales and Scotland's historic involvement in the imperial project, and all the British nations' histories of racial violence and investment in nationalist ethnocentrism.[11]

The 'mystique' of British anti-racism, with its visions of a tolerant and just white British elite handing down freedom and reform, does not incorporate the documented histories of grassroots anti-racism in the British metropole and territories.[12] Historians have demonstrated the reverse influence of the Empire, and specifically of the racialised, colonised and enslaved people who constituted that Empire, upon Britain. Priyamvada Gopal has argued that anti-colonialism in the British Empire shaped British society, intellectual life, law and governance over the nineteenth and twentieth centuries.[13] A rich historiography now shows that the boundaries and conceptions of British citizenship were renegotiated and redrawn by the migrants of the New Commonwealth, and by successive generations of Black and Asian Britons.[14] If there is a meaningful 'tradition' of British anti-racism, it was created by citizens and subjects (especially those whom Satnam Virdee has described as 'racialized outsiders') rather than by the British state or elite.[15] As Elizabeth M. Williams argues, '[t]he tradition of black radicalism in reaction to white racism in Britain has as long a history as racial discrimination itself'.[16] These actors engaged in resisting British racism, dethroning the 'mystique' of tolerance, and brokering alliances and solidarities across racial, ethnic and religious lines. This is what this book explores – the continuities and breaks, encounters and alliances, of anti-racism that resisted and challenged white British hegemony, remade British spaces and redefined British identities. It is a shifting and ongoing project of resistance with multiple points of geographic, intellectual and political origin.[17]

In tracing the history of anti-racism in Britain, we find it is characterised at one end of the spectrum by paternalism and at the other end by solidarity. The former is usually associated with liberalism, and the latter usually with socialism (although many self-described left-wing movements have not been free from paternalistic impulses). Here, we follow David Featherstone in understanding *solidarity* as 'a relation forged through political struggle which seeks to challenge forms of oppression'. It is a 'transformative relation' that can create links 'between places, activists, diverse social groups'.

It is a practice that can be forged 'from below' or through 'pressure from without'. Capturing the transnational and multiethnic coalitions that characterise anti-racism, solidarities 'are constructed through uneven power relations and geographies'.[18] We define *paternalism* as a relation characterised by a belief in the fundamental inequality of the parties. While solidarity, even if constructed through uneven power relations, at least aims toward a horizontal relation, paternalism never attempts to be anything other than a vertical one. Paternalistic anti-racists imagine themselves to be effecting change from above, and usually do not seek to unsettle social relations as broadly or as deeply as their more radical counterparts. We identify this paternalistic–solidaristic spectrum as a major axis within British anti-racist culture, and just as important as the frequently asked question of whether one *is* or *is not* an (anti-)racist.

Many would rightly argue that paternalism, rooted as it is in assumptions of superiority, is a tool of racism rather than anti-racism. However, movements of solidarity and abolition often found themselves uncomfortably sharing rhetorical and organisational space with paternalist actors. As Marc Matera argues, in the interwar period Black internationalists appropriated the practices and languages of British liberal civic society and its colonial regime (such as 'commonwealth' and 'self-government') in order 'to make political and material demands on the colonial state'.[19] The Institute of Race Relations originated in traditions of imperial paternalism, then transitioned to advising the British government on anti-discrimination and postcolonial 'integration', before a revolt among its junior staff led to its reorientation as a grassroots anti-racist organisation in 1972.[20] Recent work has detailed tensions between the postwar Anglican Church's paternalist hierarchy and the efforts of Anglican vicars based in inner-city parishes to minister to and represent the needs of Black parishioners in 1980s Britain.[21] In postwar Britain, many anti-racist organisations have found themselves having to operate at least partly within the British state's frameworks for what Alana Lentin has called 'post-racism racism management'.[22] Schofield et al. recently argued in their study of neoliberal 'enterprise' and anti-racism that '[s]eeing Black activism in the 1980s as divided into the incorporated "professionals" and the authentic radicalism of those who remained outside the state is to ignore the fact that these activists often worked in the same spaces and towards the same ends'.[23] The conference from which this volume originated closely illustrated the complexity of anti-racist movements in British history – of activists who adopted, through pragmatism or conviction, a range of rhetorical and political tools; a range of proximities to British institutions; and a range of allies, comrades and partners. Within this volume, anti-racist actors worked to hold together deeply felt commitments and sometimes fragile alliances. These alliances were sometimes fragmented by the propensity of the state and British institutions to borrow anti-racist rhetoric to justify their own ends. It is this dynamic of borrowing that allows the 'mystique' of British anti-racism to thrive, attributing the extension of civil, social and political rights to racialised people living under British rule to institutional goodwill, rather than locating its origins in those who argued and campaigned for it. This is the dynamic that weaves these two 'traditions' together.

Contributions in this volume explore the tradition and counter-traditions of anti-racism in Britain. David Killingray and Saffron East point to the role of transnational movements and relationships in creating a foundation of anti-racist practice in Britain, as political, intellectual and religious movements such as anti-colonialism, pan-Africanism, Marxist internationalism and Quakerism came into contact with one another in Britain. Killingray points to the influence of paternalist white social reformers, as well as the profound importance of activists such as Celestine Edwards and Ida B. Wells, in shaping such movements. Felix Lösing's contribution similarly explores some of the shortcomings of white paternalism. British activists who opposed the atrocities of the Congo Free State often did so in order to uphold European supremacy over Africans. Joseph Finlay's chapter highlights perhaps a missed opportunity for the creation of multiethnic solidarities, as British Jews pursued divergent aims from those of Black and Asian Britons in the creation of the Race Relations Acts of the 1960s and 1970s. As Theo Williams and Vanessa Mongey show, anti-racist movements offered a range of solutions that sometimes used or adapted liberal notions of freedom, emancipation and self-determination. As Mongey shows, some activists avoided explicitly radical arguments around the harms of colonialism, fearing that they would be seen as Communists and thus hindering their ultimate aim of African independence or self-rule. Williams paints a picture of the anti-racist British Commonwealth that was the vision of thinkers such as George Padmore, C. L. R. James and George Orwell. He emphasises, however, that Padmore and James were not deferring to tradition and hierarchy, but were seeking to overthrow an imperial order, whereas Orwell had faith in the basic 'decency' of British institutions.

This volume also demonstrates how grassroots anti-racism has often been obscured by popular or institutional histories of liberal paternalism. Talat Ahmed and Alison Holland, in their respective case studies of the Scottish Trades Union Congress's (STUC) annual St Andrew's Day Anti-Racism March and Rally, and of the Aboriginal Labour Movement, argue that the work of grassroots labour activists representing racialised communities has been erased. Other chapters pick up on moments in which institutional liberal paternalism eclipsed or neutralised more radical activism 'from below'. Sophia Siddiqui argues that many local 'self-help' initiatives were fragmented by the provision of small state grants from the 1980s onward, inhibiting alliances, particularly between communities. Finn Gleeson and Megan Hunt argue that liberal thinking sought to redefine and limit what racism (and therefore anti-racism) was. In the 1990s, Gleeson argues, racism was seen as ignorance and 'an aberration deriving from political neglect and economic alienation', and Hunt argues that in the twenty-first century British politicians limited definitions of racism to extremes of racial violence whilst making British citizenship contingent on integrating into British 'culture'.

Space, memory and the creation of anti-racist traditions

A theme that runs throughout this volume is the interplay among memory, place and migration in the generation of anti-racist thought and action. The long history of Black and Asian people travelling to and living in Britain is critical to any anti-racist British tradition. Much historical research has demonstrated that Black, Asian and other racialised people have lived in the urban and rural areas of Britain since the inception of the transatlantic slave trade.[24] African and Caribbean people came to Britain in significant numbers in the late nineteenth century as a consequence of imperial trade, and the First World War saw further arrivals of Black seafarers. Britain's position as an imperial metropolis, where trade and labour from the Empire converged, made it an imperial 'contact zone'. Michael Goebel has argued in his study of interwar Paris that 'the French capital functioned as a vantage point that clarified the contours of a global system', and that it was 'through contact, networks and connectivity that later Third World nationalists dreamed up a post-imperial world order'.[25] Imaobong Umoren argues that Britain too 'became an important space for discussions about race and empire', as travel, mobility and border-crossing shaped imperial and postcolonial politics and anti-racist action among Black women activists.[26] In the interwar period, as Marc Matera has shown, Black men and women from Africa and the Caribbean came to London to petition the Colonial Office in Whitehall, to perform music in its clubs in Bloomsbury and Soho, and to attend its universities. The imperial metropolis became 'a site of black cultural and intellectual production', where its 'social relations and spaces ... generated this work and precarious political solidarities'.[27]

After the Second World War, as metropolitan Britain sought Commonwealth labour for the rebuilding of the economy and the construction of the welfare state's institutions, hundreds of thousands of men and women from the Empire migrated to Britain. As Kennetta Hammond Perry has argued, these migrants asserted a claim to the space of the imperial metropolis and so reconfigured British citizenship. In Perry's account, this process reflected the selective adoption of a narrative of Britain as 'Mother Country' by Caribbean subjects, and an imagined Caribbean relationship with Britain that meant 'inclusion into a transnational body of British citizens whose shared rights, privileges, and freedoms were made universal in the imperial space of the metropole'.[28] This imagined sense of belonging and equality was spatialised in the places of Britain itself, and this claim was asserted through travel and mobility. Once in Britain, migrants confronted the racism of the British state and engaged in efforts 'to make cities like London the place for them'.[29] While Britain is not a space in which shared rights and freedoms are made universal, as Nadine El-Enany has written,

> the presence in Britain of racialised people with histories of colonisation has the effect of challenging and troubling white supremacist structures ... This troubling occurs in part through the taking up of physical space, but also in serving as a defiant reminder of Britain's colonial identity and the origins of its wealth.[30]

If there is a tradition of British anti-racism, then, this tradition was made and remade through its spaces. The site of metropolitan Britain drew those it had colonised and enslaved toward it, and many travelled there with visions or expectations of a postimperial order that they had formed elsewhere. Britain's spaces, hostile as they often were, were sometimes only transient homes. As Caroline Bressey and Gemma Romain show, queer Black spaces and identities in Britain in the 1920s and 1930s were not fixed by city boundaries or national borders, as queer Black people left to make homes elsewhere.[31] These spaces were transnational spaces, and Britain was one window into the 'global stage' in which Black activism and visions of freedom took shape.[32] Recent scholarship has critiqued the focus on metropolitan spaces as centres for anti-imperialism, and called us to examine 'the ways through which colonized and postcolonial subjects cultivated knowledge "sideways", meaning they inter-connected tactically, materially and intellectually without needing to call upon the imperial centre for interpretation or authorization'.[33] The anti-racist visions for new world orders that were imagined in the private rooms and public halls of Britain absolutely transcended the island itself – but the fact these visions were formed *here* is deeply meaningful for the study of British history.

Race politics – whether those of white nationalism, imperial paternalism or anti-colonialism – have been made globally. And each movement – oppressive or liberatory, reactionary or progressive – has responded to its opponents' countervailing forces and reformulated itself accordingly.[34] Britain is part of these transnational circuits in which the politics of race have been made and staged. But it also retains national particularities, which transnational historical approaches can help to tease out. As Akira Iriye has argued, 'The transnational approach to the study of history ... does not deny the existence of nations and the roles they play in contributing to defining the world at a given moment in time.'[35] Rather, national and transnational histories are fundamentally interwoven; each is necessary to illuminate the other. Richard Drayton and David Motadel have pointed to how global history can help us to understand the particularities of the nation and the local, while simultaneously safeguarding against the construction of mythologised national pasts.[36] This book, while postulating a British tradition of anti-racism, seeks to locate this tradition within broader, global traditions, which it has both shaped and been shaped by.

Just as a transnational lens demonstrates the porousness of borders to currents of anti-racist thought and action, it observes distinctive local histories, communities and spaces within nations, and the fractures and discontinuities in national identities and 'traditions' – what David Featherstone calls 'situated forms of translocal solidarity, agency and identities'.[37] This introduction opened with the toppling of Edward Colston's statue in Bristol in 2020 – an event in which a local tradition of anti-racist reckoning with Bristol's colonial past confronted those who would speak for a hegemonic British 'tradition' of tolerance and justice, in the midst of a transnational uprising following the murder of George Floyd in Minneapolis, USA. Historians have explored how distinct ecologies of local government, communities, industries and histories shaped anti-racist action (or its absence) across Britain. Daisy Payling has explored how the city council of Sheffield in the 1980s took up aspects of identity politics around race and gender 'to an extent that would not alienate white working-class voters', while Stephen Brooke's study of racial harassment in London in the same period finds that 'fear ... formed a powerful emotional community' in the East End, which led to action by local Asian communities and by the Greater London Council.[38]

This book omits a thorough examination of anti-racist action in Wales, a country with a distinct imperial and anti-racist history. Welsh people were underrepresented in the personnel of the British Empire, and their involvement particularly emphasised missionary work. The image of the Welsh missionary in the colonies was a figure of 'Welsh pride', and of pride in the Empire that many saw as more than an English project.[39] But others have argued that the Welsh mission 'provided a route into the culture for anti-imperialist ideas about race, difference and power'.[40] The South Wales coal trade drew many colonial seamen into Cardiff and the surrounding area, and Cardiff was one of the seaports where the 1919 riots broke out, the events there drawing comment from Black radicals globally.[41] Butetown was among the areas with the largest ethnic minority population in Britain before the postwar period, and was a significant local node for anti-racist resistance in early twentieth-century Britain; in recent years, the area has been a place for refugee settlement.[42] So while Wales, like England, has an entangled imperial history, longstanding multiracial communities and histories of racist violence, writers such as Charlotte Williams have argued that the position of Welshness as a minority identity also places it within a complicated relation to whiteness.[43] Future research into anti-racist thought and activism in Britain might build on the work of this volume to incorporate the local histories and practices of anti-racism in Wales into studies of British anti-racism, and ask how these practices have taken shape alongside, and been internally differentiated from, concepts of race, multiculturalism and nationhood in Britain.

A key thread running through this volume is that the existence of spaces in which racialised people could meet, talk and organise was central to anti-racist activism in Britain, and that the creation and defence of such spaces was activism in itself. Vanessa Mongey and Sophia Siddiqui both show that the need for dedicated spaces for racialised people drove mutual aid work both in 1930s north-east sailors' houses and the 1970s spaces for women and young people – and that in both instances, such spaces were seen as threatening by British institutions such as the British Sailors Society and the police. Joseph Finlay's chapter demonstrates the reluctance of the British legislature to engage with questions of equal access to schools, private clubs, hotels and private lodging in discussions about the Race Relations Acts. The volume also shows that the historically constructed meanings of spaces have shaped anti-racist movements to and in Britain. Theo Williams and Talat Ahmed explore such mythologised anti-racist spaces, with Williams considering how anti-imperialist activists were partly drawn to England in the 1930s because of visions of anti-slavery societies and radical left movements, while Ahmed deconstructs the 'exceptionalist' notion of Scotland as a tolerant space. Felix Lösing's chapter shows how European writers created a discursive spatial binary between 'Brightest Europe' and 'Darkest Africa', as well as how the British Congo Reform Movement has been mythologised as an honourable humanitarian effort that mobilised British people against the horrors of colonialism. Saffron East and Finn Gleeson's chapters – respectively case studies of 1970s Southall and the 1990s East End – illustrate how the relationship between place and the historical moment determines the articulation of both anti-racist solidarities and racism. David Killingray, Alison Holland and Megan Hunt each emphasise the importance of the transnational movement of ideas from local contexts, through which activists identified global processes of racism and colonialism, and Holland and Hunt demonstrate how states attempt to use borders to inhibit the spread of liberatory politics.

Structures of solidarity

The space of the imperial metropole as a place of encounter, and the creation of shared spaces of refuge and resistance for racialised people in Britain, were central to the forging of an anti-racist 'tradition' in Britain. However, alliances were of course not simply formed by proximity. Once people encountered one another in the spaces of the imperial metropole, partnerships, exchanges, relationships and organisations were made through the work of solidarity, as people invested in anti-racism sought to understand one another and come together not simply through a single shared identity or goal, but also to support 'the struggle of another group or individual'.[44] Priyamvada Gopal argues that it took effort, in twentieth-century anti-colonial movements, to create solidarities 'where contiguity of interests had to be argued for and forged rather than taken for granted'.[45] This work sought to undo the work of imperialism, for central to the operation of British colonialism and slavery was the deliberate fragmentation of any possible solidarities between those it had colonised and enslaved, by breaking up communities, families and those with shared languages. As James Baldwin explained to an audience at the West Indian Student Centre in London in 1968:

> If we could have spoken to each other we might have been able to figure out what was happening to us. And if we could have figured out what was happening to us we might have been able to prevent it … we would have had in short a kind of solidarity which is a kind of identity which might have allowed us – which might have made the history of slavery very different.[46]

In the period covered by this book, many anti-racist activists spoke to one another and developed solidarities in resistance to racism, colonialism and imperialism. Just as racism is 'highly contextual and can shift dramatically depending on the power relations in micro-environments within larger structures of power', the structures of anti-racist solidarity could be equally fluid, with alliances that were possible in one place or time becoming impossible in others.[47] Rob Waters has shown that while 1970s and 1980s alliances emerging from political Blackness risked the marginalisation of differences (particularly emphasising African diaspora and masculine experiences or perspectives), political Blackness was also 'embraced as a politics of complementarity and multidirectionality', often forged through shared engagement with a transnational array of political texts, music, style and countercultures, and rallying around a range of political causes.[48] Cultures of solidarity were consciously constructed and invested in by their participants.

Much historical literature has considered histories of anti-racist solidarity in Britain, and in particular how this has both operated through, and been fragmented by, the politics of class. As scholars such as Peter Fryer and Caroline Bressey have shown, some exponents of British working-class politics in the eighteenth and nineteenth centuries adopted expansive frameworks of solidarity that incorporated both the struggle of indentured or enslaved people in the colonies and the struggle of white workers in the industries of the British metropole.[49] Yet, as Bressey argues, in the twentieth century the working-class movement was split between those who subscribed to the expansive, international and anti-racist framework of equality and white workers who framed their identities through whiteness and nationalism.[50] Narratives reinforcing divisions between the Black and white working class have arguably been enshrined in historiography – recent scholarship has observed that the turn toward deindustrialisation as a metanarrative in modern British history has often implicitly framed the working class as white, even though 'just as the histories of industrialization and imperialism are inextricably bound together, so too are the histories of their unravelling'.[51] The complex intersections of class and race could also surface within and disrupt movements organised around anti-racism and anti-colonialism. Recent analyses have argued that though transnational movements for anti-colonialism or anti-racism might find 'a terrain for solidarity, commitment to emancipatory political horizons, and liberation (writ large), such a terrain also (inevitably) replicates certain hierarchies of class, race and gender'.[52]

Trade unions in postwar Britain have a long history of discrimination and neglect toward non-white workers – in particular, objections to migration and failing to challenge management colour bars. Early instances of union activism protesting workplace racism often found few allies among white union members and Race Relations Boards, and were sustained instead by support from community organisations.[53] Union activism by South Asian women was often not understood as an act of labour organisation – as with the 1976–8 Grunwick strike, which was represented in some quarters as personal, familial or cultural 'loyalty' rather read through a framework of political, collective solidarity 'based on class, race and a sense of injustice'.[54] Satnam Virdee sees, in the solidarity demonstrated with the Grunwick dispute by other unions such as the London dockers, 'the expansion of a conception and language of class that could now encompass racialised minority workers as well'.[55] Others, however, have pointed out that if there had been a change, it had been the process by which 'black and Asian workers claimed space for themselves' within trade union activism.[56] Diarmaid Kelliher, in his study of movements of solidarity in London with the 1984–5 miners' strike, identifies that alliances were constructed across lines of gender, class and race during this period. These groups often consciously recorded their histories – part of efforts to construct 'usable pasts' that might aid 'in the making of new cultures of solidarity'.[57]

This volume reflects on how various forms of class analysis could both envision solidarities and break them apart. Theo Williams and Finn Gleeson identify invocations of class consciousness: by pan-African activists in 1930s Britain who believed that white working-class racism was instilled by a ruling capitalist class, and in the 1990s and 2000s East End dominated by political narratives around a white working class 'betrayed' by Commonwealth migration. Other chapters observe that labour was a key axis across which both racism and anti-racist solidarity operated. Alison Holland and Talat Ahmed demonstrate that labour activism was an arena in which anti-racist tradition was shaped 'from below' as opposed to being constructed by political elites.

The position of women in anti-racist struggles and movements has been fraught, not least because of the gendered violence experienced by racialised women within their communities, and the failure of male-led anti-racist movements to address this violence. Sophia Siddiqui notes the 'double-edged sword' faced by South Asian women in Britain, who were subject to the racism of the state and the streets, and to patriarchal domestic relationships. Both she and Saffron East observe that South Asian women invested in political Blackness have believed in the importance of refuges run *by* South Asian women *for* South Asian women facing domestic violence.

This volume demonstrates that solidarity often responded to (or was fractured by) the involvement of the British state, as the state sought to manage the frustration and anger of Black, Asian and Jewish people to avoid international condemnation and to prevent the widespread adoption of radical politics. Vanessa Mongey, Joseph Finlay, Sophia Siddiqui and Megan Hunt all show that the British state has sought to pacify racialised communities in Britain, and split transnational solidarity movements, by making small concessions to individual groups or organisations or by incorporating limited anti-racist critique into liberal governance. In the case of the Congo Reform Movement, as Felix Lösing demonstrates, the British political elite challenged the worst excesses of the Congo Free State in order to protect European colonial rule as a whole. But the experience of being targeted or neglected by the British state was also a common experience around which otherwise different communities could form solidaristic alliances. David Killingray shows that in the late nineteenth and early twentieth centuries, pan-African organisations were formed by activists of African descent living under the aegis of the British Empire, with the purpose of appealing to local and imperial governments. Sophia Siddiqui and Saffron East both show that the experience of racialisation and state violence in Britain meant that communities with different global origins, religions or racial identities worked together to fight and protect one another from state racism.

Continuities and trajectories of anti-racism into the present

This volume holds conclusions that bear on the politics of anti-racism in Britain today. Contributions to the book reflect on the 'usable pasts' offered by these histories. Sophia Siddiqui reflects on Angela Davis's concept of 'unfinished activisms', arguing that the historical legacies of 1970s mutual aid and self-help organisations were 'reactivated' during the COVID-19 pandemic. Saffron East points to the 'alternative legacy' of the 1970s Southall youth movements, which constructed solidarity around shared common goals rather than common oppressions, and whose localism allowed them to react as much to Southall's local conservatism and religiosity as to the racism of wider British society. Talat Ahmed emphasises the importance of 'bottom-up' anti-racist action within the STUC, which integrated the anti-racist activism of its South Asian members and reoriented its structures in response, rather than imposing performative anti-racist gestures 'from above'.

These three chapters also discuss the formation, history and continued relevance of the 'Black' political identity – showing that historically, political Blackness has been used as a tool to unite racialised activists in their resistance projects. It represented a socialist and anti-colonial anti-racism that had a global outlook, despite being forged in Britain through local struggles. East, Ahmed and Siddiqui all point to the ways in which South Asian anti-racists actively constructed Black politics. Of the three, East is the most ambivalent about political Blackness, but is by no means dismissive of its strengths. She makes the case for its replacement by a concept of 'solidarity'. In common with Ahmed and Siddiqui, she articulates a vision of anti-racist politics with socialism and solidarity at its core. As such, both Ahmed and East offer critiques of efforts to commodify anti-racism in the twenty-first century. East comments on the commodification of solidarity, and its increased expression in material consumption, which fails to engage with the entanglement between racial violence and systems of global capitalism. Ahmed observes that the contemporary emphasis on 'allyship' is often paternalism in another guise – performative gestures that seek social validation and acceptance whilst being unwilling to 'sacrifice their social and economic capital to challenge the systems they benefit from'.

The histories and traditions of anti-racist solidarity in Britain are crucial in combating the dominant paternalist mythic narratives about a liberal and emancipatory British 'tolerance'. Megan Hunt argues that for many British students, histories of the United States Civil Rights movement are the first formal education they receive in histories of race and racism, and that such histories are rarely linked to concurrent anti-racist action in Britain, nor to the interlinked histories of colonialism, slavery and global capitalism that the two countries share. This volume spans over a century of anti-racist activism that articulated and challenged the injustices and legacies of British colonialism, imperialism and white supremacy, as it has manifested across the spectrum from far-right fascism to 'colour-blind' liberalism. Such histories not only lay bare the mythology of British 'tolerance', but illustrate how such a myth has served to obscure radical traditions of anti-racist solidarity. When this conference took place in early 2021, UK universities were announcing their commitments to the teaching of Black British history and the histories of race and racism in Britain, with a number of new appointments in this field. Several years on, courses on Black history at several institutions have been reduced or cut completely.[58] The implications of such decisions for histories and scholars of anti-racism and for anti-racist practice are serious.

Structure and chapter summaries

The volume is structured broadly chronologically, but each section is also thematic. The first section explores domestic, imperial and global anti-racist alliances and encounters within contexts of ongoing colonialism. David Killingray examines the relationships between Black and white opponents of 'racialism' in Britain during the late nineteenth and early twentieth centuries. He explores the role of Christian idealism in shaping the opposition to 'caste' led by white women who built on Quaker networks, and in influencing the ideas of Black anti-racist leaders such as Alice Kinloch, David E. Tobias and Henry Sylvester Williams. Killingray shows that white social reformers such as Henry Fox Bourne and John Harris were disdainful about engaging with Black people as equal partners in anti-colonial movements, but also that the condemnation of race prejudice by activists such as Celestine Edwards and Ida B. Wells, as well as lesser-known figures such as Dr Theophilus Scholes, was profoundly influential within certain sections of British social activism.

Felix Lösing uses the example of the British Congo Reform Movement to explore the colonial and racist underpinnings to the development of human rights. The movement has often been lauded as exemplary humanitarianism. Lösing, however, demonstrates that scholars have misinterpreted the movement in their portrayal of it as an antipode to the moral corrosion of New Imperialism. Through discussing prominent Congo reform activists and writers such as Roger Casement, Edmund D. Morel and Harold Spender, his chapter shows that racist beliefs in fact constituted the ideological common ground of colonising 'villains' and humanitarian 'heroes' in the great Congo controversy.

Theo Williams explores how activist-intellectuals on the British left attempted to reconcile Britishness with anti-imperialism, looking particularly at the political thought of pan-Africanists C. L. R. James and George Padmore, and at the work of George Orwell. Williams shows that Padmore and James, through embracing certain forms of British identity, made claims for the ending of colonial subjecthood and the creation of commonwealth citizenship, accompanied by the overthrow of racial capitalism achieved through alliances between pan-Africanism and a British revolutionary proletariat. These ideas influenced Orwell, who for a time advocated that the British Empire be replaced by a federation of socialist states, but also wished to draw on the resources of empire to support the British war effort during the 1940s. This episode points to an instructive example of how left-wing actors have sought to reconcile anti-imperialism with Britishness, and the fault lines they have encountered in doing so.

Alison Holland explores the influence of British anti-racism politics and activism on the anti-racist rights agenda in Australia in the 1950s and 1960s, focusing on the politics and activism of Australian feminist Jessie Street. Street was appointed by the Anti-Slavery and Aborigines' Protection Society to facilitate their attempt to improve Aboriginal conditions in Australia before the United Nations. Holland shows that Street's understanding of the position of Aboriginal people in 1950s Australia was informed by her exposure to the anti-colonial and anti-apartheid movements integral to the postwar anti-racism politics in England and in Africa. This chapter argues that just as there are strong Anglo-Australian links in Australia's racist heritage, there is also a long, thin vein of anti-racism in Australia inspired by the British tradition.

The second section explores anti-racism and the making of postimperial Britain. Vanessa Mongey explores the activities of African students in the northeast of England in the 1930s and 1940s, who launched an anti-racist campaign centred on educational events about the history and culture of West Africa, as well as creating safe spaces for Black students. Mongey argues that class played a central role in this anti-racist campaign led by mostly privileged West African students, and that class shaped how these students interacted with other Black inhabitants and migrants in the region, such as African Caribbean sailors or forestry workers. Class also informed the image of Africa that these students presented to their audiences, particularly their emphasis on 'culture', which risked predicating acceptance on respectability.

Joseph Finlay investigates the relationship of British Jewish individuals and institutions to the creation of the Race Relations Acts of 1965, 1968 and 1976. He demonstrates that for many MPs in the early 1960s, defending Jews against fascist antisemitism was a greater priority than protecting Black and Asian people from discrimination in housing, the workplace and hospitality venues. However, there remained considerable doubt about which of the given categories of 'colour, race, nationality or ethnic or national origins' Jews were supposed to fit – a situation heightened by the refusal of successive governments to include 'religion' as a protected category, despite many British Jews defining their Jewishness in religious rather than ethnic terms.[59] Finlay explores how the Race Relations Acts brought, for the first time, a racial understanding of Jewishness into British law, with ramifications for internal Jewish identity and implications for relations between Jews and other ethnic minority groups.

Saffron East develops our understanding of the rich histories of anti-racism in 1970s and 1980s Britain by exploring the specificities of South Asian engagement with Black radical politics, and particularly with concepts of Black political identity. East compares the politics of the Black People's Alliance with the later organisations, the Southall Youth Movement and Southall Black Sisters. She argues that for first-generation South Asian migrants, political Blackness was a tool for articulating anti-racist unity and uniting racialised people in Britain to protest racism, and that for the second generation, broader political frameworks of socialism, anti-racism and secularism offered opportunities for unity and solidarity within Southall's local context.

Sophia Siddiqui explores traditions of mutual aid and self-help in Britain's Black working-class communities, built on principles of care, resource sharing, building self-sufficiency and self-reliance, and commitment to community. Siddiqui discusses initiatives such as Harambee and the United Black Women's Action Group, and how such organisations operated to protect their communities against state violence and to fulfil community needs, which had been neglected by the British State. Although many Black self-help initiatives fragmented following the state's multiculturalism policies, Siddiqui argues that these histories of self-help are carried forward and reactivated in the present by creative archival projects and mutual aid activism during the COVID-19 pandemic.

The third section of the volume explores anti-racism, memory and identity in recent and contemporary British history and politics. Finn Gleeson analyses debates about racism and history in 1990s and 2000s Britain through the site of east London. The East End's position as a contact point between the industrial society of metropolitan Britain and the people and extracted resources of the Empire made it one of Britain's most vivid sites of multiculture, and of racist violence and electoral and state-based racism. In light of this, Gleeson argues that memory is significant to the history of multiculturalism at the turn of the twenty-first century, and that political engagement with the East End as a site of racism reveals that multiculturalism relied on a disavowal of histories of race and empire.

Talat Ahmed discusses the common-sense perception of 'tartan inclusivity' as a form of Scottish civic nationalism that seeks to distance itself from 'Britishness' with a Scottish national identity that is inclusive and rejects narrow concepts of race based upon birth, ethnicity, religion and ancestry. The annual St Andrew's Day March and Rally, which has gained wide political support, has become a symbol of Scottish anti-racism. Ahmed argues that the context and origins of this annual commemoration point to a different picture, whereby not only are racism and xenophobia present in Scotland, but Black and Asian communities in Glasgow, alongside trade unionists and anti-racist campaigners, worked to build an anti-racist movement and to challenge increasing racism during the 1980s and 1990s. This history destabilises the idea of 'nae [no] problem here' and demonstrates continuities and disjunctures of racism and anti-racism via a Scottish dimension.

Megan Hunt discusses the uses and misuses of 'American-centric' racial histories in British education, politics and media discussions, and the longstanding history of transatlantic solidarity and effort to combat a British political culture that considers racism an American problem. British political commentators have imported the misrepresentation of Martin Luther King, Jr, and the US ideology of 'colorblindness' in order to define and limit acceptable forms of anti-racist protest in Britain. Hunt argues that US-focused critiques of colorblind ideology offer a toolkit for undermining triumphal governmental narratives of Britain, and support demands for histories that recognise shared transatlantic histories of slavery, empire and migration.

Notes

1 Saima Nasar, 'Remembering Edward Colston: Histories of Slavery, Memory and Black Globality', *Women's History Review*, 29:7 (2020), 1218–25 (pp. 1220–2).
2 Gary Younge, 'Foreword', in Peter Fryer, *Staying Power: The History of Black People in Britain* (London: Pluto Press, 2018 [1984]), pp. xi–xii.
3 Kennetta Hammond Perry, *London Is the Place for Me: Black Britons, Citizenship and the Politics of Race* (Oxford: Oxford University Press, 2016), p. 90.
4 Ken Lunn, 'Uncovering Traditions of Intolerance: The Earlier Years of *Immigrants and Minorities* and the Sheffield School', in Jennifer Craig-Norton, Christhard Hoffmann and Tony Kushner (eds), *Migrant Britain: Histories and Historiographies – Essays in Honour of Colin Holmes* (Abingdon: Routledge, 2018), pp. 11–21; Tony Kushner and Ken Lunn (eds), *Traditions of Intolerance: Historical Perspectives on Fascism and Race Discourse in Britain* (Manchester: Manchester University Press, 1989).

5 Kennetta Hammond Perry, 'Black Futures Not Yet Lost: Imagining Black British Abolitionism', *South Atlantic Quarterly*, 121:3 (2022), 541–60 (pp. 544–5).
6 Catherine Hall, Nicholas Draper, Keith McClelland, Katie Donington and Rachel Lang, *Legacies of British Slave-Ownership: Colonial Slavery and the Formation of Victorian Britain* (Cambridge: Cambridge University Press, 2014); Linda Colley, *Britons: Forging the Nation 1707–1837* (London: Pimlico, 1994), pp. 359–60; Madge Dresser, *Slavery Obscured: The Social History of the Slave Trade in an English Provincial Port* (Bristol: Redcliffe Press, 2007).
7 Tony Kushner, 'Meaning Nothing but Good: Ethics, History and Asylum-Seeker Phobia in Britain', *Patterns of Prejudice*, 37:3 (2010), 257–76.
8 Marc Matera, Radhika Natarajan, Kennetta Hammond Perry, Camilla Schofield and Rob Waters, 'Marking Race: Empire, Social Democracy, Deindustrialization', *Twentieth Century British History*, 34:3 (2023), 552–79 (p. 560).
9 Neil Evans, Paul O'Leary and Charlotte Williams, 'Introduction: Race, Nation and Globalization in a Devolved Wales', in Charlotte Williams, Neil Evans and Paul O'Leary (eds), *A Tolerant Nation? Revisiting Ethnic Diversity in a Devolved Wales* (Cardiff: University of Wales Press, 2015), pp. 1–23 (p. 10).
10 Joseph H. Jackson, *Writing Black Scotland: Race, Nation and the Devolution of Black Britain* (Edinburgh: Edinburgh University Press, 2020), p. 38; Charlotte Williams, 'Can We Live Together? Wales and the Multicultural Question', *Transactions of the Honourable Society of Cymmrodorion*, 11 (2004), 216–30 (p. 218).
11 Neil Davidson and Satnam Virdee, 'Introduction: Understanding Racism in Scotland', in Neil Davidson, Minna Liinpää, Maureen McBride and Satnam Virdee (eds), *No Problem Here: Understanding Racism in Scotland* (Edinburgh: Luath Press, 2018), pp. 9–12 (p. 9).
12 Hakim Adi, *West Africans in Britain, 1900–1960: Nationalism, Pan-Africanism and Communism* (London: Lawrence & Wishart, 1998); Kieran Connell, *Black Handsworth: Race in 1980s Britain* (Oakland: University of California Press, 2019); David Featherstone, 'Harry O'Connell, Maritime Labour and the Racialised Politics of Place', *Race & Class*, 57:3 (2016), 71–87; Priyamvada Gopal, *Insurgent Empire: Anticolonial Resistance and British Dissent* (London: Verso, 2019); Shirin Hirsch and Geoff Brown, 'Breaking the "Colour Bar": Len Johnson, Manchester and Anti-Racism', *Race & Class*, 64:3 (2023), 36–58; Winston James, 'In the Nest of Extreme Radicalism: Radical Networks and the Bolshevization of Claude McKay in London', *Comparative American Studies*, 15:3–4 (2017), 174–203; W. Chris Johnson, '"The Spirit of Bandung" in 1970s Britain: The Black Liberation Front's Revolutionary Transnationalism', in Hakim Adi (ed.), *Black British History: New Perspectives* (London: Zed Books, 2019), pp. 125–43; Marc Matera, *Black London: The Imperial Metropolis and Decolonization in the Twentieth Century* (Oakland: University of California Press, 2015); John Narayan, 'British Black Power: The Anti-Imperialism of Political Blackness

and the Problem of Nativist Socialism', *Sociological Review*, 67:5 (2019), 945–67; Susan D. Pennybacker, *From Scottsboro to Munich: Race and Political Culture in 1930s Britain* (Princeton: Princeton University Press, 2009); Simon Peplow, *Race and Riots in Thatcher's Britain* (Manchester: Manchester University Press, 2019); Carol Pierre, 'The New Cross Fire of 1981 and Its Aftermath', in Adi, *Black British History*, pp. 162–75; Anandi Ramamurthy, *Black Star: Britain's Asian Youth Movements* (London: Pluto Press, 2013); Ron Ramdin, *The Making of the Black Working Class in Britain* (London: Verso, 2017 [1987]); Grace Redhead, ' "A British Problem Affecting British People": Sickle Cell Anaemia, Medical Activism and Race in the National Health Service, 1975–1993', *Twentieth Century British History*, 32:2 (2021), 189–211; Natalie Thomlinson, *Race, Ethnicity and the Women's Movement in England, 1968–1993* (Basingstoke: Palgrave Macmillan, 2016); Jake Thorold, 'Black Political Worlds in Port Cities: Garveyism in 1920s Britain', *Twentieth Century British History*, 33:1 (2022), 1–28; Imaobong D. Umoren, *Race Women Internationalists: Activist-Intellectuals and Global Freedom Struggles* (Oakland: University of California Press, 2018); Rob Waters, *Thinking Black: Britain, 1964–1985* (Oakland: University of California Press, 2018); Jessica White, 'Black Women's Groups, Life Narratives, and the Construction of the Self in Late Twentieth-Century Britain', *Historical Journal*, 65:3 (2022), 797–817; Daniel Whittall, 'Creating Black Places in Imperial London: The League of Coloured Peoples and Aggrey House, 1931–1943', *London Journal*, 36:3 (2011), 225–46; Elizabeth M. Williams, *The Politics of Race in Britain and South Africa: Black British Solidarity and the Anti-Apartheid Struggle* (London: Bloomsbury, 2020); Theo Williams, *Making the Revolution Global: Black Radicalism and the British Socialist Movement before Decolonisation* (London: Verso, 2022).
13 Gopal, *Insurgent Empire*.
14 Connell, *Black Handsworth*; Paul Gilroy, *There Ain't No Black in the Union Jack: The Cultural Politics of Race and Nation* (Abingdon: Routledge, 2002 [1987]); Perry, *London Is the Place for Me*; Anne Spry Rush, *Bonds of Empire: West Indians and Britishness from Victoria to Decolonization* (Oxford: Oxford University Press, 2011); Waters, *Thinking Black*. NB throughout this volume, when using the term 'Black', the capitalised form is used. This is a debated convention. We follow the model of Kimberlé Crenshaw, who capitalises Black because it 'constitute[s] a specific cultural group and, as such, require[s] denotation as a proper noun' (Kimberlé Crenshaw, 'Mapping the Margins: Intersectionality, Identity Politics, and Violence against Women of Color', *Stanford Law Review*, 43 (1991), 1241–99 (p. 1244)). This logic still applies when Black is referred to as a political category, such as in Chapter 7. In quotations the term is left as the original author has written it, which is not always capitalised.
15 Satnam Virdee, *Racism, Class and the Racialized Outsider* (Basingstoke: Palgrave Macmillan, 2014).
16 Williams, *The Politics of Race in Britain and South Africa*, p. 207.

17 Catherine Hall, 'Doing Reparatory History: Bringing "Race" and Slavery Home', *Race & Class*, 60:3 (2018), 3–21 (p. 5).
18 David Featherstone, *Solidarity: Hidden Histories and Geographies of Internationalism* (London: Zed Books, 2012), pp. 5–6.
19 Matera, *Black London*, p. 17.
20 Brett Bebber, 'The Architects of Integration: Research, Public Policy, and the Institute of Race Relations in Post-Imperial Britain', *Journal of Imperial and Commonwealth History*, 48:2 (2020), 319–50.
21 David Geiringer and Alastair Owens, 'Anglicanism, Race and the Inner City', *History Workshop Journal*, 94 (2022), 223–45.
22 Alana Lentin, 'Racism in Public or Public Racism: Doing Anti-Racism in "Post-Racial" Times', *Ethnic and Racial Studies*, 39:1 (2016), 33–48 (p. 33).
23 Camilla Schofield, Florence Sutcliffe-Braithwaite and Rob Waters, '"The Privatisation of the Struggle": Anti-Racism in the Age of Enterprise', in Aled Davies, Ben Jackson and Florence Sutcliffe-Braithwaite (eds), *The Neoliberal Age? Britain since the 1970s* (London: UCL Press, 2021), pp. 199–225 (p. 213).
24 Caroline Bressey, 'Spaces of Black History', in Craig-Norton et al., *Migrant Britain*, pp. 92–102; Kathleen Chater, *Untold Histories: Black People in England and Wales during the Period of the British Slave Trade, c. 1660–1807* (Manchester: Manchester University Press, 2009); Molly Corlett, 'Between Colony and Metropole: Empire, Race and Power in Eighteenth-Century Britain', in Adi, *Black British History*, pp. 37–51; Daniel Livesay, *Children of Uncertain Fortune: Mixed-Race Jamaicans in Britain and the Atlantic Family, 1733–1833* (Chapel Hill: University of North Carolina Press, 2018).
25 Michael Goebel, *Anti-Imperial Metropolis: Interwar Paris and the Seeds of Third World Internationalism* (Cambridge: Cambridge University Press, 2015), p. 3.
26 Umoren, *Race Women Internationalists*, pp. 6–7, 14.
27 Matera, *Black London*, p. 13.
28 Perry, *London Is the Place for Me*, p. 62.
29 *Ibid.*, p. 50.
30 Nadine El-Enany, *(B)ordering Britain: Law, Race and Empire* (Manchester: Manchester University Press, 2020), p. 230.
31 Caroline Bressey and Gemma Romain, 'Tracing Queer Black Spaces in Interwar Britain', in Justin Bengry, Matt Cook and Alison Oram (eds), *Locating Queer Histories: Places and Traces across the UK* (London: Bloomsbury, 2023), pp. 101–18.
32 Kennetta Perry, 'History beyond Borders: Teaching Black Britain and Reimagining Black Liberation', in Adi, *Black British History*, pp. 107–24 (p. 110).
33 Alina Sajed and Timothy Seidel, 'Anticolonial Connectivity and the Politics of Solidarity: Between Home and the World', *Postcolonial Studies*, 26:1 (2023), 1–12 (p. 1).
34 Daniel Geary, Camilla Schofield and Jennifer Sutton (eds), *Global White Nationalism: From Apartheid to Trump* (Manchester: Manchester University

Press, 2020); Marilyn Lake and Henry Reynolds, *Drawing the Global Colour Line: White Men's Countries and the International Challenge of Racial Inequality* (Cambridge: Cambridge University Press, 2008); Hakim Adi, *Pan-Africanism: A History* (London: Bloomsbury, 2018); Vijay Prashad, *The Darker Nations: A People's History of the Third World* (New York: The New Press, 2007).

35 Akira Iriye, *Global and Transnational History: The Past, Present, and Future* (Basingstoke: Palgrave Macmillan, 2013), p. 15.
36 Richard Drayton and David Motadel, 'Discussion: The Futures of Global History', *Journal of Global History*, 13:1 (2018), 1–21.
37 David Featherstone, 'Politicizing In/Security, Transnational Resistance, and the 1919 Riots in Cardiff and Liverpool', *Small Axe*, 22:3 (2018), 56–67 (p. 59).
38 Daisy Payling, '"Socialist Republic of South Yorkshire": Grassroots Activism and Left-Wing Solidarity in 1980s Sheffield', *Twentieth Century British History*, 25:4 (2014), 602–27 (p. 624); Stephen Brooke, 'Space, Emotions and the Everyday: The Affective Ecology of 1980s London', *Twentieth Century British History*, 28:1 (2017), 110–42 (pp. 135–6).
39 Jane Aaron, 'Slaughter and Salvation: Welsh Missionary Activity and British Imperialism', in Williams et al., *A Tolerant Nation?*, pp. 51–68 (p. 58).
40 Aled Jones, 'The Other Internationalism? Missionary Activity and Welsh Nonconformist Perceptions of the World in the Nineteenth and Twentieth Centuries', in Williams et al., *A Tolerant Nation?*, pp. 69–84 (p. 79).
41 Featherstone, 'Politicizing In/Security', 10–11; Neil Evans, 'The South Wales Race Riots of 1919', *Llafur*, 3:1 (1980), 7–16.
42 Bridget Byrne, Lindsey Garratt, Bethan Harries and Andrew Smith, 'Histories of Place: The Racialization of Representational Space in Govanhill and Butetown', *Identities*, 30:3 (2023), 373–91.
43 Alison J. Donnell, 'Welsh and West Indian, "like nothing … seen before": Unfolding Diasporic Lives in Charlotte Williams' *Sugar and Slate*', *Anthurium: A Caribbean Studies Journal*, 6:2 (2008), DOI: 10.33596/anth.120, p. 8.
44 Diarmaid Kelliher, *Making Cultures of Solidarity: London and the 1984–5 Miners' Strike* (Abingdon and New York: Routledge, 2021), p. 13.
45 Gopal, *Insurgent Empire*, p. 22.
46 James Baldwin cited in Perry, 'History beyond Borders', p. 71.
47 Naoko Shibusawa, 'Where Is the Reciprocity? Notes on Solidarity from the Field', *Journal of Asian American Studies*, 25:2 (2022), 261–82 (p. 262).
48 Waters, *Thinking Black*, p. 55.
49 Fryer, *Staying Power*; Caroline Bressey, 'Race, Antiracism and the Place of Blackness in the Making and Remaking of the English Working Class', *Historical Reflections*, 41:1 (2015), 70–82.
50 Bressey, 'Race, Antiracism and the Place of Blackness in the Making and Remaking of the English Working Class', p. 76.
51 Matera et al., 'Marking Race', p. 574.
52 Sajed and Seidel, 'Anticolonial Connectivity and the Politics of Solidarity', p. 8.

53 Sundari Anitha and Ruth Pearson, *Striking Women: Struggles and Strategies of South Asian Women Workers from Grunwick to Gate Gourmet* (London: Lawrence & Wishart, 2018), pp. 26–30.
54 *Ibid.*, p. 116.
55 Satnam Virdee, 'Anti-Racism and the Socialist Left, 1968–79', in Evan Smith and Matthew Worley (eds), *Against the Grain: The British Far Left from 1956* (Manchester: Manchester University Press, 2014), pp. 209–28 (p. 221).
56 Jack Saunders, 'Emotions, Social Practices and the Changing Composition of Class, Race and Gender in the National Health Service, 1970–79: "Lively Discussion Ensued"', *History Workshop Journal*, 88 (2019), 204–28 (208).
57 Kelliher, *Making Cultures of Solidarity*, p. 207.
58 Aamna Mohdin, 'Outrage over UK University's Plan to Cut African History Course and Its Professor', *Guardian* (23 July 2023), www.theguardian.com/education/2023/jul/23/outrage-over-chichester-university-plan-to-cut-african-history-course-and-its-professor (accessed 29 August 2023).
59 Board of Deputies, Law, Parliamentary and General Purposes Committee, London Metropolitan Archives, ACC/3121/C/13/001/017.

Part I

Domestic, imperial and global anti-racist alliances and encounters

1

Countering racial discrimination in Britain, 1880s–1913

David Killingray

In September 1905, John Hedge, an African American, was abused by white Americans in a London restaurant. Incensed at this ungentlemanly behaviour, Hedge wrote to the *Evening News*, recounting his experience. The newspaper responded with an editorial on this matter 'of considerable interest', stressing that in London 'there is no race question', although accompanying Hedge's complaint with a letter bristling with racial invective written by 'Colonist'.[1] During the next two weeks the *Evening News*, seeking to arrive at some kind of balance, printed a sample of reader's letters labelled 'Pro & Anti-Negroes'. Many readers drew on prejudices gained as settlers and soldiers in the colonies, or stereotypical views garnered from novels and ethnological displays. Contrary views stressed humanitarian values and scientific evidence of human commonality.

This chapter focuses on the presence of people of African origin and descent in Britain during a period marked by white racial imperial expansion and exploitation. First, it analyses the increase in racial antipathy toward Black people during the years after 1880. Second, and more expansively, it looks at the white and Black individuals, and the institutions they formed, who resisted racial discrimination and pointed to a more humane and inclusive civil society. These complex anti-racist ideas and actions drew on well-founded values of Christian and liberal humanitarianism rooted in Enlightenment ideas that had helped spawn the evangelical revival. Nevertheless, after the 1870s 'there was an increasing pan-Western consensus in favour of fixed, heritable, and intellectually unequal skin-colour-based racial groups'.[2] Many Christians and humanitarians stressed ideals of a common human origin, beliefs increasingly endorsed by evolving science and 'modern ethnology [which] acknowledged no permanently inferior race',[3] but their thinking was also often shaped by notions that Blackness implied mental and moral weakness. The other enduring racial canker was antisemitism, marked by the Aliens Act 1905, and by social discrimination throughout the twentieth century.

Growing racial antipathy

Many Black people living in, or revisiting, Britain commented on changed race relations over time. Frederick Douglass, the African American opponent of slavery, told a Newcastle-upon-Tyne audience in 1860 that twelve years earlier he had experienced 'not the slightest ill-feeling [of others] towards me because of my complexion'. Things had changed, and now 'American prejudice might be found in the streets of Liverpool and in nearly all commercial towns.'[4] The persistent popularity of 'minstrelsy' since the 1840s – blacked-up whites mocking 'Negro' stereotypes – angered many Black people. Catherine Impey, in 1888, influenced by the pervasiveness of racial thinking, began publishing her monthly *Anti-Caste* to warn against this rising tide. Charles Columbus Davies, a 'coloured comedian', told a London court in 1905: 'We get insulted every day because we are black.'[5] The Jamaican former medical missionary Dr Theophilus Scholes wrote in 1908 of the vulgar racial abuse by white Londoners,[6] sentiments echoed by the Sierra Leonean A. B. C. Merriman-Labor who reported similar abuse, particularly from Americans visiting the capital.[7]

Why these changes in civility and public courtesy? Four hundred years of European exploitation of African enslaved labour ingrained ideas of Black inferiority firmly in the minds of many ordinary Britons. From the late seventeenth century, white-driven polygenist ideas jostled with those of monogenists, and whether, or not, that perceived gap in the relevant stage of development to 'civilisation' might be overcome. Polygenist ideas gained leverage from the 'negrophobe' founders of the Anthropological Institute of London in 1863, which furthered a popular consensus among whites that Black people were 'savage', 'backward', 'child-like', 'lazy' and of 'limited intelligence'. Debates continued about human origins and progress, fuelled by ideas from Darwin and Spencer, accompanied by a growing popular belief that whites were superior and that Black people were inferior and would long need the guiding patronage of Europeans.[8] The Indian revolt of 1857 and the Morant Bay Rebellion in Jamaica of 1865 alienated many Britons from the idea that European influence was a civilising one for Black people. The eagerly read accounts of white 'exploration' in Africa caught the popular imagination of a continent and its people steeped in darkness and primitive savagery. Rapid industrial, urban and material progress of Europe and North America gave those states enormous military strength, buttressed by a false belief in a cultural and moral superiority over the 'lesser breeds without the law': the 'natives' of Africa and Asia who became subjects of their imperial ambitions.[9] The European 'Scramble for Africa', and partition of the continent in the post-1880s age of imperialism, helped shape new white sensibilities. Imperial control was painted as enlightened action, a 'civilising mission' to redeem Africans living in benighted darkness and ignorance. European 'savage wars' of conquest in Africa helped shape white perceptions of the continent, and the pejorative term 'n*****' markedly increased in the British press during the decade 1890–1900.[10] Service in imperial wars, particularly in South Africa, exposed many soldiers to sights and sounds prejudicial toward Africans. Across the Empire 'native' people were recruited for local colonial military forces to secure imperial territory; in Britain King's Regulations stated that officers in the army had to be of 'pure European descent'.[11]

The introduction of Empire Day in 1904 glorified imperial military activity and further entrenched notions of the white right to control large areas of distant lands and their peoples. Shortly thereafter, Robert Baden-Powell's initial idea was to call his new movement for boys the 'Imperial Scouts'. Young people had steadily been exposed to a growing market of novels and history books that portrayed Black people as 'lazy, vicious and incapable of any serious improvement or of work except under compulsion'.[12] Adult literature reinforced such prejudicial ideas, some popular novels portraying well-educated and acculturated Black men as having but a thin veneer of 'civilisation' and liable to resort to their simian and atavistic nature once they came within sight of the 'dark continent'.[13] Photographing of non-European peoples for ethnological purposes produced images that stressed exotic 'tribes' and peoples and inferior cultures.[14] Curious white audiences could visit public exhibitions of 'native' villages with living exhibits; and Black people, particularly children, were useful objects for advertisers seeking to persuade British customers to buy Pears Soap and Fry's Cocoa.[15] Hagiographic stories of white Christian missionary endeavour – the stock material of denominational magazines – and Sunday school prizes promoted ideas of pagan peoples in need of Christian 'civilisation', whose redemption depended on white patronage and moral example and, of course, finance. The pages of the scholarly eleventh edition of the *Encyclopædia Britannica* informed its readers that Africa is 'a continent practically without a history', its Indigenous peoples 'mentally inferior to the white'.[16]

A further reason for change in white–Black relations by the turn of the twentieth century was what Marilyn Lake and Henry Reynolds have termed the emergence of a sense of collective white solidarity that embraced Britain; white North America; and the white settler colonies of Australia, New Zealand and southern Africa. They argue that these white men's countries now faced a 'rising tide of colour', of population increase among Black and East Asian people, that threatened white security. To the 'Yellow Peril' – from the Boxer rising to Japan's victory at Tsushima – could be added the prospect of a 'Black Peril' following Abyssinian victory over the Italian invaders at Adwa in 1896, continued African resistance to colonial rule and the Ethiopianism of the Bambatha rising in southern Africa in 1906.[17]

Imperial racial ideas and practice had for long been imported to the metropole, a process increased in the 'age of imperialism'. It is not difficult to find reports of racial abuse in the British press in the decades before 1914. These range from abusive language to discriminatory behaviour directed against non-Europeans from all social classes; the exclusion of Black people from hotels and public houses; race discrimination on Atlantic passenger ships; and harsh treatment of coloured seamen on mercantile vessels. Criticism of Black people even extended to dress. The weekly trade paper the *Taylor & Cutter* referred to 'Ethiopians [Africans] now swarming in the London thoroughfares' and commented on the inability of 'the coloured races ... to adorn themselves with the attire of the European'.[18]

A word of caution is required. It is easy to rely heavily on reports of a few articulate Black people who complained at racial discrimination. This evidence is useful to historians, but it is incomplete. Most Black people in Britain did not publicly comment on their personal relationships. This may mean silent endurance, but it may indicate that some Black people rarely experienced any racial antipathy. Perhaps they adapted to, and were accepted into, working-class families and communities, or their middle-class professional respectability made them acceptable neighbours and colleagues. After all, Hedge commented that he had lived in Britain for some years and not encountered racial abuse, and that may well have been the story of many other Black people. National and provincial press reports about Black people often used polite social class descriptions, and occasionally precluded any mention of race and colour.[19]

The opponents of racial discrimination

In 1900 Black people in Britain numbered c. 10,000, half that number living in London, the rest mainly in major port towns. They were present in every county across the country. They were too few in any one place to be perceived by whites as a threat to jobs, housing and women, although that did not prevent individual Black people from being targeted by abuse and for discriminatory racially motivated behaviour. However, many Black people who came to Britain commented on the social, cultural and political environment that afforded them liberties unknown in their home country or colony: equality before the law; access to educational institutions; membership of professional bodies; the right to live where they chose; the right to vote subject to meeting income and property qualifications, and to marry across the colour line. Black men were elected to public office, and a few

Black clergymen pastored predominantly white congregations. Interracial marriages occurred, invariably Black men to white wives, sometimes met with hostility and ostracism from family and friends, but often not.[20] Social class was a distinction often made in British press reports that identified Black people as 'gentleman'/'lady' compared to those recorded as 'coloured man'/'woman'. Most Black people were in labouring or artisanal employ. If they encountered racial discrimination, they dealt with it locally or might take issue in the courts. The small Black elite had recourse to knowledge and to professional connections that enabled them to gain the support of white friends and patrons. Christian churches and missionary agencies, and other institutional connections, provided useful sources of help and advice. But essentially, formally educated Black people were better placed to act collectively to protect and promote their demands for civil liberties.

Throughout much of the nineteenth century Britain had a sizeable constituency of people, mainly Christians and humanitarians of all social classes, sympathetic to the welfare of Black people. The slave trade had been viewed as a 'sin', and continuing global slavery as a heinous breach of Christian charity needing to be overthrown.[21] However, since the 1830s the presence in Britain of dozens of fugitive slaves from the United States, and Black preachers, provided public examples of Black ability and civility triumphing over overwhelming odds. Hundreds of thousands of Britons heard them speak and preach and read the books they wrote, which helped shape progressive views of Black capabilities. Across the country itinerant Black preachers stayed in British hotels and lodging houses, and many private homes were open to them. After 1860 a small local minority of Christians and humanitarians condemned expanding British imperial activity and sympathised with Indigenous aims and aspirations. Friendships existed across the colour line, and Black visitors received enduring hospitality from white Christians, notably Quakers, and members of the Brotherhood Movement. This latter body, which developed from the Pleasant Sunday Afternoon movement, originated in 1875 and rapidly spread to other dissenting churches with an alternative and accessible programme of biblically based Christian worship that stressed mutual brotherly support, temperance, pacifism and racial tolerance. By 1912 there were different strands within the movement, the main federation having over 300,000 members.[22] Some Black people living in and visiting Britain were active members, including Sol Plaatje, the South African politician, who wrote that, arriving to address a Brotherhood meeting in north London, he felt at ease when he discovered it was chaired by a fellow Black man.[23]

The small town of Street, Somerset, was a local stronghold of Quakers, and the home of the unmarried sisters Catherine and Ellen Impey. The principal manufacturers in the town were the Clarks, Quaker shoemakers.

Quakers had their own tradition of independent Christian action, prominent in assailing the ills of society and in promoting high moral standards. Although numbering a few thousand their close-knit structure enabled them effectively to oppose the slave trade and slavery, and to espouse pacificism and temperance. Catherine Impey was politically aware, and on her first visit to the United States in 1878, in the cause of temperance, her interests in race relations were raised. Using her transatlantic links with African Americans, Impey, in March 1888, edited, paid for and began distributing a monthly journal, *Anti-Caste*, 'Devoted to the Interests of Coloured Races'. The aim was to alert British readers to racial prejudice (most examples were drawn from the United States) and to oppose the excesses of imperialism. Impey was prepared to shock her readers. The front-page issue of *Anti-Caste* for January 1893 carried a photograph of the body of a Black man hanging from a tree in Alabama surrounded by the lynch crowd of men, women and children viewing their tortured victim.

Impey was keen to extend the influence of her periodical and to realise a long-held idea of forming an organisation to promote its cause. This she developed with the aid of Isabella Mayo, an evangelical writer living in Scotland. In 1893 the two women launched the Society for the Recognition of the Brotherhood of Man (SRBM). They also wrote inviting Ida B. Wells, the African American anti-lynching campaigner, to extend her crusade to Britain with their financial support. Wells agreed, and arrived in London in May 1893. By then a foolish indiscretion by Impey (she proposed marriage to a Ceylonese boarder living in Mayo's home) led to a serious rift with Mayo, which divided the proposed SRBM into two bodies, and placed Wells's campaign in jeopardy, including her second tour in 1894. She chose to side with Impey, and thus was cut off by Mayo.[24]

Caught in this conflict was Jules S. Celestine Edwards, born in Dominica: a highly effective lecturer on temperance and skilful evangelical Christian apologist who attracted large audiences. As the editor of *Lux* (the organ of the Christian Evidence Society), he promoted questions of race and justice with a radical Christian socialist voice.[25] Impey registered Edwards's value to her cause and, through the offices of Dadabhai Naoroji, the Indian Liberal MP for Finsbury Central from 1892 to 1895, she invited him to join Ida B. Wells on her speaking tour.[26] This led to Edwards being asked to edit a new journal for the SRBM to replace *Anti-Caste*. The successor paper was *Fraternity*, launched in August 1893, which had below its masthead a drawing of clasped white and Black hands. Although Edwards suffered from poor health, in his next year as editor he worked vigorously to increase the number of readers and to make the paper a distinctive voice in 'the cause of the helpless races in America, India, Africa, and Australia, and wherever tribes, races, and nations have been oppressed by the accursed enemy of mankind – Caste'.[27] He condemned race prejudice in Britain, and criticised churches and missions for their compliance with a secular imperial agenda. Edwards provided Afro-centric Christian ideas, boldly challenging contemporary practice on race, religion, the conduct of commerce and empire.

Conflicting voices and ambitions muddied the cause that Impey had inspired. *Fraternity* continued, but Edwards went home to the West Indies, his health broken, where he died at the age of thirty-four in July 1894. His pan-African vision and the popular appeal of his authentic Black voice could not be duplicated by the white editors who succeeded him on *Fraternity*. Subsequently renamed *Bond of Brotherhood*, in the hands of socialist men and women its message on racial discrimination was largely replaced by a focus on imperial issues and workers' rights in Britain. Early socialist organisations, for example the Socialist League in the 1880s, had denounced British imperial activity in Africa, and Keir Hardie occasionally lent his support to those who campaigned for Black civil rights in Britain.[28] By the 1890s, as British trade unions gained strength, socialist bodies grew more active; eastern European Jewish immigration increased, particularly to east London; and the left lost sight of its traditional internationalism. The popular political climate at the end of the century, stressing nation and the working-class struggle, allowed the left to accommodate to antisemitism.[29]

Pan-African protest

For decades the conscience of Britain's expanding imperial activity had been the Anti-Slavery Society (ASS), with its roots in the campaigns to end the slave trade and slavery, and the Aborigines' Protection Society (APS), founded in 1838. The APS signalled its purpose in the masthead slogan on its journal, *Aborigines' Friend: Ab uno sanguine* ('of one blood'), being the first humanitarian body to speak out against race discrimination in the white settler colonies. At the same time both societies took a patrician watch on Black peoples who came to Britain. By the early twentieth century the APS had run out of purpose, its protective influence on Indigenous peoples at best marginal as white settler Dominions assumed greater political autonomy.[30] On the death of Henry Fox Bourne, the APS secretary, in 1909, that society merged with the larger ASS. Fox Bourne's patronising distrust of Black independent action in calling the Pan-African Conference in London in 1900, and his ambiguous role at the height of the Congo crisis, indicated the gulf between white patricians and the voice of 'aborigines'. The disdain directed by John Harris, Secretary of the ASS, toward Sol Plaatje, the representative of the South African Native National Congress in London to protest at Pretoria's 1913 Land Act, indicated his reluctance to defer to Black people as equal partners.[31]

Black and white anti-racist activity increased in Britain in the 1890s with Impey and *Anti-Caste*, Wells's campaigning lectures and the formation of the Anti-Lynching Committee, in collaboration with Edwards and the SRBM, Alice Kinloch's public damning indictments of southern African labour conditions, and the formation of the African Association in 1897.[32] The Association was the work of two students, Henry Sylvester Williams from Trinidad and Thomas J. Thompson of Sierra Leone, together with Alice Kinloch, a Coloured African from the diamond mining area of Kimberley, recently arrived in Britain. They received considerable encouragement from the Revd Alexander Crummell, a Cambridge-educated African American and ardent Anglophile, then visiting Britain. Writing to the Quaker weekly *The Friend* in late October 1897, Kinloch said that 'with some men of my race in this country, I have formed a society for the benefit of our people in Africa … I think the time has come for us to bear some of our responsibilities, and in so doing we will help the Aborigines' Protection Society.' She announced the 'initiation of "The African Association" that night' and concluded by saying that 'I am trying to educate people in this country in regard to the iniquitous laws made for blacks in South Africa.'[33] The purpose of the African Association was

> to encourage a feeling of unity, to facilitate friendly intercourse among Africans in general; to promote and protect the interests of all subjects claiming African descent, wholly or in part, in British Colonies and other places, especially in Africa, by circulating accurate information on all subjects affecting their rights and privileges as subjects of the British Empire, by direct appeals to the Imperial and local governments.[34]

The guiding committee was Black-led, with the Revd H. Mason Joseph (a West Indian Episcopalian employed in England by the Society for the Propagation of the Gospel) as president, T. J. Thompson as vice-president, H. Sylvester Williams as secretary and Alice Kinloch as treasurer. The Association was poorly supported, with limited funds and rarely more than fifty members, most being students. The status and treatment of Black people in Britain were a less prominent concern. Rather, the issues that provoked resolutions and action were the economic crisis in the West Indies; United States imperial ambitions in the Caribbean; and the demand for 'the Imperial Government to statutorily safeguard the rights of native African races, who are brought, and are being brought under British rule in southern Africa'.[35]

Although under Black direction, the Association relied heavily upon white supporters, principally Christian nonconformists, as well as liberals, radicals and humanitarians who belonged to temperance bodies and to the ASS and the APS. They provided encouragement, useful introductions and contacts, and occasionally financial support.[36] The motto of the Association was 'Light and Liberty'. Its offices were in Westminster, next to the office of the British Committee of the Indian National Congress, which was also the 'meeting place' of the Association.[37]

An international Pan-African Conference in London was probably Williams's idea. Originally intended to draw together leading Black people from the British Empire, its remit was subsequently extended to include representatives of all peoples of African origin and descent; publicity went to newspapers in Britain, the Caribbean, the United States and Africa. Nearly forty delegates and others met in London on three very hot July days in 1900. The political backcloth to the conference was the continuing South African war, the Boxer Rebellion in China, Britain's military campaign against Asante in West Africa, and echoes of other recent wars to subjugate Black and Brown people across the globe. Little attention was given by overseas delegates to race relations within the United Kingdom. American and West Indian participants highlighted racial discrimination in the Caribbean colonies and the USA, while united condemnation was directed at the official and commercial exploitive labour policies in the mines and on the farms of southern Africa. The elite delegates, mainly British citizens and subjects, remained staunchly imperial. There was no question of hauling down the Union Jack, only a demand that it fly over an Empire free of colour discrimination, where Black men and women could secure office by equal merit. All interested in the cause were invited to walk in off the street and listen to the proceedings. A written register of those present was kept, an invaluable document that appears not to have survived.

An analysis of the ideas and beliefs of the delegates indicates that most were active Christians. The chairman, Alexander Walters, was an African Methodist bishop, and a good number of others were ordained. The daily proceedings were opened with prayer, and when Walters was delayed one morning, Benito Sylvain (a devout Roman Catholic), representing his home country of Haiti and the Emperor of Abyssinia, played the piano to accompany hymn singing. The timing of the conference had originally been arranged to fit in with the international exhibition in Paris, but a final decisive matter was the London international conference of Christian Endeavor in London, at which Walters was also booked to speak. Among the delegates at the Pan-African Conference were several Black women, the most notable being Anna J. Cooper, author of *A Voice from the South* (1892), who highlighted white humanity's problem with the statement that 'God had not made black people merely for them to be wiped from the face of the earth.'[38]

The conference was widely reported in the British press. However, no photographs of the meetings are known to exist; a single pencil sketch appeared in the *Daily Graphic*, and the official *Report* failed to include a full list of delegates.[39] Few participants wrote personal accounts of the conference, and the African American historian and sociologist W. E. B. Du Bois rarely referred to his presence; when he did, he promoted his own role to the exclusion of the principal Black British actors. Nevertheless, Du Bois had a hand in writing the jointly drafted conference memorial, 'To the Nations of the World', which included the prescient statement that 'the problem of the twentieth century is the problem of the colour line', followed by the sentence 'Let not mere colour or race be a feature of distinction drawn between white and black men, regardless of worth or ability.'[40] For the first time in British history Black Britons had created their own socio-political organisation, which planned and managed an international three-day conference in the imperial capital to express their discontents and hopes in a world riven by racial discrimination. W. T. Stead's *Review of Reviews* described the conference as 'The revolt against the Paleface', a comment that Paul B. Rich says 'confessed that the notion that black men had rights was a new notion to most British peoples'.[41]

The conference produced resolutions that carried little weight in official circles. It is worth noting the number of significant Black figures who did not attend. Distance, cost, and time were good reasons. Perhaps more important were the divisive issues that occupied the minds and programmes of Black leaders in different parts of the world. For example, E. W. Blyden (d. 1912), the pre-eminent pan-Africanist of the age, objected to 'mulattos' having a leading role in Black affairs.[42] Some people of African origin and descent had their own racial distinctions, and the idea of race alone was not an easy base on which to cement an international organisation. Following the conference a Pan-African Association was formed, but it collapsed within two years because of personal rivalries, poor leadership and weak finances. It secured initial support in certain British Caribbean colonies, but little encouragement in West Africa, the United States, Canada, South Africa and Liberia, all countries with Black nascent political groupings dealing with serious domestic issues involving race.

Attempts to promote Black unity and counter racial discrimination

Most Black people in Britain, even students, appear to have had little contact with those who were politically active. Activists often complained that they had difficulty in securing support from fellow Black students who, understandably, were intent on successfully completing their studies. Building a movement from students was therefore an unreliable venture. Nevertheless, local pan-African minded groups did emerge in university towns in the years 1904–8; they tended to be short-lived, with limited reach and influence. Edinburgh University had an Afro-West Indian Literary Society in the late 1890s, which sent delegates to the Pan-African Conference. In 1902 it protested to the Colonial Office over the racial employment terms of the West African Medical Service.[43] Renamed as the Ethiopian Association in 1905, its members included future political leaders in the West African colonies, and the Nigerian Bandele Omoniyi, whose contacts were mainly with British socialists.[44] His book *The Defence of Ethiopianism*, primarily about British rule in Africa, drew attention to 'the rights and wrongs of his countryman, and advocating the claims of his race'.[45]

An Ethiopian Progressive Association was founded in Liverpool in November 1904, led by older people who were not students. It published the *Ethiopian Review*, although no known copies have survived. The Association was in existence in 1907.[46] A short-lived African Union Society was formed by two Oxford students – Isaac Pixley Seme, a South African, and Alain Locke, an African American – holding its inaugural meeting in London.[47] Some were noted in London: the United African League/African Colonial Race Society (1903), with an African Caribbean membership. Of more substance was the United African Association, called into being in February 1905 by Alfred Mangena, one of the future founders of the South African Native National Congress. The next year John Quinlan, from St Lucia, who had been a delegate to the Pan-African Conference, set up the National Society for the Protection of the Dark Races, which also published a single copy of a journal.[48] The purpose of most of these small local organisations was to bring together and represent the interests of Black peoples in Britain and around the world.

In the decade after 1900 incidents of racial discrimination in Britain appear to have increased. This may be due to greater confidence among Black people to speak out, and to write about the abuse they received. Theophilus Scholes, who retired to live in Britain in the 1890s, became a fierce critic of imperial racialism and its excesses. In the second of his intended six volumes, written primarily for white readers, he sought 'to inquire scientifically and historically into the circumstances in which the colourless peoples designate themselves as the "superior race", and in which they designate the coloured races as "inferior races"'.[49] Perhaps race became a topic more newsworthy and newspaper editors thought it worth reporting, thus the attention given to it by the London *Evening News* in 1905. Interracial marriage; boxing matches between white and Black fighters; access by Black people to public places of entertainment; the increase in the number of overseas students, particularly Indians coming to British universities (noted by Black students in London); and more Black and white visitors to the country were all commented upon in the press, sometimes at length. Eugenics, a term coined in the 1880s by Francis Galton, the British naturalist and statistician, gained a scientific foothold in the University of London in 1905. The study of the 'inborn qualities of race' now compounded the widespread belief in innate, hereditary Black inferiority.[50]

The assassination of a member of the Indian civil service by an Indian student, Madan Lal Dhingra, in London in July 1909, vividly brought home to Britons some of the abiding tensions of imperial rule and the presence of disgruntled 'natives' living in Britain.[51] Despite the Aliens Act, no restrictions were placed on Black people coming to live and work in Britain. And more importantly, from the position of Black people, acts of racial discrimination were not illegal. A stock official argument for the next sixty years was that the law should not encroach on individual liberties and private property, and that existing laws were adequate to protect the welfare and wellbeing of both white and Black citizens.

A fresh breath of brotherhood

The League of Universal Brotherhood of the 1890s staggered into the twentieth century. Renamed as the LUB and Native Races Association (LUBNRA), and despite several changes of name, a consistent driving principle remained: the advocacy of 'the universal brotherhood of humanity, without distinction of race, creed, or colour'.[52] Its dynamic secretary was the Congregational minister the Revd Charles Garnett, whose own racial Damascus road had occurred on visits to the United States, although slightly modified by the nine months he spent in southern Africa in 1908–9. Black members of the LUB included Henry Sylvester Williams; the Revd H. Mason Joseph; and Isaac Edmestone Barnes, a Jamaican mining engineer. Garnett was a staunch opponent of racial discrimination and, with Williams who had worked as a lawyer in Cape Town from 1902 to 1904, served as guide and confidant for several suppliant African delegations to London. Garnett became a critical and irritating thorn in the side of the Colonial Office as he argued for land rights for dispossessed Africans. He was no friend of the recently combined Anti-Slavery and Aborigines' Protection Society (ASAPS), being hostile to their rejection of Black and Coloured delegations protesting the creation of the unrepresentative Union of South Africa in 1909, and later their support for the Land Act of 1913. Although Plaatje knew Garnett, when he came to London in 1914 to protest the Land Act, he turned not to the LUB but to the wider national Brotherhood Movement.[53] Britain, certainly London, was more race-conscious than it had been ten years earlier. Stead's 'new notion' had been given life by Black activity in the metropole and regional cities, and by the Universal Races Congress.

The Universal Races Congress met in London in June 1911 'to discuss relations between white and so-called coloured peoples ... to encourage fuller understanding, friendly feeling, and heartier co-operation'. Several hundred delegates met at the University of London to hear papers presented in eight sessions over five days. The emphasis was on 'bringing about healthier relationships between Occident and Orient', with one session given primarily to 'the modern conscience in relation to racial questions ... the negro'.[54] Although race was referred to by several speakers, little notice was given to the subjugation and treatment of Black people under colonial rule. The Revd W. B. Rubusana, who had been elected to the Cape Parliament, used the opportunity to stress the problems of a 'white peril' in South Africa for Black people.[55] Du Bois, who had been a delegate, returned home enthused about the Congress, writing that it was 'the greatest event of the twentieth century ... because it marked the first time in the history of mankind when a world congress dared openly and explicitly to take its stand on the platform of human equality – the essential divinity of man'.[56]

If Du Bois set his sights too high, the Congress did stimulate some Black Britons into action. In July 1912, Dusé Mohamed Ali, a journalist and actor, founded the monthly *African Times and Oriental Review* (*ATOR*) 'to lay [before the British public] the aims, desires and intentions of the Black, Brown and Yellow Races with and without the Empire'.[57] With the outbreak of war in 1914, Ali emphasised his patriotic virtues, adding his hope that the conflict would achieve 'one band of Imperial British Citizenship'. During 1913 a Jamaican dreamer, Marcus Garvey, worked for a short time in the *ATOR* office. He scorned elitist pan-Africanism and espoused a populist version that became the focus of the Universal Negro Improvement Association (UNIA), which he founded in Jamaica in July 1914. The UNIA had little direct influence in Britain. However, its revolutionary reach caused deep consternation in imperial capitals, resulting in the banning of its activities in most African colonies.[58] The 1911 Congress probably gave a fillip to establish several new Black–white societies, while the racially inclusive Five Continents Club, which opened in London in late 1912, stood in marked contrast to the London University Graduates' Club (1914), which banned Black members.

The African Society, a learned body formed in London in 1901, had members drawn from African commerce, colonial administration, humanitarian bodies and missions. Original members included two Africans, E. W. Blyden and the wealthy Lagos merchant R. B. Blaize, who were later joined by other Africans. Blyden hoped that it might develop into a body directly representing African interests. That was not its remit, and following the brief flurry of Indian student political activity, the African Society consulted the Colonial Office, and along with the recently merged ASAPS, looked for means of preventing Black students from following a similar trajectory. In April 1913, the

Society called a 'Conference with Africans' with the purpose of discussing how to deal with the colour bar.[59] Forty or so Africans attended, not all students, and although some favoured the idea of a hostel most opposed any official white control.[60] Black people in general did not wish to be patronised, desiring in preference systems that gave them equality of treatment in the country. In his *ATOR*, Mohamed Ali, who attended the meeting, described the proposed hostel as 'a sort of rounding up place for West Africans'.[61] Later attempts to provide hostels for Black students from the public purse foundered on the question of who controlled such institutions.

Most Church and mission bodies would have agreed with the patronising intent of the white initiators of the 'Conference with Africans'. The missionary societies did include a few white agents who severely criticised British colonial rule, and even one or two who even supported the cry 'Africa for the Africans'. Mission societies employed Black or 'native' pastors, some of whom had been educated in Britain, but official policy was to list them separately from white missionaries and to give them different levels of pay and service. Black clergy attended international meetings in London, such as the Methodist ecumenical conference of 1881, where they met racial discrimination booking hotel accommodation, but this rarely provoked serious discussion. An Anglican conference in June 1908 included a session on 'the Church and race problems'.[62] Several Black participants were recorded, and the Bishop of Tasmania was cheered for stating that interracial marriages should be prohibited. Sir Geoffrey Lagden, from South Africa, said that 'natives' must be kept out of the hands of 'Ethiopians' and English socialists.[63] A Church Congress in Southampton in 1913 had a session on 'The relations between civilised and backward races'. No Black clergy were recorded as present, and although Sydney Olivier and Hensley Henson spoke of the perils of discrimination, and E. D. Morel warned that 'a shudder of new emotions was passing through millions of coloured men', none were as pointed as Mrs Archibald Little, who 'deprecated natives of other countries being called "backward races"'.[64] Church and mission discussions on race only reached a serious level in the late 1930s and 1940s.[65] In the meantime, several millions of children attending Sunday schools regularly sang the chorus to unknown effect that 'Jesus died for all the children ... of the world, / Red and yellow, black and white, / All are precious in His sight'.

Conclusion

From the 1880s to 1914, Black people in Britain, often recipients of direct and indirect abuse, were the most prominent in denouncing racial discrimination. Their protests, occasionally reported in the press, came from those often not named and otherwise rarely recorded – hidden voices that deserve further research and analysis. Inevitably the attention of historians has been captured by the voices of notable public Black figures who spoke and wrote demanding Black civil rights – Celestine Edwards, Alice Kinloch, H. Sylvester Williams, Samuel Coleridge Taylor (the distinguished Black British composer), Theophilus Scholes and Bandele Omoniyi. Although that focus distorts the full picture of anti-race discourse in Britain, it provides a valuable guide to the incidence of the colour bar and attempts to address and rebuff it. In the work of Edwards and Scholes, who wrote primarily for a white audience, can be seen personal experience, intellectual rigour, biblical scholarship, deep Christian faith and persuasive writing. All those named above asserted and acclaimed their racial identity in letters to the press, and on the public stage, while Coleridge Taylor demonstrated his African identity through music and by public action.

The two decades that preceded 1914 saw a growing sense of self-confidence among many people of African origin across the globe to speak and act for themselves. White racial attitudes hardened as Black people hoped their wartime loyalty would lead to greater recognition of the need for equal rights.[66] Most of the hundreds of thousands of imperial 'native' subjects enlisted for war service were employed as military labour. King's Regulations denied military commissions to Black men, although a handful overrode that barrier. British trade unions opposed the immigration of 'colonial labour' during the manpower crises of 1916, and after 1919 colonial seamen suffered discrimination from shipowners in league with white trade unions. Following the Armistice, Black soldiers were treated shabbily; denied passage home with their white wives; and blamed by civilians, police and politicians in major ports as perpetrators of race riots instigated by whites who feared even a small Black presence as a threat to jobs, housing and women. This discriminatory social and economic climate spurred and revived Black efforts to form new political pan-African associations and gatherings. As before, activists were few in number, but they were more resolved and better organised than before the war.

Notes

1 *Evening News* (23 September 1905), p. 9.
2 Edward Beasley, *The Victorian Reinvention of Race: New Racisms and the Problems of Grouping in the Human Sciences* (London: Routledge, 2010), p. 20; Douglas A. Lorimer, 'Reconstructing Victorian Racial Discourse: Images of Race, the Language of Race Relations, and the Context of Black Resistance', in Gretchen Holbrook Gerzina (ed.), *Black Victorians/Black Victoriana*

(New Brunswick, NJ: Rutgers University Press, 2003), pp. 187–207; Douglas A. Lorimer, *Science, Race Relations and Resistance: Britain, 1870–1914* (Manchester: Manchester University Press, 2013).

3 *Evening News* (23 September–3 October 1905).
4 Frederick Douglass's address in Newcastle on 'British Racial Attitudes and Slavery', 23 February 1860, quoted in David W. Blight, *Frederick Douglass: Prophet of Freedom* (New York: Simon & Schuster, 2018), p. 317.
5 *Globe* (London) (26 September 1905), p. 1.
6 Theophilus E. Samuel Scholes, *Glimpses of the Ages or the 'Superior' and 'Inferior' Races, So-Called, Discussed in the Light of Science and History*, Vol. II (London: John Long, 1908), pp. 176–84.
7 A. B. C. Merriman-Labor, *Britons through Negro Spectacles* (London: Penguin, 2022 [1909]), pp. 117–19; Danell Jones, *An African in Imperial London: The Indomitable Life of A. B. C. Merriman-Labor* (London: Hurst, 2018).
8 Paul B. Rich, *Race and Empire in British Politics* (Cambridge: Cambridge University Press, 1986); A. Rattansi, *Racism: A Very Short Introduction*, 2nd edn (Oxford: Oxford University Press, 2020 [2007]), Chapters 1 and 2.
9 Rudyard Kipling's poem 'Recessional', written for Queen Victoria's Diamond Jubilee in 1897, captures this sense of divinely endorsed imperial might. Emma Gattey, 'A Primer for Empire: Fletcher and Kipling's "School history of England"', www.uncomfortableoxford.co.uk/post/a-primer-for-empire-fletcher-and-kipling-s-school-history-of-england (accessed 9 December 2022); V. G. Kiernan, *The Lords of Human Kind: European Attitudes towards the Outside World in the Imperial Age* (London: Serif, 1969).
10 My analysis of the incidence of the term is from the digitally indexed British Newspaper Archive, www.britishnewspaperarchive.co.uk/ (accessed 15 May 2024).
11 War Office, *The Manual of Military Law* (London: HMSO, 1914), p. 198.
12 C. R. L. Fletcher and Rudyard Kipling, *A School History of England* (Oxford: Clarendon Press, 1911), p. 240.
13 Grant Allen [Charles Allen], 'The Reverend John Creedy', *Cornhill Magazine*, 41, series 2 (September 1883), 225–42; Mary Gaunt and J. R. Essex, *The Arms of the Leopard: A West African Story* (London: Grant Richards, 1904); Mary Gaunt and J. R. Essex, *The Silent Ones* (London: T. W. Laurie, 1909); Hesketh Bell, *Love in Black* (London: Edward Arnold, 1911); John Buchan, *Prester John* (New York: Houghton Mifflin, 1910).
14 Philippa Levine, 'Naked Truths: Bodies, Knowledge, and the Erotics of Colonial Power', *Journal of British Studies*, 52:1 (2013), 5–25. H. N. Hutchinson, J. Gregory and R. Lydekker, *The Living Races of Mankind* (London: Hutchinson, 1901), contained 648 images of 'natives', many unclothed.
15 Paul Greenhalgh, *Ephemeral Vistas: The 'Expositions Universelles', Great Exhibitions and World Fairs, 1851–1939* (Manchester: Manchester University Press, 1988); Anandi Ramamurthy, *Imperial Persuaders: Images of Africa and Asia in British Advertising* (Manchester: Manchester University Press, 2003).
16 *Encyclopædia Britannica*, 11th edn (New York, 1910–11), Vol. I, p. 325, and Vol. XIX, p. 344.

17 Marilyn Lake and Henry Reynolds, *Drawing the Global Colour Line: White Men's Countries and the International Challenge of Racial Equality* (Cambridge: Cambridge University Press, 2008); Felix Lösing, *A 'Crisis of Whiteness' in the 'Heart of Darkness': Racism and the Congo Reform Movement* (Bielefeld: transcript-Verlag, 2020).
18 *Taylor & Cutter* (3 September 1903), pp. 54–5.
19 This is a personal observation based on many years' reading newspaper reports on Black people in Britain for the years c. 1880–1914.
20 The enduring interracial marriages, across the social classes, merit more attention than they have received.
21 Christopher Leslie Brown, *Moral Capital: Foundations of British Abolitionism* (Chapel Hill: University of North Carolina Press, 2003).
22 David Killingray, 'Hands Joined in Brotherhood: The Rise and Decline of a Movement for Faith and Social Change, 1875–2000', in Anthony Cross, Peter J. Morden and Ian Randall (eds), *Pathways and Patterns in History: Essays on Baptists, Evangelicals, and the Modern World in Honour of David Bebbington* (Didcot: Spurgeon's College and Baptist Historical Society, 2015), pp. 319–39.
23 Brian Willan, *Sol Plaatje: A Life of Solomon Tshekisho Plaatje, 1876–1932* (Auckland Park: Jacana, 2018), pp. 274–76; 'Greetings from South Africa', *Brotherhood Journal* (October 1915), 311; 'Brotherhood Movement: West Ealing Welcomes a Speaker from South Africa', *Hanwell Gazette* (18 July 1915).
24 Caroline Bressey, *Empire, Race and the Politics of 'Anti-Caste'* (London: Bloomsbury, 2013).
25 *Ibid.*, pp. 91–2.
26 When Naoroji, for a second time, had stood for Parliament in 1888, Lord Salisbury, the Conservative prime minister, said that 'I doubt if we have yet got to that point when a British constituency will take a black man to represent them'; Rozina Visram, *Asians in Britain: 400 Years of History* (London: Pluto, 2002), p. 133.
27 *Fraternity* (July 1893), p. 7. Douglas A. Lorimer, 'Legacies of Slavery for Race, Religion, and Empire: S. J. Celestine Edwards and the *Hard Truth* (1894)', *Slavery & Abolition*, 38:4 (2012), 731–55.
28 Hakim Adi, *African and Caribbean People in Britain: A History* (London: Allen Lane, 2022), p. 185.
29 Satnam Virdee, 'Socialist Anti-Semitism and Its Discontents in England, 1884–98', *Patterns of Prejudice*, 51:3–4 (2017), 356–73.
30 James Heartfield, *The Aborigines' Protection Society: Humanitarian Imperialism in Australia, New Zealand, Fiji, Canada, South Africa and the Congo, 1836–1909* (London: Hurst, 2011).
31 *Ibid.*, pp. 82–5; James Heartfield, *The British and Foreign Anti-Slavery Society, 1838–1956: A History* (London: Hurst, 2016), pp. 389–90.
32 Keshia N. Abraham and John Woolf, *Black Victorians Hidden in History* (London: Duckworth, 2022), pp. 261–2.
33 *The Friend* (22 October 1897), p. 708.
34 Pietermaritzburg Archives, South Africa, Colenso Papers, A204, pamphlets and periodicals, C.1283/5; 'The African Association Instituted 24th September 1897,

Rules', *Annual Report 1897–1898*, p. 7; *Aborigines' Friend* (November 1897), pp. 297–8; Marika Sherwood, *Origins of Pan-Africanism: Henry Sylvester Williams, Africa, and the African Diaspora* (London: Routledge, 2011).

35 Reported in the liberal *Westminster Gazette* (26 October 1898), p. 6; *Lagos Standard* (4 January 1899, p. 2; 1 February 1899, p. 2; 8 February 1899, p. 3; 4 October 1899, pp. 2–3).

36 On prominent white members see Gwilym Colenso and Christopher Saunders, 'New Light on the Pan-African Association: Part I', *African Research & Documentation*, 107 (2008), 27–45, and 'New Light on the Pan-African Association: Part II', *African Research & Documentation*, 108 (2009), 89–109.

37 Oxford, Bodleian Library, Rhodes House Library, MSS Brit. Emp. S18 C91/6; see the headed notepaper, Williams to Travers Buxton, 2 April 1900.

38 *The Colored American* (11 August 1900), p. 14.

39 *Daily Graphic* (London) (24 July 1900), p. 8; *Report of the Pan-African Conference, Held on the 23rd, 24th and 25th July, 1900* (London: n.p., [1900]).

40 *Report of the Pan-African Conference*, pp. 12, 13. Du Bois gave oxygen to the 'colour line' phrase, adding 'the relation of the darker to the lighter races of men in Asia and Africa, in America and the islands of the sea', which appeared as the opening lines of the second essay in W. E. B. Du Bois, *The Souls of Black Folk* (Chicago: A. C. McClurg, 1903). The biographer of Du Bois, David Levering Lewis, misleadingly credits the 'Memorial' solely to him: *W. E. B. Du Bois: Biography of a Race, 1869–1919* (New York: Henry Holt, 1993), pp. 250–1.

41 *Review of Reviews* (August 1900), pp. 73–4; Rich, *Race and Empire*, p. 33.

42 Hollis R. Lynch, *Edward Wilmot Blyden: Pan-African Patriot 1832–1912* (London: Oxford University Press, 1967), p. 6.

43 Kew, The National Archives, CO96/403/11591 (19 March 1902).

44 Robert Burroughs, *Black Students in Imperial Britain: The African Institute, Colwyn Bay, 1889–1911* (Liverpool: Liverpool University Press, 2023), pp. 161–2.

45 Review of Omoniyi's book in *Labour Leader* (3 April 1908), 211. See Adi, *African and Caribbean People*, pp. 218–19.

46 Burroughs, *Black Students*, pp. 154–60.

47 Jeffrey C. Stewart, *The New Negro: The Life of Alain Locke* (New York: Oxford University Press, 2020 [2018]), pp. 143, 148–50.

48 *The Telephone* (May 1907).

49 Scholes, *Glimpses of the Ages*, Vol. II, p. ix.

50 'Eugenics', in *Encyclopædia Britannica*, Vol. IX, p. 885. See further Lorimer, *Science*, pp. 86–7; Charles King, *The Reinvention of Humanity: A Story of Race, Sex, Gender and the Discovery of Culture* (London: Bodley Head, 2019).

51 Visram, *Asians in Britain*, pp. 155–62.

52 Used in the strapline on the LUB's headed notepaper.

53 Willan, *Sol Plaatje*, Chapter 9.

54 G. Spiller (ed.), *Papers on Inter-Racial Problems* (London: P. S. King, 1911), Sixth Sessions, pp. 328–82, with papers given by J. Tengo Jabavu, Mojola Agbebi and W. E. B. Du Bois; Lake and Reynolds, *Drawing the Global Colour Line*, pp. 251–62.

55 *The Times* (29 July 1911), p. 4.
56 *Crisis* (September 1911), p. 196.
57 Ian Duffield, 'Dusé Mohamed Ali and the Development of Pan-Africanism, 1866–1945', PhD thesis, 2 vols (Edinburgh University, 1971).
58 Adam Ewing, *The Age of Garvey: How a Jamaican Activist Created a Mass Movement and Changed Global Black Politics* (Princeton, NJ: Princeton University Press, 2014), pp. 38–44.
59 The term 'colo[u]r bar' originated in the USA, and was introduced into Britain c. 1900; see *Yorkshire Evening Post* (22 August 1901), p. 2.
60 *Journal of the African Society*, 12:48 (July 1913), pp. 425–31.
61 Quoted in Hakim Adi, *West Africans in Britain 1900–1960: Nationalism, Pan-Africanism and Communism* (London: Lawrence & Wishart, 1999), p. 15.
62 *Church Times* (20 June 1908), pp. 6, 8; (26 June 1908), p. 887.
63 *Belfast News-Letter* (20 June 1908), p. 5.
64 *Westminster Gazette* (3 October 1913), p. 10.
65 David Killingray, '"To do something for the race": Harold Moody, and the League of Coloured Peoples', in Bill Schwarz (ed.), *West Indian Intellectuals in Britain* (Manchester: Manchester University Press, 2003), pp. 51–70.
66 For a useful outline see Adi, *African and Caribbean People*, pp. 231–71.

2

From racist humanitarianism to colonial human rights: The British Congo Reform Movement and the complicated history of (anti-)racism

Felix Lösing

Racism has always been contested. Given that racism is constituted as a social relation, opposition against racist formations has manifested in diverse forms of social struggle. These struggles have materialised in the realms of politics, culture and academia, as well as in everyday interactions, workplaces, streets, parliaments and legislation. 'Antiracism's meaning', as it has recently been emphasised, 'is found in this history'.[1]

However, is there genuinely a universal political tradition or a consistent ideology that binds these various anti-racisms together? If it holds true that racism is always 'historically specific', as Stuart Hall has pointed out, then every anti-racist practice is similarly situated within its specific social and political context.[2]

Furthermore, the motives, methods and objectives of those who challenge a racist formation are typically multifaceted and polyphonic, often conflictive and sometimes contradictory. Resistance against racist relations has been undertaken both by members of oppressed groups and by those belonging to the imagined community of oppressors. Practices of resistance have ranged from at times militant self-defence to acts of solidarity to state-led anti-discrimination efforts. At times, the political and discursive boundaries between racism and anti-racism have appeared less distinct than their conceptual juxtaposition suggests. This chapter delves into this complicated history of (anti)-racism by means of the historical example of the British Congo Reform Movement. Through this examination, it explores the colonial and racist origins of the modern human rights movement while simultaneously exposing a case in which the creation and mythologisation of an anti-racist tradition are intertwined.[3]

The colonial and racist underpinnings of human rights

'Racism is the negation of everything for which human rights stand for.'[4] The claim of universally shared and inalienable rights of all human beings is a powerful instrument to oppose the dehumanisation and disenfranchisement of racist policy. The International Convention on the Elimination of All Forms of Racial Discrimination, established in 1965, is one of the longest-standing international human rights agreements in the United Nations' (UN) 'arsenal to target oppression and discrimination'.[5] And yet, while the UN Human Rights Office some years ago proudly presented 'success stories' from its '50 years of fighting racism',[6] scholars of international law concede that the elimination of racism 'remains an unrealized promise of universal human rights'.[7] Even more, critics from the Global South identify 'colonial trappings and "First World" hegemonic underpinnings' in the concept of human rights,[8] understand them as part of the global 'imperiality' power matrix,[9] or an outright neocolonial tool.[10] Only recently, Amnesty International has admitted how 'racism' and 'colonial power dynamics' had shaped its 'very organisational model'.[11]

Nonetheless, the modern rights movement unquestionably forms an intrinsic part of the history of anti-racism. Popular mobilisations against major historical formations of institutionalised racism such as slavery, segregation and apartheid were milestones for the international human rights crusade. For Adam Hochschild, 'there is no tradition more honorable' than these examples 'of men and women who fought against enormous odds' for the basic freedoms shared by all human beings. During its time 'on the world stage', he concluded, the Congo Reform Movement 'was a vital link in that chain'.[12] In his popular-scientific bestseller *King Leopold's Ghost*, the American journalist has erected a literary monument to the movement against the so-called Congo Scandal. By now, it is broadly recognised as 'the first great international human rights movement of the twentieth century',[13] which had mobilised hundreds of thousands of Britons against horrendous atrocities and misgovernment in the Congo Free State.

The vast colony in Central Africa had been ruled in absolutist manner by the Belgian King Léopold II since 1885. At international conventions such as the Berlin Congo Conference of 1884/5, and in various bilateral treaties and flamboyant public declarations, the Belgian monarch had portrayed his privately controlled possession as a philanthropic, disinterested and international colony.[14] However, in the late nineteenth and early twentieth centuries, a small and initially only loosely associated group around the veteran humanitarians Charles Dilke and Henry F. Bourne,[15] the evangelist Henry G. Guinness, and the business journalist and former shipping clerk Edmund D. Morel exposed the fact that the Free State had actually established a ruthless predatory economy that violated every pledge to up-lift the population, alleged to be inherently savage, and to guarantee free access for merchants and missionaries from all so-called civilised societies. Based on troublesome testimonies from travellers, missionaries and colonial agents, and investigations into trading statistics, these early critics claimed that the extraordinary

Congolese exports of ivory and natural rubber were based on a murderous scheme of forced labour, organised by a state-run system of monopolies and concessions directly controlled by the Congolese *roi-souverain*, Léopold.[16]

Slowly but steadily, the contours of one of the biggest misdeeds in colonial history emerged that soon seriously unsettled the imperial public in Britain, but also continental Europe and the United States. A veritable public relations battle between the growing band of Congo critics and a widespread and well-organised network of Free State apologists broke out.[17] As a result, the House of Commons eventually petitioned the Conservative Balfour government to conduct a 'judicial inquiry'.[18] Vice-Consul Roger Casement was dispatched to the Congo, and collected evidences about abuses such as the cutting-off of limbs by the armed forces of the Free State and its allied concessionary companies. His report, published as a white book by the Foreign Office on 10 February 1904, largely confirmed the existence of what was now discussed as the Congo Atrocities,[19] and immediately caused turmoil in the British and international press.[20]

On Casement's initiative, a Congo Reform Association was founded in Liverpool on 23 March.[21] The organisation bound together evangelical, humanitarian and free trade milieus to form a powerful political pressure group. Under the leadership of Morel, and significantly influenced by the missionary couple Alice and John Harris, the reform association gained the support of various political, religious and economic leaders, and prominent public figures such as the famous writers Joseph Conrad and Arthur Conan Doyle, and the African explorer Harry Johnston. Moreover, the campaign reached broad spheres of the British middle and upper classes. Between 1903 and 1913, more than 400,000 Britons gathered at public Congo demonstrations or attended so-called 'atrocity lectures'.[22]

The organised Reform Movement now fought vigorously against the Free State system of monopolistic trading concessions and forced labour. Instead, as will be discussed later, they proposed a practical and more humane colonial governance based on the recognition of certain economic rights, free commercial relations and free missionising. Despite disagreements about the particular arrangement of the proposed reform policy, British reformers called for the annexation of Léopold's Free State through Belgium as the most realistic solution to the crisis of colonial policy in the Congo.[23] Confronted with rising domestic pressure and an escalating international reform campaign, the Belgian monarch eventually agreed to hand his private colony over to the Belgian State. In 1908, the Congo Free State ceased to exist and Belgian Congo was created.[24]

For the Indigenous inhabitants, this transition was only of doubtful value. The Belgian Government launched selective and limited reforms, particularly concerning the forced rubber collection, but economic exploitation including compulsory labour, political repression and cultural oppression persisted, albeit often in a less openly brutal manner.[25] The British public and activists heralded a full-scale victory of the Congo Reform Movement, though. The 'forces of humanitarianism' had prevailed, a Liverpool journal rejoiced toward the end of the campaign, 'and the cause of righteousness has triumphed'.[26]

In the past decades, this perspective on the Congo Reform Movement has stiffened to a widespread historical assessment. Of course, its international line of action, cutting-edge methods of protest (such as the use of atrocity photographs and projections through magic lanterns), and the magnitude of its subject and catalyst give the movement an outstanding place in imperial and human rights history. Nonetheless, in many academic analyses and cultural representations, an unbalanced and sometimes distorting portrayal of the political objectives and ideological constitution of the movement has dominated. These portrayals have attempted to elevate the Congo activists to valiant human rights pioneers full of empathy with the exploited in the colonies, and thus to a moral antithesis to the crimes of European colonialism, glorified as noble 'liberal altruism'[27] or modern 'heroism'.[28] However, any understanding of the Congo Reform Movement as a stronghold of 'colourless' empathy or an antagonist to the moral corrosion of New Imperialism can only be maintained if one ignores the movement's commitment to white European superiority and the related legitimate entitlement to global supremacy. The humanitarian sentiment of the Congo Reform Movement and its peculiar version of human rights were as racist as they were colonial.

The promises of Congo colonialism

In summer 1906, in the hey-day of the reform campaign, the *Contemporary Review* published an eloquent assault on the Congo Free State. Here, Harold Spender, journalist and member of the Executive Committee of the Congo Reform Association, issued a dramatic warning. In the Congo, under the very eyes of the depraved King Léopold II, and inactively observed by the neighbouring imperial powers, the 'white man's burden' was about to become the 'white man's undoing'.[29] For Spender, 'The Great Congo Iniquity' had visibly transcended the geographical and discursive boundaries of Africa or African suffering. Instead, the crisis in the colonial periphery directly pointed back to the imperial metropole and the colonising subjectivity. In nineteenth-century imperial discourse, the white man was the central embodiment of white racial superiority and the derived implementation of global white supremacy. The broadly popular imperial adventure and travel literature, colonial exhibitions and world fairs, or racist imagery of colonial advertising centrally circled around the allegedly heroic exploits of the pioneers of exploration and colonisation. Poems such as Rudyard Kipling's 'White Man's Burden' culturally bound their readers to the 'glories and difficulties' of a white 'tradition of executive responsibility towards the coloured races'.[30] As 'an idea, a persona, a style of being', the colonial white man directly distributed the 'symbolic resources of Empire' to readers, spectators and consumers, and elevated them to a superior racial and 'imperial status'.[31] According to Spender, however, the imperial tide had changed. The scandalous conditions in the Congo Free State opened up the worrying prospect of imperial failure, a perishing of the white man and the undoing of the related 'superior ontological status plus great power' it had once symbolised.[32]

To understand this ideological nexus and the profound sense of betrayal that arose from the Free State it is significant to recapitulate the immense discursive, political and social expectations invested in the colonisation of the Congo. Although it was never a British possession, the British public had a long and profound interest in the Congo Basin. After all, it was the British naval officer Verney Lovett Cameron who had been the first European to explore the region's economic potential and had given report of a 'country of unspeakable richness'.[33] The Welsh-American journalist Henry M. Stanley broadly popularised the image of the Congo as the even gloomier heart of an already 'Dark Continent'.[34] His dispatches, articles and best-selling books portrayed the inhabitants of the region as 'the most vicious and degraded of the human race',[35] who dwelled 'without the lightest veneer of artificialism over man's natural state'.[36] The Great Congo Forest became known as a dark expanse of 'ancient'[37] and 'primeval'[38] nature, a dangerous 'region of horrors'[39] fraught with a haunting spirit of 'evil',[40] but also promised untold treasures to every adventurous European conqueror. Stanley's mythologisation of alterity and inferiority quickly rose to become *the* authoritative representation of the Congo in the Western mind.

Soon, this narrative would be turned into political practice, institutionally embodied by the colony later known as the Congo Free State. The key actor in this transformation was the Belgian King Léopold II, who had followed closely all news emerging from the region. In 1876, shortly after Cameron's return, Léopold summoned an international Geographical Conference in Brussels. Here, he emphasised his dedication 'to pierc[ing] the darkness' of Central Africa and leading all coming colonisation efforts toward the Congo basin.[41] The convention ended with the formation of an 'African International Association' under Léopold's presidency, pledged to plan and conduct an ostensibly scientific, philanthropic and abolitionist mission as soon as possible.[42]

In fact, Léopold was desperate to secure himself a 'slice of this magnificent African cake'.[43] Secretly, he followed the plan to establish a dependency under his full personal control, hoped to be the seed of a future Belgian colony.[44] In the royal palaces of Brussels, Stanley's Congo writings, replete with exoticism, dramatic adventures and heroic battle stories, were regarded as letters of application. There was of course some contemporary criticism of the violence on Stanley's expedition, whose geographical discoveries were based on 'bloodshed and slaughter.'[45] In general, however, the press celebrated him and his European officers for their 'truly heroic' confrontation of the 'relentless forces of nature and barbarism'.[46] With regard to Stanley's rising popularity and demonstrated ability to thrive in the challenging Congolese environment, Léopold was convinced that he had found the right man to implement this delicate and ambitious plot.

Shortly after his initial five-year expedition, recounted in *Through the Dark Continent*, Stanley was persuaded to lead a new mission. On 14 August 1879, he returned to establish a network of stations for the African International Association and other new frontier organisations formed to conceal Léopold's geopolitical interests. Within five years, ports, stations and fortifications were constructed, along with a road and river navigation network, all secured by a small yet powerfully armed military force. It was the fateful commencement of the forceful subjugation of millions of Indigenous inhabitants.

On the international stage, Léopold and Stanley successfully portrayed themselves as guardians of Europe's historic civilising mission 'to brighten up with the glow of civilisation the dark places of sad-browed Africa'.[47] British Church leaders, Chambers of Commerce and even humanitarian organisations such as the APS viewed the state 'with a humanitarian on the throne' with 'sympathy' and 'enthusiasm'.[48] By promising indiscriminate access to undeveloped Central African markets, Léopold also garnered international political support for his endeavour. Until the final act of the Berlin Congo Conference of 1884/5, Léopold's envoys arranged the diplomatic recognition of his sovereignty by all major European powers and the United States. In view of rising internal imperial rivalries, the statesmen and diplomats assembled in Berlin lauded Léopold's commitments to forming a politically neutral colony, offering the right of 'free access' to merchants and missionaries of all nationalities and creeds.[49] On 1 August 1885, the Congo Free State was officially proclaimed. When less than a decade later the fierce resistance of pre-existing African and Arab-Muslim power structures was 'crushed out of existence',[50] the British public celebrated the establishment of a hegemonic historic structure of a collective European rule in Central Africa.[51]

British missionary societies, merchants and investors enthusiastically followed Leopold's invitation to 'open-up' the Congo.[52] Moreover, many

Britons, like other internationals, enrolled for positions in the colonial administration and its security forces. Consequently, the Free State's missionary corps, its trading agents and its civil and military officers had an extraordinarily diverse background, concerning nationality, confession and also class.[53] Nonetheless, in their daily interactions on the colonial frontier, all members of the colonial master class experienced a form of negative inclusion into a position of 'colonial whiteness' that emerged through absolute opposition to and the vilification of the African population. Integration into this imagined but socially and culturally experienced community had the capacity to mask the social fragmentation of the European metropole and foster negative cohesion.[54] The colonising subjects on the isolated state posts were awarded with what could be called a 'racist symbolic capital' through their right to control and despise the Congolese, and were of course financially participating in the colonial pillage.[55]

This accumulation of economic and symbolic capital was not limited to the periphery. The aforementioned commodification of racism and imperial culture in the nineteenth century had produced what has been called an 'empire for the masses'.[56] Stanley's mythical Congo was a central pillar of this rising 'popular imperialism',[57] processed in various forms of cultural commodities such as countless boyhood adventure anthologies, visual illustrations and artworks, advertising campaigns and postcards, and successful exhibitions. In contrast to Stanley's 'Darkest Africa', a potent pseudo-identity for an imagined racist community of 'Brightest Europe' emerged, established by the narrative of a violent confrontation and successful subjugation of the alienated Congolese space and people through a single white and 'civilised' hero.[58] Within the commodified spectacle surrounding Stanley's exploits in the Congolese jungles, broad spheres of the British society across all classes and milieus identified with his inexorable cultural and racial superiority, and developed their own ethnic mass honour and imperial status.

The colonial crisis in the Congo

At the turn of the twentieth century the first controversies emerged surrounding the actual state of colonialism in the Congo. Accounts from missionaries, former Free State agents, journalists, humanitarian networks and British envoys exposed not only carnage against the Congolese population, but instances of repression against those members of the colonial master class who were neither Belgian nor Catholic. The 'native question'[59] circulated around the so-called Congo Atrocities, encompassing mutilations, extensive flogging, massacres and the demolition of entire villages. These atrocities formed the foundation of an extensive system of forced labour fuelling the export of natural caoutchouc. The 'catalogue of horrors'[60] from the Congo shocked the public, and the 'perversion of philanthropic intentions'[61] alienated many of Léopold's former supporters. British missionaries, abolitionists and humanitarians now took the lead of the burgeoning anti-Free State campaign.

However, the impact of Léopold's exposed terror regime on British public sentiment cannot be attributed solely to humanitarian compassion for African suffering. The intense popular indignation that sparked demonstrations and protest meetings hints at a deeper discursive and political disturbance. The European question within the Congo scandal appears as a worrying corrosion of imperial alterity, in demarcation toward both an assumed savage Africa and a despotic Arab-Muslim culture.[62] The latter perspective was symbolised by the establishment of a new 'Slave State' through a supposedly progressive and abolitionist colony,[63] rendering it an 'anomaly and scandal in the modern world'.[64] The former aspect was articulated, for instance, in the allegation that the Force Publique, the Free State's army and police corps, largely comprising African recruits and conscripts, consisted of thousands of 'cannibal troops'.[65] Herewith, Léopold had actively allied himself with the 'forces of savagery', it was argued.[66]

Spender's metaphor of the undoing of the white man in this context alludes to a process of deculturalisation and a broader dissatisfaction with the concept of European civilisation. The Congo Atrocities cast, as Arthur Conan Doyle noted, a 'strange light upon the real value of those sonorous words Christianity and civilization'.[67] Reform activists interpreted the brutal profit-seeking in Léopold's colony as the symptom of a moral regress within an excessively materialistic capitalist modernity. For Spender, the 'union between greed and science' in the Congo gave birth to a 'civilised savagery' devoid of passion, guided by cold calculation and enforced through a machinery of destruction.[68] While this criticism did not explicitly contest the opposition of an irrational Africa and a rational West, it did still sharply question the moral integrity of the latter category.

Moreover, the abhorrent crimes substantially impeded the potential for racist societalisation in and around the Congo. Observers were particularly dismayed by the fall from grace of once admired colonial heroes. In this context, the undoing of the white man might well correspond to the demise of a stereotype. Indeed, contemporaries mourned the loss of the grandeur and chivalry of 'romantic whiteness' associated with their imperial boyhood heroes.[69] The Congo atrocities turned the imperial white man from a source of racial pride to a symbol of disgrace. For Roger Casement, for instance, the ill treatment of the Congolese made him 'sick at heart for the lot of these people', but at the same time 'ashamed of [his] own skin colour'.[70] The 'complicity'[71] of Britons through their participation in state administration, commerce and Church activities, and the former public sympathy for the Free State, also gave this disgrace a national dimension, since the Congo infamy stained Britain's 'dignity' and 'honour' as a nation.[72] Hence, the Congo scandal seriously eroded Stanley's vision of an imagined community of Brightest Europe. The Congo not only became a source of ethnic shame, dishonouring the imagined communities of whiteness and civilisation, but negatively affected British national consciousness.

Furthermore, the Free State similarly disrupted the allocation of more material rewards. Astonished, foreign observers noted the transformation of the once multinational state into 'a Belgian colony in all but name'.[73] Critics highlighted trading monopolies and discrimination against non-Belgian merchants and Protestant missionaries, in full 'contravention' of the General Act of Berlin.[74] As the journalist W. T. Stead complained, the 'open door guaranteed by international law has been closed and bolted in the face of the world'.[75] The outcry that the Free State harassed 'Europeans and natives alike' significantly fuelled the Congo controversy,[76] and the European question always accompanied and sometimes predominated over the native question. On a macroeconomic level, both sides were directly related. The reckless plunder in the Free State was damaging the Congolese reserves of labour, it was warned: an inexcusable consequence, since in the harsh climatic conditions of the region, only Africans could 'gather the produce of the soil the European desires', Morel reminded.[77]

In addition, the Free State's actions undermined the principal self-legitimation of New Imperialism. Léopold's colony had introduced strife, bondage and devastation where it had promised pacification, liberation and progress. This colossal deception of the very organisation that had been presented as the disinterested trustee of Europe's mission to civilise Africa exposed this narrative as the pure and hollow ideology that it was. Reform activists warned that the Congo scandal was already 'disastrous to European prestige'[78] in Central Africa and could potentially become a 'menace to white administration' across the continent.[79] In this context, the Force Publique was described as a proverbial powder-keg. Battle-hardened and well-equipped with 'modern weapons of destruction', Léopold's alleged 'great army of cannibal levies', became increasingly uncontrollable. Often mistreated by their European officers, they were 'eager to seize upon the first opportunity … of turning their weapons against their temporary masters'.[80] Reports about mutinies ignited fearful comments in Britain, in which racist tropes and geostrategic arguments were combined in an alarmist rhetoric. These insurgencies directly endangered adjacent British territories, it was claimed in the Commons, and already 'cannibal troops [had] been let loose to raid their neighbours'.[81] Throughout the Congo, an 'undying hatred of the white' was observed,[82] leading to acts of disobedience ranging from local insurrections to full-scale armed revolts from the civil population, which resulted in an escalating cycle of repression and resistance.[83] When the Congo reformers looked to Central Africa, they saw a colony on the fringe of collapsing.

Morel understood this security crisis as a continental – even global – threat, whose colour-coded representation hints at an intrinsically racial dimension. A 'great black wave' of anti-colonial resistance was created in the Congo that threatened to obliterate 'every trace of a civilization' in West Africa and to 'roll sullenly forward even unto the ocean', the leader of the British Congo reformers warned.[84] Harry Johnston similarly warned his readers that the Congo Atrocities could ignite 'such a rising against the white man ... as will surpass any revolt that has ever yet been made by the black and the yellow man against his white brother and overlord'.[85] Warnings from a global 'conflagration'[86] of anti-white resistance resonated dramatically with a public that was increasingly disturbed by worrying signs of racial decline and military setbacks all over the world.[87] Hence, the Congo transformed within decades from a symbol of the global establishment of white rule to a portent of the fragility of white supremacy itself, and even to a potential vantage point for its corrosion.

Redemption of Congo colonialism

The Congo Reform Movement's well-known political aspiration to eliminate atrocities served as its programmatic foundation, lauded and remembered until today. Its historical task, however, as it emerges from its discursive architecture, lay in addressing an interconnected crisis of racist representation, racist societalisation and racist politics. The movement's approach to the first dimension was defined by the construction of a liberation narrative. This tale revealed the colonial and racist origin of the early human rights movement, encapsulating a Congolese version of the 'dramatic humanitarian triangle',[88] in which *civilised and white saviours* rescued *helpless victims* from *savage perpetrators*. All metaphoric corners of this symbolic relation largely drew upon the pre-established racist Congo narrative pervasive in pro-colonial discourse.

In the fierce public controversy about the cutting off of hands, one of the most repulsive practices of the colonial state, prominent reformers still rejected the attempts of Léopold and Stanley to blame the 'sanguine habits'[89] and 'abominable customs'[90] of African soldiers as an obvious diversionary tactic. These mutilations were 'not native custom prior to the coming of the white man', and were 'not the outcome of the primitive instincts of savages', Casement contended, but rather a European import.[91]

Nevertheless, beyond the severed-hand debate, both sides exhibited little ideological disparity concerning the existence of these so-called primitive or savage behaviours. Central Africa was indeed 'one of the most savage regions of the world', Casement conceded.[92] Hence, when a colonial state recruited 'an admittedly savage soldiery', the root of atrocities 'need not be sought far'.[93] Recourses to cultural predispositions were frequently combined with arguments of racial determination. When the Free State's soldiers were allowed to 'do as they please', they were 'like devils', the British public was informed,[94] since '[b]lack delights to kill black'.[95] The Free State's original sin was the devolvement of its military power to Africans. The 'atrocities and misdeeds' were the 'necessary consequences'.[96]

In this way, the 'actual, though not the moral' responsibility for the Congo Atrocities was relegated to the African 'perpetrator' and his essential Africanness. The latter was even blamed with regard to the moral responsibility of the European officers, who not only commanded the marauding soldiery but frequently partook in atrocious acts. These men, Spender emphasised with a reference to Joseph Conrad's famous Congo novellas, had 'gradually descended to depths of which the modern European was assumed to be incapable'.[97] Indeed, in *Heart of Darkness* and *The Outpost of Progress*, the Polish-British author skilfully tells of isolated European colonists who dropped their thin veneer of civilisation amidst the natural savagery, spiritual darkness and deadly climate of the Congo.[98] This fictional storyline was straightforwardly echoed in the political arguments of the Reform Movement. In such a challenging environment, every European would have found it difficult to 'maintain their civilized morale' and sometimes 'yielded [...] to their surroundings', Doyle noted.[99] Essentially, the Congo Atrocities were refigured as an African crime, and the corroded boundaries between European civilisation and Congolese savagery partly re-erected.

At the same time, Europe's own painfully realised weakness in the face of a triumphing internal and external African wilderness was projected onto the Congolese sufferers of colonial violence. Primarily depicted as 'helpless women and harmless children',[100] the African victims of the Congo Atrocities embodied notions of cultural immaturity and moral innocence. Even more, victimhood was racially and culturally essentialised as an inherent characteristic of the 'helpless races' of Central Africa.[101] By appealing to different shades of the savage stereotype, the Congolese victim evolved as a safe object for pity and compassion, and herewith complemented the image of the male and adult African perpetrator.[102] Between both emerged the 'white and civilised saviour', completing the aforementioned racist dramatic triangle. Reform leaders such as Casement and Morel, 'the champion of the native races of the Congo',[103] were celebrated as a novel, humanitarian type of the imperial hero, combining the power to liberate Central Africa with a retrieved moral integrity.

This humanitarian 'heroism, classic in nature',[104] was not limited to these figureheads though, as suggested by the broad public support for the Reform Movement after Morel had successfully appealed to the 'soul' and 'honour' of the 'white races'.[105] The evangelical-styled atrocity lectures were a particular pivotal tool for the Reform Movement's popularity. Here, shocking photographs of mutilated Congolese were projected on large screens through Victorian magic lanterns.[106] Shudders, indignation, resolutions and donations were most often the intended result of these graphic confrontations with *The Reign of Terror in the Congo*.[107] However, this emotional response and expressed solidarity were ensnared within colonial metaphors and stereotypes. Right from the start, the audiences in British town halls and churches were entertained with highly stereotypical recourses to exploration and missionising, and the lectures finished with appeals to the power of the civilised spectators to safeguard once more the savage masses of the Congo.[108] The result was an identification with the objects of a racist 'phantasmagoria', and not with actual human beings living, suffering and fighting in the Congo.[109] The colonial spectacle of the atrocity meetings created a similar 'false empathy', as is observed in more recent paternalistic anti-racist struggles, understood as a counterpart to a Marxian notion of 'false consciousness', in which an oppressed people identifies with the perspectives of the aggressor and internalises their values.[110] The false empathy of the Congo reformers internalised and reproduced the racial hierarchies of imperialism and allowed the inclusion of hundreds of thousands of Britons in the group of heroic white and civilised saviours. In this way, the imperial gaze toward the Congo was once more turned into a source of ethnic mass honour.

With divergent impetus, this regained racist symbolic capital was accompanied with national pride. '[S]aving the races of Central Africa' was Britain's destiny, Morel held, and the Congo crisis actually an occasion for the 'race of Clarkson and of Wilberforce' to reconnect with its 'heritage of moral glory'.[111] Hence, the righteous cause 'to act on behalf' of the helpless millions of the Congo reaffirmed Britain and Britishness as the centre of a morally sound imperialism.[112]

On a more practical level, the Reform Movement concurrently aimed to reclaim British participation in Congo's colonisation, focusing on regaining access to the Congolese markets and resources as well as the church sector. To 're-establish the "basis of principle" set forth in the Berlin Act'[113] and return to the 'open door'[114] policy meant only to protect the 'legitimate interests'[115] of British missionaries and merchants alike.

In the case of the Congo, economic and humanitarian considerations supposedly perfectly matched. A return to a colonial system based on commercial freedom would benefit both Europeans and Africans, since it would necessarily be based on the recognition of certain 'economic rights' on the side of the African population.[116] This approach was indeed a significant departure from central motifs of contemporary colonial discourse, for instance from the myth that Central African soil had largely been uncultivated and vacant.[117] In contrast, reformers stated that the Congolese native had been 'the owner of the land and of the products of the land' before the arrival of the first Europeans.[118] Hence, the 'legitimate European enterprise in the African tropics',[119] namely the incorporation of African labour and resources into the capitalist world market, had to be achieved based on free labour, free trade and a recognition of 'immemorial'[120] and 'hereditary'[121] land rights.

Nonetheless, despite their conceptualisation in the inclusionary vocabulary of 'human rights'[122] or 'the rights of a Man',[123] the liberties demanded by the reformers were neither universal nor inalienable. They installed the African as a right-bearing individual, but rejected the African's equal footing with the imperial, white subject. Only 'certain rights' were 'common to humanity', it was clarified, and claims that 'the negro population of Africa' should be treated 'in all respects on equal terms with white men' were dismissed as 'short-sighted' and 'excessive'.[124] For Morel, just as much, 'racial and social inequality' was a fact.[125] He could not foresee any time in the future when the status of the West African societies would 'permit of the supreme governing power being shared by both races'.[126]

Hence, the reformers operated within the framework of a 'humanitarian racism',[127] in which different scales of humanity substituted the absolute dehumanisation of more exclusionary forms or racist classifications. In their rejection of all civil or political rights, they were ideologically closer to apologists of racial segregation in the New South than to an emerging anti-colonial sentiment and practice in the Global South. Colonial human rights, commercial freedom and native land tenure formed a toolkit for a more stable system of colonial rule ready to endure the new century, and were not a challenge to racist and colonial relations.

Indeed, the 'heroic' humanitarian crusade against Léopold and the Congo scandal not only restored belief in the power of European civilisation to overcome African darkness but also signified the persistence of morality and idealism in European modernity. Moreover, the Belgian annexation was eventually broadly accepted as a suitable measure to (re-)establish European hegemony over 'Darkest Africa', and a return to free trade and missionising once more allowed broader spheres of the British society to partake in the ongoing colonial plunder of the Congo.

Conclusion

There is no racism without resistance. This is evident to any researcher who diligently embarks on an investigation of the 'concrete historical "work"' of racism, as Stuart Hall once urged.[128] Researching and commemorating these historical struggles is both scientifically rewarding and politically significant. It reinstates agency for those who were objectified and discriminated against through racist discourse and practice, while challenging those who present their complicity in, or silence about, the racist relations surrounding them as being without alternatives.

Nevertheless, as the example of the Congo Reform Movement reveals, the historical struggle against racism is as intricate and contradictory as racism itself. British activists, predominantly privileged and often affluent white men, exposed and opposed one of the most atrocious regimes of the New Imperialism. Furthermore, their humanitarian stance, advocating for a minimum level of compassion transcending geographic and racial boundaries, challenged some of the most radical dehumanisations within contemporary racist discourses about Africa and the Congo. Their demand for specific colonial human rights had the potential to mitigate the profound disenfranchisement and genocidal extent of institutionalised racist exploitation. However, this specific historical protest against imperial and racist relations was concurrently an imperialist and racist struggle.

To those interested or directly involved in imperial policy in general, and the Congo in particular, Léopold's Free State, as a discursive, political and social formation, bore a transnational symbolism encompassing a trifold promise. First, its materialisation, as well as its textual representation, validated claims of a superior white race and an advanced European-Christian culture. Second, it postulated the establishment of an ostensibly unchallenged colonial hegemony in Africa. Third, it emphasised that all imperial societies and their citizens could equally benefit from the exploitation of the distant Congo colony. In all three spheres, Léopold and the Free State severely betrayed these expectations. It is this monumental failure that transformed the Congo scandal into a potential catalyst for the erosion of white supremacy and the dismantling of colonial whiteness.

Beyond and often above their concern for the cruel fate of the Indigenous population, what troubled the reform activists was how fundamentally the state in Léopold's distant colony negatively affected imperial hegemony; their personal (racial, cultural and national) identities; and the rights, privileges and benefits that they took for granted as citizens of imperial states and as white Europeans. The humanitarian empathy and colonial human rights advocated by the British Congo Reform Movement were fundamentally a project of self-redemption, aimed at resolving a historical crisis of racist discourse, racist policy and racist societalisation through the promotion of a more gentle, practical and stable colonial reform policy.

The history of the Congo Reform Movement reveals that understanding racism as the exclusive ideological domain of anti-Enlightenment reactionaries, slaveholders, proponents of apartheid or right-wing extremists dangerously underestimates its political reach and ideological adaptability. Instead, racism is a multifaceted social relation that affects all political ideologies, social classes and milieus – even those opposing (certain forms of extreme) racist discrimination. If we genuinely seek to learn from the past for the anti-racist struggles of today and tomorrow, we require empirically thorough and theoretically sound research into the oscillation of these historical struggles between solidarity and paternalism, altruism and selfishness, (false) empathy and discontent, and into the complicated, sometimes dialectical relationship between racism and anti-racism. Otherwise, we are in danger of creating new myths and legends of heroic white saviours, rather than empowering traditions.

Notes

1 Alex Zamalin, *Antiracism: An Introduction* (New York: New York University Press, 2019), p. 7.
2 Stuart Hall, 'Race, Articulation and Societies Structured in Dominance', in UNESCO (ed.), *Sociological Theories* (Paris: UNESCO, 1980), pp. 305–44 (p. 336).
3 The arguments in this chapter tie in with the comprehensive research for my dissertation, which encompasses both the British and US Congo Reform Movement's entanglement with racism and colonialism. See Felix Lösing, *A 'Crisis of Whiteness' in the 'Heart of Darkness': Racism and the Congo Reform Movement* (Bielefeld: Transcript, 2020).
4 'Rassismus ist die Negation alles dessen, wofür die Menschenrechte stehen' (my translation). Heiner Bielefeldt, 'Rassismusbekämpfung im Streit der internationalen Menschenrechtspolitik', policy paper of the *Deutsches Institut für Menschenrechte/German Institute for Human Rights*, 4 (2009), p. 3. www.institut-fuer-menschenrechte.de/fileadmin/user_upload/Publikationen/Policy_Paper/policy_paper_13_rassismusbekaempfung_im_streit_der_internationalen_menschenrechtspolitik.pdf (accessed 19 May 2024).
5 Committee on the Elimination of Racial Discrimination, 'International Convention on the Elimination of All Forms of Racial Discrimination: 50 Years of Fighting Racism', www.ohchr.org/en/treaty-bodies/cerd/international-convention-elimination-all-forms-racial-discrimination-50-years-fighting-racism (accessed 9 June 2024).
6 Ibid.
7 Anna Spain Bradley, 'Human Rights Racism', *Harvard Human Rights Journal*, 32 (2019), 1–58.
8 Ratna Kapur, 'Human Rights in the 21st Century: Taking a Walk on the Dark Side', *Sydney Law Review*, 28:4 (2006), 665–87 (p. 684).
9 Revathi Krishnaswamy, 'Postcolonial and Globalization Studies: Connections, Conflicts, Complicities', in Revathi Krishnaswamy and John C. Hawley

(eds), *The Postcolonial and the Global*, new edn (Minneapolis: University of Minnesota Press, 2008), pp. 2–210 (p. 12).
10. See Fidèle Ingiyimbere, *Domesticating Human Rights* (Cham: Springer, 2017), pp. 97–114.
11. 'Statement from the International Board on Amnesty International, Racism, and Black Lives Matter', email sent to all staff on 15 June 2020, as reproduced in the appendix of Howlett Brown, *Amnesty International Focus Group Report* (Amnesty International, 2020), p. 24.
12. Adam Hochschild, *King Leopold's Ghost: A Story of Greed, Terror, and Heroism in Colonial Africa* (Boston, MA: Houghton Mifflin, 1999), p. 306.
13. *Ibid.*, p. 2.
14. See Thomas Pakenham, *The Scramble for Africa* (London: Abacus, 1991), pp. 225–55.
15. On the longer traditions of imperial humanitarianism in Britain, as represented by Fox Bourne and his Aborigines' Protection Society, and its ambivalences between critique and paternalism, see David Killingray, 'Countering Racial Discrimination in Britain, 1880s–1913', Chapter 1 in this volume.
16. For a detailed discussion of this period of early exposure, see Lösing, *A 'Crisis of Whiteness'*, pp. 81–7.
17. *Ibid.*, pp. 88–97.
18. Arthur J. Balfour, 'Congo Free State', 122 Parl. Deb., HC (20 May 1903), col. 1331.
19. Roger Casement, 'Report on My Recent Journey on the Upper Congo', in Foreign Office (ed.), *Correspondence and Report from His Majesty's Consul at Boma Respecting the Administration of the Independent State of the Congo* (London: printed for HM Stationery Office by Harrison and Sons, 1904), pp. 21–82.
20. Dean Pavlakis, 'The Development of British Overseas Humanitarianism and the Congo Reform Campaign', *Journal of Colonialism and Colonial History*, 11:1 (2010), DOI: 10.1353/cch.0.0102.
21. Catherine A. Cline, *E. D. Morel, 1873–1924* (Dundonald: Blackstaff Press, 1980), pp. 42–4; Dean Pavlakis, *British Humanitarianism and the Congo Reform Movement, 1896–1913* (London: Routledge, 2016), pp. 58–65.
22. Pavlakis, *British Humanitarianism*, pp. 104–5.
23. Jules Marchal, *E. D. Morel contre Léopold II: L'histoire du Congo, 1900–1910*, 2 vols (Paris: L'Harmattan, 1996), Vol. II, pp. 263–4, 325–6.
24. *Ibid.*, p. 352.
25. Georges Nzongola-Ntalaja, *The Congo from Leopold to Kabila* (London: Zed Books, 2002), p. 26.
26. 'A Liverpool Hero and His Work', *Liverpool Echo* (31 May 1911), reproduced in Lord Cromer [Evelyn Baring] et al. (eds.), *The Public Presentation to Mr. E. D. Morel: Among Those Associated with the Effort for Reform of Conditions of the Congo, Whitehall Rooms, Hotel Metropole, on May 29th, 1911* ([London?]: n.p., [1911?]), p. 40.
27. Neal Ascherson, *The King Incorporated* (London: Allen & Unwin, 1963), p. 260.

28 Hochschild, *King Leopold's Ghost*, subtitle.
29 Harold Spender, 'The Great Congo Iniquity', *Contemporary Review*, 90 (July/December 1906), 46.
30 Edward Said, *Orientalism* (London: Penguin, 2003 [1978]), p. 226.
31 David Trotter, 'Colonial Subjects', *Critical Quarterly*, 32:3 (1990), 3–20 (p. 5).
32 Said, *Orientalism*, p. 226.
33 Letter of Verney L. Cameron, reproduced in 'Royal Geographic Society', *The Times* (11 January 1876), 3. See also Verney L. Cameron, *Across Africa*, 2 vols (London: Daldy, Isbister, 1877).
34 Henry M. Stanley, *Through the Dark Continent*, 2 vols (New York: Harper & Brothers, 1878); Henry M. Stanley, *The Congo and the Founding of Its Free State*, 2 vols (London: Sampson Low, Marston, Searle & Rivington, 1885); Henry M. Stanley, *In Darkest Africa* (New York: Charles Scribner's Sons, 1890). For colonial representations of the Congo, see Kevin C. Dunn, *Imagining the Congo* (New York: Palgrave Macmillan, 2003); Johnny van Hove, *Congoism* (Bielefeld: Transcript, 2017); and Frits Andersen, *The Dark Continent?* (Aarhus: Aarhus University Press, 2016).
35 Stanley, *In Darkest Africa*, Vol. II, p. 88.
36 Stanley, *The Congo*, Vol. II, p. 373.
37 A. L. Bruce, 4 September 1888, reproduced in 'Letter from Mr Stanley: The Explorer's Narrative of His Experiences', *Scotsman* (2 April 1889), 5.
38 Stanley, *In Darkest Africa*, Vol. I, p. 141.
39 *Ibid.*, p. 138.
40 Stanley, *Through the Dark Continent*, Vol. II, p. 137.
41 'Speech Delivered by the King at the Opening of the Conference: Léopold II at the Brussels Geographical Conference, 12 March 1876', reproduced in the appendix of Emile Banning, *Africa and the Brussels Geographical Conference* (London: Sampson Low, Marston, Searle & Rivington, 1877), p. 152.
42 Ascherson, *The King Incorporated*, pp. 93–101.
43 'une part de ce magnifique gâteau africain' (my translation). Léopold II to Baron Henry Solvyns, 17 November 1877, reproduced in Pierre van Zuylen, *L'échiquier congolais; ou, Le secret du roi* (Brussels: Charles Dessart, 1959), pp. 43–4.
44 Ascherson, *The King Incorporated*, pp. 109–11.
45 'Letters of Henry Stanley from Equatorial Africa to the *Daily Telegraph*', *Edinburgh Contemporary Review*, 147 (1878), 166–91 (p. 167).
46 'London, Monday, April 28, 1890', *The Times* (28 April 1890), 9.
47 Speech of Henry M. Stanley in front of the London Chamber of Commerce, 19 September 1884, as quoted in Edmund D. Morel, *Affairs of West Africa* (London: W. Heinemann, 1902), p. 312.
48 Herbert Samuel, 'Congo Free State', 122 Parl. Deb., HC (20 May 1903), cols 1300–1.
49 'Art. II, General Act of the Conference of Berlin Concerning the Congo, Signed at Berlin, February 26, 1885', *American Journal of International Law*, 3: S1 (1909), 7–25.
50 Sidney L. Hinde, *The Fall of the Congo Arabs* (London: Methuen, 1897), p. 22.

51 Lösing, A 'Crisis of Whiteness', pp. 210–15.
52 'Speech Delivered by the King', p. 152.
53 Lewis H. Gann and Peter Duignan, *The Rulers of Belgian Africa, 1884–1914* (Princeton: Princeton University Press, 2015 [1979]), pp. 59–60, 69–70, 100–7.
54 Lösing, A 'Crisis of Whiteness', pp. 275–9.
55 Anja Weiß, 'Racist Symbolic Capital', in Wulf D. Hund, Jeremy Krikler and David Roediger (eds), *Wages of Whiteness and Racist Symbolic Capital* (Berlin: Lit, 2010).
56 William H. Schneider, *An Empire for the Masses* (Westport, CT: Greenwood Press, 1982).
57 Jan Nederveen Pieterse, *White on Black: Images of Blacks in Western Popular Culture*, repr. edn (New Haven: Yale University Press, 1998), p. 77. See also Wulf D. Hund, 'Negative Societalisation: Racism and the Constitution of Race', in Hund et al., *Wages of Whiteness*, pp. 57–96 (p. 72).
58 Lösing, A 'Crisis of Whiteness', p. 126.
59 Henry R. Fox Bourne, *Civilisation in Congoland* (London: P.S. King and Son, 1903), p. 298.
60 John G. Leigh, introduction to Guy Burrows, *The Curse of Central Africa* (London: R. A. Everett, 1903), p. xvi.
61 Aborigines' Protection Society, *The Aborigines' Protection Society* (London: P. S. King & Son, 1899), pp. 52–3.
62 Jeff D. Bass, 'Imperial Alterity and Identity Slippage', *Rhetoric & Public Affairs*, 13:2 (2010), 281–308.
63 Edmund D. Morel, *The Congo Slave State* (Liverpool: J. Richardson & Sons, 1903).
64 Herbert Samuel, 'The Congo State and the Commission of Inquiry', *Contemporary Review*, 88 (December 1905), 881.
65 See, for instance, Morel, *The Congo Slave State*, pp. 18, 97; Edmund D. Morel, *King Leopold's Rule in Africa* (London: W. Heinemann, 1904), pp. 174n, 104, 176–7, 219.
66 Bourne, *Civilisation in Congoland*, p. 303.
67 Arthur Conan Doyle, introduction to Edmund D. Morel, *Great Britain and the Congo* (London: Smith, Elder, 1909), p. xv.
68 Spender, 'The Great Congo Iniquity', p. 45.
69 Felix Lösing, 'From the Congo to Chicago: Robert E. Park's Romance with Racism', in Wulf D. Hund and Alana Lentin (eds), *Racism and Sociology* (Zurich: Lit, 2014), pp. 107–22 (p. 115).
70 Roger Casement, as quoted in Robert M. Burroughs, *Travel Writing and Atrocities: Eyewitness Accounts of Colonialism in the Congo, Angola, and the Putumayo* (New York: Routledge 2011), p. 57; also see Morel, *King Leopold's Rule*, p. 243.
71 Morel, *Great Britain*, p. 127.
72 Henry Norman, 'Congo Free State', 184 Parl. Deb., HC (26 February 1908), col. 1861.
73 Jesse S. Reeves, *The International Beginnings of the Congo Free State* (Baltimore: Johns Hopkins University Press, 1894), p. 90.

74 George Grenfell to Alfred H. Baynes, August 1903, quoted in Kevin Grant, *A Civilised Savagery* (New York: Routledge, 2005), p. 46.
75 William T. Stead, 'Leopold, Emperor of the Congo', *The American Monthly Review of Reviews*, 28:1 (1903), 38.
76 Lionel Decle, 'The Murder in Africa,' *New Review*, 13:79 (1895), 587.
77 Morel, *King Leopold's Rule*, pp. 35–6.
78 *Ibid.*, p. xii.
79 Harry Johnston, quoted in 'Congo Reform Meetings in Liverpool', *Glasgow Herald* (20 March 1907), 8.
80 Morel, *Affairs of West Africa*, p. 351.
81 Samuel, 'Congo Free State', col. 1292.
82 Morel, *Affairs of West Africa*, p. 351.
83 Aldwin Roes, 'Towards a History of Mass Violence in the Etat Indépendant du Congo, 1885–1908', *South African Historical Journal*, 62:4 (2010), 634–70 (p. 635); Nzongola-Ntalaja, *The Congo*, p. 22.
84 Edmund D. Morel, *The British Case in French Congo: The Story of a Great Injustice, Its Causes and Its Lessons* (London: W. Heinemann, 1903), p. 11.
85 Harry H. Johnston, as quoted in Edmund D. Morel, *Red Rubber: The Story of the Rubber Slave Trade Flourishing on the Congo in the Year of Grace 1906* (London: T. Fisher Unwin, 1907), pp. 209–10. Further citations are to this edition unless otherwise indicated.
86 *Ibid.*, p. 209.
87 For instance, the British setbacks through the Mahdi revolt in Sudan (1885–95) and the failed Jameson Raid in South Africa (1895–96), the Ethiopian victory over Italy (1896), and the Russian defeat by the Japanese army (1904–05).
88 Jane Lydon, *Photography, Humanitarianism, Empire* (London: Bloomsbury, 2016), p. 6.
89 '"Letter from the King of the Belgians", Léopold II, 16 June 1897', reproduced in the appendix of Guy Burrows, *The Land of the Pigmies* (London: C. Arthur Pearson, 1898), p. 286.
90 Henry M. Stanley, quoted in Bourne, *Civilisation in Congoland*, p. 52.
91 Casement, 'Report on My Recent Journey', p. 76.
92 *Ibid.*, p. 21.
93 *Ibid.*, p. 59.
94 Diary of the missionary Joseph Clark, reproduced in Morel, *Red Rubber*, p. 53; and Arthur Conan Doyle, *The Crime of the Congo* (New York: Doubleday, Page, 1909), p. 48.
95 Edward J. Glave, 'New Conditions in Central Africa,' *Century Magazine*, 53 (1897), 908. Also reproduced in Bourne, *Civilisation in Congoland*, p. 183; and Doyle, *The Crime of the Congo*, p. 28.
96 Harry H. Johnston, *George Grenfell and the Congo* (London: Hutchinson, 1908), Vol. I, p. 464.
97 Spender, 'The Great Congo Iniquity', p. 46.
98 See Joseph Conrad, 'An Outpost of Progress', in Joseph Conrad, *Tales of Unrest* (London: Eveleigh Nash & Grayson, 1897); and Joseph Conrad, *Heart of Darkness*', in Paul. B. Armstrong (ed.), *'Heart of Darkness': Authoritative*

Text, Backgrounds and Contexts, Criticism, 4th edn (New York: W. W. Norton, 2006 [1902/1899]).
99 Doyle, *The Crime of the Congo*, p. 85.
100 *Ibid.*, p. 33; Bourne, *Civilisation in Congoland*, p. 210.
101 Lord Monkswell and Edmund D. Morel, *A Reply to the Belgian Manifestos* (London: Congo Reform Association, [c. 1909]), p. 3.
102 Lösing, *A 'Crisis of Whiteness'*, p. 186.
103 'Honouring Mr. Morel', *Bristol Times* (30 May 1911), as reproduced in Cromer, *The Public Presentation*, p. 41.
104 Félicien Challaye, quoted in Cromer, *Public Presentation*, p. 17.
105 Arthur Conan Doyle, quoted in *ibid.*, p. 22.
106 On the Victorian projectors, see Steve Humphries, *Victorian Britain through the Magic Lantern* (London: Sidgwick & Jackson, 1989).
107 The title of a successful lecture series by Henry Grattan Guinness; see 'Congo Reign of Terror', *Preston Herald* (30 March 1904), p. 4; Grant, *A Civilised Savagery*, pp. 61–2.
108 Lösing, *A 'Crisis of Whiteness'*, pp. 329–38.
109 Sharon Sliwinski, 'The Childhood of Human Rights: The Kodak on the Congo', *Journal of Visual Culture*, 5:3 (2006), 333–63 (p. 353).
110 Richard Delgado, *The Coming Race War?* (New York: New York University Press, 1996), p. 12.
111 Morel, *Red Rubber*, p. 200.
112 Resolution of the Congo Reform Association, quoted in Edmund D. Morel, *Red Rubber*, new and rev. edn (Manchester: National Labour Press, 1919), p. 224.
113 Edmund D. Morel and Congo Reform Association, *The Crisis in the Campaign against Congo Misrule* (Liverpool: John Richardson & Sons, 1907), p. 28.
114 Morel, *The British Case*, p. 186.
115 *Ibid.*, p. 148.
116 Morel, *Great Britain*, p. 187.
117 Grant, *Civilised Savagery*, pp. 12, 36.
118 Morel, *Great Britain*, p. 187.
119 Morel, *Red Rubber*, p. 201.
120 Morel, *Great Britain*, pp. 84, 218; Bourne, *Civilisation in Congoland*, p. 71.
121 Bourne, *Civilisation in Congoland*, pp. 132, 134.
122 For instance, Edmund D. Morel and Congo Reform Association, *A Memorial on Native Rights in the Land and Its Fruits in the Congo Territories Annexed by Belgium (Subject to International Recognition) in August, 1908* (London: Edward Hughes, 1908), p. 28.
123 Morel, *Red Rubber*, p. 205.
124 Samuel, 'Congo Free State', cols 1297–8.
125 Edmund D. Morel, *Nigeria* (London: Smith, Elder, 1911), p. 216.
126 *Ibid.*, p. xii.
127 Neil MacMaster, *Racism in Europe 1870–2000* (Houndmills: Palgrave, 2001), p. 13.
128 Hall, 'Race, Articulation and Societies Structured in Dominance', p. 338.

3

George Orwell, pan-Africanism and reconciling anti-imperialism with 'Britishness'

Theo Williams

In July 1939, George Orwell (1903–50) published a remarkable article in the *Adelphi*, a British left-wing literary journal. Orwell argued that in the compounding emergencies of the late 1930s ' "anti-Fascism" and "defence of British interests" are discovered to be identical'. The British ruling class had been forced against its will into an anti-Nazi position, and even Communists were 'waving Union Jacks'. The country was rushing inexorably toward a war against fascism and for 'democracy'. Nevertheless, some politicians and intellectuals held out hope for peace. In the article, Orwell paid special attention to Clarence Streit's recent book *Union Now*. Streit was a US journalist who advocated the federation of fifteen of the world's major democracies – including the United States, several northern and western European powers, and the Dominions of the British Empire – so as to ensure the peaceful continuation of the liberal world order. To Orwell, who had served as an imperial police officer in Burma during the 1920s, this smelled of 'hypocrisy and self-righteousness'. He observed that 'Mr Streit has coolly lumped the huge British and French empires – in essence nothing but mechanisms for exploiting cheap coloured labour – under the heading of democracies!' Indeed, 'the overwhelming bulk of the British proletariat' lived in Africa and Asia, rather than Britain. With regard to imperialism, it had 'become the first duty of a "good anti-Fascist" to lie about it and help to keep it in being.'[1]

In discussing George Orwell's (anti-)imperialism, scholars have been particularly concerned with his Burma writings – especially the essays 'A Hanging' (1931) and 'Shooting an Elephant' (1936) and the novel *Burmese Days* (1934) – all of which were influenced by Orwell's time as an imperial police officer. For some scholars, Orwell's experiences in Burma alerted him to the horrors of colonial rule; 'he wrote that his opposition to oppression was driven by "the immense weight of guilt I had got to expiate" as a consequence of his colonial service'.[2] To others, however, Orwell was concerned only, or at least primarily, with the suffering of the white man in the colonies. His opposition to empire stemmed from the realisation that 'when the white man turns tyrant it is his own freedom that he destroys'.[3] He was not interested in, and was unable to represent, the anti-colonial yearnings of the Burmese people, whom he generally portrayed as cowardly, shiftless and backward, a mass devoid of individual human personalities.[4] As Barry Hindess has observed, Orwell's Burma writings expressed a 'civilised distaste for imperial rule', in which his anti-colonialism belonged to a 'strand in liberal political thought which feels that the dirty work of empire is just too much to stomach'.[5] More recently, Douglas Kerr has commented on the 'bad fit between [Orwell's] indictments of empire and his disparaging of local resistance to it'.[6]

Even if Orwell's Burma writings were, in a sense, anti-imperialist, we might find the words of Chinua Achebe instructive. Achebe remarked that scholars of Joseph Conrad's novella *Heart of Darkness* (1899) often claim that:

> Conrad is concerned not so much with Africa as with the deterioration of one European mind caused by solitude and sickness. They will point out to you that Conrad is, if anything, less charitable to the Europeans in the story than he is to the natives, that the point of the story is to ridicule Europe's civilizing mission in Africa.[7]

For Achebe, however, this is precisely the problem: *Heart of Darkness* sees 'Africa as setting and backdrop which eliminates the African as human factor'.[8] Achebe further comments on Conrad's 'fixation on blackness'. For instance, Conrad wrote, 'A black figure stood up, strode on long black legs, waving long black arms', to which Achebe adds 'as though we might expect a black figure striding along on black legs to wave *white* arms!'.[9] We might think of Orwell's descriptions of a 'sea of yellow faces' and the 'black Dravidian coolie' in 'Shooting an Elephant', as well as the essay's foregrounding of colonialism's psychological impacts on the coloniser, to get a sense of how Achebe's critique could be transposed to Orwell's depiction of colonial Burma.[10]

By the late 1930s, however, Orwell's stance on imperialism had become more strident, as illustrated by his article in the *Adelphi*. In this article, Orwell glumly concluded that 'Nothing is likely to save us except the emergence within the next two years of a real mass party whose first pledges are to refuse war and to right imperial injustice. But if any such party exists at present, it is only as a possibility, in a few tiny germs lying here and there in unwatered soil.'[11] Orwell did not explicitly identify these 'few tiny germs', but one of them was undoubtedly the Independent Labour Party (ILP), the party of which Orwell was a member. The ILP was founded in 1893 in order to pursue socialism through electoral means. It later joined the newly formed Labour Party, but disaffiliated from the larger party in 1932 and underwent a revolutionary turn. During the second half of the 1930s, the left was divided in accordance with how its various factions conceptualised the interlocking relationships among capitalism, colonialism, fascism and war. Communist parties, including that of Britain, declared in 1935 that they would pursue a 'Popular Front' of socialists, social democrats, liberals and even anti-appeasement conservatives in order to oppose fascism. Because of this imperative to form anti-fascist alliances that included bourgeois elements, Communists suspended talk of socialist and anti-colonial revolution. (Some Communist activists – especially those of colour – continued to be involved in anti-colonial struggles during this period, but they were certainly going against the grain of the Communist movement institutionally.)[12] By way of contrast, the ILP, influenced by the growing pan-Africanist and anti-imperialist movements, declared imperialism to be as great an evil as fascism, and challenged forms of anti-fascism that did not simultaneously aim to overthrow capitalism and imperialism.[13]

Orwell was exposed to these theoretical and programmatic differences while fighting against Francisco Franco's Nationalist forces in the Spanish Civil War. He described the factional infighting of his own side during 1937 as 'the antagonism between those who wished the revolution to go forward and those who wished to check or prevent it'.[14] His sympathies were with the revolutionaries – the anarchists and the ILP's sister party, the Partido Obrero de Unificación Marxista – who faced Communist and Republican repression. It was as he was still reeling from his Spanish experience that Orwell joined the ILP. As he wrote in the party's newspaper, the *New Leader*, in June 1938,

> The things I saw in Spain brought home to me the fatal danger of mere negative 'anti-Fascism'. Once I had grasped the essentials of the situation in Spain I realised that the I.L.P. was the only British party I felt like joining – and also the only party I could join with at least the certainty that I would never be led up the garden path in the name of Capitalist democracy.[15]

In this context, he adopted the party's strain of anti-imperialism that dovetailed so neatly with his contempt for the Popular Front.

The ILP's anti-imperialist position during the late 1930s was largely informed by the ideas of a number of Black activist-intellectuals associated with the International African Service Bureau (IASB), who were also vocal critics of the Popular Front. They were not formal members of the ILP, but worked closely with the party. In conjunction with sympathetic members such as Arthur Ballard and Fenner Brockway, they were responsible for shaping its militant anti-imperialism.[16] The ILP, despite a diminishing national profile, was particularly strong in London (where the IASB was based) and in Glasgow. The latter city provided all four of the party's MPs by the late 1930s. In 1938, the ILP and the IASB collaborated to stage an anti-imperialist 'counter-exhibition' to the Empire Exhibition in Glasgow.[17] The Trinidadian Marxist George Padmore was the IASB's central figure, and he was joined by the likes of Amy Ashwood Garvey (from Jamaica), C. L. R. James (from Trinidad), Chris Jones (from Barbados), Jomo Kenyatta (from Kenya), T. Ras Makonnen (from British Guiana) and I. T. A. Wallace-Johnson (from Sierra Leone). The IASB formed the most radical wing of a rich pan-Africanist movement in Britain (see also David Killingray and Vanessa Mongey's contributions to this volume for discussions of Britain's pan-Africanist movement). The relationship between the IASB and the ILP continued a tradition of Black and white interracial cooperation in efforts to combat racial oppression and inequality, although these largely solidaristic relationships were sometimes punctuated by moments of white paternalism (again, see Killingray's chapter). Black anti-racist and anti-colonial activists, including those who constituted the IASB, have been particularly likely to find white comrades in the socialist and labour movements, as Talat Ahmed's chapter in this volume illustrates. While the IASB and the ILP maintained a comradely relationship, the IASB had a more antagonistic relationship with other sections of the British left, including the Communist Party.

In *Africa and World Peace* (1937), Padmore criticised the Popular Front by arguing that ' "Democratic" Imperialism and "Fascist" Imperialism are merely interchanging ideologies corresponding to the economic and political conditions of capitalism within a given country on the one hand, and the degree to which the class struggle has developed on the other.'[18] Importantly, he suggested not only an equivalence between fascism and colonialism, but also a causative relationship between the two. Fascism was, in part, the result of the frustrations of the European powers that had missed out on or been denied colonial plunder. Moreover, while the spoils of colonialism helped to check the development of fascism in imperial countries, colonialism propped up capitalism and was the main cause of war. Therefore, the struggle against colonialism and for socialism was central to the struggles against fascism and war. The IASB accordingly advanced a socialist pan-Africanism in which anti-colonialism intersected with global proletarian solidarity.

The influence of these ideas on the ILP was profound. In June 1938, the *New Leader* declared that 'One of the worst features of the Popular Front Policy advocated by the Communist Party is the betrayal of the colonial workers which it involves.'[19] While it was probably only the more theoretically inclined socialists who grappled with the complex relationship between colonialism and fascism postulated by the likes of C. L. R. James and George Padmore, many more could at least recognise the hypocrisy of overlooking one form of racially stratified authoritarian rule (colonialism) in order to oppose a different form of racially stratified authoritarian rule (fascism). It was this hypocrisy that Orwell, whose politics were usually informed by moral outrage and empirical observations rather than Marxist theory, so pointedly remarked upon in the *Adelphi*. Orwell's appeal was still at its heart a moral one and, unlike his comrades, he continued to show limited recognition of the revolutionary potential of colonised peoples. While Orwell's politics were more radical than those of the Congo Reform Movement a generation earlier (see Felix Lösing's chapter in this volume), he shared elements of the movement's paternalism with regard to the capabilities and character of colonised peoples. Yet he nevertheless identified the anti-colonial struggle as one of the two most pressing concerns of the British socialist movement, alongside resisting war.[20] As Christian Høgsbjerg observes, 'such relative clarity from Orwell ... on this question owes a great deal not only to Orwell's experiences of being part of the apparatus of British colonial oppression in Burma but also the impact made by the anti-colonialist writings and pan-Africanist activism of figures like James and Padmore'.[21]

Orwell moved in the same circles as the IASB during the late 1930s. In September 1938, Brockway, Orwell, Padmore and a number of other British socialists and pacifists were co-signatories to a manifesto titled 'If War Comes, We Shall Resist', which blamed the present crisis in large part on the imperialist policy of the British government. In order to achieve lasting peace, 'a new world order based on fellowship and justice' would have to be built.[22] Orwell and James attended parties hosted by the socialist anti-Stalinist publisher Fredric Warburg, whose firm published books by both men.[23] Orwell read James's history of the Communist International, *World Revolution, 1917–1936* (1937), and, in agreement with James's anti-Stalinism, referred to it as 'that very able book'.[24] For his part, James later in life called Orwell's account of the Spanish Civil War, *Homage to Catalonia* (1938), 'a very fine book and it's typical of Orwell: Orwell went and he saw that the Stalinists had ruined the revolution and he wrote it'.[25]

The confluence of Orwell's socialism with pan-Africanist politics during the late 1930s is an interesting enough story in itself. What this chapter further suggests, however, is that examining this pan-Africanism, which exerted some influence on Orwell's views, allows us to explore the attempts of activist-intellectuals to reconcile anti-imperialism with 'Britishness' or 'Englishness'. This chapter's actors used the words 'Britishness' and 'Englishness' sometimes interchangeably, but Orwell spoke more frequently of 'Englishness', and pan-Africanists of 'Britishness', probably reflecting the fact that 'Britishness' was more likely to be understood as an imperial (rather than national) and therefore non-racially exclusionary identity.[26] Orwell can productively be read in conjunction with figures such as James and Padmore for a number of reasons: perhaps most obviously because of the synchronicity of their works and their shared association with the ILP and the British left more broadly, but also because each held a sense of 'Britishness'/'Englishness' that was forged in a colonial context. On 25 June 1903, three days before Padmore was born in the British crown colony of Trinidad and Tobago, Orwell was born in British India to a family that was part of the imperial world. As Ben Clarke has argued with reference to Orwell, on the basis of Robert Young's scholarship on the idea of 'English ethnicity',

> Englishness was 'created for the diaspora' and 'paradoxically became most itself when it was far off'. It was reproduced in everyday colonial life, in the ways people interacted, dressed, and ate, and partially extended to subjugated populations through practices including the teaching of literature, which was central to the production of Englishness as a system of values rather than a matter of citizenship.[27]

The Black subjects who formed the IASB belonged to these subjugated populations to whom Englishness had been partially extended. Padmore's father's professional ambitions had been hindered by the racism and colourism of Trinidad.[28] C. L. R. James, like Padmore dark-skinned and middle-class, wrote of the obstacles faced by such men: 'Socially racial lines were clear. The whites, the browns and the blacks each kept their own company. The best positions were shared (very unequally) by the first two … It was on the black as opposed to the brown middle class that the discrimination fell hardest and George was a member of that class.'[29] The young Padmore 'was very sensitive to all this', and was especially angered by the racism he faced when working for the *Trinidad Guardian*.[30] The racial and class formations of the Caribbean therefore played an important role in Padmore's political development.

Despite the IASB's militant anti-imperialism, its members enjoyed a complex relationship with Britain and Britishness. James, for instance, remembered leaving Trinidad for Britain in 1932 as a case of the 'British intellectual … going to Britain'.[31] Indeed, colonial subjects from the British West Indies particularly identified with Britishness. Kennetta Perry has observed how West Indian migrants to Britain 'made choices to exercise their imperial citizenship' and 'subsequently remapped the very boundaries of what it meant to be both Black and British'.[32] Anne Spry Rush similarly argues that 'West Indians participated in a complex process of cultural transition – a struggle to re-define Britishness and their relationship to it – not only as Caribbean peoples but also as Britons'.[33] Both Perry and Rush demonstrate that Britishness has been contested and reshaped by colonial subjects from the Caribbean as a racially inclusive identity rather than one defined by whiteness. 'Britishness' was something that was being constituted by colonial residents of the metropole – even by those who sought the end of empire – during the 1930s and 1940s. Pan-Africanist identities were fluid, and, as Stephen Howe has observed, one could 'think of oneself as Trinidadian or Antiguan, *and* West Indian, *and* British'.[34] West Indians had long claimed collective rights based not only on their own distinctive identity but also on their imperial status, which Catherine Hall dates back to J. J. Thomas's *Froudacity: West Indian Fables Explained* (1889).[35] Furthermore, Howe reminds us that the role of Britishness in shaping Caribbean societies 'should not glibly be reduced to colonial mimicry, to false or divided consciousness'. Rather, 'this Britishness was part of a rich, complex, internationally open and distinctively modern cultural mix'.[36]

James and Padmore's complex position in Trinidadian society, and by extension the British imperial system, goes some way to explaining their relationship with Britishness. James belonged to a middle-class, intellectual family, which was shaped by Victorian values of respectability.[37] Bill Schwarz has highlighted 'the unusually deep penetration of the institutions of Victorian civic life into the cultural organisation of the colonial Caribbean'.[38] Those from middle-class, intellectual backgrounds, such as James and Padmore, were particularly shaped by these institutions. James was an ardent cricketer. In following this passion, he joined Maple (the club of the brown-skinned middle class) over Shannon (the club of the dark-skinned lower-middle class). He later recalled: 'My decision cost me a great deal ... Faced with the fundamental divisions in the island, I had gone to the right and, by cutting myself off from the popular side, delayed my political development for years.'[39] James devoured English literature, especially Shakespeare and Thackeray, and it was partly his immersion in this culture that prompted him to consider his first voyage to Britain as something of a homecoming. The IASB's pamphlet *The West Indies To-day* (1938) described Caribbean people as 'almost entirely European in outlook'.[40] This denial of the survival of African diasporic cultures was clearly incorrect, and probably stemmed from James and Padmore's middle-class backgrounds. However, James and Padmore were part of a long line of Caribbean intellectuals who invoked ideas of Britishness in the service of demands for democratic rights and self-government.[41] This strand within James and Padmore's political thought was contradictory, as it demanded colonial liberation while denying colonial cultures.

One of the IASB's central objectives was to foster links between the socialist movement in Britain and the anti-colonial movements in the empire. In doing so, they hoped to tap into a particular strain of Englishness. The Guianese activist Ras Makonnen recalled that Black activists went to the metropole 'because they held the belief that there were two Englands – the

England of the colonies, the settlers and the plantocrats, and the England of Westminster, the anti-slavery societies, and the rebel movements of the Left'.[42] Cedric Robinson has written of this attitude:

> To [Makonnen and Padmore] and many of their fellows, England ... was the embodiment of fair play and deep moral regulation. It was an ideal, then, that even the most committed anti-imperialists among them found difficult to shake. Not even the gross imperfections and racism they confronted in the metropole dissuaded them. It was as though they had come to accept that as Black Englishmen a part of their political mission was to correct the errant motherland.[43]

However, the IASB did not hold out hope for every section of the motherland's society. Pan-Africanists regarded the British ruling class as an adversary to be defeated. The IASB, while aware of racism within the British working class, believed the metropolitan proletariat to be of great progressive potential. Padmore believed the ruling class and the labour aristocracy were responsible for stirring up working-class racism.[44] James commented on the lack of racism in Nelson, a town known for its socialist militancy, where he lived from 1932 to 1933.[45] He fondly recalled that at meetings at which there was competition to speak, white workers would ask that James be able to share his thoughts, precisely because he was Black.[46] James and Padmore, as Marxists, concluded that the most class-conscious British workers were also the most committed anti-racists. Their 'Britishness' should be understood not as a reactionary deference to tradition and hierarchy, but rather as a claim to imperial citizenship and culture. They looked to Britain as, in part, a force of progressive change and a progenitor of radicals and rebels, and remained committed to the overthrow of the imperial ruling class. It was the British (and European) proletariat who, alongside the colonised peoples, would remake the world and signal the end of racism, imperialism and capitalism. As the IASB wrote to the 'workers of Britain' as the Second World War approached: 'Though you have neglected us in the past, today in this hour of common crisis, we want you to know that we Blacks bear you no ill-will. The imperialists are the common enemy. Our freedom is a step towards your freedom.'[47]

How did pan-Africanist invocations of 'Britishness' compare to those of Orwell? My contention is not that these invocations were identical, but rather that each hinged on recovering and reinterpreting what the respective actor considered to be radical traditions of Britishness or Englishness in order to serve a contemporary left-wing end. As Ben Clarke has argued, ' "Englishness" ... is not only a discourse within which [Orwell's] texts operate but a concept reinterpreted within them. Orwell attempted, particularly after 1939, to figure patriotism as a component or even basis of "democratic Socialism".'[48] Moreover, Orwell's and pan-Africanists' conceptions of Britishness or Englishness had been shaped by imperial identities and experiences. As James himself argued in a 1964 lecture, Orwell's incisive commentary on metropolitan society was facilitated by his time spent in the colonial world, and this was something he had in common with Caribbean writers: 'after he had seen the colonial world in Burma, he came back to become the finest, most original journalist in England. You see, you have to come from outside, to be able when a civilisation is shaking to see and carry to a conclusion the things that are being developed.'[49] In this lecture, James, unlike in some of his earlier works, positioned Caribbean peoples (as well as people like Orwell) as outside of, as well as constitutive of, British culture.

It is worth noting that the period in which Orwell's invocations of 'Englishness' became most pronounced corresponded to his political divergence from the IASB. While in 1938 he was a co-signatory to an anti-war manifesto alongside Padmore, he left the ILP shortly after the outbreak of the Second World War, as he was unable to reconcile himself to the party's anti-war position. In 'My Country Right or Left' (1940), Orwell

> revealed ... that in a dream on the eve of the Ribbentrop–Molotov Pact of late August 1939 he felt that the war had started, and believed then (and only for the first time clearly) 'that I was patriotic at heart, would not sabotage or act against my own side, would support the war, would fight in it if possible'.[50]

He articulated this patriotism more fully in *The Lion and the Unicorn* (1941). As Gregory Claeys has written of the essay, patriotism represented to Orwell 'the essential decency and democratic bias of British customs and institutions, which he believed could be wedded to socialism without producing totalitarianism'.[51] Orwell argued that the British ruling class was decadent, but that, unlike its continental neighbours, it was not prone to fascism:

> However unjustly England might be organized, it was at any rate not torn by class warfare or haunted by secret police. The Empire was peaceful as no area of comparable size has ever been ... As people to live under, and looking at them merely from a liberal, *negative* standpoint, the British ruling class had their points. They were preferable to the truly modern men, the Nazis and Fascists.[52]

Owing to a profound sense of national solidarity, England was simply 'a family with the wrong members in control'.[53] In response, a 'revolution' was needed. By 'revolution', Orwell meant 'a fundamental shift in power', which could happen 'with or without bloodshed' and did not mean 'the dictatorship of a single class'. Anyone who could 'grasp what changes are needed' could play a role in this revolution.[54] The 'proletarian revolution' was, accordingly, 'an impossibility'.[55]

What did Orwell's support of the British war effort mean for his anti-imperialism? Perhaps most obviously, he worked for the BBC's Eastern Service from 1941 until 1943, producing war propaganda to be broadcast to India. Even as the Indian National Congress launched the Quit India Movement and its leadership was imprisoned as a result, Orwell urged Indian loyalty to the Empire in the name of anti-fascism.[56] The discontinuities of Orwell's political positions should be clear. As John Newsinger has observed, Orwell was always 'a work in progress'.[57] During the Spanish Civil War, Orwell had aligned himself with those who did not wish to postpone the revolution and had joined the ILP on the basis that he 'would never be led up the garden path in the name of Capitalist democracy'. Yet as soon as the Second World War began, he urged national and imperial unity in order to fight Nazi Germany. In 1939, he criticised Clarence Streit for advocating a liberal world union that concealed the realities of imperialism. Yet in 1941, he published *The Lion and the Unicorn* with Searchlight Books, the intention of which was to 'stress Britain's international and imperial responsibilities and the aims of a planned Britain at the head of a greater and freer British Commonwealth, linked with the United States of America and other countries, as a framework of world order'.[58] Aside from a concession that the Commonwealth should be 'freer', Searchlight Books' programme was remarkably similar to Streit's. Nevertheless, Orwell retained a degree of anti-imperialism. His six-point programme in *The Lion and the Unicorn* included 'Immediate Dominion status for India, with power to secede when the war is over', and 'Formation of an Imperial General Council, in which the coloured peoples are to be represented'.[59] It seems reasonable to conclude that Orwell's anti-imperialism was partial and conditional. Even during the late 1930s, he had never fully abandoned his paternalism and was mostly unable to recognise the great masses of colonised peoples as historical agents.

In *How Russia Transformed Her Colonial Empire*, written during the Second World War but not published until 1946, Padmore argued that:

> If it is possible for the former colonies of the Czarist Empire to come together in fraternal co-operation, there is no reason at all why a Socialist Britain, for example, should fear to extend the Right of Full Self-Determination to the subject peoples of the British Empire. Once these dependent territories are given the right to plan their future, in their own interests, they would link up with the more advanced sections of the new Socialist Commonwealth.[60]

For Padmore and other pan-Africanists, self-determination did not necessarily mean a rupture from Britain. Rather, there were various imaginings of what a postcolonial world might look like. Formal independence won out, and during the postwar period pan-Africanist politicians and intellectuals devoted greater energies to seeking federation with one another than with their former colonial rulers.[61] But, especially before 1945, many pan-Africanists genuinely entertained the idea of creating postimperial federations along the lines of former empires, even if, as Richard Drayton has noted, citing the example of T. A. Marryshow's *Cycles of Civilisation* (1917), these visions could be 'joined to arguments that conjectured subversive post-British futures'.[62] For Padmore and the IASB, a British postimperial federation was dependent on a socialist revolution in the metropole and the immediate renunciation of colonial rule. For Orwell, by way of contrast, colonial reforms were needed in order to support the more urgent task: winning an anti-fascist war. Nevertheless, what both programmes had in common was the imagination of a British Commonwealth in which socialism and democracy replaced – by varying methods – oppression and coercion.

In 1942, Orwell argued that 'All left-wing parties in the highly industrialized countries are at bottom a sham, because they make it their business to fight against something which they do not really wish to destroy.' Living standards in Britain were supported by 'robbing Asiatic coolies', and, while the 'enlightened' around Orwell maintained 'that those coolies ought to be set free', the British standard of living 'demands that the robbery shall continue'. On this basis, a 'humanitarian is always a hypocrite'.[63] This was a somewhat ironic argument for Orwell to make, given that three years earlier he had left the one British political party that opposed the British war effort on the basis of anti-imperialism. Ben Clarke argues that Orwell's comment 'is not an argument against socialism, but [is an argument] against the limitations of its dominant Western forms in the 1930s and 1940s. The development of an effective left-wing practice in England depends upon the recognition of empire as a component of Englishness, destabilizing the boundary between the local and the global.'[64] The likes of James and Padmore would no doubt have agreed that destabilising the boundary between metropole and colony was crucial to left-wing practice, but it is doubtful that they would have seen Orwell as embodying this politics during the Second World War. Rather than Orwell's liberal conception of *humanitarianism*, they sought *solidarity* between colonised peoples and the British proletariat, in order to reconstitute the British Empire along socialist and anti-imperialist lines. Orwell never really succeeded in his attempt to reconcile Englishness with anti-imperialism. He was, though, not the only person to attempt to crack this puzzle.

Notes

1 George Orwell, 'Not Counting N******' (1939), in George Orwell, *The Collected Essays, Journalism and Letters of George Orwell*, 4 vols, ed. Sonia Orwell and Ian Angus, Vol. I, *An Age like This, 1920–1940* (Harmondsworth: Penguin, 1970 [1968]), pp. 434–8.
2 Ben Clarke, '"A Humanitarian Is Always a Hypocrite": George Orwell, Englishness, and Empires', in Ken Seigneurie (ed.), *A Companion to World Literature* (Chichester: Wiley Blackwell, 2020), Vol. 5a, pp. 2865–75 (p. 2868). See also Christopher Hitchens, *Why Orwell Matters* (New York: Basic Books, 2002); Stephen Ingle, 'The Anti-Imperialism of George Orwell', in John Horton and Andrea T. Baumeister (eds), *Literature and the Political Imagination* (London: Routledge, 1996), pp. 218–37; and John Newsinger, *Hope Lies in the Proles: George Orwell and the Left* (London: Pluto Press, 2018).
3 George Orwell, 'Shooting an Elephant' (1936), in Orwell, *The Collected Essays, Journalism and Letters*, Vol. I, pp. 265–72 (p. 269).
4 Mohammed Sarwar Alam, 'Orwell's "Shooting an Elephant": Reflections on Imperialism and Neoimperialism', *IIUC Studies*, 3:1 (2006), 55–62; Elleke Boehmer, *Colonial and Postcolonial Literature* (Oxford: Oxford University Press, 1995), pp. 160–3; Barry Hindess, 'Not at Home in the Empire', *Social Identities*, 7:3 (2001), 363–77; Douglas Kerr, *Orwell and Empire* (Oxford: Oxford University Press, 2022); Pavan Kumar Malreddy, 'Imperialist Shame and Indigenous Guilt: George Orwell's Writings on Burma', *European Journal of English Studies*, 23:3 (2019), 311–25; Paul Melia, 'Imperial Orwell', *Atlantis*, 37:2 (2015), 11–25.
5 Hindess, 'Not at Home in the Empire', p. 369.
6 Kerr, *Orwell and Empire*, p. 76.
7 Chinua Achebe, 'An Image of Africa', *Research in African Literatures*, 9:1 (1978), 1–15 (p. 9).
8 Ibid.
9 Ibid., p. 10. Emphasis in original.
10 Orwell, 'Shooting an Elephant', pp. 267, 269.
11 Orwell, 'Not Counting N******', p. 438.
12 Tom Buchanan, '"The Dark Millions in the Colonies Are Unavenged": Anti-Fascism and Anti-Imperialism in the 1930s', *Contemporary European History*, 25:4 (2016), 645–65; David Featherstone, 'Maritime Labour, Circulations of Struggle, and Constructions of Transnational Subaltern Agency: The Spatial Politics of the 1939 Indian Seafarers' Strikes', *Antipode*, 55:5 (2023), 1411–32.
13 Buchanan, 'The Dark Millions in the Colonies Are Unavenged'; Theo Williams, 'Collective Security or Colonial Revolution? The 1938 Conference on Peace and Empire, Anticolonialism, and the Popular Front', *Twentieth Century British History*, 32:3 (2021), 325–49.
14 George Orwell, *Homage to Catalonia* (London: Secker & Warburg, 1967 [1938]), p. 125.

15 George Orwell, 'Why I Join the I.L.P.', *New Leader* (24 June 1938), 4.
16 Priyamvada Gopal, *Insurgent Empire: Anticolonial Resistance and British Dissent* (London: Verso, 2019), Chapters 8–9; Williams, 'Collective Security or Colonial Revolution?'. For more on the IASB and its members, see Christian Høgsbjerg, *C. L. R. James in Imperial Britain* (Durham, NC: Duke University Press, 2014); Leslie James, *George Padmore and Decolonization from Below: Pan-Africanism, the Cold War, and the End of Empire* (Basingstoke: Palgrave Macmillan, 2015); W. O. Maloba, *Kenyatta and Britain: An Account of Political Transformation, 1929–1963* (Cham: Palgrave Macmillan, 2018); Minkah Makalani, *In the Cause of Freedom: Radical Black Internationalism from Harlem to London, 1917–1939* (Chapel Hill: University of North Carolina Press, 2011); Marc Matera, *Black London: The Imperial Metropolis and Decolonization in the Twentieth Century* (Oakland: University of California Press, 2015); Carol Polsgrove, *Ending British Rule in Africa: Writers in a Common Cause* (Manchester: Manchester University Press, 2009); and Daniel Whittall, 'Creolising London: Black West Indian Activism and the Politics of Race and Empire in Britain, 1931–1948', PhD thesis (Royal Holloway, University of London, 2012).
17 Sarah Britton, '"Come and See the Empire by the All Red Route!": Anti-Imperialism and Exhibitions in Interwar Britain', *History Workshop Journal*, 69:1 (2010), 68–89.
18 George Padmore, *Africa and World Peace* (London: Secker & Warburg, 1937), p. 252.
19 'Communists and Colonial Workers', *New Leader* (3 June 1938), 4.
20 Orwell, 'Not Counting N******', p. 438.
21 Christian Høgsbjerg, 'C. L. R. James, George Orwell and "Literary Trotskyism"', *George Orwell Studies*, 1:2 (2017), 43–60 (p. 46).
22 'If War Comes, We Shall Resist', *New Leader* (30 September 1938), 4–5.
23 Høgsbjerg, 'C. L. R. James, George Orwell and "Literary Trotskyism"', p. 53.
24 *Ibid.*, p. 52; Newsinger, *Hope Lies in the Proles*, p. 43.
25 Høgsbjerg, 'C. L. R. James, George Orwell and "Literary Trotskyism"', p. 52.
26 Anne Spry Rush, 'Imperial Identities in Colonial Minds: Harold Moody and the League of Coloured Peoples, 1931–50', *Twentieth Century British History*, 13:4 (2002), 356–83 (p. 362); Robbie Shilliam, 'Ethiopianism, Englishness, Britishness: Struggles over Imperial Belonging', *Citizenship Studies*, 20:2 (2016), 243–59 (p. 244).
27 Clarke, '"A Humanitarian Is Always a Hypocrite"', p. 2866; Robert J. C. Young, *The Idea of English Ethnicity* (Malden, MA: Blackwell, 2008), pp. 1–2.
28 James R. Hooker, *Black Revolutionary: George Padmore's Path from Communism to Pan-Africanism* (London: Pall Mall, 1967), p. 2.
29 New York, Columbia University, Rare Book and Manuscript Library, C. L. R. James papers, box 5, folder 21, C. L. R. James, 'Notes on the Life of George Padmore', p. 16.
30 C. L. R. James, 'George Padmore: Black Marxist Revolutionary – A Memoir' (1976), in *At the Rendezvous of Victory: Selected Writings* (London: Allison & Busby, 1984), pp. 251–63 (p. 253).

31 C. L. R. James, *Beyond a Boundary* (London: Hutchinson, 1963), p. 59.
32 Kennetta Hammond Perry, *London Is the Place for Me: Black Britons, Citizenship, and the Politics of Race* (New York: Oxford University Press, 2015), p. 6.
33 Anne Spry Rush, *Bonds of Empire: West Indians and Britishness from Victoria to Decolonization* (Oxford: Oxford University Press, 2011), p. 1.
34 Stephen Howe, 'C. L. R. James: Visions of History, Visions of Britain', in Bill Schwarz (ed.), *West Indian Intellectuals in Britain* (Manchester: Manchester University Press, 2003), pp. 153–74 (p. 161). Emphasis in original.
35 Catherine Hall, 'What Is a West Indian?', in Schwarz, *West Indian Intellectuals in Britain*, pp. 31–50 (p. 46).
36 Howe, 'C. L. R. James', p. 159.
37 Høgsbjerg, *C. L. R. James in Imperial Britain*, Chapter 1; Kent Worcester, *C. L. R. James: A Political Biography* (Albany: State University of New York Press, 1996), Chapter 1.
38 Bill Schwarz, 'Introduction: Crossing the Seas', in Schwarz, *West Indian Intellectuals in Britain*, pp. 1–30 (p. 12).
39 James, *Beyond a Boundary*, p. 59.
40 IASB, *The West Indies To-Day* (London: IASB, 1938), p. 5.
41 Richard Drayton, 'Commonwealth History from Below? Caribbean National, Federal and Pan-African Renegotiations of the Empire Project, c. 1880–1950', in Saul Dubow and Richard Drayton (eds), *Commonwealth History in the Twenty-First Century* (Cham: Palgrave Macmillan, 2020), pp. 41–60.
42 T. Ras Makonnen, *Pan-Africanism from Within* (London: Oxford University Press, 1973), p. 150.
43 Cedric J. Robinson, *Black Marxism: The Making of the Black Radical Tradition* (Chapel Hill: University of North Carolina Press, 2000 [1983]), pp. 264–5.
44 George Padmore, *How Britain Rules Africa* (London: Wishart, 1936), p. 4.
45 C. L. R. James papers, box 4, folder 7, C. L. R. James, 'Autobiography, 1932–38', p. 6.
46 C. L. R. James papers, box 12, folder 8, Alan J. Mackenzie, 'Marxism and Black Nationalism: A Discussion with C. L. R. James' (c. 1975), p. 7.
47 Kew, The National Archives, MEPO 38/91, IASB, 'Manifesto against War' (September 1938).
48 Ben Clarke, 'Orwell and Englishness', *Review of English Studies*, 57:228 (2006), 83–105 (p. 86).
49 C. L. R. James, 'A National Purpose for Caribbean Peoples' (1964), in *At the Rendezvous of Victory*, pp. 143–58 (p. 148).
50 Gregory Claeys, '*The Lion and the Unicorn*, Patriotism, and Orwell's Politics', *Review of Politics*, 47:2 (1985), 186–211 (p. 191).
51 *Ibid.*, p. 186.
52 George Orwell, *The Lion and the Unicorn: Socialism and the English Genius* (1941), in George Orwell, *The Collected Essays, Journalism and Letters*, Vol. II, *My Country Right or Left, 1940–1943* (Harmondsworth: Penguin, 1970 [1968]), 74–134 (p. 91). Emphasis in original.
53 *Ibid.*, p. 105.

54 *Ibid.*, p. 108.
55 *Ibid.*, p. 116.
56 Douglas Kerr, 'Orwell's BBC Broadcasts: Colonial Discourse and the Rhetoric of Propaganda', *Textual Practice*, 16:3 (2002), 473–90; Jutta Paczulla, '"Talking to India": George Orwell's Work at the BBC, 1941–1943', *Canadian Journal of History*, 42:1 (2007), 53–70.
57 Newsinger, *Hope Lies in the Proles*, p. 2.
58 Claeys, '*The Lion and the Unicorn*, Patriotism, and Orwell's Politics', p. 192.
59 Orwell, *The Lion and the Unicorn*, p. 119.
60 George Padmore with Dorothy Pizer, *How Russia Transformed Her Colonial Empire: A Challenge to the Imperialist Powers* (London: Dennis Dobson, 1946), p. 63.
61 Adom Getachew, *Worldmaking after Empire: The Rise and Fall of Self-Determination* (Princeton: Princeton University Press, 2019).
62 Drayton, 'Commonwealth History from Below?', p. 47.
63 George Orwell, 'Rudyard Kipling' (1942), in Orwell, *The Collected Essays, Journalism and Letters*, Vol. II, 215–29 (p. 218).
64 Clarke, 'A Humanitarian Is Always a Hypocrite', p. 2869.

4

British anti-racism in Australia: Exploring the nexus through the anti-racist activism of Jessie Street, 1950–60

Alison Holland

When a full history of anti-racism in Australia is written, what Hakim Adi refers to as a British anti-racism tradition will be a feature.[1] This chapter explores a critical moment in the translation of this tradition in postwar Australia, when leading Australian feminist Jessie Street pursued justice and human rights for Indigenous Australians through her peace and activist networks in England between 1950 and 1960. Her prescient identification of Australian postwar assimilation policy as a form of apartheid demonstrated the connections she was making between Australia's record of separate race-based exclusion of Aboriginal people with the similar settler-colonial state of South Africa. Of particular importance was her work as an envoy of the Anti-Slavery Society (ASS), which had maintained a continuous interest in Australian conditions since the early nineteenth century. Important, too, were her feminist, peace and labour connections both in Australia and England, including counsel from two anthropologists associated with Max Gluckman's Manchester School of Marxist anthropology, which emerged after the war.[2] As a Cold War exile from Australia because of her Communist sympathies, and residing in England between 1950 and 1960, her interpretation of Australia's ongoing racial discrimination of Aboriginal people was strongly influenced by developments in the postwar British anti-racism movement.

One of the aims of this volume is to explore the relationship between a British anti-racist tradition and global and imperial anti-racist movements. There is also a concern to think through what the former looks like and whether it is characterised by solidarity. Street's anti-racist activism demonstrates the transnational and multiethnic coalitions that characterised anti-racist solidarities (see introduction in this volume). That it occurred in the context of British anti-racist solidarity is nonetheless important. She took up this work in the context of the decline of Britain as a global power, including shifting relations with Australia conditioned by its experience of war in the Pacific during the Second World War.[3] Nationalist movements in Asia informed her activism but the Cold War made it impossible for her to undertake anti-racist work domestically. Connecting to an older British tradition of anti-racist investments enabled her to develop her thinking around Australia's particular racist and colonialist heritage in relation to colony and empire. It connected her to a transnational rights movement that was cross-fertilised by a diverse range of other liberatory commitments and politics.

There is a rich, if dispersed, body of work on anti-racist activism in relation to Indigenous Australians. Together with a significant body of work on nineteenth-century anti-slavery interventions in colonial governance, work on Indigenous rights-claiming and humanitarian activism before the Second World War has been a feature.[4] Despite some notable accounts of the biracial postwar advancement movement in Australia, as well as an account of anti-racist activism in the 1960s, the period between 1940 and 1960 is less well historicised.[5] This is partly because of the way the postwar Indigenous rights movement is understood as a changing discourse from civil to land rights, to self-determination across the twentieth century. In a postcolonial context the latter is understood to be the most salient for understanding an Indigenous rights agenda. The former is less so because it is characterised as mostly white-led and because the era is understood as overwhelmingly assimilationist in emphasis and, thus, less relevant to anti-racist histories.

This is encapsulated in one of the leading historian's interpretations of the period. According to Marilyn Lake, the shift from the pre- to the postwar era was characterised by a movement from paternal/maternal protectionism to leftist assimilationism shaped by labour ideals of anti-discrimination after the war.[6] This characterisation has curtailed more critical readings of anti-racism after the war and impacted understanding of activists such as Street. Her commitment to Aboriginal rights has been interpreted as a liberal project of assimilation as against the avowed liberatory ethics of anti-colonialism and self-determination she promoted for places such as China and Ghana after the war.[7] This interpretation not only fails to understand the wider context of Street's anti-racist activism, it fails to appreciate how the labour movement's response was itself shaped by Indigenous political mobilisations.

As this suggests, the characterisation of the anti-discrimination politics of the Aboriginal civil and human rights movement after the war as assimilatory is not helpful in terms of tracking an anti-racism history in Australia. As David Theo Goldberg argues, although working in different directions, the one effecting national independence and the other national integration, anti-colonial and civil rights mobilisations are both anti-racist movements because they seek 'to undo histories of racially ordered social structures and conceptual colonialisms'.[8] Thus, the interpretation described above not only fails to see Street's anti-racism and anti-colonialism, it cordons off

Australian anti-racist/anti-colonial struggle from the circuits of discursive and activist mobilisation that characterised it. It speaks to an anti-racism history in Australia that is yet to be written.

Background

There is a long thin vein of anti-racism in relation to Indigenous people in Australian history that has been influenced by the British anti-racist tradition (see Lösing in this volume). At the same time, conditions at the Australian colonial periphery have been a source of concern for and intervention by anti-racist activists in England. This activism includes anti-slavery campaigns, interventions around Aboriginal protection, and civil and human rights claiming. Emblematic of imperial humanitarianism, this local and imperial activism situated Australian conditions within an arc of humanitarian concern around the empire.[9] At the local level, an explicitly anti-colonial agenda developed from within communist ranks in response to punitive state intervention in Aboriginal lives in the 1920s.[10] In a landmark moment in 1939 the labour movement called for justice for Aborigines against the discriminatory aims of the states where assimilation was declared as future policy. The labour movement's 'New Deal' for Aborigines (1939) critiqued assimilation as protecting white economic interests and transforming Aboriginal people into exploitable workers, with loss of land and culture the corollary. It demanded retention of culture and ownership of land and resources instead.

A leading feminist, Street joined the labour and peace movements in the late 1930s in response to the challenges the war posed and her sense that feminism needed to work for structural change. As a founding member of the International Peace Campaign (New South Wales) in 1937 with affiliations to the National Peace Council in Britain, she lobbied for an international settlement that progressed Indigenous peoples' self-determination at war's end. The postwar women's charter conferences she organised in Australia in the 1940s and 1950s were an expression of her new political commitments. Modelled on the Atlantic Charter, they developed a set of women's reforms for postwar reconstruction. In what was the first explicitly anti-colonial feminist position in Australia the charter declared Aborigines to be part of the world's colonised peoples whose rights and independence as minorities must be recognised.

This language of minority rights demonstrated the fusion of labour and pacifist ideology around notions of national independence for colonial peoples after the war. By the late 1940s the British and Australian labour movements' promotion of democratic self-determination for the 'suppressed peoples of Empire' was greatly strengthened by pacifist ideology. Influenced by movements toward decolonisation, peace activists argued that colonialism and imperialism, and the conditions of dependence, subjugation and monopoly they implied, were incompatible with the new world order heralded by the United Nations (UN). Race conflict was understood to be one of the main impediments to international cooperation.

This context helped shape Street's postwar activism for Aboriginal rights. She was the only female representative in the Australian delegation to the conference that established the UN in 1945, where she helped to found the Status of Women subcommission.[11] She was active in numerous international organisations, including the Women's International League for Peace and Freedom.[12] The latter had consultative status with the Economic and Social Council of the UN, which played an important role in raising international concern about Indigenous peoples after the war and in the formation of the Sub-Commission on the Prevention of Discrimination and Protection of Minorities in 1948.

By the time Street left Australia for England in 1950 all the threads of her anti-racist activism in relation to Aboriginal Australians had emerged, particularly investments in labour and peace movements in Australia and England. Her feminist and UN commitments positioned her as a transnational activist and exposed her to frameworks for thinking about the distinct position of Aboriginal people as national minorities. Her time in England gave her the space and distance to critique Australian conditions and policies.

Street in England

Historians have documented how the politics of the Cold War made Street a political target in Australia.[13] Not a Communist herself, she was a long-term friend of the Soviet Union and had productive working relationships with Communist friends and allies.[14] The Charter conferences exposed deep fissures in the feminist movement as conservative women's groups boycotted them and attacked Street's capacity for national feminist leadership. This hostile climate saw her move to England to pursue her peace and feminist work, and here she became an executive member of the World Peace Council and participated in a vibrant transnational politics of peace, labour and feminist, as well as anti-apartheid, anti-colonial activism.

By 1950, a local human rights movement for Aborigines had emerged.[15] A shifting landscape of individuals and groups comprising Indigenous and labour activists, humanitarians, Christian socialists, Communists, feminists, civil libertarians and pacifists saw in the postwar world a chance to end racial discrimination and remind governments of their responsibility to Aboriginal people.[16] The links between a growing local and British anti-racist movement were strengthened in the context of Britain's postwar atomic testing in central and northern Australia immediately after the war.[17] The testing of rockets across the Central Aboriginal reserve saw local activists work with representatives of the British peace movement, the ASS, the League of Coloured Peoples and the Royal Anthropological Institute to critique the testing as a breach of the Atlantic Charter and the 'final chapter in the dark history of Australia's treatment of her minority race'.[18]

The UN Charter of Human Rights was a key impetus for the establishment of the Council for Aboriginal Rights (CAR), a Victorian-based group that formed in 1951 using the Declaration of Human Rights as a basis for reform. With leading Communists among its leadership, the CAR was one of the few groups explicitly to reject assimilation in its reform programme. Yet, the movement was largely subterranean. Just as the Cold War constrained Street's activities in Australia, demands for Aboriginal rights were labelled suspicious and targeted for surveillance by the 1950s (see Mongey, Chapter 5).[19]

While the postwar policy of assimilation promised equality and citizenship for all, in fact policy remained deeply embedded in race ideology and practice.[20] Discussion of needing to eliminate 'colour prejudice' was beginning to be heard in progressive circles, but it took a number of well-publicised cases of injustice into the 1950s to expose the full extent of ongoing discrimination and mistreatment. The emergent rights movement was not an anti-colonial one at this stage. Most of the activists in the 1950s and 1960s, including many Indigenous activists, were campaigning for equal citizenship, as Aboriginal people were uniformly excluded from most of the rights enjoyed by non-Aboriginal citizens, including the vote, access to education, welfare provision and equal wages.[21]

Street's exposure to the changing British postwar anti-racist movement was critical in this context.[22] Furthermore, her attendance at major international forums within the UN plunged her into this shifting landscape and exposed her to the global politics of decolonisation, anti-apartheid and anti-colonialism then taking shape in England, led by prominent activists such as Michael Scott and Paul and Eslanda Robeson, whom she counted as friends.

Street's anti-slavery mission

Historians note how older humanitarian groups such as the ASS lost authority in this postwar context. To Amaliz Forclaz they remain a white philanthropic enclave undertaking strategic lobbying, circulating specialist knowledge and cultivating political contacts.[23] Their invitation to Street to join their executive in 1954 was illustrative of this. Their decision to do so demonstrated their enthusiasm for the Human Rights Commission as opening the way for Aboriginal conditions in Australia to be brought under the international spotlight.

A historic condition of their intervention in local affairs was first-hand knowledge of conditions via Australian affiliates. Since the late 1920s Australian correspondents had appealed to the Society about aspects of Aboriginal policy and had requested their assistance in bringing about more humane conditions. One of their long-term correspondents was Mary Montgomerie Bennett (1880–1961), who consistently raised concerns about the loss of liberty and rights of Aboriginal people under abusive legislative regimes.[24] By the 1950s several others had alerted the Society to the discriminatory nature of Aboriginal legislation, including the ways in which it trapped them in systems of abuse and exploitation. They raised doubts about Aborigines' status and lack of human rights.

Street was considered an ideal ally because of her active role in public life and her UN experience. Not only had she been involved in the setting up of the UN, but she was also Australia's representative on the Commission on the Status of Women in 1947–48. During this time she had attended meetings of the Sub-Commission on the Protection of Minorities. She had also attended the World Peace Council and joined the British section of the Women's International League for Peace and Freedom. Her feminist internationalism was an attempt to put pressure on national governments on the question of sex discrimination. She now did the same on race discrimination, subsequently reflecting on their connection: 'the discriminations practised against coloured people were the same ... as the discriminations practised against women ... the reason for these discriminations was to protect the status, rights and privileges of the white man vis-à-vis women and the coloured races'.[25]

For its part the Society had gained consultative status with the UN Economic and Social Council. Its move to expose Aboriginal conditions at the UN was influenced by the Belgian thesis, which was a response to the limited interpretation of Article 73 of the UN Charter.[26] This Article stipulated that member states were to assume responsibility for the administration of territories whose peoples had not yet attained full self-government. In the decade since the establishment of the UN, member states had applied it solely to inhabitants of recognised dependencies, such as colonies, protectorates or mandated territories.

In 'The Question of the Aborigines before the United Nations', Belgium's permanent representative to the UN argued that the interpretation of this Article had been too narrow. He argued that the original intention of the

Article was to apply to all Indigenous people, whether living in colonies or in the metropolitan territories of member states. The limited interpretation disadvantaged groups in a metropolitan country who had not yet attained equal civil and political rights, effectively absolving the international community of any responsibility. In support of this argument the ASS cited the Australian Aboriginal people, making a submission to the UN that the right to decide to whom Article 73 applied should be vested in the UN, not the administering state.[27]

The Society decided to canvass humanitarian opinion in Australia about their plans before proceeding. They sent a copy of their draft letter to the Sub-Commission on the Protection of Minorities to their Australian contacts, including government ministers and bureaucrats, emphasising that they were acting in a *de facto* role until a national lobby group in Australia could do the same. Importantly, they believed that the Sub-Commission's definition of minorities, first published in 1949, applied to Aboriginal people.[28] The Society requested that the Sub-Commission consider the treatment of Aboriginal people as urgent. They argued that while Article 2(7) of the UN Charter specifically precluded member states from intervening in the domestic affairs of other nations, under articles 55(c) and 56, where responsibilities 'to work for universal respect for and observance of human rights and freedoms irrespective of race' had been abrogated, member states were not entitled to protection under Article 2(7).[29]

Their letter was not received well in Australia. In particular, the Federal Minister for Territories, Paul Hasluck, rejected the proposal, reminding the Society that his government held the principle of domestic jurisdiction 'quite unyieldingly'.[30] Fearing that they were in danger of alienating Hasluck, the Society cancelled the plan, instead sending Street on an investigatory trip to Australia to canvass opinion and investigate conditions before taking further action. They prepared a lengthy questionnaire to be sent to all Australian correspondents and contacts. It aimed to provide information on all points where the treatment of Aborigines did not conform to the UN Charter and was divided into nine categories including administration, civil rights, land, cultural rights and employment.

Street returned to Australia in December 1956 at a pivotal moment in the local setting. Her arrival coincided with the 'Warburton Affair', a series of allegations and evidence tabled in the Western Australian Parliament regarding the severe malnutrition and disease of the Aboriginal people forced to move to less productive country in the Warburton Ranges from central Australia and Maralinga because of British atomic testing. The report also provided a trenchant critique of Aboriginal child removal, which was happening apace in the region as a result of assimilation, with devastating consequences for family and community life, describing it as an inhumane practice.[31]

This moment galvanised the local activist groups, and Street's visit became the catalyst for establishing the first biracial national lobby group, the Federal Council for Aboriginal Advancement (FCAA).[32] While in Australia, she undertook a nine-week investigation of Aboriginal reserves, government stations and missions in Western Australia, South Australia and the Northern Territory. The highlight was her visit to the successful mining cooperative that had been established by striking Aboriginal workers in north-west Western Australia in 1946. Having walked off their stations to demand better wages and conditions, they established their own mining venture with the help of a white prospector, Communist Don McLeod. The ASS had maintained interest and connection with this development, having long advocated cooperative enterprises as a form of economic safeguard for Indigenous groups in the decolonisation phase. Up to 1953 the group had achieved considerable economic success, basing itself largely on prospecting for minerals. At the height of its operation, the Aboriginal workers had bought four stations with profits and attracted up to 600 station workers to the cooperative.

However, when financial difficulties set in in 1953, the company they had formed was liquidated. In addition, the Department of Native Affairs took control of the company's station assets including Yandeyarra station, which had been the base of their enterprise.[33] In an effort to retain some of these, McLeod formed Pindan Pty Ltd, in which, apart from himself and one other white person, only Aborigines were shareholders. For the next six years Pindan operated as a cooperative mining venture. It employed a significant number of workers; built houses; started a school; developed a kibbutz-style camp for children; and had communal washing, dining and kitchen facilities.[34]

This was a landmark development. After the war, cooperatives remained a progressive model of economic reform and recovery, particularly for Aboriginal communities clustered on reserves and government stations increasingly vulnerable to closure under assimilation policies. The Christian cooperative movement was launched by the Australian Board of Missions in Cape York in the 1950s, and Tranby Co-Operative in Sydney became a metropolitan centre for Aboriginal leaders to learn new trades and skills.[35] Underpinning their development was an ideal of sympathetic adaptation to modernity that had long motivated humanitarian reformers, but there were also secularists who proposed cooperative enterprises around mining and pastoralism to enable Aboriginal communities to become independently and economically viable as communal entities and to stay on their own reserve lands.[36]

Yet, in the context of a postwar mining boom in the north, cooperative enterprises were anathema to Aboriginal policy. Indeed, Hasluck argued that the resumption of reserves and pursuit of assimilation were the twin imperatives of native administration in the Northern Territory.[37] At the same time the Western Australian government constantly attempted to frustrate the Pindan initiative and defame McLeod. Even the Christian cooperative movement experienced difficulty getting financial backing in this context. By 1956 there was a general humanitarian understanding that Pindan and McLeod were being persecuted by a hostile government anxious to counteract such efforts toward Aboriginal autonomy. In March 1956 McLeod informed the Council for Civil Liberties of endless litigation and persecution of the Pindan group, and the denial of the Aborigines' struggle through the portrayal of him as a Communist infiltrator.[38]

Street's exposure to the Pindan cooperative was a pivotal moment in her thinking and activism around Aboriginal rights. In her report to the ASS she described it as one of the few places she visited where the Marrngu people had independence and a shared objective. After discussions with the people she took their grievances to leading businessmen in the area, arguing that not only did they resent their discriminatory treatment in wages and living conditions, but they grieved the loss of Yandeyarra station, which was the biggest and had been the base of their enterprise prior to Pindan's formation.[39] She argued that the station should be returned and a new approach to the building of viable Aboriginal economies was needed.

Street believed that cooperatives such as Pindan represented a sympathetic form of adaptation because they resembled what she termed 'the historical way of life of the Aborigines'. She argued that governments needed to devise labour schemes to heal Aboriginal economies demoralised by past and present policies aimed at breaking tribal organisation. To be effective, such schemes needed to recognise the differences between Aboriginal and non-Aboriginal culture. She informed the Society that all previous attempts to impose white civilisation on Aboriginal people had failed because concepts of white racial superiority had blinded 'us' (non-Aboriginal Australians) to the fact that Aboriginal people were as attached to their way of life as 'we were to ours'.[40] Furthermore, policy needed to be framed with an appreciation of the fundamentally different nature of Aboriginal and non-Aboriginal civilisations, the latter being individualistic, acquisitive and competitive, and the former more communally oriented.

Street and the Marxist anthropologists

Street's argument about Aboriginal cultures as historical demonstrated the shaping of her thinking by two leading Marxist anthropologists of the day, both with Australian experience. Before returning to Australia on the ASS's mission she made contact with Peter Worsley (1924–2013), who was then a sociologist at Hull University publishing articles in the socialist press in Australia and Britain on the 'Aboriginal question' stimulated by his recent experience of fieldwork in Australia. Trained in anthropology at Cambridge University, he went on to be a student of Max Gluckman, the founder of the Manchester School of Marxist anthropology.[41]

Founded in 1947, the Manchester School represented a shift in British anthropological practice and theory from structural functionalism. The latter emerged around the late nineteenth century influenced by the work of Bronisław Malinowski. Against the backdrop of heightened imperialism in Africa he developed an interpretation of culture as a complex mechanism wherein the function of each of its parts was linked and conditioned by the rest. As a result, 'native' cultures were understood as vulnerable in the context of contact with outsiders. Scientific knowledge was thus needed to steer so-called backward peoples toward modernity. The theory provided an intellectual framework for imperial humanitarian ideals of trusteeship.[42]

Gluckman's contribution was to combine structural functionalism with a Marxist focus on inequality and oppression and to take an interdisciplinary approach, drawing on economics and sociology. In this way he developed a critique of colonialism from structuralism and applied it to social justice issues such as apartheid and class conflict. It was partly Worsley's avowed anti-racism that attracted Gluckman, who offered him a research studentship at Manchester in the late 1940s. In the context of the Cold War, when Worsley's Marxist commitments made it difficult for him to advance, Gluckman suggested he apply to complete a doctorate in the new department of anthropology at the Australian National University in Canberra. Yet, his plans to study the people of the Central Highlands of New Guinea were thwarted too, as he was denied an entry permit by the Department of Territories in Australia.[43] His Communist sympathies thus hampered his plans in both England and Australia.

However, at the suggestion of his good friend, fellow anthropologist Fred Rose (1915–91), he was permitted to do fieldwork on Groote Eylandt instead, where he studied the language and kinship system of the Anindilyakwa between 1952 and 1954. From this experience he saw that tribal cultures were disappearing, and that Aborigines were 'now proletarians not nomads', but the issue was not class-based alone.[44] His advice to Street demonstrated the development of his anti-colonial consciousness. In 1956 he informed her that to see Aboriginal rights as about class alone ignored the national characteristics of the Aboriginal people and ultimately played into the hands of the 'capitalist assimilators', who denied the Aboriginal people the right to develop their own cultures.[45] This view was confirmed at the time by Commander Fox-Pitt of the ASS, who informed Street that the Australian states denied Aboriginal people minority status within the UN on the basis that they had no desire to preserve their own culture.[46]

Worsley's argument was illustrative of his own political and scientific maturation in relation to colonial affairs. His thinking was profoundly shaped by leftist historians with whom he interacted in the British Academy, such as E. P. Thompson and E. J. E. Hobsbawm, as well as the emergent anti-colonial movement galvanised in moments such as the Mau Mau uprising in Kenya (1952–60), on which Worsley subsequently wrote.[47] On the one hand leftist historians were writing important new histories of Western capitalism, and on the other anti-colonial uprisings in Africa forced an appreciation of the dialectics of colonialism.[48] As Worsley would later claim, understanding that colonialism was not just a top-down process but one that met with and intersected 'native' worldviews was a revelation, not least in terms of himself as, in his words, 'a privileged white man in a country where every single aspect of everyday life was governed by the colour bar'.[49] He suggested that Street get in contact with Fred Rose.

For his part, Rose had left Australia under a Communist cloud in March 1956, bound for the German Democratic Republic and a position in anthropology at Humboldt University. However, he remained deeply interested in and engaged by the question of Aboriginal rights, despite being continuously refused re-entry to Aboriginal reserves to continue fieldwork in Australia. Born in England, Rose had studied biology and anthropology at Cambridge before coming to Australia to undertake fieldwork in 1937. Taking up a position as a meteorologist in the Bureau of Meteorology enabled him to pursue his interest in anthropology, being posted to Darwin and Broome. He performed most of his fieldwork at Groote Eylandt between 1938 and 1941. Having been exposed to left-wing politics at Cambridge, he joined the Australian Communist Party in 1942. He then went on to hold a number of public service positions until 1953, resigning from the Department of Territories when his position was abolished.[50] He was hauled before the Royal Commission on Espionage (Petrov Commission) in 1954 on allegations of being involved in a Soviet spy ring.[51]

Valerie Munt has explored the intersections of anthropology, ideology and political repression in Rose's experience in Australia.[52] Worsley later claimed that he had been victimised by officialdom's fear of his Communist affiliations.[53] Munt shows how this extended to his research, pointing out that the significant contributions he made to anthropology were withheld by a conservative academic establishment and the politics of the Cold War. Yet, Rose's Communist sympathies helped to shape his anti-racism as well as his anthropological research. In 1939 he read *We Europeans: A Survey of Racial Problems* by Julian Huxley and Alfred Haddon, which was a damning scientific and political criticism of Nazi antisemitism and US racism.

It caused him to reflect on anthropology's role in the general movement against racism.[54]

As we have seen, Communists took a lead in developing an anti-colonial critique of Australian Aboriginal policy as they did elsewhere.[55] Although only beginning to emerge in the postwar period, Marxist anthropology was important for articulating concepts of Aboriginal rights as part of the wider global anti-colonial struggle. One of the reasons for this was the loosening of the stranglehold that structural functionalism had on British and Australian anthropology, which was facilitated by the Manchester School. In particular, a Marxist framework focused on historical and economic explanations for understanding Aboriginal societies.[56] Like Worsley's, Rose's thinking changed significantly between his fieldwork experience, which focused on the method and theory of kinship classification amongst the Groote Eylandt Aborigines, and the final publication of his research in Germany in 1960.[57]

Knowledge of the kinship structures of Aboriginal societies had been dominated by the Sydney School of structural functionalists led by A. P. Elkin at Sydney University.[58] In Munt's framing, structural functionalism buttressed assimilation policy because it presumed that Aboriginal culture was static, leading to the conclusion that its survival rested on adaptation to the capitalist economy. Elkin and the Sydney School had long maintained the view that, as symptomatic of 'backward peoples', Aboriginal culture was doomed to destruction. The dominance of this view led to a methodology in which the economies of Aboriginal societies went largely unacknowledged, including their economic dependence on the land.

Via his own fieldwork, and drawing on historical/material and economic explanations for the social organisation of Aboriginal peoples, Rose instead utilised a Marxist explanatory frame.[59] This led him to a different conclusion. He argued that Aboriginal society was not static but dynamic and flexible, constantly in a process of social evolution. Aborigines had adapted to changes in their environments to maximise economic productivity necessary for reproduction and survival. This included kinship, which was always in a state of flux.[60] In Munt's terms, Rose argued that land, as well as human and political rights, were essential for the continuance of their own historical development and self-determination.[61]

Street and Rose's correspondence confirmed what Worsley had advised.[62] In particular, Rose reiterated Aboriginal peoples' cultural and economic distinctiveness and enhanced Street's appreciation of their historicity and the class dimensions of the question. By the 1950s Rose had also helped to shape the Communist Party's shift in their policy on Aborigines. In particular, the emphasis was on encouraging an appreciation of them as an oppressed national minority whose distinctiveness should be maintained and supported, including in the encouragement of their leadership of the struggle.[63] The latter was particularly pertinent for Street. As she noted to Brian Fitzpatrick of the Council for Civil Liberties in 1957:

> The position of women vis-à-vis men is akin to the position of the coloured races vis-à-vis the white race. As coloured people have been kept doing the menial work and routine and lesser jobs of the colonial society, so are women in the western world ... It is just as important that men should be ready to accept the leadership of outstanding women as the white races should be ready to accept the leadership of outstanding coloured people.[64]

Aboriginal people as a national minority

Street's engagement with Worsley and Rose came at a pivotal moment in her activist work. In particular, her sense of Aboriginal people as national minorities led her to make direct comparisons with similarly placed groups around the world. Against the backdrop of decolonising movements, including anti-apartheid, she began to articulate a critique of the Aboriginal peoples' position in Australia as about colonial repression. Her references to needing to abolish apartheid in Australia were linked to her leftist, anti-discrimination politics. As she wrote, 'until all traces of apartheid are expunged from our laws ... we cannot claim that Australia is a country in which all people enjoy freedom'.[65] This was the spirit of the broader human rights movement. However, her coupling of Aboriginal historical experience to colonialism and contemporary decolonisation movements was a nuanced position within the mainstream rights agenda of the time.

This was demonstrated at Pindan, where she noted that the position of Aboriginal workers was related to their lack of citizenship, which in turn increased their colonial dependency. In her report she criticised the system of exemptions via which, under assimilation, Aboriginal people could become either 'exempted persons' or full citizens minus their Aboriginality. She noted how the people critiqued this, and assimilation more broadly, as humiliating.[66] They resented having to separate from their families, which was a condition of exemption, with many refusing to apply. She even noted that those who had been granted exemption suffered loneliness and unhappiness to the point of surrendering it. Similarly, she singled out the Commonwealth's *Welfare Ordinance* of 1953 as illustrative of colonial repression, as it earmarked all but six full-descent Aborigines in the north as citizens, the rest remaining 'wards of the state'.

The ASS questioned the credibility of this law, arguing that it was out of step with developments elsewhere. They pointed to the 'Eskimo' minority in Canada and Greenland, who held unqualified citizenship, and noted that their inclusion had not had any negative consequences for the majority.

Street also pointed to developments in Australia's neighbouring countries, where minorities were gaining independence and the extension of civil and political rights previously denied. She suggested that similar policies were being adopted by the governments of Egypt, Tunisia, Morocco, the Sudan, Ghana and Pakistan, whose populations were no more 'developed' than Australian Aboriginal people.[67]

Her report to the ASS focused on the benefits of cooperative enterprises for promoting Aboriginal independence, as well as detailing the incompatibility of Australian policy with UN resolutions on human rights and the anti-colonial movements among Australia's Asian neighbours. When the ASS submitted her report to Hasluck they supported these claims, arguing that cooperatives had been successful amongst Indigenous populations in Mexico, Guatemala and Bolivia.[68] The official response was to refute their possibility in Australia. The government reminded the Society of the principle of domestic jurisdiction and suggested that Aborigines were apathetic to any venture that required initiative. Community settlements were dismissed as impeding the process of assimilation, Yandeyarra was not returned to the people of Pindan and Street's report was dismissed as biased.[69]

In the context of the late 1950s and against Hasluck's implacable resistance, the Society backed away from their UN move altogether. As Forclaz shows, they had all but lost their authority in the postwar context, not least because their attempts to redirect the language of trusteeship to welfare imperialism were out of step with the anti-colonial mood of the times.[70] It is notable, however, that it wasn't just the Society that walked away from the issue. At the time of the Warburton crisis, Mary Bennett tried to get the Aboriginal question raised in the British Parliament, particularly as it was British weapons-testing that was largely responsible. However, the leftist politician and anti-colonial advocate Fenner Brockway informed Street of the British Parliament's refusal to debate the issue, on the strength of Australia's domestic jurisdiction in the matter.[71]

That Street had a more expansive vision was demonstrated in her resolve to pursue her investigation of minority rights and search for alternative policies to assimilation once the Society's campaign was abandoned. In 1958 she travelled to the Soviet Union and China to investigate their policies of minority rehabilitation, arguing that their more sympathetic policies demonstrated the absurdity of Australia's position. In a tour of these regions she found that in both instances previously illiterate minorities who were without civil or political rights had been rehabilitated by policies of health and education, land and self-government. She argued that, following the defeat of Chiang Kai-shek in 1949, minority groups in China were even encouraged to elect their own representatives to the national and provincial parliaments, and Institutes of Minorities were established to train the people in the application of new policies and developmental schemes. Citing Nehru's integration policy in India, she stressed the importance of preserving culture while advancing economic, educational and welfare reforms.[72]

The period of the early 1960s, the decade before her death, represented the peak of her input on this issue, in which she drove an argument about Australian colonial rule and regressive apartheid-like regimes. In 1960 she wrote from London to the Australian Prime Minister, Robert Menzies, emphasising the more progressive policies of men in the 'home governments' who were extending the franchise, self-government and independence to colonial peoples.[73] In a government inquiry on Aboriginal voting rights, she pointed out that for 300 years the British in India, the French in Indo-China and the Dutch in the Dutch Indies had denied votes and political and civil rights to the Indigenous inhabitants on the same basis that they denied them to women: that they were incapable of using them. She added that after the Russian revolution in 1917 the whole population were given the right to vote from the age of eighteen at a time when nearly 90 per cent of the population were illiterate. Similarly, in India, Pakistan, Ceylon, Indonesia, China and South East Asia, the population had been granted the franchise upon gaining independence.[74]

She repeatedly observed how Australia's reputation for the abuse of Aboriginal human rights was regularly noted abroad, arguing that, with the Portuguese colonies, South Africa, the southern states of the USA and the Middle East, Australia practised the worst abuses and had the most backward conditions anywhere in the world.[75] Her final attempt to have Aboriginal conditions raised at the UN in 1963 was in the context of economic exploitation in the north via mining, which had resulted in the confiscation of Aboriginal reserve land. She believed that Aboriginal conditions resembled those she had heard aired in the Trusteeship Council of the UN by Black African activists, and argued that Australia's discriminatory treatment of Aborigines made the protection of domestic jurisdiction invalid.[76] She pointed out that the argument about domestic interference in the nation was the same argument used when the right of a man to beat his wife had first been raised.[77]

Working with a younger female activist in the CAR, she suggested obtaining the advice of the Reverend Michael Scott, the experienced and respected anti-apartheid activist whose championship of the Herero people of South West Africa provided hope for Black people throughout the world. The news was not promising. He pointed out that there was no mechanism within the UN for small groups within sovereign states to be heard. He noted that the idea of a subcommittee on the 'Aboriginal question' had been mooted but, because of a lack of information and funds, had not eventuated. He suggested further investigation was required before representations could be made.[78] By the mid-1960s Street was unable to get the support of either the ASS or the newly formed FCAA for this cause.[79]

Conclusion

This hesitancy about international exposure of Australian conditions demonstrated just how idiosyncratic Street's position was on this question from the local perspective. While the period between 1940 and 1960 saw significant shifts and important developments in anti-racist activism and consciousness in Australia, there was a limited lexicon for understanding Aboriginal people as dependent minorities under colonial rule at this time, much less articulating the rights movement as part of a global decolonising one. While the Communist Party certainly referenced a history of colonialism in Australia, there was no written history or discourse around Australian colonialism or empire in the 1950s, and Street was the first to label Australian policy as apartheid.[80] At a time when Australia's responses to the South African regime were shaped by needing to deflect attention from its own institutions of white supremacy, this was a radical anti-racist position.[81]

Goldberg argues that anti-racism requires historical memory, recalling the conditions of racial degradation, and relating contemporary to historical and local to global conditions.[82] Clearly Street's transnationalism facilitated this process, as did her interaction with a complex web of transnational anti-racist politics. In presenting Hasluck with a copy of Mark Twain's *King Leopold's Soliloquy* – his searing satire on the Belgian King's ruthless exploitation of the Congo Free State – in 1959 (see Lösing in this volume), she noted that the white man had a terrible heritage to live down, demonstrating Australia's inclusion in a wider story of British colonialism that was largely anathema to Australia's historical consciousness at the time.

Exploring her activism and this politics enables us better to see the influence of British anti-racist traditions on a rights agenda in Australia. Just as there are strong Anglo-Australian links in Australia's racist heritage, there is a vein of anti-racism in Australia influenced by the British tradition. In this chapter, we have seen how it was shaped by the labour movement, as it was in postwar Britain, as well as by the much longer tradition of anti-slavery intervention. The discourse about human rights was an important development but it only went so far. Street's interventions demonstrated the way in which appreciating Aborigines as a national minority with specific cultural needs and rights ultimately required an epistemic shift from an anthropological paradigm to an historical one. Street's story demonstrates how the anti-racism of the hour exposed the muddied colonial history underpinning the Anglo-Australian alliance and the Australian settlement. Her exposure to an anti-racist politics in England significantly broadened her anti-racist message and shaped her timely input to this politics 'at home', even as the Cold War climate constrained its possibilities.

Notes

1 Hakim Adi, Keynote Address, *Anti-Racism in Britain: Histories and Trajectories*, online conference, 20 and 27 February 2021.
2 Frederik Barth, Andre Gingrich, Robert Parking and Sydel Silverman, *One Discipline, Four Ways: British, German, French and American Anthropology* (Chicago: University of Chicago Press, 2005).
3 Kate Darian-Smith, 'World War 2 and Post-War Reconstruction, 1939–1945', in Alison Bashford and Stuart Macintyre (eds), *The Cambridge History of Australia*, Vol. II (Cambridge: Cambridge University Press, 2013), pp. 88–111 (pp. 94–5).
4 For example, Alan Lester and Fae Dussart, *Colonisation and the Origins of Humanitarian Governance* (Cambridge: Cambridge University Press, 2014); Jane Lydon, *Anti-Slavery and Australia: No Slavery in a Free Land?* (London: Routledge, 2021); Bain Attwood, *Rights for Aborigines* (Sydney: Allen & Unwin, 2003); William Cooper, *An Aboriginal Life Story* (Melbourne: Melbourne University Press, 2021); John Maynard, *For Liberty and Freedom: The Origins of Australian Aboriginal Activism* (Canberra: Aboriginal Studies Press, 2007).
5 Jennifer Clark, *Aborigines and Activism: Race, Aborigines and the Coming of the Sixties to Australia* (Crawley: University of Western Australia Press, 2008); Jack Horner, *An Insider's Memoir of the Movement for Aboriginal Rights 1938–1978* (Canberra: Aboriginal Studies Press, 2004); Sue Taffe, *Black and White Together FCAATSI: The Federal Council for the Advancement of Aborigines and Torres Strait Islanders, 1958–1973* (St Lucia: University of Queensland Press, 2005).
6 Marilyn Lake, 'Feminism and the Gendered Politics of Antiracism, Australia, 1927–1957: From Maternal Protectionism to Leftist Assimilationism', *Australian Historical Studies*, 110 (1998), 91–108.
7 Chloe Ward, 'Jessie Street: Activism without Discrimination', in Stefan Berger and Sean Scalmer (eds), *The Transnational Activist: Transformations and Comparisons from the Anglo-World since the Nineteenth Century* (London: Palgrave, 2018), pp. 227–56.
8 David Theo Goldberg, 'Buried Alive', in *The Threat of Race: Reflections on Racial Neoliberalism* (Oxford: Blackwell Publishing, 2009), pp. 1–31 (p. 14).
9 Lester and Dussart, *Colonisation and the Origins of Humanitarian Governance*; Penny Edmonds, 'Activism in the Antipodes: Transnational Quaker Humanitarianism in the Troubled Politics of Compassion in the Early Nineteenth Century', in Berger and Scalmer, *The Transnational Activist*,

pp. 31–59; Penelope Edmonds and Zoe Laidlaw, 'The British Government Is Now Awakening: How Humanitarian Quakers Repackaged and Circulated the 1837 Select Committee Report on Aborigines', in Samuel Furphy and Amanda Nettelbeck (eds), *Aboriginal Protection and Its Intermediaries in Britain's Antipodean Colonies* (London: Routledge, 2019), pp. 38–57.

10 Padraic Gibson, '"Stop the War on Aborigines": The Communist Party of Australia and the Fight for Aboriginal Rights, 1920–1934', PhD thesis (University of Newcastle, 2020).

11 Andree Wright, 'Jessie Street, Feminist', *Labour History*, 29 (1979), 59–68 (p. 67).

12 Lenore Coltheart (ed.), *Jessie Street: A Revised Autobiography* (Sydney: The Federation Press, 2004).

13 Heather Radi, 'Organising for Reform', in Heather Radi (ed.), *Jessie Street: Documents and Essays* (Sydney: Women's Redress Press, 1990), pp. 107–17; Peter Sekuless, *Jessie Street: A Rewarding but Unrewarded Life* (Brisbane: University of Queensland Press, 1978), pp. 117–25.

14 Heather Radi, 'Street, Lady Jessie Mary (1889–1970)', in *Australian Dictionary of Biography* (2002), https://adb.anu.edu.au/biography/street-lady-jessie-mary-11789/text21089 (accessed 6 August 2021).

15 Don Watson, *Brian Fitzpatrick: A Radical Life* (Sydney: Hale and Iremonger, 1970), p. 203.

16 Deborah Wilson, *Different White People: Radical Activism for Aboriginal Rights 1946–1972* (Perth: University of Western Australia Publishing, 2015).

17 Elizabeth Tynan, *Atomic Thunder: The Maralinga Story* (Sydney: NewSouth Publishing, 2016).

18 'Rocket Tests in Central Australia', *The White Ribbon Signal* (December 1946), 151; 'British Groups Protest Proposed Australian Rocket Range', *The White Ribbon Signal* (March 1947), 22.

19 Ann Curthoys and John Merritt (eds), *Australia's First Cold War, 1945–1953*, Vol. I, *Society, Communism and Culture* (Sydney: Allen & Unwin, 1984); Ann Curthoys and John Merritt, *Australia's First Cold War 1945–1959*, Vol. II, *Better Dead than Red* (Sydney: Allen and Unwin, 1986).

20 Anna Haebich, *Spinning the Dream: Assimilation in Australia 1950–1970* (Fremantle: Fremantle Press, 2008).

21 Taffe, *Black and White Together*.

22 Rob Skinner, 'The Moral Foundations of British Anti-Apartheid Activism, 1946–1960', *Journal of Southern African Studies*, 35:2 (2009), 399–416.

23 Amalia Forclaz, *Humanitarian Imperialism: The Politics of Anti-Slavery Society Activism, 1880–1940* (Oxford: Oxford University Press, 2015), pp. 204–5.

24 Alison Holland, *Just Relations: The Story of Mary Bennett's Crusade for Aboriginal Rights* (Perth: University of Western Australia Publishing, 2015).

25 Jessie Street, *Truth or Repose* (Australia: Australasian Book Society, 1966), p. 2.

26 'Aborigines' (editorial), *The London Times* (15 August 1955), 7.

27 Lord Winster and Dr Hubert Murray, 'Aborigines and Slaves Responsibility of the UN', *The London Times* (30 August 1955), 9.

28 The definition of minority was a group whose members shared a common ethnic origin, language, culture or religion and were interested in preserving either their existence as a national minority or their particular distinguishing characteristics.
29 ASS, draft letter to the Secretary of the Sub-Commission for the Prevention of Discrimination and the Protection of Minorities (1956), Street Papers, National Library of Australia (NLA), MS2683, series 10.
30 Paul Hasluck, draft letter to the ASS, sent to the administrator of the Northern Territory (July 1956), National Archives of Australia (NAA), A452/1, 55/694, Anti-Slavery and Aborigines' Protection Society – Aboriginal Welfare, Northern Territory.
31 Holland, *Just Relations*, pp. 283–91.
32 Taffe, *Black and White Together*.
33 Sarah Holcombe, 'Indigenous Organisations and Mining in the Pilbara, Western Australia: Lessons from a Historical Perspective', *Aboriginal History*, 29 (2005), 107–35.
34 For an account of the strike, see Anne Scrimgeour, *On Red Earth Walking: The Pilbara Aboriginal Strike 1946–1949* (Victoria: Monash University Publishing, 2020).
35 Noel Loos and Robin Keast, 'The Radical Promise: The Aboriginal Christian Co-Operative Movement', *Australian Historical Studies*, 99 (1992), 286–301.
36 Olive Pink, 'Is Social Science and Social Anthropological Research – or Is Emotionalism – to Decide the Fate of the Wailbri-Speaking Tribe in the Northern Territory of Australia?', paper read to Section F (Anthropology) ANZAAS Conference, Adelaide, August 1946, Olive Pink Papers, Australian Institute for Aboriginal and Torres Strait Islander Studies, Canberra, MS 2638.
37 Australia, House of Representatives 1952, *Debates*, Vol. 218, 46.
38 Don McLeod to Brian Fitzpatrick (28 March 1956), Street Papers, NLA, MS 2683/10/70.
39 Jessie Street, *Report on Aborigines in Australia* (Sydney: published by the author, 1957), pp. 29–30.
40 *Ibid.*, 7.
41 Robert J. Gordon, *The Enigma of Max Gluckman: The Ethnographic Life of a 'Luckyman' in Africa* (Lincoln: University of Nebraska Press, 2018).
42 Freddy Foks, 'Bronislaw Malinowski, "Indirect Rule", and the Colonial Politics of Functionalist Anthropology, ca. 1925–1940', *Comparative Studies in Society and History*, 60:1 (2018), 35–57.
43 Peter Worsley, *An Academic Skating on Thin Ice* (New York: Berghahn Books, 2008), p. 83.
44 Peter Worsley, 'A New Stage in the Development of the Aboriginal People', *Communist Review*, 153 (September 1954), 282–5.
45 Peter Worsley to Jessie Street (1 June 1956), Street Papers, NLA, MS 2683, series 10.
46 Commander Fox-Pitt to Jessie Street (13 December 1956), Street Papers, NLA, MS 2683, series 10.

47 Peter Worsley, 'The Anatomy of Mau Mau', *The New Reasoner*, 1 (Summer 1957), 13–25.
48 Interview between Alan Macfarlane and Peter Worsley, Worsley's House (25 February 1989), www.youtube.com/watch?v=sWKMzd8YFL4 (accessed 29 May 2024).
49 Worsley, *An Academic Skating*, p. 115.
50 Peter Monteath and Valerie Munt, *Red Professor: The Cold War Life of Fred Rose* (Adelaide: Wakefield Press, 2015).
51 Peter Monteath, 'Rose, Frederick George (1915–1991)', *Australian Dictionary of Biography* (2016), https://adb.anu.edu.au/biography/rose-frederick-george-19126/text30701 (accessed 19 August 2021).
52 Valerie Munt, 'Australian Anthropology, Ideology and Political Repression: The Cold War Experience of Frederick G. G. Rose', *Anthropological Forum*, 21:2 (2011), 109–29.
53 Ibid., 123.
54 J. S. Huxley and A. C. Haddon, *We Europeans: A Survey of Racial Problems* (London: Jonathan Cape, 1935).
55 Oleksa Drachewych and Ian McKay, *Left Transnationalism: The Communist International and the National, Colonial and Racial Questions* (Montreal: McGill-Queen's University Press, 2019).
56 Munt, 'Australian Anthropology', p. 123.
57 F. G. G. Rose, *The Classification of Kin, Age Structure and Marriage amongst the Groote Eylandt Aborigines: A Study in Method and a Theory of Australian Kinship* (Berlin: Academie-Verlag, 1960).
58 Geoffrey Gray, *A Cautious Silence: The Politics of Australian Anthropology* (Canberra: Aboriginal Studies Press, 2007); Tigger Wise, *The Self-Made Anthropologist: A Life of A. P. Elkin* (Sydney: Allen & Unwin, 1985).
59 Munt, 'Australian Anthropology', p. 122.
60 *Ibid.*, p. 121.
61 *Ibid.*, p. 123.
62 Frederick Rose, general correspondence (c. 1930–91), State Library of New South Wales, MLMSS 10167, boxes 1–26, 34, 77.
63 W. G. Smith, 'Communists and the Aborigines', *Social Survey*, 12 (1963), 229–43.
64 Jessie Street to Brian Fitzpatrick (10 May 1957), Street Papers, NLA, MS 2683, series 10.
65 Jessie Street, 'Report from the Select Committee on Voting Rights for Aborigines', Council for Aboriginal Rights, *Papers*, MS 12913, La Trobe Collection, State Library of Victoria, box 9/7.
66 Jessie Street, 'A Visit to Pindan Camps', *The Dawn* (December 1957), 18.
67 Jessie Street to Cyril Gare (5 August 1957), Street Papers, NLA, MS 2683, series 10.
68 C. W. W. Greenidge to Paul Hasluck (17 December 1957), NAA, F1, 58/77, Welfare Branch, ASS representations re welfare of Aborigines, 1957–61.
69 Paul Hasluck to C. W. W. Greenidge (5 March 1958), NAA, F1, 58/77, Welfare Branch, ASS representations re welfare of Aborigines, 1957–61.

70 Forclaz, *Humanitarian Imperialism*, pp. 202–10.
71 Fenner Brockway to Jessie Street (18 November 1957), Street Papers, MLA, MS 2683, series 10.
72 Jessie Street, 'Visit to Tashkent: report May 1958', in Radi, *Jessie Street*, pp. 252–5.
73 Jessie Street to Robert Menzies (9 March 1960), Street Papers, NLA, MS2683, series 10.
74 Jessie Street, 'Evidence to the Select Committee on Voting Rights', Parliament of the Commonwealth of Australia, House of Representatives, *Report from the Select Committee on Voting Rights of Aborigines* (Canberra: printed and published for the Government of the Commonwealth of Australia by A. J. Arthur, 1961), pp. 503–4, https://aphref.aph.gov.au/house/committee/reports/1961/1961_h%20of%20r%201.pdf (accessed 9 June 2024).
75 Jessie Street to C. A. Kelly, MLA (12 January 1961), Street Papers, NLA, MS2683, series 10, box 27.
76 Jessie Street, 'The Question of Discrimination against Aborigines and the United Nations', letter to Shirley Andrews (7 January 1963), Street Papers, NLA, MS 2683, series 10.
77 Street, *Report on Aborigines*, p. 1.
78 Michael Scott to Shirley Andrews (9 August 1963), MS 12913, Council for Aboriginal Rights, Papers, La Trobe Manuscript Collection, State Library of Victoria, box 8.
79 Commander Fox-Pitt to Jessie Street (29 April 1963), MS 12913, Council for Aboriginal Rights, Papers, La Trobe Manuscript Collection, State Library of Victoria, box 8.
80 Jessie Street to Eslanda Robeson (16 April 1961), MS 12913, Council for Aboriginal Rights, Papers, La Trobe Manuscript Collection, State Library of Victoria, box 2/10.
81 Roger Bell, *In Apartheid's Shadow: Australian Race Politics and South Africa, 1945–1975* (Melbourne: Australia Scholarly Publishing, 2019).
82 Goldberg, 'Buried Alive', p. 21.

Part II

Anti-racism and the making of postimperial Britain

5

Celebrating African culture in the north-east of England, 1930s–40s

Vanessa Mongey

'Do you beat the tom-tom drum in your bush?' Victor Oyenuga, a Nigerian PhD student in nutritional biochemistry, found himself at a loss for words when his classmate posed this question as they both sat in a lecture hall in King's College (now Newcastle University). Oyenuga realised that the Africa he knew had little to do with the distorted perceptions held by his white English classmates.[1] The uncomfortable interaction prompted Oyenuga and six other students to establish the African Friendship Society in 1947. Their aim was to dispel prejudices prevalent in the region. The north-east was home to a range of anti-racist activities in the 1930s and 1940s. Recognising that culture had been weaponised in British colonial discourse to portray African culture as 'primitive' and 'uncivilised', African students embarked on a counter-discourse to challenge these damaging stereotypes. Central to their efforts was the celebration of African culture, which became the cornerstone of their anti-racist activism.

In their efforts to challenge stereotypes and combat discrimination, African students discovered shared experiences across national and regional differences, and forged alliances with other people of African descent. They established and joined various organisations and launched a campaign to celebrate African culture. By actively promoting a 'respectable' representation of African culture to the British public, these individuals asserted the principle of equality between metropole and colonies. In doing so, they created a space for themselves within the imperial landscape of Britain.

This campaign to celebrate African culture is an opportunity to explore the dynamics that Africans and individuals of African descent encountered. These dynamics were not only limited to their interactions with the British state, but also extended to their relationships with each other and with other colonial populations. Moreover, the campaign shows their active participation in broader discussions surrounding the British Empire and British citizenship. Many Africans and West Indians leading this campaign were students and middle-class professionals, but they did not act alone. Working-class groups, mutual aid associations and sailors' associations were also active at the time. These latter groups did not much use this anti-racist campaign as a means to advocate self-determination or reconsider the dynamics between metropole and colonies; instead they focused on leveraging the campaign to advocate for increased employment and educational opportunities, thereby securing their future in Britain.

Located near the North Sea, the Newcastle region serves as a remarkable case study for comprehending the complicated construction of Black unity through anti-racist practices. African and African Caribbean individuals residing in the region possessed diverse racial, national and class-based identities. The north-east was a point of transit for colonial and migrant populations, linking the region to the wider empire. Merchant shipping attracted maritime workers, while the presence of a prestigious university attracted students to the area. In that sense, the north-east mirrored the national patterns observed in the relationships between metropolitan Britain and the wider Empire. The first half of the twentieth century witnessed increased numbers of people from Africa and the Caribbean living in Britain. Excellent studies have traced how cultural and political associations, such as the West African Students' Union (WASU) and the League of Coloured Peoples (LCP) in London, built transnational solidarity. Hakim Adi and Marc Matera, for instance, have shown how these associations of students, intellectuals and artists became more radical and openly anti-colonial in the mid-1930s through a combination of internationalism, pan-Africanism and anti-imperialism.[2]

The north-east has largely been overlooked in research on race and Britain. This absence of attention is reflective of a broader dearth of studies on Black history and anti-racism in Newcastle, particularly when compared to cities such as London, Liverpool and Bristol. As David Killingray points out in his chapter in this volume, local pan-African groups appeared in various university towns at the dawn of the twentieth century. The superficial 'whiteness' of the north-east, both historically and contemporarily, has come under scrutiny.[3] This chapter builds upon existing work on ethnic minority communities in the early twentieth century, specifically focusing on the Arab communities in South Shields. By bringing this work into dialogue with research on Afro-centric activism in London and the paternalism prevalent among certain members of the formally educated middle class, the chapter aims to shed light on the complexities of the north-east's racial landscape.[4]

Unlike many other organisations in London, the associations in the north-east included a more diverse range of participants, extending beyond students and middle-class professionals. This chapter expands the current scholarship on anti-racism by venturing beyond London and showcasing how grassroots organisations, albeit small and short-lived, managed to mobilise across different social classes. This movement not only championed pan-African ideas but also advocated for local social issues. While studies of Black organisations focus on networks of students, middle-class professionals and artists in London, the campaign to celebrate African culture in the north-east transcended these boundaries, with networks of students and sailors collaborating. However, as this chapter reveals, the celebration of African culture often ended up reflecting the West African, formally educated and Christian backgrounds of the middle-class organisers.

The chapter explores the web of organisations and historical figures in the north-east who challenged various forms of inequality and racism faced by Africans and people of African descent. These organisations included the Colonial Students' Club, the African Friendship Society and the Society for the Cultural Advancement of Africa, mostly led by students. These clubs collaborated with other associations in the region, including the West African Society, the West African Women's Association, the International Colonial Mutual Aid Association and two sailors' boarding houses: the West Indies Sailors House in Newcastle and the Colonial House in North Shields. What sets the history of anti-racist collaboration in the north-east apart is the fact that the supervisors of the sailors' boarding houses were Africans, rather than white British individuals, unlike the other clubs and hostels for seafarers and specialised workers from the colonies established throughout the country during that time.[5] Often at great personal cost, these individuals played a pivotal role in fostering unity among diverse communities in the region.

These associations and organisations championed intellectual and cultural production around Africa as a catalyst for change. Their primary objectives were threefold: first, to challenge stereotypes and racial biases prevalent among white English audiences; second, to cultivate a sense of community and solidarity among individuals from the African Diaspora; and third, to establish a cultural and intellectual foundation that would pave the way for a new relationship between the metropole and the colonies.

Fighting racial prejudices

During the 1940s, approximately 2,000 African students resided in Britain, with between sixty and 100 of them calling Newcastle their home. Hailing from Nigeria, Sierra Leone, the Gold Coast (Ghana) and The Gambia, these students had received scholarships to pursue studies in medicine, agriculture, engineering and education.[6] A few kilometres from Newcastle, in North Shields, maritime workers from the Caribbean and West Africa settled and married local women. Their number grew in the early years of the war when merchant sailors and other war workers ended up in the region.[7]

When they arrived in the north-east, young Africans encountered daily forms of racism and prejudice.[8] Some churches did not accept them, and they were forced to listen to white passengers on trains lecturing them about the 'primitive conditions' in Africa.[9] The students were part of an extended network linking Newcastle and West Africa. They either came from the same schools (for example, Fourah Bay College in Freetown, Sierra Leone, which was affiliated with Durham University at the time) or had family connections in the region.[10] When they arrived, most of them joined the Newcastle International Club, which had served as a community centre since its founding in 1930. As the number of African students grew in the 1940s, many decided to form their own associations to accommodate their needs and interests.[11] They became convinced that ignorance was at the root of the prejudice they experienced. In response, they put together a strategy to promote 'African culture'.

This belief in culture as an instrument of change is apparent with the African Friendship Society, founded in 1945 with fifteen students coming from Nigeria, Sierra Leone and the Gold Coast. The Society blamed the legacy of the transatlantic slave trade and colonialism for the image of Africa in Britain as a 'backward' and 'inferior' continent. Ignorance, they observed, produced an 'erroneous and unhealthy conception of Africa in the average English mind'.[12] These students often worked with other groups in the region, notably the Newcastle International Club, but the African Friendship Society was for Africans only. The members of this society insisted that Africans should attend to their own history because only those who 'have sojourned in that land [Africa] can grasp the significance and understand the meaning of African culture'.[13] By restricting membership to Africans, the African Friendship Society claimed that their events and activities represented an authentic image of Africa.

These attempts to dispel stereotypes around Africa and Africans in the north-east had started before the 1940s. Several students had protested the so-called native African village at the North East Coast Exhibition in 1929. The West African Students' Union in London, as well as students in Newcastle, wrote that 'as educated Africans', they objected 'to making a show of native life in such a way as to draw attention to the more backward side of African life', and insisted that such a discourse would increase feelings of racial prejudice. The organisers disregarded these concerns.[14] Over 4 million people visited the exhibition.[15] Newspapers commented that Africans in the village were using 'primitive utensils' and were 'practically savages'.[16]

The success of the African village of 1929 meant that this image of Africans as people with a 'primitive' or 'uncivilised' culture was the prevalent view until university students and graduates began their campaign ten years or so later. While these students built upon the campaign led by WASU in 1929, they did not draw a distinction between an 'educated' and a 'backward' Africa; they organised concerts and art exhibitions to educate white English audiences on the richness of African culture. When Oyenuga's classmate mentioned the 'tom-tom drum' in the African bush, Oyenuga and the African Friendship Society invited African drum artists to perform, encouraging them to perform in English and different African languages. The presence of musicians among the sailors and stowaways in the region probably accounts for the importance of these musical performances.

The students' anti-racist campaign identified music as a way to reach across local audiences. A popular initiative was a concert series of 'native songs'. It was well attended by both white and Black audiences, especially during the Christmas season. Local newspapers publicised the story of Titus Henry Nunoo, a young Gold Coast musician, who had reached Newcastle stowed away as a greaser in a ship's engine room. Nunoo performed in various locations around the region and recorded several songs in English, Creole and Ga, praising the contribution of West African soldiers in the war.[17]

The African Friendship Society was not the first association of its kind in the region. When Robert Wellesley Cole came from Sierra Leone in 1928 to study medicine in Newcastle, he soon became the nexus of the African community in town and ran several organisations. He became president of the Newcastle International Club, and founder and president of the Society for the Cultural Advancement of Africa in 1940 with his sister Irene, who had also come to Newcastle to study medicine. Another association was the Colonial Students Club, founded in 1944, with limited support from the Colonial Office, to accommodate students outside term time, since they could not easily find lodgings in the city. These various organisations implemented initiatives to promote African culture. They contacted schools, youth groups and religious groups in the region and offered to give talks about the history and culture of West Africa.[18] Many never responded, but the members of these clubs ended up giving talks at a few places, including the International Friendship League and the Workers' Educational Association in Newcastle and in Sunderland.[19]

These organisations joined the war effort when Britain entered the Second World War. Many feared what would happen if Italy and Germany won the war. One group appealed to all its members to support British war efforts by explaining that '[The Germans] have no time for Jews, and they will have less time for us, we coloured men.'[20] The Colonial Students' Club and the International Club organised lectures on events in Europe and Africa with one lecture on the daily workers' fights against antisemitism and race prejudice.[21] They saw their efforts to undermine prejudices against Africans and people of African heritage as part of the same fight against antisemitism in Europe.[22]

These associations also celebrated African culture through art. In 1943, the Society for the Cultural Advancement of Africa organised the exhibition 'Africa to Tyneside' at an art gallery at the university.[23] They invited guests from London, including the secretary-general of the West African Union of Great Britain, to give lectures on African culture and history. They also arranged for the distinguished Nigerian musician Fela Sowande to perform.[24] Robert Wellesley Cole, who helped organise the exhibit in Newcastle, later worked on another exhibition in Oxford, promoting African artworks as artistic pieces, and not as ethnographic or religious artefacts. White English audiences needed to shift their perspective, Wellesley Cole argued.[25] He insisted that 'the field was ripe for further investigation. It was up to West Africans to encourage investigations and research.' He also encouraged the government and private collectors to commission contemporary works that could stock the galleries of future West African museums.[26]

Africans also used the British Broadcasting Corporation (BBC) as a platform to broadcast their stories and claim their place as valued members of British society. A prominent member of the Newcastle Black community, Koi Obuadabang Larbi (or O'Larbi), arranged for the BBC to interview West Africans and West Indians in the region to show 'just how strong the coloured peoples on Tyneside were'. The BBC interviewed a few people, including an engineer in the Royal Army Service Corps and two West African students: Irene Cole – sister of Robert Wellesley Cole – who was a medical student and a Krio from Sierra Leone, and Folayegbe M. Akintunde-Ighodalo, who was studying teaching and was a Yoruba from Nigeria.[27] Irene's brother Robert gave a series of talks on the history of West African cities.[28] He was contacted again by the BBC for a series on the colour bar and racial discrimination in England. He refused to participate, explaining that 'for an African especially, the [colour bar] is a living organic experience, and not a museum piece to be discussed in calm detachment as to its historical origins, as if this was the only thing that mattered'.[29]

While Wellesley Cole acknowledged the legacy of the slave trade and colonialism in creating the 'historical origins' of the colour bar, he preferred to celebrate the accomplishments of African culture instead of delving into the racial prejudices that existed in England. Colonialism – and the prejudices it had produced – shaped past relationships between English and Africans. However, Wellesley Cole argued, colonialism would not shape the future of Africa and Africans. Wellesley Cole wanted to foreground the stories of Africans and the historical and cultural importance of Africa. Focusing on the colour bar would divert attention away from these accomplishments and recentre racist perceptions held by some white British audiences.

Students often navigated racial tensions by deploying their respectability as formally educated elites. When students were prevented from joining churches based on their race, they mobilised their connections with white inhabitants. They also used their educational credentials to convince church leaders to invite them to give talks on African culture. The strategies deployed by the student groups were not confrontational. While they exchanged stories of everyday racism amongst themselves, they framed these prejudices as stemming from ignorance. In that sense, most of these associations shared the ideology of the League of Coloured Peoples in London, which advocated for equality for all inhabitants of the British Empire.[30] Associations in the north-east did not openly advocate for an overhaul or even dissolution of the British Empire. They worked to celebrate African cultures and disseminate African historical and cultural achievements, convinced that this counter-discourse would eventually prevail over the dominant discourse of Africa as 'less than' Britain – an Africa that needed Britain's protection and colonial rule.

Students and middle-class professionals also mobilised their connections with the British state. Some of them contacted the Colonial Office to protest the discrimination they experienced in the north-east. These concerns prompted the Colonial Office to send two representatives in 1941 to meet a few community leaders and students to discuss the situation.[31] One of the representatives already had connections to the region: Ivor G. Cummings was one of a few Black senior officials in British government at that time. His mother, a white British nurse, and his father, a Black doctor from Sierra Leone, had met at Newcastle's Royal Victoria Infirmary. The Colonial Office, including Cummings, was eager to respond to these concerns publicly, as they feared that frustration in the Black community would drive them to more radical politics, notably Marxism.[32]

While students and university graduates promoted culture as an instrument of social and political change, others adopted a different strategy to confront the discrimination they experienced. Cinemas, pubs and dance halls frequently refused service to people of African descent. When a few sailors were prevented from entering a pub, they protested the colour bar by destroying the pay box window.[33] Others simply refused to work in protest at the mistreatment and the lower wages they received.[34] These examples show that anti-racism extended beyond the campaign to celebrate African culture run by students and middle-class professionals. Anti-racism also included more confrontational forms of resistance by people in the working class. This resistance came at a heavy price, and often resulted in the protesters being fined or even briefly jailed.[35]

Pan-African spaces and identities

Organising cultural events for white audiences to fight stereotypes of Africa was not the sole objective of these groups and associations. African students wished to create a safe place to discuss cultural and political questions.

The campaign to celebrate African culture in the north-east was ideologically close to the LCP, which was one of the less radical organisations for social progress in the 1930s and advocated for moderate reforms within the British Empire, as Anne Rush, David Killingray, Daniel Whittall and Simeon Marty have shown.[36] In a letter to Harold Moody, the president of the LCP, Robert Wellesley Cole explained that his aim with the Society for the Cultural Advancement of Africa in Newcastle was 'to bind the students here, African, West Indian, and America negro, in a self-conscious and race-conscious unit'.[37] Wellesley Cole had opened a medical practice in Newcastle after graduation, and nurtured a network of African students.

Even when Africans were keen to debate contemporary political events, they were careful not to appear too radical, as they were already under suspicion.[38] A secretary of the International Seamen Union in North Shields, for example, opposed any form of organising by Africans and people of African descent because, he argued, it could only lead to Communism.[39] Africans learnt to navigate these suspicions and avoided virulent critiques of British racism or colonialism in public. In correspondence with the Colonial Office, Wellesley Cole, as president of the West African Society, insisted that unlike African students in London, Africans in Newcastle were not interested in politics.[40] In practice, the number of talks given about African politics seems to undermine his claim. Nevertheless, these groups and associations avoided calls for full independence and anti-colonialism. They worked instead to garner British public support for a moderate programme, whereby West Africa and the Caribbean would secure more rights of self-government in the colonies. The first step was to convince metropolitan audiences that African culture was rich, thriving and sophisticated.

By trying to educate white audiences about Africa culture, these students also educated each other. While Irene Cole was putting the 1943 'Africa to Tyneside' exhibition together, she felt pride in seeing all these objects and craftwork in the space of the museum. 'In fact', she wrote to her brother, 'it's helped me to appreciate the arts of other countries'.[41] This pan-African solidarity persisted even after students returned to West Africa. When a prominent member of the Newcastle community, Albert Odulate, who had studied and trained for six years at the medical school, died in a road accident in Nigeria, the Colonial Students' Club announced a memorial fund in his name.[42]

These efforts to create a pan-African consciousness and unity were sometimes in tension with local working-class groups, which were more concerned with the living and social conditions of Black families in the north-east. Black students in Newcastle were not all Africans. A few local inhabitants also attended the university to study nursing, engineering and teaching. While they probably attended the events organised by West African students and interacted with them at university, these local students lived at home, often in North Shields, and stayed in the region after graduation.[43] African students initially promoted African culture to counteract racial stereotypes and reinforce solidarity in the small Black community of Newcastle. However, through their interactions with other groups, African students grew aware of other forms of discrimination, especially related to employment.[44]

The links among student clubs, sailors' houses and mutual aid associations were tight in such a small community. The same individuals served on the committees of different associations. When the war broke, Koi Obuadabang Larbi, who had come from Ghana to study law, paused his career and became the superintendent of the sailors' boarding house that opened in October 1941, a few blocks from the university, called the West Indies House Sailors Hotel.[45] He collaborated with students and sailors to organise concerts, dances and lectures. He even carried a pool table back and forth between the boarding house and the Colonial Students' Club.[46] While class differences persisted, students and sailors often worked together. These collaborations across social classes were rare at the time, with such organisations of students and intellectuals as WASU and LCP remaining separate from workers' groups such as the Coloured Seamen's Association.[47]

The reason students, and middle-class and working-class individuals, often worked together in the north-east is probably that two Africans oversaw the sailors' houses in the region. These two figures served as nodal points connecting different groups. Several seamen's hostels opened during the Second World War, with responsibility given to the Colonial Office, but only in Tyneside were these hostels run by Africans.[48] Occupying this space was not easy. Larbi often clashed with the British Sailors' Society, which wanted the West Indies House to host European sailors. Larbi insisted that the space should be reserved for Black sailors, especially with the influx of colonial populations during the war. Between 700 and 900 workers from British Honduras (today's Belize) came to cut timber in Scotland to support the war effort. The foresters complained about low wages and living conditions, and organised a strike in 1942.[49] The workers sometimes travelled to Newcastle while on leave and stayed at the West Indies House. Some of them looked for other forms of employment in town. The boarding house became a point of contact for people of different national origins and social backgrounds. This process was accelerated through the debate clubs and study groups that Larbi set up in which current affairs in the colonies were discussed. Since public libraries did not let people of African descent use their facilities, Larbi launched a book donation drive to create a reading room at the West Indies House.[50]

The Colonial Office took over the administration of the hostel in June 1942. Throughout the war, the Colonial Office pushed the government to address the grievances of African and West Indians living in Britain.[51] While most hostels of this type in Britain employed white supervisors, Africans ran the boarding houses in Tyneside: Larbi at the West Indies House in Newcastle and Charles Udor Minto at the Colonial House in North Shields, which opened in May 1943. Minto was a former middle-weight boxer from Calabar, Nigeria, who came to the north-east as a sailor and married a local woman. The Colonial House welcomed 600 people every year.[52] It was supported by the Colonial Office, since Minto refused to work with the British Sailors' Society, probably because of Larbi's experience in the West Indies House in Newcastle. Minto leveraged the work he had been doing as the president of the International Coloured Mutual Aid Association (ICMAA) and convinced the Colonial Office that he was the best person to become the warden of the hostel.

At the centre of the Black community in North Shields was the ICMAA created in 1935.[53] The ICMAA was a Christian organisation that aimed to improve the welfare of Black people living in the region. Some members of the Black community felt that organisations such as the ICMAA worked too closely with the Colonial Office and the British imperial state to the detriment of more radical or anti-imperialist actions.[54] The ICMAA split up into two groups in 1939 because of tensions around politics and clashes between West Africans and West Indians. The other association proved short-lived. Striving to create solidarity across racially, nationally and politically heterogeneous groups, Minto became president of the ICMAA and collaborated with members from Barbados, Nigeria, Liberia, Sierra Leone and South Africa. The Association claimed 126 members in 1941.[55] Inspired by Christian idealism, Minto argued that all people were equal before God; the association's motto was 'One aim, one goal, one destiny'.[56] While the ICMAA often collaborated and worked with students to run events about the history and culture of Africa, they mostly wanted to offer a safe space and a source of support for Black families.

Mutual aid associations and boarding houses were spaces of solidarity, belonging and financial support. Unlike other pan-African organisations that campaigned against British colonial rule, the ambitions of the North Shields groups were mostly driven by local concerns. Minto assisted with securing housing and employment, acted as a liaison officer for sailors and workers, and organised social activities. He celebrated African culture so that the next generations could feel proud of their heritage.

The mutual aid associations in port cities were particularly preoccupied with the welfare and the lack of cultural and educational opportunities for children. Some lived in poverty, their fathers being often away at sea. The ICMAA provided clothing to children, and financial aid to send them to school.[57] The ICMAA saw education as a way for younger generations to move away from poorly paid occupations such as seafaring for men and domestic work for women. It set up a scheme with the Red Cross and Tynemouth Education Authority to compensate working-class parents when they sent their children to secondary school instead of sending them to work. It also provided grants for academic and vocational training.[58]

The ICMAA also tackled employment and educational discrimination. Minto and members of the ICMAA visited factories, shipowner offices and labour exchanges.[59] They confronted compensation issues with the Shipping Office, demanding equal pay for sailors. When sailors became disabled, Minto attempted to secure work opportunities for them on shore.[60] Most employers, including public utilities such as coal boards and railways, refused to employ them.[61] The ICMAA tried to set up a 'colonial store' that could provide African food and employ local workers.[62] This fight for social justice was a family affair. One of Minto's daughters, Edna, was secretary of the ICMAA; she worked at the Colonial House and served as a social worker to assist West Africans and West Indians in the region.[63]

Minto also worked to garner support outside the Black community. He often reached out to white officials and politicians, union officers, and councillors to secure immediate and concrete support: 'My main aim', he reminisced in 1950, 'was to establish a centre where coloured people and white people could get together and know and understand each other'.[64] Minto's wife was a white woman who organised many events. With the help of his wife and daughter, the Colonial House ran cinema screenings, dances, lectures and concerts, and publicised them as open to everyone.[65] Minto encouraged children to bring their white friends to these events, which combined films, music and refreshments.[66]

Sailors' hostels in both Newcastle and in North Shields encouraged sports. There was a billiard table at the Colonial House; games of checkers and dominoes were frequent.[67] Improving interracial relationships drove many of these initiatives led by mutual aid associations. With the help of a West African secretary, a member of the British Council set up an athletic club to encourage the participation of West African and West Indian local players, mostly sailors, as well as to 'improve the relation between white and coloured people'.[68]

The ICMAA continued to help with employment and housing discrimination until the Colonial House closed in June 1950 and the ICMAA stopped its activities.[69] University graduates also experienced employment discrimination. Robert Wellesley Cole, for example, was denied a residency appointment in 1950. Reflecting on this experience, Wellesley Cole noted 'I felt I was blocked because they [other doctors] were jealous, because I was beating them and they hated the idea of a black chap doing that.'[70] Wellesley Cole moved his medical practice to Nottingham until he joined the Nigerian

Civil Service as a consultant surgeon. Like him, many African students turned their attention to anti-colonial efforts in West Africa, especially when the Second World War ended.

Africa for Africans

Diverse groups and associations promoted African culture as key to an anti-racist discourse and a sense of community, but their ambitions were ultimately different. On the one hand, mutual aid groups in North Shields thought that these prejudices had a direct impact on the working, living and educational conditions for Black adults and children living in the region. On the other hand, student associations in Newcastle wanted to pave the way for extended opportunities for Africans in Africa.

When they arrived in the metropole, many students had already experienced racial discrimination, as Africans were excluded from administrative service in British West Africa, with colonial elites protecting their privileges.[71] Many members of the student associations understood their presence in England as temporary. They came to Britain to gain an education and a network, and, for some of them, to use this experience to become the doctors, educators and politicians that West African countries would need after independence. Although most students did not call for independence openly (they often pushed for dominion status instead), many of them became more interested in West African nationalism when the war ended and they worried that racist stereotypes would hinder popular support for self-rule in West Africa.[72]

The West African Society, founded in 1947 and headquartered in Newcastle, promoted research on history, folklore, art and culture 'in preparation fully to play our part in the new community of nations'.[73] The Society embraced the idea that racial unity and political liberation could be built through cultural work, especially through the production of shared historical memories. Its motto was 'For culture and learning' and it encouraged the kind of national consciousness that would eventually lead to the end of British colonialism.[74] The members of the society wanted to provide the intellectual and cultural foundation for self-governing West African countries to flourish.

The reports of the West African Society show how its members conceptualised culture. They defined 'culture' as almost exclusively a written and academic form of knowledge. The Society insisted on the need to record and document African accomplishments. When it came to promoting African culture as a tool of political legitimacy, they foregrounded written records over oral traditions and songs. African accomplishments, they argued, were only known through verbal and 'other more or less ineffective forms' of communication.[75] The European style of historical production and scientific research was the lens through which the Society defined culture. One of the Society's projects, for instance, was to produce a series of biographies of Africans, mostly men.

While the cultural enterprise of these groups often focused on telling or retelling the accomplishments of African men, women played a key role in the anti-racist and pan-African activism of the era, as Marc Matera, Imaobong D. Umoren and others have shown.[76] Irene Cole not only founded the Society for the Cultural Advancement of Africa with her brother, Robert, but also founded women's groups such as the West African Women's Association.[77] She ran this group alongside managing her brother's medical practice while he visited West Africa as a member of the Colonial Office Advisory Committee in 1945–46. Personal relationships often sustained these associations. When people left the region, these associations dissolved. Irene and Robert Wellesley Cole from Sierra Leone, and two other siblings, Albert and Folake Odulate from Nigeria, were part of the same circles. Albert was studying medicine while Folake studied English, Latin, mathematics, education and law. Both returned to Nigeria, Folake marrying a Nigerian doctor she had met in Newcastle and establishing a law firm in 1966 – the first by a Nigerian woman.[78]

For these women, securing gender, racial and political equality was part of the same struggle. Irene Cole argued that self-government in West Africa could only be assured through expanding women's educational and employment opportunities in West Africa.[79] She presented a paper on women's role in education, social services and public health to the WASU Conference on West African problems in August 1942.[80] Irene married a Nigerian lawyer, Samuel Ighodaro, in front of a large crowd in Newcastle in 1947.[81] A few years later, the couple moved to Nigeria, where Irene continued her career as a physician and a social reformer.

The West African Society not only aimed at providing a cultural foundation for African countries, but also wanted to provide training for future elites. The Society launched a recruitment campaign to convince West African students to join the Society and draft articles for its magazine *Africana*. Members of the Society toured student clubs, hoping that the new recruits would not only help create records of African historical accomplishments, but would also allow the Society to grow its presence in West Africa when these students returned home.[82]

The Society had offices in Sierra Leone, the Gold Coast and Nigeria, and sent issues of *Africana* to the United States.[83] They struggled to get a foothold in the Gambia.[84] The Society and its members placed themselves in a diasporic perspective to link Africans and members of the African diaspora across Britain, West Africa and the United States through culture. At the core of their mission was the idea that Africans should drive this cultural enterprise to protect the Society from white influences.[85] The Society barely broke even financially and ceased its activities around 1950.

Despite their divergent interests, students, sailors and middle-class professionals frequently collaborated and formed friendships and alliances. However, these collaborations seem to have been limited to their own communities and did not extend to other colonial subjects in the region. South Shields, a port town, housed various communities, including many sailors from Yemen, Pakistan and Somaliland.[86] When the sociologist Sidney Collins conducted research in the area in 1950, he observed a sense of suspicion between the Black communities in North Shields and their Yemeni neighbours in South Shields. He also noted the absence of multiethnic solidarity, attributing it to religious and cultural differences.[87] Similarly, there was no apparent effort to establish connections with Black communities in other parts of Europe or to engage with other colonial subjects from the French West African colonies.[88] Pan-Africanism in the north-east remained predominantly anglophone and framed within the confines of the British Empire.

Tensions between these local groups and the British state became increasingly frequent after the war. The superintendent of the West Indies House, Koi Larbi, clashed with the Colonial Office, which restricted Larbi's authority and paid him a low salary. Larbi resumed his legal career and pushed for the right to self-determination in the British Empire. A member of the Pan-African Federation, Larbi attended the All Colonial Peoples' (or Subject Peoples') Conference in London in 1945 and advocated for a policy and programme for the unconditional and immediate ending of all colonial systems.[89] Many Africans, like others in the British Empire, hoped that postwar peace would bring freedom and equality for all, including for those living under colonial rule. They were no longer willing to compromise. Larbi returned to the Gold Coast and supported the colony gaining its independence in 1957 as the country of Ghana.

Conclusion

Diverse groups and associations actively conducted a campaign to celebrate African culture during the 1930s and 1940s. They recognised that cultural production, encompassing music, art and history, was key to countering the prevailing stereotypes and caricatures of Africans in Britain. The north-east region offers a compelling case study for understanding the collaborations among students, middle-class professionals and maritime workers that characterised anti-racism during this period. The role played by the two heads of the sailors' houses in the region, Larbi and Minto, was pivotal in facilitating these alliances. Larbi's direct connections to the university as a former student, along with Minto's prominence as a community leader, explain their ability to bring together distinct groups. In addition to the significance of places such as Newcastle and North Shields as vibrant hubs of Black politics, this chapter argues that grassroots associations, by celebrating African culture, actively engaged in a broader discussion concerning the place of people of African descent within the British Empire. This discussion gained momentum in the years following the 1950s.[90]

These groups and associations fought against racism and the injustices of empire and colonial status. They were interwoven into the fabric of the region, with student meeting rooms and sailors' boarding houses serving as sources of support, guidance and creativity. Students, seafarers, doctors and manual workers personally experienced the detrimental impact of racist stereotypes on their daily lives in Britain. Despite their differences, they organised a series of events, including exhibits, concerts, dances and lecture series, to celebrate African culture and envision a future free from racial discrimination. Through these social and educational activities, they performed and articulated a form of African culture that brought together individuals from different regions, countries and ethnicities. However, they ultimately promoted a pan-African culture that reflected their own backgrounds as British West African elites who were formally educated and predominantly Christian. By promoting a 'respectable' African culture to the British public, these different actors asserted the equality between the metropole and the colonies, and carved out a space for themselves within the metropolitan space of imperial Britain.

Social class played a significant role in shaping the narrative of this campaign to celebrate African culture. Students and middle-class professionals meticulously curated their image as educated Africans, aiming to promote formal and intellectual knowledge and establish equality between the empire and its colonies. Additionally, class influenced the portrayal of Africa by these students, particularly their emphasis on 'culture', which risked basing acceptance on respectability. On the other hand, other Black inhabitants and migrants in the region, such as sailors or forestry workers, had their own distinct priorities. For instance, while student clubs in Newcastle requested books from the Colonial Office, the mutual aid association in North Shields asked for warm clothing.[91] Because of their access to the media and their ability to produce their own historical records, students and middle-class professionals took over the campaign to celebrate African culture, and centred the campaign on English-speaking West Africa.

The celebrations of African culture held in various locations in the northeast were part of dynamic politics led by student activists and community leaders in the region. The aim was to bring visibility to African culture and contribute to the diverse cultures of anti-racism. However, following the war, the hopes of achieving equality within the British Empire gradually faded away. The closure of sailors' hostels and mutual aid societies, together with the rise of African nationalism, led to the gradual disappearance of the network of pan-African organisations by the early 1950s. Members of these groups either relocated to other regions in Britain, or moved to West Africa and the Caribbean to focus on achieving independence from the British Empire. Meanwhile, other colonial and migrant groups moved to the region, forging new connections and networks.[92]

Notes

1 Adebayo Adesoye, *Sojourn: Emeritus Professor V. A. Oyenuga's Biography* (Pittsburgh: RoseDog Books, 2010), p. 49. The current Newcastle University was originally an extension of Durham University and was known as King's College (a merger of the School of Medicine and Armstrong College) from 1937 until 1963, when it became Newcastle University, independent of Durham.
2 Hakim Adi, 'West African Students in Britain, 1900–60: The Politics of Exile', *Immigrants & Minorities*, 12:3 (1993), 107–28; Hakim Adi, *Pan-Africanism* (London: Bloomsbury Academic, 2019); Marc Matera, *Black London: The Imperial Metropolis and Decolonization in the Twentieth Century* (Berkeley: University of California Press, 2015). See also David Killingray, '"A Good West Indian, a Good African, and, in Short, a Good Britisher": Black and British in a Colour-Conscious Empire, 1760–1950', *Journal of Imperial and Commonwealth History*, 36:3 (2008), 363–81; and Priyamvada Gopal, *Insurgent Empire: Anticolonial Resistance and British Dissent* (London: Verso, 2019).
3 Anoop Nayak, '"White English Ethnicities": Racism, Anti-Racism and Student Perspectives', *Race, Ethnicity and Education*, 2:2 (1999), 177–202.
4 Richard Lawless, *From Ta'izz to Tyneside: An Arab Community in the North-East of England during the Early Twentieth Century* (Exeter: University of Exeter Press, 1995); Craig Armstrong, 'Aliens in Wartime: A Case Study of Tyneside, 1939–45', *Immigrants & Minorities*, 25:2 (2007), 119–40; Laura Tabili, *Global Migrants, Local Culture: Natives and Newcomers in Provincial England, 1841–1939* (London: Palgrave Macmillan, 2011); Jacqueline Jenkinson, 'Black, Arab and South Asian Colonial Britons in the Intersections between War and Peace: The 1919 Seaport Riots in Perspective', in H. Ewence and T. Grady (eds), *Minorities and the First World War* (London: Palgrave Macmillan, 2017), pp. 175–98; Youssef Nabil and Tina Gharavi, *Last of the Dictionary Men: Stories from the South Shields Yemeni Sailors* (London: Gilgamesh, 2013); Vanessa Mongey, 'Paths across Waters: Black British Stories in the North East', www.pathswaters.wixsite.com/tyne (accessed 15 February 2023).

5 Sarah A. Milne, 'Accounting for the Hostel for "Coloured Colonial Seamen" in London's East End, 1942–1949', *National Identities*, 22:4 (2019), 1–27.
6 J. L. Keith, 'African Students in Great Britain', *African Affairs*, 45:179 (1946), 65–72.
7 Kew, The National Archives (TNA), CO 859.76.5, letter from Charles Udor Minto to Ivor G. Cummings (9 April 1941).
8 School of Oriental and African Studies, University of London (SOAS), papers of Dr Robert Wellesley Cole, PP MS 35, box 20, file 149, letter from Wellesley Cole to Nicholson (28 February 1948).
9 Reference to Anglican churches in Newcastle is in Adesoye, *Sojourn*, p. 53. Reference to the train ride is found in a letter from Mai Clarissa Jones to Wellesley Cole, SOAS, PP MS 35, box 1, file 5 (7 April 1958); Jones wrote that 'I let her [the train passenger] off lightly, But I do not know whether the next offender will not be left off with a legion of fleas or barbs in his or her ear.'
10 Durham University was affiliated with Fourah Bay College between 1876 and 1967 and with Codrington College in Barbados between 1875 and 1965.
11 Adi, 'West African Students'; Matera, *Black London*.
12 Adesoye, *Sojourn*, pp. 54–5.
13 *Ibid*.
14 *Wasu*, 2:1 (January 1933), 19–20. Deborah L. Hughes, 'Debating the "African Village" at the North East Coast Exhibition, Newcastle, 1929', in Celia Pearce, Bobby Schweizer, Laura Hollengreen and Rebecca Rouse (eds), *Meet Me at the Fair: A World's Fair Reader* (Pittsburgh: ETC Press, 2014), pp. 61–9.
15 Michael Barke, 'The North East Coast Exhibition of 1929: Entrenchment or Modernity?', *Northern History*, 51:1 (2014), 153–76.
16 *Sunderland Daily Echo and Shipping Gazette* (23 July 1929); *Newcastle Chronicle* (16 February 1929).
17 *Shields Daily News* (20 July 1944). Mentions of concerts or musical events appear, for instance, in *Shields Daily News* (27 April 1943); and *Newcastle Journal* (29 November and 1 December 1941).
18 Adesoye, *Sojourn*, p. 52; *Shields Daily News* (27 November 1942).
19 Adesoye, *Sojourn*, p. 53; SOAS, PP MS 35, box 20, file 156, letter from Wellesley Cole to Workers' Educational Association (4 May 1946).
20 TNA, CO 859/76/5, letter from Minto to J. L. Keith (14 August 1941).
21 Robert Wellesley Cole, *An Innocent in Britain; or, The Missing Link* (n.p.: Campbell Matthews, 1988), pp. 260–1.
22 Stephen Bourne, *Mother Country: Britain's Black Community on the Home Front, 1939–1955* (London: History Press, 2010).
23 *Newcastle Journal* (10 June 1943).
24 *Colonial Cinema*, 1:9 (November 1943), p. 3.
25 *Africana*, 1:2 (April 1949), p. 26.
26 *Ibid*.
27 'Talk by Michel Yanni,' *Calling West Africa*, recorded at West Indies House, Newcastle, 13 June 1942, transmitted to Africa, 11 July 1942, BBC Written Archives; 'Two West African Women in 1940s Britain: Dr Irene Cole-Ighodaro

and Folayegbe M. Akintunde-Ighodalo', cited in A. A. Y. Kyerematen, 'West Africa in Transition', *African*, 1:2 (1949), 3–4.
28 SOAS, PP MS 35, box 38, file 199, BBC talk (28 October 1948).
29 *Ibid.*
30 Anne Rush, 'Imperial Identity in Colonial Minds: Dr Harold Moody and the League of Coloured Peoples, 1931–50', *Twentieth Century British History*, 13:4 (2002), 356–83; David Killingray, '"To do something for the race": Harold Moody, and the League of Coloured Peoples', in Bill Schwarz (ed.), *West Indian Intellectuals in Britain* (Manchester: Manchester University Press, 2003), pp. 51–70; Daniel Whittall, 'Creating Black Places in Imperial London: The League of Coloured Peoples and Aggrey House, 1931–1943', *London Journal*, 36:3 (2011), 225–46; Simeon Marty, 'Thinking Black in the Blitz: Harold Moody, the League of Coloured Peoples and Its Shift of Pan-African Ideas in Second World War London', *Esboços*, 28:48 (2021), 407–26.
31 *Shields Daily News* (28 June 1941).
32 On Cummings, see John Flint, 'Scandal at the Bristol Hotel: Some Thoughts on Racial Discrimination in Britain and West Africa and Its Relationship to the Planning of Decolonisation, 1939–47', *Journal of Imperial and Commonwealth History*, 12:1 (1983), 74–93; and Sonya O. Rose, 'Race, Empire and British Wartime National Identity, 1939–45', *Historical Research*, 74:184 (2001), 220–37.
33 *Shields Daily News* (26 October 1950).
34 *Shields Daily News* (10 November 1944).
35 See Christopher Fevre, 'Race and Resistance to Policing before the "Windrush Years": The Colonial Defence Committee and the Liverpool "Race Riots" of 1948', *Twentieth Century British History*, 32:1 (2021), 1–23.
36 Rush, 'Imperial Identity in Colonial Minds'; Killingray, 'To do something for the race'; Whittall, 'Creating Black Places in Imperial London'; Daniel Whittall, 'Creolising London: Black West Indian Activism and the Politics of Race and Empire in Britain, 1931–1948', PhD thesis (University of London, 2012); Marty, 'Thinking Black in the Blitz'.
37 SOAS, PP MS 35, box 20, file 151, letter from Wellesley Cole to Harold Moody (2 June 1942).
38 On issues around accommodation and politics in the interwar and war periods, see Whittall, 'Creating Black Places'; and Sarah A. Milne, 'Accounting for the Hostel for "Coloured Colonial Seamen" in London's East End, 1942–1949', *National Identities*, 22:4 (2020), 395–421.
39 TNA, CO 859/76/5, letter from Keith to Minto (22 July 1941).
40 SOAS, PP MS 35, box 20, file 149, letter from Wellesley Cole to Marjorie Nicholson (29 February 1948).
41 SOAS, PP MS 35, box 1, file 7, letter from Irene Cole to Wellesley Cole (5 July 1947).
42 *Africana*, 1:2 (April 1949), p. 29.
43 Sidney Collins, '"Moslem" and "Negro" Groupings on Tyneside: A Comparative Study of Social Integration in Terms of Intra-Group and Inter-Group Relations', PhD thesis (University of Edinburgh, 1952), p. 85.

44 SOAS, PP MS 35, box 20, file 147, letter from Wellesley Cole to Moody (2 June 1942).
45 *Shields Daily News* (31 July 1941).
46 SOAS, PP MS 35, box 7, file 73, report of Colonial Students' Club (December 1946).
47 On working-class organisations, see Laura Tabili, *We Ask for British Justice: Workers and Racial Differences in Late Imperial Britain* (Ithaca: Cornell University Press, 1994).
48 Colonial Development and Welfare Act of 1940.
49 TNA, CO 876/41, letter by A. Slater (18 September 1942). More on forestry workers can be found in Marika Sherwood, *Many Struggles: West Indian Workers and Service Personnel in Britain (1939–1945)* (London: Karia Press, 1985).
50 *Newcastle Evening Chronicle* (15 May 1944).
51 Hakim Adi, *African and Caribbean People in Britain: A History* (London: Allen Lane, 2022), pp. 356, 383.
52 *Shields Daily News* (1 January 1949).
53 *Shields Daily News* (15 May 1939).
54 *The Negro Worker* (July–August 1935).
55 TNA, CO 859/76/5, Minto's application (22 July 1941).
56 For another example of how Christianity informed Harold Moody's belief in racial equality, see Killingray, 'To Do Something', pp. 55–7.
57 TNA, CO 859/76/5, letter from Minto to Cummings (9 April 1941).
58 *Shields Evening News* (11 September 1943); *Newcastle Journal* (23 September 1943).
59 TNA, CO 859/76/5, letter from Minto to Keith (10 July 1941).
60 *Shields Daily News* (28 June 1941).
61 *Shields Daily News* (13 August 1948). See Gavin Schaffer, 'Fighting Racism: Black Soldiers and Workers in Britain during the Second World War', in Caroline Bressey and Hakim Adi (eds), *Belonging in Europe: The African Diaspora and Work* (New York: Routledge, 2013), pp. 142–56.
62 *Shields Daily News* (3 September 1947).
63 *Shields Daily News* (15 February 1943).
64 *Shields Daily News* (18 July 1950).
65 For example, *Shields Daily News* (23 December 1940) reported on the Christmas party: 'About 120 children representing various nations in the British Empire were entertained by [the] Association to a cinema show, games and a special Christmas tea.'
66 *Shields Evening News* (8 May 1944).
67 *Shields Evening News* (30 September 1941 and 7 September 1946).
68 Athletic Club's report (undated) cited in Collins, '"Moslem" and "Negro" Groupings', pp. 142–4.
69 See Sophia Siddiqui's chapter in this volume on the resurgence of Black self-help and mutual aid associations in the 1960 and 1970s whose efforts were often localised, but who, unlike the ICMAA, had a complicated relationship with receiving financial support from the British state.

70 Gary Stewart, 'Robert Wellesley Cole at 80', *Sierra Leone Journal Dispatches from Pre-War Freetown and Beyond* (1987), www.sierraleonejournal.org/cole.html (accessed 15 December 2022).
71 Flint, 'Scandal', pp. 80–1. A shortage of staff during the war prepared the ground for reforms, but racial exclusion and discrimination remained in place in British West Africa until 1947.
72 Gabriel Olusanya, *The West African Students' Union and the Politics of Decolonization 1925–1958* (Ibadan: Daystar Press, 1982).
73 SOAS, PP MS 35, box 21, file 156, International Press Bureau (11 December 1948).
74 *Ibid*.
75 SOAS, PP MS 35, box 21, file 156, progress report of the West African Society (June 1949).
76 Matera, *Black London*; Imaobong D. Umoren, *Race Women Internationalists: Activist-Intellectuals and Global Freedom* (Oakland: University of California Press, 2018).
77 SOAS, PP MS 35, box 1, file 7, letter from Irene Cole to Wellesley Cole (24 January 1946); Irene Ighodaro, *A Life of Service* (Lagos, Oxford: Malthouse Press, 1996), pp. 27–30; Matera, *Black London*, pp. 213–28.
78 Adesoye, *Sojourn*, pp. 64–6.
79 SOAS, PP MS 35, box 1, file 7, letter from Irene Cole to Wellesley Cole (24 January 1946).
80 Irene Cole, 'Social Problems in West Africa', *Wasu*, 10:1 (May 1943), 24–5.
81 SOAS, PP MS 35, box 1, file 7, letter from Irene Cole to Wellesley Cole (1 January 1947).
82 SOAS, PP MS 35, box 21, file 156, chairman's report (26 July 1949).
83 For example, Special Collections and University Archives, University of Massachusetts Amherst Libraries, W. E. B. Du Bois Papers, MS 312, letter from Hugh H. Smythe to West African Society (20 December 1948).
84 *Ibid.*, progress report of the West African Student Union (June 1949).
85 *Ibid.*, editorial report (July 1949).
86 Lawless, *From Ta'izz to Tyneside*; Tabili, *Global Migrants*; Nabil and Gharavi, *Last of the Dictionary Men*.
87 As a West Indian researcher, Collins recognised that he had more facility surveying West Africans and West Indians: 'Groupings', pp. 13–19 (the quote is on p. 18). More research might uncover collaborations across the different groups, especially around left seafarers' politics and the Colonial Seamen's Association. See Tabili, *We Ask for British Justice*; and Christian Høgsbjerg, 'Mariner, Renegade, Castaway: Chris Braithwaite, Seamen's Organiser and Pan-Africanist', *Race and Class*, 53:2 (2011), 36–57.
88 Laurence Brown, 'Afro-Caribbean Migrants in France and the United Kingdom', in Leo Lucassen, David Feldman and Jochen Oltmer (eds), *Paths of Integration: Migrants in Western Europe (1880–2004)* (Amsterdam: Amsterdam University Press, 2006), pp. 177–98; Robbie Aitken and Eve Rosenhaft, *Black Germany: The Making and Unmaking of a Diaspora Community, 1884–1960* (Cambridge: Cambridge University Press, 2013); Michael Goebel, *Anti-Imperial*

Metropolis: Interwar Paris and the Seeds of Third World Nationalism (New York: Cambridge University Press, 2015); Annette K. Joseph-Gabriel, *Reimagining Liberation: How Black Women Transformed Citizenship in the French Empire* (Champaign: University of Illinois Press, 2019).
89 Marika Sherwood, 'The All Colonial Peoples Conferences in Britain, 1945', *Leeds African Studies Bulletin*, 79 (Winter 2017/18), 113–24.
90 On the postwar period, see Kennetta Hammond Perry, *London Is the Place for Me: Black Britons, Citizenship, and the Politics of Race* (Oxford: Oxford University Press, 2015); and A. J. Stockwell, 'Leaders, Dissidents and the Disappointed: Colonial Students in Britain as Empire Ended', *Journal of Imperial and Commonwealth History*, 36 (2008), 487–507. East Germany became a destination for many African students; see Sarah Pugach, *African Students in East Germany, 1949–1975* (Ann Arbor: University of Michigan Press, 2022).
91 SOAS, PP MS 35, box 7, file 73, report of Colonial Student Club (December 1946); and TNA, CO 859/76/5, letter from Cummings to Minto (3 July 1941).
92 On postwar multiculturalism in the north-east, see Dave Renton, *Colour Blind? Race and Migration in North East England since 1945* (Sunderland: University of Sunderland Press, 2007); Sarah Hackett, 'The Asian of the North: Immigrant Experiences and the Importance of Regional Identity in Newcastle upon Tyne during the 1980s', *Northern History*, 46:2 (2009), 293–311; and Anoop Nayak, 'Race, Religion and British Multiculturalism: The Political Responses of Black and Minority Ethnic Voluntary Organisations to Multicultural Cohesion', *Political Geography*, 31:7 (2012), 454–63.

6

British Jews and the Race Relations Acts

Joseph Finlay

In 1965, Harold Wilson's Labour government (with a majority of just two) passed the Race Relations Act, a landmark piece of legislation. For the first time Britain introduced legally binding protections against discrimination – though these were initially very limited – and a country without a written constitution took the first steps toward what Anthony Lester and Geoffrey Bindman called 'a statutory declaration that everyone in Britain was to be treated on the basis of individual merit, irrespective of colour or race'.[1] The primary motivation for the legislation has been remembered as having been the protection of Black and Asian Britons who arrived from New Commonwealth countries after the Second World War, as well an attempt to 'balance' the restrictive 1962 Commonwealth Immigrants Act.[2] Another motivation for the Act has attracted far less attention: the desire to protect Britain's Jewish community from fascist verbal and printed attacks. Jews were both a group that legislators sought to protect, and a group heavily overrepresented amongst those lobbying for legislation. According to many MPs who spoke during the Act's parliamentary passage, and during the unsuccessful passage of several precursor Bills, a major aim was to combat the neofascist groups enjoying a resurgence in the early 1960s, some of whom made naked antisemitism their priority. Jewish communal organisations, led by the Board of Deputies' Defence Committee (itself under pressure from new Jewish anti-fascist groups), argued that existing laws were failing to prevent such groups meeting and inciting hatred against Jews, and found a receptive audience amongst parliamentarians. A small number of Jewish progressive lawyers were also highly influential in drafting, reshaping and commenting on the Act, most notably Lester, but also Bindman, Jeffrey Jowell and others.[3]

Recent academic accounts of the Act underplay this Jewish contribution. Erik Bleich has minimised the impact of Jewish communal lobbying for protection against incitement, observing that Home Office officials believed Jewish leaders were more concerned about swastika daubing than verbal incitement.[4] In his study of the creation of the first Race Relations Board

Simon Peplow omitted issues of Jewishness altogether, despite the inclusion of the Jewish politician Bernard Langton as one of the three eventual Board members.[5] The protection of Jews as a possible motivation for the creation of the Act was absent from Harry Goulborne's overview of the field, despite its assertion that British anti-racist history, particularly in the law, 'is incomplete without the clear recognition of the paramount role played by individuals from the Jewish, Irish and other communities'.[6] And while Satnam Virdee's landmark work on the influence of 'racialized outsiders' on British radical politics pays attention to Jewish trade unionism and Communism at the turn of the twentieth century and mentions the large number of Jewish organisers of the Anti-Nazi League in the 1970s, it says nothing about Jews and the Race Relation Act or the fascist incitement that preceded it.[7] The only account to pay close attention to the Jewish-focused element of the Act has thus far been Gavin Schaffer's: examining the incitement clause in the context of a study of how sophisticated racists evaded legal sanction, while a number of Black radicals were prosecuted.[8] I will expand on Schaffer's study, suggesting that the process that led to the Act demonstrated the relative concern for Jews amongst many MPs, in contrast to a lack of sympathy for Black and Asian people. My focus will be on discussions of Jews in the *Hansard* record of parliamentary debates; key to my study will be a series of unsuccessful Private Members' Bills in the late 1950s and early 1960s that set the terms of the debate for the eventual 1965 Act. A number of underlying themes will be explored: the tendency of both parliamentary proponents and opponents of the Act to use Jews to make their case whilst being far more occupied with Jewish concerns than those of other racialised minorities; the narrow focus on incitement by Jewish communal bodies and their disinclination to be included in a broader piece of 'race' legislation; and the placing of measures protecting Jews in a separate part of the Act from those protecting Black and Asian Britons, a separation that would persist for decades through the twin camps of anti-fascism and anti-racism.

Prehistory of the Act

The demand for legislation to protect Jews from incitement was a long-standing one. The only law limiting fascist meetings was the Public Order Act of 1936, which merely prohibited the wearing of uniforms and the intentional stirring up of violence. The toothlessness of the sedition laws in relation to anti-Jewish incitement was demonstrated when the publisher of a Morecambe local paper was acquitted, despite having published an article suggesting that Jews had brought the 1947 antisemitic riots upon themselves.[9] His successful defence was that while he had intended to cause offence to Jews, he had not intended to stir up violence. The 1948 Porter Report on Defamation considered the idea of group libel, to offer the possibility of prosecuting defamatory speech against groups of people rather than individuals, but rejected it on traditional freedom-of-speech grounds.[10] In the parliamentary debate leading up to the 1952 Defamation Act, Labour's Lord Silkin proposed an amendment to the effect that a defamatory statement 'concerning any group of persons distinguishable as such by race, creed or colour' could be prosecuted by any individual who identified as a member of that group, referring to 'wicked statements' in connection to antisemitic blood libel claims. Other Peers expressed concern about antisemitic publications, such as the *Protocols of the Elders of Zion*, and expressed sympathy for the 'Jewish race' and plight of Jewish refugees in the wake of the Nazi genocide. They went on to claim, however, that in contrast to Jews in other countries, those in Britain needed no special protection, and that to provide it might incite antisemitism, at which point the amendment was withdrawn.[11] In the activist realm, the founding meeting of the anti-fascist 43 Group in 1946 made lobbying Parliament 'to illegalise racial incitement and make it an offence punishable by imprisonment' one of its two strategic aims.[12] The wave of 1940s fascism had sufficiently subsided by 1950 for the 43 Group to disband voluntarily,[13] and by the early 1950s the Board's Defence Commitee felt that threats to the Jewish community had substantially decreased. The Committee was, however, aware of the activities of various fascist groups, and believed that their focus on Black and Asian immigrants might change in the future. While noting that Oswald Mosley had in recent years 'played down the anti-Jewish side of his campaign', it suggested that 'any success he may have on one plain of prejudice would soon be extended to others, including that against Jews'.[14] The Board continued to desire new legislation, but did not make it a priority.

In this climate Fenner Brockway launched his first unsuccessful attempt at a Racial Discrimination Private Member's Bill in 1957. The Bill's short debate contained substantial discussion of Jews. Brockway's primary opponent, the Conservative MP (and later Monday Club member) Ronald Bell, argued that the Bill was unnecessary, saying:

> There is probably no country in the world where there is less feeling on account of race than in Britain. The Jews have lived here happily at peace and enjoying full equality under the law for many generations. There is no country in the world where there is less feeling against them as a community than there is in Britain.[15]

For Bell, Jews were the litmus test of discrimination. If, as he supposed, there was no discrimination against Jews, there was no need for additional legislation. Leslie Plummer and Barnett Janner (then Board of Deputies

President) pointed to ongoing cases of discrimination against Jews, such as those in golf clubs.[16] Bell claimed to oppose such discrimination, but argued that these would be excluded by the Bill because they were private clubs.[17] The opponents of new legislation were more careful and less dismissive when discussing anti-Jewish discrimination in comparison to discrimination against Black and Asian people, such as Bell's criticism of those who 'build up for themselves and in the minds of others a belief that there is something specific, definable and wicked in a colour bar'.[18] This discrepancy was testament to the higher status and parliamentary representation enjoyed by Jews relative to other minorities, a trend that remained constant through the 1960s parliamentary debates on the subject.

The start of the 1960s proved to be something of a turning point, when an international wave of swastika daubing broke out (initially in Cologne), beginning in Britain with 'Juden Raus' scrawled on the doors of Notting Hill Synagogue, located opposite the headquarters of Mosley's Union Movement, followed by around 160 incidents across the country.[19] In February 1960 Plummer introduced a 'Racial and Religious Insults Bill', explicitly giving the swastika outbreak as its primary impetus. In an emotive speech, Plummer brought together fascist incitement against Jews with anti-Black language:

> I complain of the insults to hundreds of thousands of British Jews who are good citizens, as good citizens as every one of us in the House today. I am complaining of and trying to legislate against the insults to the coloured citizens of this country and of the Commonwealth who are publicly insulted every day by seeing signs like, 'N*****s get out' and 'Keep Britain white.'[20]

While Plummer was deeply concerned with both anti-Jewish and anti-Black incitement, his language of 'good citizens, as good citizens as every one of us' as opposed to 'coloured citizens' alludes to the higher social status of Jews in comparison to Black and Asian people, at least in the minds of some parliamentarians. Unlike Brockway's Bills, Plummer's left out the more contentious question of discrimination – more contentious because it was seen to relate to New Commonwealth citizens and to be a much wider issue. This Bill was supported by a lobbying campaign run by the Board in which deputies wrote to members of Parliament, though only sixteen MPs gave a positive response.[21]

Introducing his 1960 Race Discrimination Bill, his fifth attempt at passing legislation, Brockway made prominent mention of Jews in his early remarks, saying 'My Bill would deal not only with discrimination on the grounds of colour, but also of race and religion. It would include the Jewish race and the Jewish religion. I have been disturbed by the extent of prejudice against that race and their religion.'[22]

Brockway's reference to Jews in his speech was designed to elevate the importance of the Bill in the minds of its parliamentary critics, utilising the social unacceptability of antisemitism to build a case for the criminalisation of other forms of racism. In a sixth attempt, later that year, he again mentioned Jews whilst conceding that discrimination was 'most prevalent in the experience of coloured persons searching for private lodging', saying that he had found 'that it happens sometimes to members of the Jewish race'.[23] Here he referred to Jews purely as a 'race', possibly representing an acceptance that including religion in a Bill would be an added source of complication that would give ammunition to critics. At his seventh attempt, in December 1961, Brockway did not speak of Jews directly, but for the first time tied together the issue of racial incitement and discrimination in the purpose of his Bill and included religion as one of the protected categories.[24]

The issue gained urgency in July 1962 with the National Socialist Movement's notorious meeting in Trafalgar Square, which featured the slogan 'Free Britain from Jewish Control.' The Board of Deputies, and its many Jewish critics, was outraged that the meeting had not been blocked, and that there was no legal means by which Colin Jordan and John Tyndall could be prosecuted for their antisemitic speeches.[25] In fact, Jordan and Tyndall were charged under the Public Order Act for intending to incite a breach of the peace, and were initially convicted, but Jordan's conviction was overturned at appeal, with the judge ruling that his speech came 'very, very near the borderline' but just failed 'to step over the edge'.[26] Jewish anger in relation to the seemingly free rein being given to fascists on the streets of the capital was not heard in the chambers of power: Harold Macmillan's Conservative government was unmoved and Private Members' Bills all failed owing to a lack of government support.

In January 1963 Brockway argued that the anti-incitement section of his by now annual Bill had become increasingly urgent 'because of a resurgence of Fascist propaganda in our country', and listed 'the Jewish community' as supporting the Bill alongside the churches and the National Council of Women.[27] At his tenth legislative attempt, in January 1964, Brockway held up a card he had been sent by the 'Council for the Final Solution of the Jewish Question'. Describing it as 'too revolting to describe to this house' he went on to say that 'a humanly civilised society would not give those who spread this disease the protection of the law which they now receive'.[28]

The 1964 election proved a turning point, as the Labour Party committed to new legislation in its manifesto. Another change was the United Nations (UN) process which would culminate in the December 1965 International Convention on the Elimination of All Forms of Racial Discrimination. That process had itself begun in response to antisemitism, specifically the international swastika outbreak of 1959–60, which was condemned by the Sub-Commission on Prevention of Discrimination and Protection of Minorities, which recommended that the UN General Assembly organise a convention against racial hatred.[29] In an interesting parallel to the passage of the British Race Relations Act, there was a proposal for antisemitism to be specified in Article 3 of the Convention, alongside segregation and apartheid. This was dropped in response to Soviet demands that if antisemitism was to be condemned then so should Nazism and Zionism.[30] At the international and UK government level, Jews were viewed as covered by anti-racist measures, but were not mentioned by name, for a range of diverse political reasons.

Individual Jewish activists

Several Jewish lawyers were active in the fight for anti-discrimination legislation in Britain. The Society of Labour Lawyers set up a Committee on Racial Discrimination, which was highly influential in drafting the new legislation, and on it four out of the seven members were Jewish, or of Jewish origin (Peter Benenson, Anthony Lester, Fredman Ashe Lincoln and Michael Zander), to whom was added Jim Rose (formally Elliot Joseph Benn Rose, author of the 1969 report *Colour and Citizenship*) as a co-opted member. Benenson, a founder of Amnesty, was from a Russian Jewish background; Lester a British Jewish lawyer and activist; Lincoln a British Jew who had been a naval officer and a prospective Conservative parliamentary candidate in 1945 and 1950; Zander a legal scholar who had come to Britain with his German-Jewish parents in 1937, at the age of four. Lester and Zander also sat on the Campaign against Racial Discrimination's (CARD) legal committee, alongside the South African Jew Jeffrey Jowell.[31] This small group of key Jewish lawyers were disproportionately involved in race relations in the 1960s. Anthony Lester in particular suggested that his Jewish background was a significant motivating factor in his life's work as an anti-discrimination lawyer and activist, saying:

> I cannot be sure why I have spent my adult life fighting for these ideas. It had to do with my upbringing by Jewish parents whose European relatives had been murdered in the Holocaust and who sympathised with disadvantaged people. It had to do with ... with feeling the pinpricks of English anti-Semitism during National Service.[32]

A number of Jewish Labour parliamentarians were also active in the drive for legislation, such as Maurice Orbach, Reg Freeson and Paul Rose, with the latter two, alongside Maurice Miller, going on to vote against the 1965 Act on the grounds that its discrimination provisions did not go far enough.[33] While some figures, like Orbach, linked Jewish experiences of prejudice to the need for new legislation, other figures such as Home Secretary Frank Soskice (whose father was an émigré Ukrainian Jewish lawyer) showed lukewarm support for the Bill and hoped that it would never need to be used. The example of Soskice demonstrates that having Jewish heritage was no guarantee of fulsome support for anti-racist legislation.

Lobbying by the Board of Deputies

Cases of anti-Jewish discrimination persisted in the 1950s and early 1960s. In 1958 the Board of Deputies' Trades Advisory Council raised complaints of anti-Jewish discrimination in hotels, and a failed attempt to persuade the British Travels and Holiday Association to pass a resolution against the practice specifically connected anti-Jewish and anti-Black discrimination.[34] Discrimination against Jews in golf clubs came to public attention in the late 1950s and early 1960s and led to the creation of Jewish-run alternative clubs across Jewish suburban areas.[35] Reports in the early 1960s suggested that many independent schools operated a Jewish quota of around 10 per cent,[36] and in 1961 Isaiah Berlin resigned from St Paul's School's alumni association, the Old Pauline Club, when it was revealed that the school had been capping the proportion of Jewish students at 15 per cent.[37] Such quotas discriminated against Jews on grounds of religion rather than race, as prestigious independent schools sought to uphold their 'Christian character', meaning that they would not fall under the provisions of the 1965 Act, or any of its successors. Despite these ongoing cases of anti-Jewish discrimination, the Board of Deputies paid little attention to the issue and a document submitted by the Board to Soskice concentrated almost entirely on incitement. Despite welcoming the anti-discrimination measures being proposed, it did not see these as a primarily Jewish concern, saying 'Social and economic discrimination has in the past affected Jews to a considerable extent, but over the last years this has decreased.'[38] A report to the World Jewish Congress explained that while there were some ongoing instances of discrimination against Jews in hotels and clubs, 'there has been no demand from Jewish quarters for protection by law'.[39] The decision by the Board to play down anti-Jewish discrimination may have been motivated by a desire for Jews not to be seen as requiring the same protections as Black and Asian people; it certainly accentuated the separation between groups who might otherwise have been able to unite around a common cause. It also emphasises that the Board was purely focussed on anti-incitement; it did not wish for such measures to become part of an umbrella Act concerned with broader questions of 'race'.

The Act's parliamentary passage

In moving the second reading of the Act in May 1965, Frank Soskice explained that the government's motivation in this legislation was to cover 'issues which arise from the presence with us of between 800,000 and one million coloured citizens'.[40] Soskice explained that the government had sought a form of words that would cover 'every possible minority group in the country', specifying Cypriots, the Maltese and 'people of that sort' as borderline groups that he wanted to cover. He was immediately challenged by the gentile Essex MP Bernard Braine as to whether this would include Jews 'because it is widely held by many authorities that Jewish citizens are of British race'. Soskice assured his colleague that Jews were included, by way of an answer that demonstrated longstanding confusion over the nature of Jews and an unwillingness (by Jews or non-Jews) to lay down a categorical definition:

> I would have thought a person of Jewish faith, if not regarded as caught by the word 'racial' would undoubtedly be caught by the word 'ethnic', but if not caught by the word 'ethnic' would certainly be caught by the scope of the word 'national', as certainly having a national origin. He would certainly have an origin which many people would describe as an ethnic if not a racial origin.[41]

Surprisingly, vague assurances like this reassured the Board, despite the longstanding principle that parliamentary statements could not be used by the judiciary in interpreting legislation. Solicitor General Dingle Foot supported the absence of religion from the Bill and suggested that 'attacks upon the Jews … are not directed merely against those who observe the Mosaic law. They are directed against Jews as a race.'[42] The *Jewish Chronicle* was unconvinced, saying that being Jewish 'has very little to do with being part of a racial, ethnic or national group and a great deal to do with religion. The absence of any reference to religion in the Bill means that antisemitism is likely to be excluded from its operation.'[43]

Jewish parliamentarians such as Barnett Janner raised the spectre of Nazism in defence of the Bill, suggesting that those who opposed the Bill on free speech grounds were in an analogous position to citizens of the Weimar Republic who failed to foresee the threat of fascism. Members of Parliament treated his, and other comments relating to Jews, respectfully, whilst simultaneously playing down the size and influence of fascist groups and suggesting that existing legislation was sufficient to deal with them. Anthony Buck described antisemitism as 'what concerns most of us more than anything else', and Dingle Foot foregrounded anti-Jewish hate in his defence of the Bill, saying that 'nothing is more loathsome and more contemptible than expressions of anti-Semitism'. Even those who opposed the incitement provisions, Clause 6 of the Bill, did so, like former Home Secretary Henry Brooke, on the basis that Jews were already adequately protected from fascists by the revised Public Order Act of 1963. There was far less sympathy for anti-discrimination measures, which MPs understood as designed to protect Black and Asian Britons, with Conservative MPs frequently denying the existence of any 'colour bars'. The recently and controversially elected Peter Griffiths, MP for Smethwick, suggested that it existed only in the minds of 'people who are sensitive to the fact that they are coloured in a community which is largely white', who, he alleged 'frequently imagine that they have been discriminated against in circumstances in which no discrimination whatever has existed'.[44]

Following the first reading, Soskice made major concessions, removing criminal sanctions from the discrimination measures, and replacing them with a system of conciliation modelled on provisions of the 1964 US Civil Rights Act. This was largely to appease the Conservative opposition, who ended up abstaining on the Bill, but it had also been lobbied for by CARD's legal committee because it believed that criminal sanctions would be unenforceable and would reduce public sympathy with the aims of the bill.[45] The support of CARD for the move was based on Lester's trip to the USA in the summer of 1964, which convinced him that Britain had 'little to teach and much to learn from the United States about combating racial discrimination', and that the US experience had proved the success of conciliation over criminalisation.[46]

Criminal sanctions remained in place for the anti-incitement provisions, a point that was uncontroversial, with some Conservatives going out of their way to pronounce their support for that part of the Bill, out of solidarity with their Jewish constituents and a feeling that 'the Jewish people had suffered enough in our life-time'.[47] As a result, the final Act that gained Royal Assent in November 1965 maintained very different structures and legal remedies for the measures designed to protect Jews from those designed to protect Black and Asian people, with the former far stronger than the latter.

The Act led to the creation of the Race Relations Board in 1966; of its three members one was Jewish, the Labour councillor and Lord Mayor of Manchester Bernard Langton. Langton had recently launched Manchester Brotherhood week and the Manchester Council for Community Relations, making him a suitable candidate for the role.[48] The combination of Langton, alongside the West Indian cricketer Sir Learie Constantine and the wealthy white liberal Mark Bonham-Carter made the Board a telling microcosm of liberal race relations in the mid-1960s. In addition, the radical Jewish lawyer Geoffrey Bindman was appointed legal advisor to the Board, a position he held until 1976.[49]

Towards the 1968 Act

Jews were active in lobbying for the strengthening of the Act which began almost immediately after the 1965 Act was passed. The Campaign against Racial Discrimination campaigned to extend the areas in which discrimination should be outlawed, launching (on the suggestion of Anthony Lester) a campaign to send complaints of discrimination to the Race Relations Board, 90 per cent of which were outside the scope of the Act.[50] The Board of Deputies, in contrast, sought to strengthen Clause 6, ruefully conceding that 'the principal interest of other organisations was in the discrimination clause, and the Board was more or less alone in requesting amendments to section six'.[51] The Defence Committee campaigned to remove the requirement to prove 'intent' to incite racial hatred and to remove the exemption for private clubs (exploited by fascists via the creation of 'book clubs'), and proposed that the consent of the Director of Public Prosecutions should be sufficient for prosecution, not that of the Attorney General.[52] They considered pushing for the inclusion of 'religion' as one of the protected categories, an anomaly that Colin Jordan had attempted to exploit in his unsuccessful 1967 appeal against his conviction. Jordan had claimed to have a letter from the Chief Rabbi's Secretary stating that 'the Jewish community was a religious one', supposedly demonstrating that the Act did not protect Jews.[53] The Board decided not to press this point, fearing that it would be too controversial and thus put other amendments at risk. It did, however, argue for the addition of protection for religion in the anti-discrimination sections of the Bill, noting that 'there was some evidence of religious groups being discriminated against on these grounds' without specifying Jews, though presumably referring to the fact that lingering anti-Jewish discrimination was more likely to be on grounds of faith than ethnicity.[54]

Just as the Board pressed for the strengthening of Section 6, anti-racist activists were calling for its abolition. This was due to one of the surprising outcomes of the Act, that many of those charged under it were Black Power activists whose militant language could be successfully prosecuted under the Act in a way that pseudo-respectable groups such as the Racial Preservation Society could not.[55] *Colour & Citizenship*, issued by the Institute of Race Relations and edited by the Jewish journalist Jim Rose, viewed the inclusion of Section 6 in the 1965 Act as an anomaly, and called for it to be removed (or at least incorporated into a public order Act). It criticised the incitement provisions for limiting freedom of speech, for arousing sympathy for those prosecuted under it and for giving publicity to tiny fascist groups whilst leaving more sophisticated operators untouched. It rued the fact that its criminal sanction led to the misapprehension that the act *in toto* was penal, and thus made the Race Relations Board's task more difficult.[56] Thus Jewish communal organisations once again found themselves on the opposite side of the argument from bodies seeking to represent Black and Asian Britons.

The Home Secretary, James Callaghan, declined to abolish Section 6, but also rejected the calls of a delegation from the Board of Deputies to strengthen it, arguing that if Section 6 was amended it would lead to hostile amendments seeking to water it down, and that it was thus better to leave it as it was. Callaghan gave an assurance that he would monitor the situation and introduce new legislation to protect Jews if needed.[57] Just as in 1965, the government gave private assurances to the representatives of the Jewish community rather than write them definitively into the law. While official British Jewish bodies had more access and influence than Black- or Asian-led groups they were not influential enough to win the foolproof legal protections for Jews that their representatives sought.

Despite its success in demonstrating the need for a strengthened antidiscrimination law, this period saw CARD collapse, largely because of internal arguments over whether it needed to be exclusively Black and Asian run, or because, as Lester put it, it was 'taken over by militant Maoists and other militant tendencies, brought together under the tattered banner of "Black Power"'. Lester called the end of CARD 'a severe blow to those of us who had worked to build a multiracial movement for racial equality, led by members of the ethnic minorities, and reflecting their needs and aspirations'. In its place was formed the group Equal Rights, an organisation created purely to pass the 1968 legislation, in which Lester was a key member.[58] The collapse of CARD also led to the formation of the Runnymede Trust in 1968 by Lester and Rose, which would become the leading liberal race relations charity in the coming decades.[59]

Jews were again discussed in the parliamentary debates preceding the 1968 Act. Shadow Home Secretary Quintin Hogg, opposing the Bill, drew attention to the absence of protection for religion, saying that Sikhs and Catholics could be attacked on such grounds, and elaborated: 'If I wanted to attack the Jews … I could attack their dietary laws, their methods of slaughter. I could invent some imaginary political conspiracy of rabbis.'[60] Maurice Orbach spoke of his work on anti-Jewish discrimination with the Trades Advisory Council in the 1940s and, supporting the sanctions in the Bill, noted that the Council had often found success on account of employers' conspiratorial beliefs that the Council held powers that it did not actually have. Conservative MP Dudley Smith opposed the legislation, taking the view that without legislation there would be 'a gradual growth of acceptance and tolerance', noting that Jews had suffered 'extreme prejudice in the 1920s and 1930s' but were now 'largely accepted and assimilated by society. They are unremarkable people and they do not stand out in any particular respect.' Smith recounted speaking to 'a Jewish man yesterday' who had conceded that antisemitism had 'passed away' but had presented a caricature of 'the bad Jew' who 'imagined' ongoing antisemitism and found in it 'a refuge for his own lack of success or disappointment in life'. Smith's Jewish contact opposed the Bill 'because he fully expects the prejudice against coloured people to be exacerbated and that the bad coloured man may well take a line similar to that taken by the bad Jewish man'.[61] Thus, for some Conservative spokespeople, looking to oppose the Bill whilst claiming to abhor discrimination, Jews could be utilised to justify opposition to the Bill, on the grounds that the absence of a religion clause meant that Jews were insufficiently protected by it, or that it was unnecessary, since antisemitism was (supposedly) over.

Toward the 1976 Act

The last of the three Acts was not only motivated by Jewish concerns but was drafted by a Jewish lawyer. After the return of the proto-multiculturalist Roy Jenkins to the post of Home Secretary in March 1974, Anthony Lester left his work at the Bar to become a Special Advisor to Jenkins.[62] The government intended to legislate on both sex and race discrimination, but sex discrimination was tackled first as a means to create a less hostile climate for the latter.[63] Lester drafted both White Papers, against opposition from Home Office civil servants who sought a narrower approach to combating discrimination.[64] His Race Relations White Paper began with highly idealistic language:

> The Government's proposals are based on a clear recognition of the proposition that the overwhelming majority of the coloured population is here to stay, that a substantial and increasing proportion of that population belongs to this country, and that the time has come for a determined effort by Government, by industry and unions, and by ordinary men and women, to ensure fair and equal treatment for all our people, regardless of their race, colour, or national origins.[65]

The Bill was a major advance over the previous two, extending anti-discrimination to private clubs and political parties, including the selection of parliamentary candidates. It also introduced the notion of 'indirect discrimination', in which, as Lester put it, 'Neutrally framed and well-intentioned practices and procedures were made unlawful, if they have a disproportionate adverse impact on ethnic minorities and lack any objective justification.'[66]

Once again, the Board focused on strengthening the anti-incitement provisions, and here they had the support of the Bill's drafters. Jenkins and Lester's 1975 White Paper suggested that there had been 'a decided change in the style of racialist propaganda. It tends to be less blatantly bigoted, to disclaim any intention of stirring up racial hatred, and to purport to make a contribution to public education and debate.'[67] A lack of intention to incite racial hatred was thus removed as a defence, although in relation to written material there was a possible defence that an accused person 'was not aware of the content of the written matter in question and neither suspected nor had reason to suspect it of being threatening, abusive or insulting'.[68] The Board regretted another missed opportunity to add the term 'religion' to the legislation, with the Chair of the Board's Law, Parliamentary and General Purposes Committee arguing that 'Jews were legally neither a race nor of common ethnic origin, but they were a religious sect'. A committee meeting, which included the Chief Rabbi, declined to push for this, continuing to rely on the assurance of past Home Secretaries that Jews were included, somewhere, in the categories of 'colour, race, nationality or ethnic or national origins'.[69] The *Jewish Chronicle* paid attention to this failing in the legislation, noting in an editorial that 'most Jews regard themselves as members of a religion rather than of a racial, ethnic or national group, and there could be circumstances when it would be difficult to bring about a successful prosecution'.[70]

Jews were mentioned just once in Roy Jenkins's speech proposing the second reading of the Bill, when he stated that it would not be 'in the public interest for clubs to be permitted to operate a colour bar or, say, a Jewish quota as part of their policy', glossing over the fact that the Bill would only prevent such a Jewish quota if it discriminated against Jews on racial, rather than religious, grounds.[71] Jewish concerns were only raised twice in the debate that followed, on both occasions by Jewish MPs. In response to Enoch Powell's warnings regarding the rate of 'New Commonwealth births', the Jewish Scottish Labour MP Maurice Miller argued that similar warnings had been made about Jews seventy years earlier and that the Jewish population was 'no higher now than in those days', suggesting that fears of demographic change due to immigration were unfounded. Paul Rose called for religion to be added to the protected categories, stating that 'it is so easy – as the National Front and the British Movement do – to concentrate on Sikhs, Hindus, Jews or Muslims'.[72] In contrast, an attempt to insert religion into the Bill via an amendment in the House of Lords led to far greater discussion of Jews. Fenner Brockway reminded his colleagues that he had sought to include religion in his bills, arguing that some 'opposition to the Jewish community' was on the grounds of 'religious views', and he was supported by George Brown, who, presumably referring to his Jewish wife Sophie (née Levene), described himself as living in 'an Anglican-Jewish atmosphere'. Drawing on his Jewish connections, Brown suggested that:

> It is exceedingly difficult to distinguish between that which is called racial and that which is called religious. So many of my Jewish friends in this country deny

that they are of a different race, and indeed they have every reason to so deny. They have lived here for as many generations as the rest of us – and scratch any of us and you will find somebody else. But they either practise a different religion, or even where they do not practise it they are assumed to be of it.[73]

It was challenging to describe the identity of Jews who did not practise Judaism without using the language of ethnicity, or at least ethnicity's more subtle proxy 'culture', but Brown was in touch with much of British Jewish opinion in seeking to avoid this implication. Former Shadow Home Secretary Lord Hailsham (Quintin Hogg) then expounded an eccentric account of Jewishness, positing that Jews come in all shapes, sizes and colours: 'There are black Jews called Falashas in Ethiopia; there are yellow Jews called something else in China; and there are white Jews with fair hair and blue eyes, with the best Aryan characteristics, in Europe.' Because of this, he argued that Jews were 'not a race … but some of them … have a religion. If you want to discriminate against Jews, it is no use discriminating against people with long noses: you must discriminate against people who will not eat bacon – and that is a religious discrimination.'[74] In this Hogg perpetuated a Jewish racial (i.e. nasal) stereotype while arguing against treating Jews as a race, demonstrating the widespread confusion over how Jews should be categorised and understood.

Greville Janner, in his response, identified himself as a member of the 'Jewish religion', but did not see the inclusion of religion as a major issue, suggesting that it was only 'from time to time' that attacks were made Jews on 'religious grounds'.[75] The amendment was withdrawn, thus leaving in place the constitutional anomaly that, as Lester put it: 'it is unlawful to discriminate on religious grounds in Northern Ireland, but not in Great Britain: it is unlawful to discriminate on racial grounds in Great Britain, but not yet in Northern Ireland'.[76]

The passing of the 1976 Act ended the sequence of race relations legislation, although the precise position of Jews under it would not be confirmed until a court ruling in 1983, in which Bindman represented the Commission for Racial Equality (CRE).[77] Only at that point were Jews legally considered an 'ethnic group' for the purposes of the Race Relations Act. Ironically, a few years later, anti-incitement laws were moved into the 1986 Public Order Act. With this, the uneasy amalgamation of anti-incitement and anti-discrimination measures into a single Act came to a close after just over two decades.

Conclusion

The official Jewish community never sought to be included in a 'Race Relations Act', still less to be defined through case law as an 'ethnic group'.

The Board of Deputies, alongside anti-fascist groups such as the 43 Group and the Jewish Aid Council of Britain (JACOB), sought simply to criminalise fascist hate speech against Jews. These organisations engaged little in campaigns against the 'colour bar' or for the welfare of Black and Asian citizens in general, at least until the late 1960s, and even then, only to a very limited extent. The fact that the anti-incitement provisions that the Board and others had long sought, and which were widely supported in Parliament, ended up being combined in a single Act with anti-discrimination laws designed to protect Black and Asian people was a historical coincidence, one unsought by Jewish communal bodies.

The 1965 Act created two opposing outcomes in terms of how it positioned Jews relative to Black and Asian people. On the one hand, through the Act's title and the fact that Jews were one of the groups it was widely assumed to cover, it placed Jews under the legal umbrella of 'race'. Despite popular (and antisemitic) understandings that racialised Jews, British law had hitherto understood Jews primarily as a religious sect, hence the historical ability of individual Jews to escape the terms of discriminatory measures through conversion or willingness to recite Christian oaths.[78] There had long been a degree of legal ambiguity around the definition of Jews, which continued in postwar legislation, with the 1949 Marriages Act regulating marriages between those 'professing the Jewish religion according to the usages of the Jews'. This language simultaneously recognised the existence of a Jewish religion but defined it as belonging to a fixed (presumably ethnic) group called 'the Jews'. In response to fascist racialisation of Jews in the early 1960s the Race Relations Act implicitly brought a racial understanding of Jewishness into law, in a context that unwittingly connected Jews to the new subject of racial fears: Black and Asian immigrants from the Commonwealth.

At the same time the Act implicitly placed Jews in a separate legal category from other racialised minorities. The anti-discrimination measures were designed to protect Black and Asian people, while the anti-incitement measures were focused squarely on protecting Jews from fascists. The difference between these provisions reveals the differing levels of influence enjoyed by these communities – while incitement was criminalised, allowing prosecutions to be brought (by the Attorney General), discrimination was dealt with under a far weaker conciliation mechanism. Instances of discrimination had to be reported to the Race Relations Boards, and only in 1976 did the new CRE gain the ability to launch its own investigations rather than being required to wait for complaints from victims of discrimination. Aside from differing levels of communal influence the disparity may well have been down to a perception of scale: while the government believed that the anti-incitement measures were targeted at a small number of fascists who did not enjoy popular support, discriminatory practices, and unspoken support for them, were too widespread to criminalise directly (a tacit acceptance of how commonplace racist attitudes were in 1960s Britain). Finally, the Act helped perpetuate and formalise a situation in which Jewish organisations were primarily concerned with words – criminalising anti-Jewish speeches and publications, while Black and Asian groups (and white-led or even Jewish-led groups that sought to support them) were primarily focused on structures – on structural oppression in government agencies such as the police, the education service and immigration services. While the differences were largely bridged in the campaign against the National Front in the late 1970s, they became all too clear in the 1980s, when anti-fascism and radical anti-racism became distinct and sometimes fractious worlds.[79]

While British Jews were not the primary group the Acts sought to protect (nor the primary group that 1960s anti-immigration legislation sought to keep out), in terms of individual involvement and parliamentary discussion they played a significant part in the Act's prehistory, its 1965 origins, and its development in 1968 and 1976. Just as Jews have been largely omitted from the history of British race relations more generally, this chapter has sought to reinsert them into the story of how the combating of racial discrimination and incitement was first legislated in Britain. It has uncovered a lack of inter-minority solidarity and cooperation – sometimes because of the actions of MPs and the British state, who prioritised the protection of some minorities over others, and sometimes because of minority communal representatives declining to connect their struggles with wider anti-racist politics. The account has raised several underlying issues: the complex meanings of 'race' and ethnicity, the status of religious discrimination in law, how anti-semitism and racism relate to one another, the political behaviour of historically racialised minorities after they have begun to improve their social status, and the societal choice of whether to focus on the extreme hatred of a small far-right minority or on the more wide-ranging prejudices held by the majority. These questions have remained live since the 1960s and continue to provoke discussion and controversy in the present day.

Notes

1 Anthony Lester and Geoffrey Bindman, *Race and Law* (London: Penguin, 1972).
2 See for example Michael Banton, *Promoting Racial Harmony* (Cambridge: Cambridge University Press, 1985), pp. 69–98; White Paper on Immigration from the Commonwealth, Kew, The National Archives (TNA), HO 376/1.
3 Some early commentary on the Act was written by Jewish lawyers and scholars such as Bob Hepple, Louis Kushnick and Ira Katznelson. See Louis Kushnick, 'Race Relations: Cooperation or Conflict?', *Pointer*, 4:1 (Autumn

1968); Bob Hepple, *Race, Jobs and the Law* (London: Allen Lane, 1968); and Ira Katznelson, *Black Men, White Cities: Race, Politics, and Migration in the United States 1900–30, and Britain, 1948–68* (New York: Oxford University Press, 1973).
4 Erik Bleich, *Race Politics in Britain and France: Ideas and Policymaking since the 1960s* (Cambridge: Cambridge University Press, 2003), p. 51, p. 42 n. 14.
5 Simon Peplow, 'The "Linchpin for Success"? The Problematic Establishment of the 1965 Race Relations Act and Its Conciliation Board', *Contemporary British History*, 31:3 (2017), 430–51.
6 Harry Goulbourne, *Race Relations in Britain* (Basingstoke: Palgrave Macmillan, 1998), p. 153.
7 Satnam Virdee, *Racism, Class and the Racialized Outsider* (Basingstoke: Palgrave Macmillan, 2014).
8 Gavin Schaffer, 'Legislating against Hatred: Meaning and Motive in Section Six of the Race Relations Act of 1965', *Twentieth Century British History*, 25:2 (2014), 251–75.
9 On the 1947 riots, see Tony Kushner, 'Anti-Semitism and Austerity: The August 1947 Riots in Britain', in Panikos Panayi (ed.), *Racial Violence in Britain 1840–1950* (Leicester: Leicester University Press, 1996), pp. 149–68.
10 E. Hall Williams, 'Committee on the Law of Defamation: The Porter Report (Cmd. 7536/48)', *The Modern Law Review*, 12.2 (1949), 217–23.
11 178 Parl. Deb., HL (28 July 1952), cols 326–74.
12 Morris Beckman, *The 43 Group* (London: Centerprise Publication, 1993), p. 26.
13 *Ibid.*, p. 197.
14 'Race Riots in England' (September 1958), London, Wiener Library (WL), 1658/10/37.
15 569 Parl. Deb., HC (10 May 1957), cols 1425–38.
16 For a full treatment of discrimination against Jews in golf clubs, see David Dee, *Sport and British Jewry: Integration, Ethnicity and Anti-Semitism 1890–1970* (Manchester: Manchester University Press, 2013).
17 *Ibid*.
18 *Ibid*.
19 See Nigel Copsey, 'A Defining Decade? Swastikas, Eichmann and Arson in 1960s Britain', in Tom Lawson and Andy Pearce (eds), *The Palgrave Handbook of Britain and the Holocaust* (London: Palgrave Macmillan, 2021), pp. 303–24.
20 616 Parl. Deb., HC (2 February 1960), cols 796–801.
21 Board of Deputies (BoD), Law, Parliamentary and General Purposes Committee (LPGPC) (9 May 1960), London Metropolitan Archives (LMA), ACC/3121/C/13/001/016.
22 621 Parl. Deb., HC (12 April 1960), cols 1088–90.
23 631 Parl. Deb., HC (7 December 1960), cols 1270–2.
24 651 Parl. Deb., HC (13 December 1961), cols 451–3.
25 See Joshua Cohen, *British Antifascism and the Holocaust, 1945–1979* (London: Routledge, 2022).
26 'Jordan Wins Appeal', *Guardian* (5 September 1962), 4.

27 670 Parl. Deb., HC (23 January 1963), cols 97–100.
28 687 Parl. Deb., HC (14 January 1964), cols 42–5.
29 Egon Schwelb, 'The International Convention on the Elimination of All Forms of Racial Discrimination', *International & Comparative Law Quarterly*, 15.4 (1966), 996–1068 (pp. 997–8).
30 *Ibid.*, pp. 1011–15; UN, A/C.3/SR.1302, https://digitallibrary.un.org/record/807048?ln=es&v=pdf (accessed 13 June 2024)
31 Lester and Bindman, *Race and Law*, pp. 110–11.
32 Anthony Lester, *Five Ideas to Fight For: How Our Freedom Is under Threat and Why It Matters* (London: Oneworld Publications, 2016), p. 9.
33 Lester and Bindman, *Race and Law*, p. 116.
34 'Prejudice at Hotels', *Jewish Chronicle* (24 October 1958), 19.
35 See Dee, *Sport and British Jewry*, for a full treatment of the subject.
36 'Jewish Quota for Schools', *Jewish Chronicle* (12 June 1961), 5.
37 David Caute, *Isaac and Isaiah: The Covert Punishment of a Cold War Heretic* (New Haven: Yale University Press, 2013), p. 241.
38 BoD Defence Committee (DC), 'Observations on Racial Discrimination and Incitement and Racial Hatred' (6 January 1965), WL, 1658/10/37/3/22.
39 BOD DC, WL, 1658/10/37/3/93.
40 711 Parl. Deb., HC (3 May 1965), col. 926.
41 *Ibid*.
42 *Ibid.*, col. 1043.
43 'Race, Religion and Law', *Jewish Chronicle* (7 May 1965), 7.
44 711 Parl. Deb., HC (3 May 1965), col. 926.
45 Benjamin W. Heineman, *The Politics of the Powerless* (Oxford: Oxford University Press, 1972), p. 116.
46 Brett M. Bebber, '"Standard Transatlantic Practice": Race Relations and Antidiscrimination Law across the Atlantic', *Journal of Civil and Human Rights*, 4:1 (2018), 5–36; Anthony Lester, *Justice in the American South* (London: Amnesty International, 1965).
47 716 Parl. Deb., HC (16 July 1965), col. 1063.
48 See 'Brotherhood Week Plea by Manchester Lord Mayor', *Jewish Chronicle* (8 October 1965), 20.
49 'Sir Geoffrey Bindman KC (Hon.), Senior Consultant, Public Law and Human Rights', Bindmans, www.bindmans.com/our-people/sir-geoffrey-bindman-kc-hon/ (accessed 24 March 2023).
50 Heineman, *The Politics of the Powerless*, pp. 131–3.
51 BoD DC minutes (5 February 1968), LMA, ACC/3121/C6/001/001.
52 BoD DC minutes (8 January 1968), LMA, ACC/3121/C6/001/001.
53 WL, 1658/10/37/4/81.
54 'A Memorandum on the Race Relations Act 1965' (22 February 1968), LMA, ACC/3121/A/042.
55 See Schaffer, 'Legislating against Hatred'.
56 E. J. B. Rose & Associates, *Colour & Citizenship: A Report on British Race Relations* (London: Oxford University Press, 1969), pp. 686–7.

57 'Report of Home Office Deputation' (March 1968), LMA, ACC/3121/C6/001/001.
58 Lester and Bindman, *Race and Law*, pp. 132–3.
59 Anthony Lester, 'The Politics of the Race Relations Act 1976', in Muhammad Anwar, Patrick Roach and Ranjit Sandhi (eds), *From Legislation to Integration? Race Relations in Britain* (London: Palgrave Macmillan, 2000), pp. 24–39 (p. 27). For a history of CARD, see Heineman, *The Politics of the Powerless*.
60 763 Parl. Deb., HC (23 April 1968), cols 53–198.
61 *Ibid.*
62 For Jenkins's famous speech on integration and diversity, see Roy Jenkins, 'This Is the Goal', in Brian MacArthur (ed.), *The Penguin Book of Modern Speeches* (London: Penguin, 2012), pp 362–7.
63 See Lester, 'The Politics of the Race Relations Act 1976', p. 33.
64 Lester, *Five Ideas to Fight For*, p. 57.
65 White Paper on Racial Discrimination (11 September 1975), TNA, CAB 129/184/18.
66 Lester, 'The Politics of the Race Relations Act 1976', p. 33.
67 White Paper on Racial Discrimination (11 September 1975), TNA, CAB 129/184/18.
68 Race Relations Act 1976.
69 BoD LPGPC, LMA, ACC/3121/C/13/001/017.
70 'Racial Hatred', *Jewish Chronicle* (26 March 1976), 24.
71 906 Parl. Deb., HC (4 March 1976), cols 1547–67.
72 *Ibid.*, cols 1568–669.
73 374 Parl. Deb., HL (27 September 1976), cols 25–83.
74 *Ibid.*
75 374 Parl. Deb., HL (27 September 1976), cols 25–83.
76 Lester, 'The Politics of the Race Relations Act 1976', p. 35.
77 *Mandla v. Dowell Lee* [1983] UKHL 7 1 All ER 1062. See also *Seide v. Gillette Industries Ltd* [1980] IRLR 927, EAT.
78 See for example, the United Synagogue Act of 1870, which provided for 'places of worship for persons of the Jewish religion who conform to the Polish or German ritual'. See also Lester and Bindman, *Race and Law*, p. 157.
79 From 1979 onward the Campaign against Racism and Fascism (CARF) was published as a dedicated section of the anti-fascist magazine *Searchlight*. The acrimonious end of the relationship in 1991, over allegations that *Searchlight* prioritised antisemitism over other forms of racism, is a prime example of the fracturing of the anti-racist movement.

7

South Asian political Blackness in Britain: Lessons and limitations of anti-racist solidarity

Saffron East

How and why did political Blackness develop in South Asian communities in Britain? What was its significance? In this chapter I analyse three instances when political Blackness was engaged with by South Asian actors: the Black People's Alliance (BPA), Southall Youth Movement (SYM) and Southall Black Sisters (SBS). Through comparing these movements, the chapter develops our understanding of the rich histories of anti-racism in 1960s, 1970s and 1980s Britain by exploring the specificities of South Asian engagement with Black radical politics.[1]

For certain activists at specific moments, the term 'Black' encompassed all racialised people and communities from colonised or formerly colonised nations, not only those of African Caribbean or African diasporic origins or heritage (as Blackness is most often defined as today). In postwar Britain, Black political identity was constructed as an anti-racist and socialist response to British state and societal racism, bringing together legacies of colonial oppression and experiences of racism in Britain. Jenny Bourne and Rosie Wild have both explicitly charted the history of the use of Black as a political umbrella in Britain, with Wild in particular exploring the position of the BPA within the broader British Black Power movement.[2] This chapter develops this work by focusing on the role of the BPA within the broader historical context of South Asian engagement with political Blackness.

More broadly, the chapter adds to scholarship that records the activism of racialised community anti-racists, from the more recent historical work of Rob Waters, who explores the prevalence of Black political thought in anti-racism in Britain in the 1960s and 1970s, to the work of SBS; Beverley Bryan, Stella Dadzie and Suzanne Scafe; Ron Ramdin; and Ambalavaner Sivanandan; who among others have documented decades of Black activism in Britain. Though these volumes cover a variety of case studies, they share the common theme of preserving Britain's rich history of political Blackness and racialised historical actors engaging in socialist and anti-racist activism.[3] Southall Black Sisters and Bryan, Dadzie and Scafe specifically highlight the role of racialised women in forging Black politics, while Waters traces the ways that locality, postcoloniality and a commitment to particular socialisms impacted Blackness in Britain. This connects the study of Black British activism with broader scholarship on Black British citizenship, namely Kennetta Perry's study into the ways that Black migrants articulated belonging in Britain as a form of activism, building on Peter Fryer's *Staying Power*, which highlights the longevity and resilience of Black communities in Britain.[4]

The case studies in this chapter highlight the historically and generationally contingent nature of South Asian political Blackness. For the first generation, political Blackness was a tool for articulating anti-racist unity, to bring different national and ethnic groups together to protest racism in Britain. For the second generation, the political frameworks of socialism and anti-racism were more important for articulating radicalism and secularism within the local context of Southall. I also demonstrate that the specificities of local context (place) and period determined the particular contours of the articulations of Blackness that emerged in postwar Britain. I analyse the limitations of South Asian activists' use of the Black political banner as well as the lessons we can draw from this history. Finally, I explore new lexicons of anti-racist resistance, arguing that the histories of political Blackness explored here have created a foundation upon which a contemporary politics of solidarity can further develop. This connects with the work of Talat Ahmed, whose chapter in this volume explores potentials for multiethnic unity in socialist and anti-racist organising, which intersects with my perspectives on potential futures of anti-racist unity through the concept of solidarity.

The first case study, the BPA, founded in 1968, was a collective of community groups that were themselves based on national identities related to the places of origin of their members. The BPA brought together Caribbean and South Asian anti-racist activists under the Black banner so that the different groups were enabled to support each other's action, which was locally contingent, and collectively demonstrate on national issues. Wild, one of just a handful of scholars to engage with the history of the BPA and its role in shaping British Black Power, writes that there were over fifty organisations in the BPA, including Pakistani and Indian Workers' Associations.[5] Exploring the history of the BPA thus allows us to understand a moment – however brief – when anti-racist unity was at its peak.

With the near-historical context of the BPA in mind, the remaining case studies, SYM and SBS, allow us to understand the ways that the lived experience of being a 1.5- or second-generation South Asian migrant shaped practical articulations of political Blackness. Southall Youth Movement, formed in 1976, was a grassroots collective made up of young men from the local area, created in direct response to police brutality. Its activism took the form of on-the-street demonstrations. Southall Black Sisters was a non-hierarchical collective formed in 1979 by a handful of local young women. It not only served as a vehicle for on-the-street protest, its members also engaged in activism in other ways, through legal aid, setting up women's shelters, and in more individual and domestic ways through political education and writing groups. Understanding how racialised women sought to raise each other's consciousnesses and help each other to develop Black feminist praxes connects my research with that of Sophia Siddiqui, whose chapter in this volume historicises the role of 'self help' in racialised women's activism in modern Britain. For readers, her work might prove a useful place to pick up where this chapter ends in its analysis of SBS's work with domestic violence survivors/victims.

Although both SYM and SBS collaborated with Black organisations that were not South Asian-led, both represented a departure from the practice of Blackness of the BPA, as active collaboration with African Caribbean or other African diasporic groups was not central to their practices. I argue that, instead, their Black politics was shaped more by their socialist politics and their commitment to uniting different South Asian communities, as opposed to the pursuit of anti-racist unity in the practice of activism. Both SYM and SBS framed themselves as secular organisations, open to 'Black' people of all religious and national backgrounds. Both movements' Blackness was also shaped by their youth politics. Youth and rebellion thus played a role in the Blackness of SYM and SBS in a way that connected both organisations' politics with the local context. One core feature of this context comprised the relative social conservatism and patriarchal structures of families and broader South Asian communities. As a result of this, for SYM and SBS, political Blackness was a useful tool in developing a secular identity around which to organise, allowing both movements to recruit members from a range of religious backgrounds. Rejecting religion was a way for them to reject parental values, which they perceived, for diverging reasons, as stifling local anti-racist unity, even if parents were not particularly religious.

The methodology I use in this chapter primarily involves archival research, using the records of these three movements, as well as reviewing the scholarship and oral testimony of former members. Thus, the primary source material I employ in the chapter has solely been created by racialised historical actors, whose history the chapter writes and analyses. This approach is significant, developing the methodologies of scholars such as Perry, Shirin Hirsch, Priyamvada Gopal and Waters, who also create historical narratives about race and resistance using primary sources created by the racialised actors whose lives they write about.[6] I use this method to preserve the agency of the historical actors in question, and I cross-examine the records of different activists and organisations in order to address inherent biases in this approach (namely, that writing a history of an organisation using only their own records would result in omissions and partiality).

The origins of political Blackness and the Black People's Alliance (BPA)

Whether South Asian migrant communities belong within a Black polity in Britain was and is contested. Although some anti-racist activists engaged with Black political identity as an umbrella to encompass all racialised migrants to Britain, others chose not to. Scholars of racialised communities, identities and organisation also debate the utility of political Blackness. Tariq Modood is perhaps the most prominent example of a scholar who has rejected the concept of the Black political umbrella throughout his career, as he argues that this theoretical framework was not representative of most people's lived experiences, senses of self or political persuasions. In doing this, Modood suggests that Black political identity was wrongly attached to South Asian actors, to whom it did not apply.[7]

In this chapter I conversely argue that certain South Asian actors actively constructed Black political identities, using this to inform their activism. I demonstrate that Black political identity was shaped directly by people who had migrated to Britain from South Asia (most often India), or who were of South Asian diasporic descent. Thus, I argue that there are many cases when, historically, South Asian people were active participants in the Black political project. At the core of this argument is the theoretical intervention of Waters, who builds on the work of Sivanandan and Hall by observing that for those who saw themselves as politically Black, their alignment with Blackness described a particular political framework, as opposed to describing 'the public of this politics'.[8] In other words, political Blackness did not describe racialised communities, and therefore cannot be applied incorrectly; instead, engagement with Black political identity represented a commitment to socialism and anti-racism. It was something that people subscribed to not only on the basis of physicality (bodies, skin or material culture), but also on the basis of political affiliation. In making this argument, Waters's scholarship historicises the cultural theory of Stuart Hall, who argues that 'it is not because of [people's] skins that they are Black in their heads'.[9]

This is not to dispute the claim that most people did not identify as Black, but instead adds nuance to the debate by highlighting the agency of the South Asian individuals and groups who did – and in some cases still do – identify in this way. Those in question intentionally aligned themselves with a political project that reflected unity across ethnic and national lines in the fight against racism and for socialism. The agency behind the decision to organise as Black, I argue, represents an assertion of unity that was in itself tied up with specific socialist and anti-racist politics. This label therefore spoke to the racialised community, particularly other anti-racist activists, and signified either a common politics or a politics of difference, depending on the specific context.

According to Bourne, in the wake of the 1968 Kenyan Asian 'crisis' and Enoch Powell's infamous Rivers of Blood speech, the BPA was conceived of as a necessary vehicle to unite Black people across Britain, through which collective action could be organised.[10] It was intended that the various member organisations would operate as normal at the local level, working with the communities in which they were situated. The BPA is thus an example of Black unity in practice, as organisations across different localities in Britain, with members who originated from different localities across the globe, worked together to fight British state racism and local conflicts, using international political theories. This highlights the translocal nature of political Blackness, which Perry argues shaped the Black political landscape in postwar Britain via the transnational exchanges of ideas, global concepts of Blackness and the local British context.[11] At the same time, particularly for second-generation South Asian politically Black movements, which were more diverse in terms of place of origin and religion, the Black banner provided a framework for conceptualising a secular identity and politics that was used to unite people from a range of family and community backgrounds.[12]

Theoretically, the BPA built on the foundations for Black unity in anti-racist practice, which were laid in the interwar period. It was at this time that networks were formed between radical African, African Caribbean and Asian student associations in Britain. These associations sought to organise collectively on two issues that they saw as inherently connected: racism in Britain and anti-colonialism.[13] It was these students' experiences of life in the imperial metropole that made clearer 'the connections – between colonialism and racism'.[14] In other words, it was through coming to Britain that people from various colonised nations better understood the universality of their experiences. Through forging communicative networks these associations built transnational solidarity between themselves, in Britain, and anti-colonial nationalist movements across the British Empire. In this way, concepts of racialised migrant unity were developing in the interwar period. Black political identity, as it developed in Britain, was constructed as part of a translocal network of solidarity.[15]

Following increased migration to Britain after 1948, Sivanandan writes that through the 1950s and early 1960s the pursuit of anti-racist and anti-colonial activism 'was beginning to break down island and ethnic affiliations and associations and to re-form them in terms of the immediate realities of social and racial relations, engendering in the process strong community bases'.[16] In other words, the ideological basis of organisations formed on national, 'island' (referring to the Caribbean) or 'ethnic' lines shifted toward broader unity as a result of migrants' experiences of life in Britain. The 'community bases' Sivanandan describes had a fundamental role in shaping concepts of non-white, anti-racist unity. He argues that through the specific experiences that communities had, as a result of where they were (i.e. the specific, local context), 'there was no one unity – or two or three – but a mosaic of unities'.[17] Practically, this 'mosaic of unities' resulted in the formation of multiple organisations and coalitions of organisations that claimed to speak to the racialised migrant experience universally. This included the BPA, and other prominent examples were the Universal Coloured People's Association (UCPA) and the Campaign against Racial Discrimination (CARD).

The BPA was formed to connect local movements on national campaigns. In practice, this often took the form of providing coaches from the Midlands to London so member organisations could participate in national demonstrations. One example of this was the 1969 demonstration against police brutality and 'the extradition and plot to murder Bobby Seale, chairman of the Black Panther Party, USA', flyered as 'All Black and White Militants Demonstrate on Sunday March 15.'[18] 'Black' here refers to all racialised people in Britain at the time. This demonstration highlights the practical application of transnational solidarity between Black radicals in the BPA and in the USA, as well as the use of political Blackness. The flyer ends by stating:

DEMONSTRATE AGAINST THE BRUTAL TREATMENT OF BOBBY SEALE.

DEMONSTRATE AGAINST AMERICAN AND BRITISH IMPERIALISM.

DEMONSTRATE AGAINST THE AMERICAN AND BRITISH TERRORISM OF BLACK PEOPLE.

DEMONSTRATE FOR AFRO-AMERICAN LIBERATION IN THE U.S.[19]

Here, the BPA highlighted the parallels between experiences of racism in Britain and the USA, seeking to incite solidarity between anti-racism in the two nations. This suggests an intentional linking of the BPA with global anti-racist and socialist movements. Hence, the BPA connected local organisations across Britain and connected them – at least in terms of showing solidarity – with activism outside Britain.

By calling for racialised people in Britain to 'demonstrate for Afro-American liberation in the U.S.' the BPA provides us with an instance of South Asian people participating in Black unity activism, as these South Asian people were protesting the mistreatment of a US Black Panther, who was Black/African American. The language connecting British and American imperialism also reflects the way that this demonstration was presented as part of a translocal Black politics that in this case stemmed from a Black

Marxist perspective. Black Marxism combined material analysis of global history and the development of the nation-state and capitalism taken from Marxism, with the Black radical thinking of Malcolm X, Frantz Fanon and Stokely Carmichael (Kwame Ture). In combination this produced a worldview that recognised the 'material force of racism'.[20]

The BPA also explicitly made links between British imperialism and racism in Britain. For example, another BPA flyer published in 1969, 'Racialism in Britain Is Imperialism in Our Countries. Overthrow Both', stated:

> Africans, Indians, Pakistanis, West Indians – we are all black people ... We share a common past: enslavement; we share a common present: the exploitation of our homelands by colonialism – old and new – and its black puppets; we share a common hope; to liberate our countries and people from the yoke of imperialist oppression and racialism which is rooted in empire.[21]

Here, the BPA made connections between Black unity ('we are all black people') and a common history of homelands having been colonised, as well as between empire and racism. The language in this flyer reflects Carmichael's dialectics, showing his widespread influence. The BPA's Black Marxist perspective uniquely cemented the existing connections between anti-racist and anti-colonial activism in Britain.[22] This had a practical impact on BPA activism, as it fought for the rights of Black people as workers. The BPA helped Black workers to strike when they were not supported by British trade unions. These strikers happened to be predominantly people from South Asia who had taken work in foundries, factories, mills and plants in Britain. Without trade union support, local Indian Workers' Associations and Pakistani welfare associations were required to assist strikers, and BPA solidarity reinforced these strikes.[23]

The BPA is a clear example of a movement in which South Asian people at the leadership and membership levels were directly involved in Black activism in Britain. This precedent, however, did not result in a long-term adoption of Black unity in anti-racism, though it did lay the foundations for the theoretical interventions made by the second generation, namely SBS and SYM, who reinterpreted these theories through a secular lens, based on their lived experiences. For contemporary activists, the BPA represents a moment when Black unity was possible, providing a historical reference for promoting solidarity and anti-racist unity in the present.

The second generation: Southall Youth Movement (SYM) and Southall Black Sisters (SBS)

The activism of the BPA served as a first-generation example of the potential that Black political identity had for South Asian people in Britain for the second generation. Synchronously, Southall's local Indian Workers' Association (IWA Southall) chose not to align itself with the Black banner. It was a first-generation organisation, like the BPA. Hence, for SYM and SBS activists, their local anti-racist organisation was not a direct model. Instead, for these movements, Blackness came to signify a radical departure from their parents' anti-racism, while also building on first-generation Blackness elsewhere in Britain (BPA) since both movements' Blackness was socialist, anti-racist and secular. By looking at the activist theory and practice of SYM and SBS, this section of the chapter demonstrates that the agency of South Asian actors in forging Black politics and identities is just as evident in the cases of SYM and SBS as with the BPA.

In practice, SBS and SYM definitions of Blackness meant that the inclusion of non-South Asian politically Black people was not prioritised by either organisation. Hence, I argue that for SYM and SBS their definition of Black politics was informed by their locality and lived experiences in Southall, making it necessarily characterised by secularism, a category that was itself informed by the gender and generation of both groups. I also argue that Black unity was not demonstrated by either SYM or SBS in practice; this was a purely theoretical element of their Black politics. In other words, for both SBS and SYM, political Blackness was less about theoretical ties with African Caribbean and other African diasporic people, and more about demonstrating ties with people from different religious backgrounds within the South Asian population of Southall.

Today, SBS still operates as a charity supporting racialised women facing domestic violence in West London, whereas SYM and the BPA have stopped operating at the front lines of anti-racist activism. While, in this section of the chapter, I point to the limitations of SBS's Blackness alongside those of SYM, it is important to note that SBS is the only movement still operational today. This is, in part, a result of their shift in approach to focusing on one specific issue: the intersections of race, class and gender in domestic violence. This has meant that their practice of political Blackness has also shifted, as SBS no longer protest British state racism and capitalism directly, on the streets, but instead address the complexities of the quotidian experiences of these broad societal issues, working exclusively with survivors/victims of domestic abuse. Thus, I suggest that today the 'Black' in SBS indicates their serving of a community of racialised women more than a specific Black politics, with which the movement aligned much more overtly when it was founded. The socialist nature of their work is still present in their representation and assistance of working-class women, demonstrating a practical application of radical anti-racism in the context of racialised austerity, but this is no longer directed toward the central state, and has less resonance with anti-colonialism.[24]

Both SYM and SBS were New Social Movements (NSMs), referring to their focus on identifiers beyond class structures: namely youth, race and, for SBS, gender.[25] While much of the literature on NSMs explores how identity and experience shaped these movements' activism, as opposed to class-based ideology, Aziz Choudry argues that analysis of participation in social movements tells us more about 'self-realization rather than contesting state/political power'.[26] In other words, exploring the activism of SYM and SBS adds nuance to our understanding of these movements as youth cultures. Southall Youth Movement can be categorised as a grassroots anti-racist movement, as it was formed during an organic, mass demonstration. It was the first of many Asian Youth Movements (AYMs) to form across Britain, making up a network of solidarity among local nodes in Britain, based on the notion of shared experiences of racism and shared identity.[27]

Southall Black Sisters was a slightly different type of NSM: an anti-racist and socialist 'non-hierarchical' activist collective, founded by a group of four women, exclusively for women, in order to give them a space to discuss their views and to organise as anti-racist activists, without losing their autonomy or being subjected to gender-based oppression. The smaller, collective nature of SBS made it differ at the organisational level from SYM. These distinctions in definition provide context for understanding the nuances in the articulations of Black politics, and activism more broadly, of the two movements. Both SYM and SBS were made up of second-generation young people, who were in school, had just finished school or were at university. While literature about NSMs often focuses on generational shifts and identities that 'transcend class structures' (in these cases youth and gender), Stanley Aronowitz argues that NSMs are also class-based movements, and so they should not be as divorced from workers' movements as they often are.[28] Indeed, while SBS and SYM were both youth movements, both also understood their members' lived experiences as tied up with their position in British society on class and racial lines. In this sense, as each claimed, both organisations were politically Black.

More specifically, for SYM, political Blackness represented a radical youth politics that was socialist and anti-racist. Anandi Ramamurthy writes that the movement's Blackness reflected theoretical anti-racist unity without denying cultural differences, and its secularism symbolised religious pluralism under the Black political banner.[29]

She argues that this specific Black and secular identity stemmed directly from experiences of racism in Britain, which called for a united, anti-racist front. Building on this, I posit that the name, Southall Youth Movement, was therefore specifically formulated to encompass this ideology. In conversation with Ramamurthy, Balraj Purewal, a SYM founder, explains that the name was based on two things: SYM did not want to discriminate on national lines, to exclude any Asians or any African Caribbean youth; and they did not want to specify that they were 'not white' because that wasn't 'anything special' in Southall – they *were* the youth of Southall'.[30] Purewal also argues that the name SYM was 'influenced by black politics and a version of secularism that became a unifying force', as the group wanted to choose a name that could not only be seen to represent any young Black people in Southall, but could be actively used to unite the local community, particularly those from different religious backgrounds or places of origin with South Asian heritage.[31]

The limits of SYM's Black unity can be seen in the fact that, as the movement spread to different localities across Britain, the new local organisations were named Asian Youth Movements, thereby excluding non-South Asian people upon entry. According to Sivanandan, SYM and other AYMs worked with non-South Asian Black organisations, namely youth groups for African Caribbean men.[32] However, this is not apparent in testimony from SYM members, suggesting that this was not of high significance to them. Black identity reflected the content of SYM politics but not the practice of working with other Black racialised groups. Instead, Blackness was employed to evoke a secularism that allowed young men from different religious backgrounds and places of origin to come together.

Like SYM, SBS also framed itself as secular through Blackness. For example, it published an anonymous poem, 'Southall', in its 1980 newsletter, in which the author presents secularism in terms of different religious communities working together, and presents secularism and Blackness as sources of 'togetherness, strength and pride'.[33] The poem states that 'Southall has Gurdwaras and Masjids' to demonstrate connections across these lines. It describes Southall as religiously diverse – but this, the poem asserts, is not a line on which Southall residents are divided. At the same time, in this poem, SBS frame their Black political identity as something that was born of the local context, in reaction to local events and instances of state racism. Like SYM, in practice, SBS's Black identity was more about secularism to unite South Asian people of differing religious backgrounds and places of origin, as it was less practical, locally, to unite people with African Caribbean and other African diasporic heritage with South Asian people; at least, in practice, this was something SBS found to be the case.[34]

The secularism of SYM and SBS was also reflective of local demographics. Southall, by 1979, was a more religiously diverse community than it had been in the late 1950s, 1960s and early 1970s as a result of South Asian migration to Southall from East Africa, bringing people from a more diverse range of backgrounds in terms of place of origin in India and religion. The original South Asian community in Southall was predominantly Punjabi and Sikh, whereas migrants from East Africa largely came from Gujarati backgrounds and were Hindu and Muslim.³⁵ Southall's diversity along these lines was significant to SBS's Black politics because it was a point of difference between their activism and that of the older generation (IWA Southall). For example, further demonstrating its pride in its secularism, SBS writes of its locality:

> We have been lucky too. Southall is a very mixed community. Asians who settled there were mainly from ... Punjab. Sikhs, Hindus and Muslims are all represented in Southall. There is a long tradition of radical secular organising which stretches back to India when young communist and nationalist activist workers settled in Britain and brought their politics and their organisational experience with them.³⁶

The reference here to Southall as a community made up of Sikhs, Hindus and Muslims is an intentional choice made by SBS in this publication to demonstrate its secular nature through highlighting collaboration among the three religious communities. This reflection by SBS on the context out of which it emerged also reflects the ways that anti-racist activism in Britain was informed not only by the local and national contexts, including the demographics of the local community as described here, but also by the international movement of ideas about activism. The 'young communist and nationalist activist workers' mentioned here were IWA activists, who brought their own radical ideas and traditions with them from India. Hence, SBS's organisation had roots in the South Asian-led Black activism of the 1960s, namely the BPA.³⁷

Despite no direct experience of living under colonial rule, language of anti-imperialism and solidarity with global anti-racist and anti-colonial movements was central to SYM's Black activist identity. This position connected SYM in solidarity with other Black activist groups in Britain, as well as across the globe. This theoretical internationalism became a tangible part of their activism. For example, SYM demonstrated against apartheid in South Africa and in solidarity with Palestine. Similarly, SBS reflected on the intersections of race, class and gender in contemporary movements in El Salvador and India.³⁸ These connections were drawn for the purpose of political education, to inform and radicalise readers. Building global solidarity was part of both of these movements' political aims for the education of their local memberships, so that they could situate themselves within a global political order.

In practice, some of the limitations of this framework of solidarity can be seen in a paper that SBS gave at a 1981 study group hosted by the Organisation of Women of African and Asian Descent (OWAAD) at the Brixton Black Women's Centre. Though the presence of SBS at the conference suggests a certain level of collaboration with Black women's groups led by women of African Caribbean or other African diasporic heritage, the paper explicitly stated that African Caribbean and South Asian women could show solidarity but needed to organise independently in practice.[39] It reads:

> as a group who have attempted to put [political Blackness] into practice, we feel that it completely ignores differences we have found it essential to take into account at all levels of organisation ... whilst we are both oppressed as women, the specific nature of that oppression takes different forms ... the Asian sisters in our group tend to have greater problems coming to meetings due to strong family commitments, where resistance holds the distinct possibility of ostracism, whilst [African Caribbean] sisters will have family problems they do not face the same fear of being cut off from their whole community.[40]

The argument presented here shows that SBS did not feel they were able to work with non-South Asian Black women in their practice of activism through their domestic violence shelter and other related work. Yet, as mentioned, SBS have continued to call themselves Black to this day as a way to reflect the politics of the organisation, as opposed to anti-racist unity with African Caribbean or other African diasporic groups. While this represents a continuation of SBS's approach to political Blackness since the mid-1980s, it is nonetheless quite a departure from the Blackness of the BPA, which existed specifically to bring together various national and ethnic groups for on-the-street demonstrations. If the political Blackness of the first generation brought different groups together in practice, and the second generation's political Blackness was a theoretic framework of reference, what is the future of this concept?

Is Black political identity still relevant? New lexicons of resistance in contemporary anti-racism

The histories of SBS, SYM and the BPA teach us that political Blackness has been a useful tool for South Asian communities developing anti-racist theories and practices in Britain. Thus far this chapter has highlighted the ways that the BPA sought to bring together different anti-racist groups, which organised on national lines, in order to support each other and build a united anti-racist front. Then, SBS and SYM used the socialist and anti-racist politics of Blackness to respond specifically to their local environment while also building a globally conscious politics of anti-racism. The nature of each movement's ideas about political Blackness varied, but looking at each case highlights that South Asian people have actively participated in Black politics and activism in Britain, albeit in varied ways.

Yet, South Asian inclusion in Black politics continues to be a source of contention in anti-racist activism in Britain. The ambiguity surrounding contemporary understanding of the concept of *political* Blackness may stem from the lack of consistency in its use, now and historically. As Modood argues, 'Asians are sometimes "black" and sometimes not depending not upon the Asians in question (i.e. upon whether they accept the terminology), but upon the convenience or politics of the speaker or writer.'[41] While my research suggests that this argument might obstruct the agency of the South Asian individuals who chose to call themselves Black, and organise as Black, Modood nonetheless exposes a key source of the confusion surrounding political Blackness.

When the question of South Asian inclusion under the Black banner is raised in the broader public sphere today, it is still discussed with ambiguity. For example, in 2016, the University of Kent's Student Union (Kent SU) was met with criticisms for using images of Sadiq Khan and Zayn Malik in its Black History Month (BHM) campaign. According to a *Guardian* article published during that BHM, many students whom the article identified as 'Black' at the University of Kent, and the BHM UK official Twitter account, were opposed to the fact that these two South Asian people were included. Kent SU explained that the decision was a result of employing the political definition of Blackness.[42] The next day, Kehinde Andrews, Amrit Wilson and Vera Chok co-penned another *Guardian* article entitled 'Is Political Blackness Still Relevant Today?'.[43] The short answer, from their perspective, was no, and this article reinforced the notion that Kent SU had made a mistake with their decision to categorise the 'Black' in BHM as political. Andrews, who in particular does not advocate for South Asian inclusion in any form of Black identity, writes in the article that 'Solidarity shouldn't mean creating a shared identity.'[44] So why did Kent SU include two South Asian, Muslim men?

Part of the reason for this is not only the history of political Blackness in Britain but also the racialised position of Muslims in contemporary Britain and their relationship with the state through programmes such as Prevent. As Jed Fazakarley points out, Muslims are othered in specific ways, which makes this cultural-religious category of identity more important than that of South Asian (and other geographic and ethnic categories).[45] At the same time, as Gareth Jenkins argues, class is still an important element of people's sense of self and identity – including constructions of political Blackness.[46] He writes that 'the modern Conservative Party may wish to show its inclusivity by having a Muslim chairperson, but the presence of a successful business woman is more likely to reassure the aspiring Muslim shopkeeper than appeal to Muslims who work in factories or on the buses, alongside non-Muslims'.[47] Crucially, this highlights that the position of different racialised communities in Britain is far more stratified than it was in the post-*Windrush* phases of migration to Britain. The inclusion of South Asian communities within political Blackness has become more complicated to legitimise through shared colonial heritage and experiences of racism. In addition, African diasporic Black identities have increasingly developed toward the Black Atlantic paradigm, and away from the definition that includes all racialised people. Thus, to include South Asian communities in BHM not only risks homogenising different experiences (which critics of political Blackness have always suggested) but also risks a misappropriation of histories of enslavement and the continued institutional racism faced by many in the British African Caribbean community.[48]

For those who are approaching anti-racist activism without the lived experiences of 1970s and 1980s Britain, the question of Black political identity is therefore understandably confusing. In Reni Eddo-Lodge's podcast on political Blackness, she discusses the need for improved political education for racialised communities in Britain, as the histories of Black unity and anti-racist activism are still not widely taught.[49] Thus, political Blackness cannot be widely understood today without a significant shift in the intergenerational transfer of knowledge among activists. Equally, we have different language to express common experiences and politics along racialised lines today. Examples include 'Black and brown', 'Black and Global Majority', person/people of colour (PoC) and BIPOC in the US context (Black, Indigenous and People of Colour). These terms, like political Blackness, all not only reflect the commonality of being racialised and experiencing racism, but also express political values. 'Black and brown', for example, is used by the Stuart Hall Foundation in their copy, reflecting the specificities of the British context while acknowledging some of the limitations of political Blackness. The Black-and-brown umbrella may not describe all racialised people in the UK today, but it reflects the history of migration to Britain from (formerly) colonised places being predominantly made up of people of the African and South Asian diasporas. 'Black and Global Majority' has also gained traction in the UK more recently, reflecting a more diverse racialised community as well as a more internationally oriented politics.

Returning to Andrews's statement 'Solidarity shouldn't mean creating a shared identity', I would go further to argue that the foundations of political Blackness – shared experiences of racism in Britain – are not a necessary guarantee for solidarity in the present. This has been articulated by Osman Yousefzada, an artist who wrote an article on Black and brown solidarity for the *Observer*, in which he states:

> If political blackness is dead, then maybe we need a new set of ideas with its own terminology, a language that allows us to come together to fight, especially as often our struggles have more in common than not. A term that doesn't divide us or fragment us, that doesn't pitch us against one another

fighting for scraps of regenerational grants from an elitist system built on race and class privilege. Together, we are stronger! [50]

Here, Yousefzada makes an explicit reference to the types of funding streams employed by SBS and other anti-racist community organisations, suggesting that a new approach might be useful in bringing together a fractured anti-racist movement. I conversely argue that solidarity, which is not a new concept, could serve this purpose. To be more precise, solidarity is 'broadly understood as a commitment to the struggle of "others"' at local, national and global scales.[51] This makes it a translocal phenomenon, much like that which was encouraged by the advocates of political Blackness explored in this chapter. However, as Rebecca Peters argues, 'the casual usage of the term to describe everything from purchasing a handbag, to donating money, signing a petition, or wearing a bracelet risks undermining solidarity's potential' for transformative social change, locally, nationally or across the globe.[52] She goes on to argue that:

> the danger of connecting the practice of solidarity with the consumptive activity of shopping is that it threatens to undermine the power of the term to encourage people to engage in a structural critique of the patterns of global capitalism that are contributing to the continued impoverishment of many of the poorest of the poor. [53]

In other words, today, the notion of solidarity as a practice is being commodified to the extent that its origins and purpose are distorted. This mirrors the ambiguities surrounding political Blackness, and it may be the case that this language too loses coherence as a uniting socialist concept. Historically, as is highlighted in this chapter, racialised communities in Britain shared experiences of racism across 'ethnic' lines. At the same time, there were – and still are – many differences in the experiences of racism for different individuals and groups, as well as differences in terms of culture (for example religion, language, work). Political Blackness, as a shared identity, did not seek to homogenise these differences, but served as a tool for politicisation, and fostering solidarity and a sense of unity.

Is Solidarity the new political Blackness? Certainly it has the potential to educate and unite people in similar ways. Muna Abdi, anti-racist scholar of education, highlighted this when she tweeted:

> Patriarchy, Racism ... all oppressive systems ... are not our fault, but if they allow us to live in safety at the cost of other people's lives, it IS our RESPONSIBILITY to dismantle them.
>
> Solidarity means your freedom is dependent on mine.[54]

This not only evokes the notion of solidarity, which Abdi here expresses as an understanding that – even without any sense of shared identity – 'your freedom is dependent on mine', but also gives an insight into the ways that Intersectionality theory has come to the fore in contemporary debates about solidarity in anti-racist activism. Yet, today, the term 'intersectionality' is often misused as simply referring to an awareness of intersecting modes of oppression. Hence, as was the case with Black political identity in 1970s Britain, the nature of the concept of intersectionality as nuanced and complex is too ambiguously understood by many at the fore of anti-racist activism. This means that activists are not always able to utilise the concept and advocate on intersectional lines. Nonetheless, the concepts and languages of intersectionality and solidarity do have the potential to work as unifying terms, as political Blackness has done at specific historical moments. As, for example, Kimberlé Crenshaw also argues, for Black women, the categories of 'race' and gender can be sources of empowerment rather than labels of oppression.[55] If intersectionality is understood in this way, combined with a nuanced understanding of solidarity that does not require a shared identity, yet 'means your freedom is dependent on mine', there is potential for these concepts to be useful for contemporary anti-racists seeking to politicise and radicalise their peers and wider society. Solidarity provides a route through which activism moves toward a common goal (rather than being formed on the basis of common oppression) and can be pursued by anyone who shares that goal. Thus, solidarity allows disparate groups to support each other without requiring a common sense of selfhood, meaning the term is able to address the concerns of SYM and SBS in relation to religion being a source of division for racialised communities in Britain.

As the previous sections of this chapter have shown, this approach to anti-racist socialism is not much of a departure from the Black politics of the BPA, SYM and SBS, at least in practical terms. Therefore, engagement with the history of these movements may be useful for contemporary activists who wish to develop on their theoretical interventions, insofar as they highlight the limitations of anti-racist unity in practice in Britain. For example, SYM and SBS shared a vision of a fairer society, in which racialised communities could be treated on equitable terms with their white counterparts, yet the two movements were unable to work together despite being part of the same locality. Understanding this history may help contemporary activists overcome these historical struggles, in part through the utilisation of specific language, such as that of solidarity.

Conclusions

If political Blackness has been replaced with new vocabularies both in terms of identity and resistance to racism, then how useful are histories of political Blackness in the current contemporary context? I have argued that these histories are useful in understanding the active role played by South Asian actors in developing Black politics in Britain, and therefore provide a model for anti-racist unity and broader solidarity in activism. With shifts in the demographics of racialised communities in Britain, the language of solidarity is a more useful tool than political Blackness today, as it is more flexible and less reliant on the notion of shared experiences. Nonetheless, exploring histories of South Asian political Blackness can be a tool to reflect on essential ideas about race, ethnicity and identity, as well as approaches to socialist and anti-racist activism.

The cross-case-study analysis in this chapter has demonstrated that, historically, the Black activism of first-generation South Asian migrants to Britain was implemented in their practice much more overtly than that of the second generation. For the BPA, the practice of bringing together organisations with members from different nationalities was important, to create strength in numbers for on-the-street protest. This was informed by direct shared experience of having lived under colonial rule before migrating to Britain, and then experiencing similar racialised class struggles when living here.

For SYM and SBS, Black politics was much more about speaking to their local environment. Their approach to activism relating to national and even global issues was filtered through the local context. This was informed by the positions of members of both groups as young people who grew up in Southall, experiencing police and judicial racism and inequality in education, at the same time as feeling that their parents' generation were not doing enough to fight the racism they faced. This shift in positionality between the first and second generation was in part why SBS and SYM's Black unity was more limited than the BPA's in practice; their Blackness focused instead on secularism and generational radicalism oriented toward their local context. Particularly in the case of SBS, their active decision to adapt to the needs of the local community in a way that allowed them to access local authority funding has led to longevity and the ability to provide practical help to women facing domestic violence to this day. The fact that SBS's Blackness is more about rebellion against Southall's local conservatism and religiosity makes sense and is just as valid as the Black unity-oriented politics of the BPA – and indeed provides an alternative legacy for contemporary activists to draw from if they choose to.

Notes

1 It is important to note the prevalence of anti-Blackness in South Asian communities in Britain when writing a history of South Asian political Blackness. In doing this, I also note the lack of scholarship on South Asian anti-Blackness,

and suggest that this is an important area for further study. It is difficult to grapple with South Asian Blackness without understanding this important counterpart, so this is an unfortunate omission that I have not had the space to address in this chapter or in my broader work to date.
2 Jenny Bourne, 'When Black was a Political Colour: A Guide to the Literature', *Race & Class*, 58:1 (2016), 122–30; Rosie Wild, ' "Black Was the Colour of Our Fight": The Transnational Roots of British Black Power', in Robin Kelley and Stephen Tuck (eds), *The Other Special Relationship: Race, Rights and Riots in Britain and the United States* (New York: Palgrave Macmillan, 2015), pp. 25–46.
3 Rob Waters, *Thinking Black: Britain, 1964–1985* (Berkeley: University of California Press, 2019); SBS, *Against the Grain – a Celebration of Survival and Struggle: Southall Black Sisters 1979–1989* (Nottingham: Russell Press, 1990); Beverley Bryan, Stella Dadzie and Suzanne Scafe, *The Heart of the Race: Black Women's Lives in Britain* (London: Virago Press, 1985); Ron Ramdin, *The Making of the Black Working Class in Britain* (Aldershot: Gower, 1987); Ambalavander Sivanandan, *A Different Hunger: Writings on Black Resistance* (London: Pluto Press, 1983).
4 Kennetta Hammond Perry, *London Is the Place for Me: Black Britons, Citizenship and the Politics of Race* (Oxford: Oxford University Press, 2015); Peter Fryer, *Staying Power: The History of Black People in Britain* (London: Pluto Press, 1984).
5 Rosie Wild, 'Black was the Colour of Our Fight: Black Power in Britain, 1955–1976', PhD thesis (University of Sheffield, 2008), p. 134.
6 Perry, *London Is the Place for Me*; Shirin Hirsch, *In the Shadow of Enoch Powell: Race, Locality and Resistance* (Manchester: Manchester University Press, 2018); Priyamvada Gopal, *Insurgent Empire: Anticolonial Resistance and British Dissent* (London: Verso, 2019); Waters, *Thinking Black*.
7 Tariq Modood, ' "Black", Racial Equality and Asian Identity', *Journal of Ethnic and Migration Studies*, 14:3 (1988), 398–400.
8 Waters, *Thinking Black*, p. 49.
9 Stuart Hall, 'Old and New Identities, Old and New Ethnicities', in Les Back and John Solomos (eds), *Theories of Race and Racism: A Reader* (London: Routledge, 2000), pp. 144–53 (p. 149).
10 Bourne, 'When Black Was a Political Colour', pp. 125–6.
11 Perry, *London Is the Place for Me*, pp. 10–11.
12 This was a finding of oral history interviews conducted as part of my doctoral research, in which I spoke with activists who had been involved with Southall Black Sisters and the Southall and Asian Youth Movements.
13 Sivanandan, *A Different Hunger*, p. 7.
14 *Ibid.* NB Sivanandan defines *racialism* as related to individual and collective prejudices and beliefs, and suggests this was present in British society as a direct result of British imperialism. He defines *racism* as structural, and argues that a particular form of postwar British racism toward Black (ex-)colonial migrants emerged in the 1960s. Racism is therefore more closely tied with the class

struggle, as racialised labourers have a specific relationship with the means of production in postwar Britain. For more on South Asian students in Britain, see Sumita Mukherjee, *Nationalism, Education and Migrant Identities: The England-Returned* (London: Routledge, 2010).
15 Ramdin, *The Making of the Black Working Class in Britain*, p. 5.
16 Sivanandan, *A Different Hunger*, p. 8. For more on this, see Jed Fazakarley, 'Race as a Separate Sphere in British Government: From the Colonial Office to Municipal Anti-Racism', *Callaloo*, 39:1 (2016), 185–235; and Sasha Josephides, 'Organisational Splits and Political Ideology in the Indian Workers Associations', in Pnina Werbner and Muhammad Anwar (eds), *Black and Ethnic Leaderships in Britain: The Cultural Dimensions of Political Action* (London: Routledge, 1991), pp. 253–76.
17 Sivanandan, *A Different Hunger*, p. 8; Kalbir Shukra, *The Changing Pattern of Black Politics in Britain* (London: Pluto Press, 1998), pp. 16–18.
18 BPA flyer, 'All Black and White Militants Demonstrate on Sunday March 15 …', Wolfson Centre, Birmingham Library, MS2141/c/4/3.
19 *Ibid.*
20 Cedric Robinson, *Black Marxism: The Making of the Black Radical Tradition* (London: Zed Press, 1983), p. 228.
21 BPA flyer, 'Racialism in Britain Is Imperialism in Our Countries. Overthrow Both.', Wolfson Centre, Birmingham Library, MS2141/c/4/5.
22 Sivanandan, *A Different Hunger*, pp. 20–1.
23 *Ibid.*, pp. 22–3.
24 For more on the ways that racialised women have developed practices of anti-racism and self-help at the local, quotidian level, see Sophia Siddiqui's chapter in this volume.
25 Hank Johnston, Enrique Laraña and Joseph Gusfield, 'Identities, Grievances, and New Social Movements', in Hank Johnston, Enrique Laraña and Joseph Gusfield (eds), *New Social Movements: From Ideology to Identity* (Philadelphia, PA: Temple University Press, 1994), pp. 3–35 (p. 6).
26 Aziz Choudry, *Learning Activism: The Intellectual Life of Contemporary Social Movements* (Toronto, ON: University of Toronto Press, 2015), p. 47.
27 Anandi Ramamurthy, *Black Star: Britain's Asian Youth Movements* (London: Pluto Press, 2013); Sivanandan, *A Different Hunger*; Paul Almeida, *Social Movements: The Structure of Collective Mobilization* (Berkeley: University of California Press, 2019).
28 Stanley Aronowitz, *How Class Works: Power and Social Movement* (New Haven, CT: Yale University Press, 2003), p. 141; Johnston et al., 'Identities, Grievances, and New Social Movements'.
29 Anandi Ramamurthy, 'The Politics of Britain's Asian Youth Movements', *Race & Class*, 48:2 (2006), 38–60 (p. 39).
30 *Ibid.*, pp. 42–3.
31 *Ibid.*, p. 39.
32 Sivanandan, *A Different Hunger*, pp. 39–40.
33 SBS Newsletter (c. 1980), Institute of Race Relations Special Collections, 01-04-03-02-146.

34 Paper presented by SBS at Afro-Asian Unity day school organised by Organisation of Women of African and Asian Descent (OWAAD) Study Group at the Brixton Black Women's Centre, Institute of Race Relations Special Collections, 01-04-04-01-10-07-049.
35 Maya Parmar, 'Reading the Double Diaspora: Representing Gujarati East African Cultural Identity in Britain', *Atlantis*, 35:1 (2013), 137–55 (p. 139).
36 SBS, *Against the Grain*, p. 4.
37 Ramamurthy, 'The Politics of Britain's Asian Youth Movements', pp. 45–6.
38 SBS newsletter (c. 1980), Institute of Race Relations Special Collections, 01-04-04-01-12.
39 Paper presented by SBS at Afro-Asian Unity day school organised by OWAAD Study Group at the Brixton Black Women's Centre, Institute of Race Relations Special Collections, 01-04-04-01-10-07-049.
40 *Ibid.*
41 Tariq Modood, 'Political Blackness and British Asians', *Sociology*, 28:4 (1994), 859–76 (p. 863).
42 David Batty, 'Student Union Promotes Black History Month with Zayn Malik Picture', *Guardian* (26 October 2016), www.theguardian.com/world/2016/oct/26/student-union-black-history-month-zayn-malik-sadiq-khan-kent-university (accessed 3 June 2024).
43 Amrit Wilson, Kehinde Andrews and Vera Chok, 'Is Political Blackness Still Relevant Today?', *Guardian* (27 October 2016), www.theguardian.com/commentisfree/2016/oct/27/political-blackness-black-history-month-zayn-malik-sadiq-khan (accessed 3 June 2024).
44 *Ibid.*
45 Jed Fazakarley, 'Muslim Communities in England, 1962–92: Multiculturalism and Political Identity', PhD thesis (University of Oxford, 2014), p. 24.
46 Gareth Jenkins, 'In Defence of Multiculturalism?', in Michael Lavalette and Laura Penketh (eds), *Race, Racism and Social Work: Contemporary Issues and Debates* (Bristol: Bristol University Press, 2014), pp. 131–50 (p. 135).
47 *Ibid.*
48 This is particularly important considering the prevalence of anti-Blackness in certain circles within South Asian communities in Britain, a phenomenon that deserves far more dedicated research than this chapter has space to explore.
49 Reni Eddo-Lodge and Renay Rich, *About Race*, podcast, Episode 4, 'Political Blackness' (April 2018), accessed on Spotify.
50 Osman Yousefzada, 'Shades of Unity in Hope of a New Brown and Black Coalition', *Observer* (22 November 2020), www.theguardian.com/society/2020/nov/22/osman-yousefzada-designer-and-writer-essay-on-tackling-race-in-britain-identity (accessed 22 November 2021).
51 Elisabet Dueholm Rasch and Pooyan Tamimi Arab, 'Introduction: Solidarity', *Etnofoor*, 29:2 (2017), 7–10 (p. 7).
52 Rebecca Todd Peters, *Solidarity Ethics: Transformation in a Globalized World* (Minneapolis: 1517 Media, 2014), p. 30.

53 *Ibid.*
54 Muna Abdi, tweet published 29 November 2021, https://twitter.com/Muna_Abdi_Phd/status/1465302772903985154 (accessed 28 April 2022).
55 Kimberlé Crenshaw, 'Mapping the Margins: Intersectionality, Identity Politics, and Violence against Women of Color', *Stanford Law Review*, 43 (1991), 1241–99 (p. 1242).

8

'Unfinished activisms': From Black self-help to mutual aid organising today

Sophia Siddiqui

During the COVID-19 pandemic, there was an upsurge in solidarity in the form of thousands of mutual aid groups that sprung up across the UK, filling urgent needs that had been long neglected. Groups were set up on the basis of mutual aid, not 'charity', such as people organising for migrants with no access to public funds; collective hardship funds for those who found themselves without work; and efforts to distribute masks to care homes, foodbanks and homeless shelters. All these efforts recognised that our strength lies in looking after each other as a way of responding to structural violence.[1]

The principles of mutual aid – of recognising the importance of caring for each other, sharing resources and maintaining a commitment to the community – have a long, and often overlooked, history here in the UK, a tradition led by Black working-class communities. Whilst mutual aid as a political concept is drawn from the work of Russian anarchist and scientist Peter Kropotkin, who argued in 1902 that it was human cooperation, not competition, that facilitated the survival of our species,[2] self-help movements led by Black working-class communities in Britain continued this mode of organising from the mid-1960s to the early 1980s. Emerging in the mid-1960s, Black self-help initiatives flourished, including the setting up of supplementary schools, community bookshops, art centres, domestic violence refuges and youth support groups. This chapter seeks to fill the gap in the literature on mutual aid and anti-racism, by showing the role of community self-help organising in Britain and exploring its links to present-day mutual aid activism. Self-help organising is often not seen to be an integral part of the left tradition because of political blind spots that render the role of looking after a community as secondary to what were believed to be more pressing political concerns. However, the anti-racist movement in Britain, influenced by Black Power politics from the USA, saw this as a false dichotomy: creating spaces to make life liveable within the current system was as important as the need to challenge the state directly. This exploration provides an opportunity to retrieve the work of local campaigns from the margins, which helps to broaden our understanding of the variety of tactics and organising methods that make up the anti-racist movement, historically and in the present day.

This chapter will begin by tracing the origins of the self-help movement in Britain. What aspects of state racism were communities responding to? Which groups were set up, how did they organise and how did they navigate issues around funding? What was the influence of Black Power on such groups? The following section will explore three self-help initiatives, including Harambee, a community youth rescue project in Islington set up in 1969; the United Black Women's Action Group (UBWAG), which began at Campsbourne Estate in Haringey and later joined the Organisation of Women of African and Asian Descent (OWAAD); and Awaz, the first feminist Asian women's collective, formed in 1977. This anti-racist history is also a feminist history, and I will explore the role of Black and South Asian women in these movements. Actively engaging with this underexplored aspect of anti-racism, mutual aid and Black feminism can shed light on our current conditions, marked by multiple crises of state violence, police racism, neoliberalism and gendered violence.

The final section of the chapter will look at how this history is built upon and carried forward by activists engaged in mutual aid organising today. Although many Black self-help initiatives eventually fragmented, I argue that histories of self-help do not have a specific end date but are reactivated through mutual aid activism, which made a resurgence during the pandemic. Historical legacies are not static; they are 'unfinished activisms' that are carried forward in the present day.[3]

The emergence of self-help activism in Black communities

Context of post-war Britain

In his pivotal essay 'From Resistance to Rebellion: Asian and Afro-Caribbean Struggles in Britain', written in October 1981, A. Sivanandan charts the emergence of self-help activism in postwar Britain.[4] This self-help activism, based on self-organisation and self-reliance, organised to meet the needs of the community that were being neglected by a racist state, or were being caused by it – by brutalising policing; lack of housing provision; educational neglect; or racist immigration laws that wanted cheap labour, but not the social costs of the labourer. Racial discrimination was enshrined in law and racist attacks were a regular part of immigrant life,[5] often fanned by inflammatory political rhetoric that brought far-right views into the frame of respectable debate on immigration.[6] It was in this context that Black self-organisation and self-reliance grew – out of necessity, in order for communities to survive. As Sivanandan writes, 'The loom of British racism had been perfected, the pattern set. The strands of resistance were meshed taut against the frame.'[7] The various resistance struggles of Black communities – the threads – operated within and against the loom of British racism. Under the signifier of 'Black', activists created a collective political identity that united Asian, African and Caribbean communities in a joint struggle against racial injustice, bound by their shared experiences of colonial rule and the subsequent racism faced in Britain.[8]

Whilst in this chapter I focus on the legacies of self-help from the mid-1960s onward, it should be noted that this mode of self-organising in the Black community can be traced back even further, and does not have a fixed start date or end date. After the 'race riots' of 1919 in Liverpool, Cardiff, Hull, London and other port areas, groups formed with the explicit aim of challenging racist discrimination against 'coloured' seamen, who were viewed as 'undesirable'. In Cardiff, the Colonial Defence Association and the South Wales Association for the Welfare of Coloured People were formed to support the seamen and their families.[9] In London, where a 'colour bar' discriminated against Black people across many spheres of life, groups such as the Negro Welfare Association, formed in 1931, organised trips for children and campaigned for support for trade unions in the Caribbean and against the 'colour bar' in Britain.[10]

The role of Black Power

A host of militant Black organisations sprung up around the country to address various needs, often drawing on traditions brought from their home countries, but also increasingly politicised by the Black Power movement. Britain had its own Black Power movement, inspired by its US counterpart, but rooted in the particularities of anti-colonialism and the experiences of Commonwealth immigrants in Britain.[11] Following Malcolm X's visit to London in February 1965, the Radical Action Adjustment Society (RAAS) and the Universal Coloured Peoples' Association (UCPA), headed by Obi Egbuna, were formed. Stokely Carmichael's visit to London in 1967 further catalysed discussions around Black Power in Britain, leading to the formation of the Black Unity and Freedom Party (BUFP) in 1970 and the Black Liberation Front (BLF) in London in 1971.[12]

Many activists who were involved with and politicised by organisations such as RAAS, UCPA, BUFP and BLF went on to set up a range of self-help groups. Supplementary schools, such as the Kwame Nkrumah School, the Malcolm X Montessori Programme, the George Padmore School, the South-East London Summer School and the Marcus Garvey School, were set up in response to the inadequate education system and West Indian children being branded as 'educationally subnormal', and the Free University for Black Studies was founded for older students.[13] Hostels and youth clubs were set up, such as Harambee and Dashiki, created by Brother Herman and Vince Hines respectively, who were both involved in RAAS, in order to provide holistic support for alienated Black youth.[14] To meet cultural needs, groups such as Keskidee taught arts, sculpture and creative writing, and various community bookshops were set up, such as the Black People's Information Centre, Unity Bookshop and New Beacon Books. Community newspapers and journals such as *Black Voice* (the journal of the BUFP), *Grassroots* (the official journal of the BLF) and *Freedom News* (the organ of the Black Panthers) were established to speak to communities and amplify their concerns. Self-help groups were not confined solely to the capital – in Manchester, Gus John helped to set up the George Jackson Trust, which provided accommodation, education and employment training for Black young people, and in Birmingham, the African-Caribbean Self-Help Organisation (ACSHO) ran a supplementary school and welfare advice service.[15]

And as the Black Women's movement, formed in response to the neglect of Black women's concerns by both the Black Liberation Movement and the Women's Liberation Movement,[16] gained momentum in the late 1970s, a host of groups were set up not only to address Black women's needs, but to campaign for the community as a whole. Groups including Brixton Black Women's Group, UBWAG, Elbow and Awaz came together under an umbrella organisation, OWAAD, 'one of the most decisive influences on Black women's politics in this country'.[17] Black feminist groups were also connected to and influenced by Black Power, with key activists such as Olive Morris and Gerlin Bean, who were foundational to Brixton Black Women's Group and OWAAD, also involved with British Black Power groups.[18]

The principles of self-help

The notion of self-help itself was influenced by Black Power. As Rosie Wild writes, 'self-help had always been a key tenet of Black Power philosophy and community work was a central feature of Black Power groups' activities'.[19] The Black Panther Party in the USA recognised that addressing basic needs and direct relief was the first step in fostering revolutionary consciousness in communities, and set up a food programme in the 1960s that provided free breakfast to inner-city neighbourhoods. As encapsulated by Fred Hampton, 'First you have free breakfasts, then you have free medical care, then you have free bus rides, and soon you have FREEDOM!'.[20]

Similarly in Britain, Black Power groups were small and localised, providing essential services for the poor and underresourced, and built on the principles of self-help. As noted in a tribute to Brother Herman, who is considered one of the founders of Black self-help in Britain, given by Wilfred Wood and Shona Edwards at the Ninth Annual Martin Luther King Lecture:

> Self-help means *self reliance* for a community. And, to achieve that, black people must return their skills to the community, learn not to be distracted by monies that come with strings, create our own opportunities without relying on outside agencies to provide them. Self-help is not the same as group selfishness. Genuine self-help will create *genuine unity* within a community.[21]

Here we can see some of the key principles of self-help articulated: sharing resources, rather than competing with each other for them; being self-sufficient without reliance on state funding; operating on the basis of solidarity, not charity; and a wider political agenda of organising against the violence of structural oppression, which either neglects a community's needs, or causes them in the first place. Underlying self-help organising is an awareness that the conditions in which we are made to live are unjust, and that we must organise collectively to meet those needs. Self-help is not an individualistic endeavour, but a way of strengthening communities through forging a unity that recognises that our ability to survive depends on each other.

Despite the term 'self-help' bringing connotations of rugged individualism and notions of 'pulling yourself up by your bootstraps', self-help has a radical meaning. Self-help forges community, through a recognition that our strength lies in looking after each other as a way of responding to structural violence. There are clear resonances between the terms 'self-help' and 'mutual aid' – defined by activist Dean Spade as the 'collective coordination to meet each other's needs, usually from an awareness that the systems we have in place are not going to meet them'.[22] I argue that the histories of self-help and mutual aid are intertwined and overlapping, and are carried forward by activists in the present day.

Now that I have mapped out the history and the politics of self-help organising led by Black communities in Britain, the following section will outline the work of three key organisations that were part of this history – Harambee (1969), UBWAG (1977) and Awaz (1977). I will trace the emergence of these organisations, how they provided for the community, what principles underpinned their work and what was their relation to the British state, particularly around the role of funding.

Harambee: Working together with young people

Brother Herman, an Antiguan builder, arrived in Britain in 1955, at a time when 'racism was stark, raw and unmediated'.[23] His concern for the Black community combined with his interest in Black Power led him to become one of the key figures in Black self-help initiatives. He built and taught at the Black House on Holloway Road, London, a cultural centre, hostel for the homeless and meeting place for local groups that was run by and for the Black community, initiated by RAAS.[24] The Black House was a source of inspiration for many people, described by Herman as 'one of the first times we built something for black people in England'.[25] It was eventually raided by the police and shut down, but many of its members went on to set up their own self-help initiatives.

After seeing how alienated Black young people perpetually fell into vicious cycles of homelessness or imprisonment, Herman set up Harambee (meaning 'working together' in Swahili) in Islington in 1969 after leaving the Black House. Harambee provided a range of services for young people, including educational programmes, bail hostel accommodation, prison visiting and teaching practical skills such as the physical restoration of buildings. It put into practice a 'holistic vision of rescue and regeneration' that went beyond liberal paternalism in order to help young people to help themselves and each other.[26] This involved restoring in young people a sense of self-confidence and self-reliance, which was often stripped away after being subjected to state violence and neglect, through a broad programme of rehabilitation by drawing on the support of lawyers, architects and teachers in the wider Black community who engaged with young people. Additional bases were set up in Haringey and Hackney.

Interactions with the state

Herman understood that self-help projects were about not just meeting a particular social need, but also defending such projects from attacks – whether from the media, the police or the local council. Whilst Harambee was focused on creating opportunities for young people, the state responded by raiding the premises and confiscating typewriters and books, allegedly motivated by the fear of Black Power spreading.[27] Because of the the racism of the state, and how it trickled down to every sphere of life for many, Black people had to organise to provide care for their communities themselves: 'No one expected a racist government to provide; no one wanted a racist social worker or teacher or race professional to intervene.'[28]

Initially, Harambee functioned without government money, relying instead on support from volunteers, the Church and the energies of young people to keep it going, enabling the people it served to determine the direction of the group. However, as Herman writes, 'the destruction [of Harambee] started with the intervention of government personnel and government money'.[29] Local councils could apply to the government for funding through the Urban Programme (known colloquially as the Urban Aid Programme), which singled out Black self-help groups for funding – groups that often had close associations with Black Power.[30] Many activists were critical of the Urban Programme. To receive funding, groups had to fit with the local council's aims, often leading to the dilution of their political messaging. Some activists viewed the Urban Programme as a strategy to bring radical self-organised groups into a state framework, which could be more easily controlled, monitored and subservient to government funding. The Urban Programme left activists in a difficult bind around the question of whether state funding could be used to achieve radical ends or whether it would inevitably dilute the political thrust of the movement.[31] On principle, Herman refused to take government money for many years before eventually accepting it.[32] As Wild writes, 'If the strategic aim of the Urban Programme was to separate the practical work of the Black Power movement from its ideological base and bring it into the orbit of the state, it was indeed successful.'[33] The question of how to acquire funds whilst remaining autonomous and committed to the group's principles remains a key issue that mutual aid activists navigate today.[34]

United Black Women's Action Group (UBWAG): Campaigning for the community

United Black Women's Action Group was formed in the summer of 1977 on Campsbourne estate in Haringey, north London, by a group of Black women who 'got together to bridge the widening gap between us from different parts of the world yet have many things in common'.[35] Tenants on the estate would meet regularly at the local dominos club, but when women began to use the space to discuss the issues they faced, their concerns were dismissed by men who wished to use the club as a space to escape everyday life. This pushed the women, mainly Black mothers, to set up UBWAG to address their needs.

As one of the founding members, Martha Osamor, recounts, a focus on *issues* united diverse communities and overcame colonial divisions, by bringing people together to fight for common goals.[36] Their aim, as articulated in their campaign material, was to assist Black women to help themselves, to meet the cultural and social needs of Black women and to take up the issues of concern for Black women.[37]

The need for Black women to be collectively and individually self-sufficient was at the heart of their activism, but also, the scope of their campaigns went beyond this, as they campaigned on issues around education, housing and policing for the community as a whole. Knowing one's rights was a crucial first step in building stronger communities, so they began by hosting workshops teaching women about their rights – rights on arrest, housing rights, women's rights, and their children's rights around education and school suspension.

Protecting Black youth – from schooling to policing

As Black mothers shared information, they began to build up a picture of what was happening across their communities, particularly in the education system. Young Black children were being suspended, excluded or demarcated as 'educationally subnormal'. Rather than seeing cases as one-off incidents, they began to see trends and patterns in the ways their children were being treated in schools. In response, UBWAG set up their own after-school club, as well as a pressure group that researched exclusions and shared information on how to appeal. This was at a time when up and down the country, galvanised by the 1971 publication of Bernard Coard's *How the West Indian Child Is Being Made Educationally Subnormal in the British School System*,[38] communities embraced the message of self-reliance and set up Saturday and supplementary schools across the country in response to racist assumptions about the intelligence of Black children.

A key tenet of self-help movements was community protection against state violence, and this was put into practice by UBWAG in their response to the policing of Black youth. Black mothers shared and documented how their children were being policed by the 'sus' law, a section of the 1824 Vagrancy Act that was used to prosecute young Black men before any offence had been committed.[39] In response, UBWAG helped to spearhead the Scrap Sus campaign, mainly led by Black mothers, which led a series of coordinated actions to stop police racist harassment and to protect Black neighbourhoods. The sus law was eventually repealed in 1981 following riots in Brixton and the resulting Scarman Report, although the legacies of sus live on through police stop-and-search powers that continue to target Black working-class communities.[40]

Building coalitions

Collaboration and coalition building were key to UBWAG's work, which involved linking up with other groups and encouraging them to take up the issues they raised, as well as joining groups and getting involved in their campaigns. As Martha Osamor recounts:

> We realised what was happening to us was happening all over the place. The idea grew of linking what we were doing and making a network to be an effective force. If you are going to have a law repealed, you are going to have to galvanise quite a lot of people.[41]

They joined the Haringey branch of the Organisation for Sickle Cell Anaemia Research to raise funds and awareness about the disease, and held public meetings as well as a forum for parents, children who suffered from the condition, doctors and social workers to meet. They also collaborated with the Haringey Labour Movement to organise a demonstration in support of Tony Anderson, a young Black boy who was harassed by the police for many years and eventually imprisoned.[42]

As UBWAG realised that what was happening in their estate in Haringey was mirrored in other parts of London, they joined OWAAD, a Black feminist umbrella movement that united many member organisations including Brixton Black Women's group, East London Black Women's Organisation and Awaz, the first feminist Asian women's collective in the UK. OWAAD campaigned not only for their own rights as women, but fought for the rights of the community as a whole – including around immigration, domestic violence, policing of Black communities – and for adequate health and welfare provision. Joining OWAAD and attending its first national conference in 1979 brought many more members to UBWAG.

Self-help groups were generative, with individuals going on to help set up or support other initiatives in nearby communities. Martha Osamor went on to support Dolly Kiffin, a mother of Jamaican heritage, who in 1981 founded the Broadwater Farm Youth Association (BWFYA), which became a haven for Black youth in Tottenham and across North London.[43] This was another key self-help group, which helped to create a community centre, a nursery, a women's centre and a tenants' room on the estate, driven by the visions of young people, as well as encouraging residents to give back to the community by becoming governors of schools and looking after the elderly.[44] But rather than being seen as an empowering space for young people, BWFYA was seen as a threat by police, and it was targeted repeatedly from 1982 to 1987.[45] As community campaigner Stafford Scott told researcher Jessica Pandian, 'I just think that police have an issue with young Black people who try to do for self. Police wanna criminalise and contain Black people, control how we move and where we go. And they have a real issue with Black empowerment.'[46]

Awaz: Challenging racism and sexism

Awaz, meaning 'voice' in Urdu, was the first South Asian women's collective in Britain, set up in 1977 by a handful of young South Asian women. Similarly to the other self-help groups outlined above, Awaz responded directly to needs; 'we desperately needed a way of addressing our needs and those of other Asian women', recounts anti-racist feminist activist Amrit

Wilson, one of the group's founding members.[47] South Asian women in Britain faced a double-edged sword – the racism of the state meant that they were often working in difficult and low-paid jobs and often faced racist violence on the streets as well as the paternalistic and colonial attitudes of the middle classes, but they also often faced patriarchal relationships at home. Whilst the predominantly male Black movement ignored issues around sexism, the predominantly white women's liberation movement did not see issues around racism as part of their remit. South Asian women were drawn to Awaz, as they needed a space they could claim as their own whilst taking a stand against both racism and sexism simultaneously.

Responding to needs in the community

As well as responding to specific needs, like other self-help initiatives, Awaz had a wider political purpose of fighting state racism. As Wilson explains, Awaz took a two-pronged approach: 'we exposed and confronted the state's racism and violence against women ... and at the same time demanded that the state provide services to Asian women in the context of domestic violence'.[48] One of their long-term projects was their campaign to set up refuges run by Asian women for Asian women facing domestic violence. For South Asian women, domestic violence was, and is, often compounded by state violence: insecure immigration status, poverty, inadequate housing and heavy-handed policing can all make it more difficult to leave an abusive relationship. There was therefore a need for specialist services that could provide holistic support. So, in the early 1980s they worked in collaboration with the Asian Women Community Workers Group to set up a refuge in south London that was to be a precursor of the Asha refuge.

The refuge was one of many Asian women's organisations that established themselves across the country, including Southall Black Sisters (SBS), a leading feminist organisation in London that helped women facing domestic violence.[49] As Anjona Roy explained to Wilson:

> These refuges and resource centres were set up by women who had identified problems and then came together to solve them. They had ownership of the issues, and looked at them in depth and holistically. It was because of their own experiences that they integrated educational work (about women's oppression or about how to manage in a racist society) into service provision.[50]

By recognising that minoritised women needed support that incorporated an understanding of larger societal issues – such as racism, sexism, cultural expectations and economic hardship – Awaz was able to provide holistic support *for* Asian women and *run by* Asian women who often had experience of dealing with domestic violence.

Exposing state brutality

But as well as filling an immediate need, Awaz also had a wider political purpose, which was to challenge the racism of the state and particularly the gendered aspects of immigration regimes. In 1979, they drew attention to the practice of virginity testing that some South Asian women were subjected to by immigration officials upon arrival in Britain. Under immigration laws, fiancées did not need a visa to join their soon-to-be husbands in the UK, but upon arrival they would be subject to a vaginal examination to 'check' they were virgins, to prove their eligibility for a visa.[51] This horrific form of state sexual abuse rested on patriarchal and misogynistic notions of virginity, and was also used against young girls to claim that they were too old to come to Britain to join their parents as dependants. To shed light on virginity testing, which was so often shrouded in shame, Awaz organised a powerful picket at Heathrow Airport, as well as a sit-in with OWAAD.

On 9 June 1979 they jointly organised a national demonstration against state brutality with Brixton Black Women's Group and the Indian Workers' Association (IWA). Holding a banner with the slogan 'Black people against state brutality', members of Awaz wore saris as a symbol of protest against rampant racism directed toward the South Asian community. Awaz also protested against poor working conditions by supporting the historic Grunwick strike in north-west London – a two-year strike lasting from 1976 until 1978, led mainly by Indian women who challenged their treatment by their employers – and also the lesser-known strike at Futters, a light engineering firm in Harlesden, north London, in 1979, where mainly Asian women workers walked out in protest at low wages, poor health and safety conditions, and victimisation of union activists.

The breakdown of the tradition of self-help

What happened to this tradition of self-help? Individual self-help endeavours broke down for a variety of reasons, but also changes to the state meant that the tradition as a whole began to fragment. After the uprisings of 1981 and 1985 and the resulting Scarman report, racial *disadvantage* was seen as the cause, with equal opportunities held up as the solution. Funds, such as the Urban Programme, became available to groups on an ethnic basis, which meant that groups began competing against one another for funding. This was in context of the Thatcher era, where cuts to public services and attacks on voluntary services were rife, meaning that self-help organisations were precarious and thus had to rely on state funding. Coming within the orbit of the state, when previously self-help groups had been self-funded, brought its own problems, including the professionalisation of self-help groups, often diluting their political aims, which were replaced with 'outputs' that had to be achieved in order to receive funding. As Sivanandan notes, this resulted in the breakdown of Black unity, which had previously been the basis of organising: 'groups began to fight one another for funds on an ethnic basis; they were no longer fired by the needs of the whole community'.[52]

Multiculturalism further cemented differences between Black communities, which fragmented into African Caribbean, African and Asian cultural identities, seeing each other as competitors rather than as part of the same struggle, and the race relations industry took equal opportunity programmes into local authorities and government departments. As Sivanandan summarises, 'in effect, it transferred Black politics from the streets into the town halls'.[53]

'Unfinished activisms': Tracing the continuities to the present day

Although many self-help initiatives fragmented and broke down during this period, I would argue that this history of community self-help does not have a fixed end date. The principles of self-help live on through mutual aid organising, which made a resurgence during the COVID-19 pandemic, with activists carrying forward this history to the present day. In a memorial lecture for Steve Biko held in Pretoria, South Africa, in 2016, Angela Davis drew attention to the relationship between past struggles and present-day activism:

> The struggles of our contemporary times should be thought of as productive contradictions, because they constitute a rupture with past struggles, but at the same time, they reside on a continuum with those struggles, and they have been enabled by activisms of the past. They are unfinished activisms.[54]

Using this notion of 'unfinished activisms' I argue that histories of self-help are reactivated in the present day by activism that carries this legacy forward. Activists today not only create a 'rupture' with past struggles but also disrupt the violence of the state using a variety of methods.

Responding to COVID-19

As demonstrated in the examples of Harambee, UBWAG and Awaz, mutual aid grows in the context of insufficient state support or action, so it is unsurprising that in times of deep social and economic crises, mutual aid groups flourished globally. The COVID-19 pandemic exacerbated deeply embedded race, class and gender inequalities, and overwhelmed public health, medical care and disaster support systems across the world. Governments and state agencies were ill prepared to contain and suppress outbreaks, and often it was mutual aid groups that filled the gap. In the UK, mutual aid groups mobilised to support people on the margins – in particular the homeless, those without recourse to public funds, the elderly and the undocumented. Mutual aid groups built on the history of self-help groups by responding directly to the communities' needs. Set up on the basis of mutual aid, not charity, groups provided groceries and medicine deliveries; organised collective hardship funds; sourced phones and laptops for children who had to attend school virtually from home; distributed masks to foodbanks, care homes and homeless shelters; and provided emotional support to isolated people who were shielding at home. As the pandemic spread globally, so did forms of mutual aid and solidarity, with thousands of mutual aid groups emerging across the world.

At a time when capitalism reduces us to consumers with competition at the bedrock of free-market ideology, mutual aid (the antithesis of competition) thrived during the COVID-19 crisis, built on the premise that there is enough for everyone if we redistribute our resources and organise collectively. However, it is worth pointing out that COVID-19 mutual aid groups are not monolithic, and there was a multiplicity of views within groups that did not always cohere around a radical politics, leading to tensions and contradictions over questions such as who is prioritised within community organising, whether to work with local authorities such as the police, how to create processes of accountability and how to navigate cooption by the state.[55]

Resisting police violence: Bail funds and prisoner support groups

As COVID-19 raged on through 2020, another crisis was foregrounded – the epidemic of police violence. Video footage of the police killing of George Floyd rocked the world, and a global mass movement protesting police brutality erupted into the foreground. As scholar-activist Barbara Ransby noted, this was a 'watershed moment'.[56] In the UK, one such watershed moment was the pulling down of the statue of seventeenth-century slavetrader Edward Colston, which was rolled into the river at a Black Lives Matter protest in Bristol.[57] But for every action there is a reaction, and the sustained backlash to Black Lives Matter's mobilisations in response to oppression and unjust conditions has been fierce.[58] At least 135 people were arrested at protests in the summer of 2020, and in Bristol, four people, now known as the 'Colston Four', were selected from a crowd of hundreds and charged with criminal damage.

An often-overlooked aspect of mutual aid organising is fundraising for defence funds and prisoner support organising for those facing state repression as a result of participation in direct action. This was put into practice by the community in Bristol who launched a campaign to support the

Colston Four by encouraging in-person and virtual attendance at the trial, raising money for trial costs and holding a teach-in as well as an eight-minute silence to remember those enslaved by Colston.[59] Bristol Solidarity Defendant Group[60] is a grassroots group that organises to support activists imprisoned following the 'Kill the Bill' demonstration against the Police, Crime, Sentencing and Courts Bill in Bristol in March 2021.[61] They continue to organise letter writing campaigns and fundraisers, as well as publicising the messages of activists from inside prison to the wider public. This is an important aspect of mutual aid that shows imprisoned activists that they are not alone and maintains a network between those in prison and those outside.

Resistance to immigration raids: Building networks of resistance

On 13 May 2021 an exhilarating image circulated on social media – the photo of two men, beaming with their fists raised in the air, as they were released from an immigration removal van on Kenmure Street, Glasgow, after an eight-hour stand-off on the streets.[62] Hundreds of locals and people from across the city, including Muslim families who were celebrating Eid, surrounded the van, stopping it from moving, chanting 'These are our neighbours, let them go', whilst one activist from the No Evictions network squeezed under the van for nearly eight hours. This inspiring collective action cannot be divorced from the long history of refugee and migrant solidarity in Glasgow, which laid the groundwork enabling groups to mobilise quickly on the day.[63] In the year following the action on Kenmure Street, a flurry of resistance to immigration raids happened across the country, including in Dalston and Peckham in London, in Nicholson Square in Edinburgh, and in Chorlton in Manchester.[64]

Whilst community rejection of immigration raids has a rich history that goes back decades, it's clear that the acceleration of resistance to raids is a cumulative result of anger at the conditions facing asylum seekers, the building of anti-raid networks that connect people locally, as well as the power of social media in reaching the wider community.

Anti-raids mutual aid groups such as the Anti-Raids Network (ARN) in London engage in a multiplicity of tactics including physically blocking raids, providing training on rights and legal knowledge about raids, collecting intelligence on raids, and sharing real-time information on when a raid is happening. Central to their work is building a network of resistance that brings together communities to fight immigration controls – 'our weapon is our solidarity'.[65]

As with most mutual aid groups, ARN supports resistance based on 'doing it ourselves' without any interference from the state or from political parties. As well as responding directly to raids, they have a wider political purpose of standing against all forms of state oppression and understanding resistance against raids as 'one way we can come together with our neighbours and create communities of mutual aid that can challenge racism, capitalism and social control'.[66]

Conclusion: Responding to an evolving crisis

Times of crisis, as well as being points of upheaval and collapse, can also be pivotal points of political awakening. It is no surprise that COVID-19 led to the proliferation of mutual aid groups, which held the potential to engage millions of people globally into a mode of organising that seeks to understand and address the root causes of systemic, interlocking crises. However, as Dean Spade writes, 'we need groups and networks that do not disappear after the peak of the crisis, but instead become part of an ongoing, sustained mobilization with the capacity to support people and keep building pressure for bigger wins'.[67]

From the ferment of the late 1970s, when racism was 'raw, stark and unmediated', groups such as Harambee, UBWAG and Awaz emerged to respond to community needs, and to fill specific gaps that were neglected by, or caused by, the state. We have seen a return to this mode of community organising in the years following the outbreak of the COVID-19 pandemic. Tracing the lineages of self-help organising in mutual aid activism today reveals many continuities – the importance of cross-coalitional organising and connecting to other groups on the ground; the need to be autonomous and an awareness of the pitfalls of working with the state, particularly around the question of funding; and the need to protect initiatives and individuals from state repression. By combining direct relief with a broader political purpose that attempts to understand why the crisis is happening in the first place, both self-help initiatives and mutual aid groups hold the potential to transform our conditions radically through building new futures, based on community care, solidarity and liberation. As writer Rebecca Solnit notes:

> I sometimes think that capitalism is a catastrophe constantly being mitigated and cleaned up by mutual aid and kinship networks, by the generosity of religious and secular organisations, by the toil of human-rights lawyers and climate groups, and by the kindness of strangers. Imagine if these forces, this spirit, weren't just the cleanup crew, but were the ones setting the agenda.[68]

Rather than temporary responses, mutual aid and kinship networks have always existed – operating on a continuum with the past whilst also breaking with it in a 'productive contradiction'.[69] Because of changes to the state and particularly the entrenchment of neoliberalism, and the violence of austerity combined with the normalisation of racism, mutual aid groups operate today on a very different political landscape from that of self-help groups in the 1960s and 1970s. Creeping authoritarianism and the changing nature of state repression have eroded the right to protest and criminalised mutual aid efforts. Austerity cuts to services mean that community-based provisions are working in a more difficult environment and are increasingly relied upon to fill the gap, whilst the far right is able to exploit economic issues to push a racist agenda. Police powers have become more advanced and more diffuse, operating not just on the streets but in schools too, which means that strategies to resist have also had to adapt. Racism, and particularly the hostile environment, has made it even harder for those without papers to be able to resist. In this context, solidarity across differences can be hard to forge, particularly as differences can be easily weaponised, pitting groups against each other and encouraging us to turn inward. But despite the changing nature of the world, mutual aid organising continues to respond to needs and remains an antidote to the atomisation of neoliberalism.

This history of self-help led by Black communities is rarely known, even by activists who continue to forward their legacy through mutual aid organising, which is a gap this chapter seeks to fill. History is a powerful tool. It gives us context for the world we live in today, and hope when we hear stories of resistance and struggle. Important archival work is already happening at the grassroots, with connections between past struggles and the present day being creatively explored, often by young people who seek out this history. For instance, the *Stop Sus!* project, led by a group of year 10 students, sought to explore the history of the sus laws in the context of the present day. The group interviewed activists (including Martha Osamor from UBWAG), and created a zine, poems and learning resources for an anti-racist curriculum. As one member of the group said, 'this is the history they want us to forget'.[70] Retrieving this history and ensuring that memories of resistance are more accessible is crucial, as it connects us back in time to those who have come before us and provides historical context for the struggles that continue in the present day.

Notes

1. Sophia Siddiqui, 'We Starved but We Shared', *IRR News* (7 May 2020), https://irr.org.uk/article/we-starved-but-we-shared/ (accessed 18 December 2022).
2. Peter Kropotkin, *Mutual Aid: A Factor in Evolution* (London: Heinemann, 1908).
3. Angela Y. Davis, Seventeenth Steve Biko Memorial Lecture (2 September 2016), University of South Africa, quoted in Brenna Bhandar and Rafeef Ziadah (eds), *Revolutionary Feminisms* (London and New York: Verso, 2020), p. 2.

4 A. Sivanandan, 'From Resistance to Rebellion: Asian and Afro-Caribbean Struggles in Britain', *Race & Class*, 23:2/3 (1981), 111–52.
5 The Commonwealth Immigrants Act created a second class of non-white British citizens.
6 Jenny Bourne, 'The Beatification of Enoch Powell', *IRR News* (21 November 2007), https://irr.org.uk/article/the-beatification-of-enoch-powell/ (accessed 11 January 2023).
7 Sivanandan, 'From Resistance to Rebellion', p. 136.
8 For an analysis of the relationship of South Asian actors to 'political Blackness' and how this has changed over time and between generations, see Saffron East's chapter in this volume.
9 St Clair Drake, 'The "Colour Problem" in Britain: A Study in Social Definitions', *The Sociological Review*, 3:2 (1955), 197–217.
10 Hakim Adi, 'Forgotten Comrades? Desmond Buckle and the African Communists', www.hakimadi.org/articles-2 (accessed 1 June 2024).
11 Rosie Wild, '"Black Was the Colour of Our Fight": Black Power in Britain 1955–1976', PhD thesis (University of Sheffield, 2008).
12 John Narayan, 'British Black Power: The Anti-Imperialism of Political Blackness and the Problem of Nativist Socialism', *Sociological Review*, 67:5 (2019), 945–67.
13 Bernard Coard, *How the West Indian Child Is Being Made Educationally Subnormal in the British School System: The Scandal of the Black Child in Schools in Britain* (London: New Beacon Books, 1971).
14 Vince Hines went on to set up the National Federation of Self-Help Movements in 1975, an umbrella organisation that aimed to lead and support collective self-help efforts.
15 This is a non-exhaustive list of examples. For a further, often overlooked, example of self-help activism in the local community, see Talat Ahmed's chapter in this volume, which explores the work of the Scottish Asian Action Committee (SAAC), a community organisation based in Glasgow that offered individual support for the Asian community and promoted collective anti-racist action.
16 Nydia A. Swaby, '"Disparate in Voice, Sympathetic in Direction": Gendered Political Blackness and the Politics of Solidarity', *Feminist Review*, 108:1 (2014), 11–25.
17 Beverley Bryan, Stella Dadzie and Suzanne Scafe, *Heart of the Race* (London: Verso, 2018), p. 164.
18 See *ibid.*, pp. 140–8, for the relations between Black women and Black Power.
19 Wild, 'Black Was the Colour of Our Fight', pp. 173–4.
20 Fred Hampton quoted in Joshua Bloom and Waldo E. Martin, Jr, *Black against Empire: The History and Politics of the Black Panther Party* (Oakland: University of California Press, 2016), p. 177.
21 Wilfred Woods and Shona Edwards, 'Brother Herman: Tribute to a Founder of Black Self-Help in Britain', *Race & Class*, 37:4 (1996), 71–9.
22 Dean Spade, *Mutual Aid: Building Solidarity during This Crisis (and the Next)* (London and New York: Verso, 2020), p. 17.

23 Woods and Edwards, 'Brother Herman'.
24 Wild, 'Black Was the Colour of Our Fight', p. 112.
25 Woods and Edwards, 'Brother Herman', p. 73. There was some controversy around the workings of the Black House, and particularly the leadership of Michael X. See Wild, 'Black Was the Colour of Our Fight', pp. 112–14.
26 Woods and Edwards, 'Brother Herman', p. 74.
27 *Ibid.*, p. 75.
28 *Ibid.*, p. 74.
29 *Ibid.*, p. 75.
30 £7,00,000 was granted by the Home Office to the Urban Programme. Some of the Black self-help groups that received aid included Harambee, Southall Education and Community Project, Pakistani Association Youth and Community Centre, and the George Jackson House Trust. See A. Sivanandan, 'Race, Class and the State: The Black Experience in Britain', *Race & Class*, 17:4 (1976), 347–68 (p. 364).
31 Wild, 'Black Was the Colour of Our Fight', pp. 171–6.
32 Herman eventually accepted a grant but refused to follow the rules on how it should be spent or accounted for, resulting in his serving short prison sentences for embezzlement; see *ibid.*, p. 175.
33 *Ibid.*
34 Spade, *Mutual Aid*, pp. 154–9.
35 Black History Collection, Institute of Race Relations, London, 01-04-04-01-04-02-28, UBWAG.
36 Harmit Athwal and Jenny Bourne, 'It Has to Change: An Interview with Martha Osamor', *Race & Class*, 58: 1 (2016), 85–93 (p. 89).
37 Black History Collection, Institute of Race Relations, London, 01-04-04-01-04-02-28, UBWAG.
38 Coard, *How the West Indian Child Is Being Made Educationally Subnormal*.
39 Institute of Race Relations, *Policing against Black people* (London: Institute of Race Relations, 1979).
40 Joseph Maggs, 'Fighting Sus! Then and Now', *IRR News* (4 April 2018), https://irr.org.uk/article/fighting-sus-then-and-now/ (accessed 1 June 2024); Leslie George Scarman, *Scarman Report: The Brixton Disorders, 10–12 April 1981* (London: HMSO, 1981).
41 Athwal and Bourne, 'It Has to Change', p. 89.
42 Black Cultural Archives, London, UBWAG (1978), https://artsandculture.google.com/asset/RQEmVbPilLhtpQ?childAssetId=5AEwUCcjkQ7GcA (accessed 1 June 2024).
43 'Broadwater Farm: A "Criminal Estate"? An Interview with Dolly Kiffin', *Race & Class*, 29:1 (1987), 77–85.
44 Athwal and Bourne, 'It Has to Change', pp. 90–1.
45 Jessica Pandian, 'The Policing of Black Youth Project: From Broadwater Farm to the Present', *IRR News* (20 October 2020), https://irr.org.uk/article/policing-of-black-youth-projects/ (accessed 1 June 2024).
46 *Ibid.*

47 Amrit Wilson, *Dreams, Questions, Struggles: South Asian Women in Britain* (London: Pluto Press, 2006), p. 161.
48 *Ibid.*, p. 163.
49 Rahila Gupta, *Homebreakers to Jailbreakers: Southall Black Sisters* (London: Zed Press, 2003).
50 Amrit Wilson, *Dreams, Questions, Struggles*, p. 164.
51 Amrit Wilson, *Finding a Voice: Asian Women in Britain* ([Montreal]: Daraja Press, 2018), pp. 87–90.
52 Kwesi Owusu, 'The Struggle for a Radical Black Political Culture: An Interview with A. Sivanandan', *Race & Class*, 58:1 (2016), 6–16 (p. 12).
53 *Ibid.*, 14.
54 Davis, Seventeenth Steve Biko Memorial Lecture, quoted in Bhandar and Ziadah, *Revolutionary Feminisms*, p. 2.
55 Amardeep Singh Dhillon, 'The Politics of Covid-19: The Frictions and Promises of Mutual Aid', *Red Pepper* (4 May 2020), www.redpepper.org.uk/the-politics-of-covid-19-the-frictions-and-promises-of-mutual-aid/ (accessed 11 January 2023).
56 Jenny Bourne, '"This Is What a Radical Intervention Could Look Like": An Interview with Barbara Ransby', *Race & Class*, 62:2 (2020), 14–23.
57 Haroon Siddique and Clea Skopeliti, 'BLM Protesters Topple Statue of Bristol Slave Trader Edward Colston', *Guardian* (7 June 2020), www.theguardian.com/uk-news/2020/jun/07/blm-protesters-topple-statue-of-bristol-slave-trader-edward-colston (accessed 1 June 2024).
58 Adam Elliott-Cooper, '"Britain Is Not Innocent": A Netpol Report on the Policing on Black Lives Matter Protests in Britain's Towns and Cities in 2020', *Netpol* (2020), https://netpol.org/wp-content/uploads/2020/11/Britain-is-not-innocent-web-version.pdf (accessed 1 June 2024).
59 The Colston Four were eventually found not guilty in January 2022; see Damien Gayle, 'BLM Protesters Cleared over Toppling of Edward Colston Statue', *Guardian* (5 January 2022), www.theguardian.com/uk-news/2022/jan/05/four-cleared-of-toppling-edward-colston-statute (*sic*) (accessed 1 June 2024).
60 https://twitter.com/bristoldefenda1 (accessed 2 June 2024).
61 Tom Anderson, 'Bristol Protesters Sentenced to over Five Years in Prison Last Week Refuse to Be Silenced by the Courts', *The Canary* (15 November 2022), www.thecanary.co/uk/news/2022/11/15/bristol-protesters-sentenced-to-over-five-years-in-prison-last-week-refuse-to-be-silenced-by-the-courts/ (accessed 1 June 2024).
62 Immigration raids in the UK, led by Immigration Compliance and Enforcement teams, target migrants in the UK, at their homes, at their places of work or in public places, tearing up and terrorising communities. See Corporate Watch, *The UK Border Regime: A Critical Guide* (2018), https://corporatewatch.org/wp-content/uploads/2018/10/UK_border_regime.pdf (accessed 1 June 2024).
63 Teresa Piacentini, Smina Akhtar, Ashli Mullen and Gareth Mulvey, '"It's Not Like It Just Happened That Day": Anti-Racist Solidarity in Two Glasgow Neighbourhoods', in Stamatis Poulakidakos, Anastasia Veneti and Maria

Rovisco (eds), *Social Movements and Everyday Acts of Resistance: Solidarity in a Changing World* (London: Routledge, 2023), pp. 72–86.
64 Tassia Kobylinska, '"Let Them Go": Dalston Stands Up to Police Immigration Raid', *Counterfire* (16 May 2022), www.counterfire.org/article/let-them-go-dalston-stands-up-to-police-immigration-raid/ (accessed 1 June 2024); Xander Richards, 'Edinburgh: Nicolson Square Protests "Force Home Office to Abandon Raid"', *The National* (5 May 2022), www.thenational.scot/news/20118425.edinburgh-nicolson-square-protests-force-home-office-abandon-raid/ (accessed 1 June 2024); Benny Hunter, 'How Our Community in Peckham Fought the Hostile Environment – and Won', *Open Democracy* (13 June 2022), www.opendemocracy.net/en/evan-cook-close-peckham-immigration-raid-home-office/ (accessed 1 June 2024); Adam Maidment and Stephen Topping, 'Protesters "Barricade" Themselves in Front of Immigration Vehicles as Officers Attempt Raid', *Manchester Evening News* (14 August 2022), www.manchestereveningnews.co.uk/news/greater-manchester-news/protesters-barricade-themselves-front-immigration-24755395 (accessed 1 June 2024).
65 ARN, 'About', https://antiraids.net/about/ (accessed 1 June 2024).
66 *Ibid.*
67 Spade, *Mutual Aid*, p. 53.
68 Rebecca Solnit, '"The Way We Get through This Is Together": Mutual Aid Organising under Covid-19', *Guardian* (14 May 2020), www.theguardian.com/world/2020/may/14/mutual-aid-coronavirus-pandemic-rebecca-solnit (accessed 11 January 2023).
69 Davis, Seventeenth Steve Biko Memorial Lecture, quoted in Bhandar and Ziadah, *Revolutionary Feminisms*, p. 2.
70 Maggs, 'Fighting Sus!'.

Part III

Anti-racism, memory and identity

9

Memory, multiculturalism and anti-racism in east London, 1990–2006

Finn Gleeson

The 1980s and early 1990s brought fundamental shifts in the institutional bases, organising principles and cultural perceptions of anti-racism in Britain. In the early 1980s, greater numbers of activists from street-based, direct action organisations achieved footholds in city councils, where they won new support from the state through three primary means. These were, as Adam Lent notes, the adoption of hiring practices pursuing greater diversity in council workforces, the organisation of set-piece public events celebrating radical politics such as the 'London against Racism' Festival, and a large increase in public funds given to anti-racist campaigning groups.[1] Many of these new council employees retained their connections with those outside the state, feeding funds and vocal support back to direct action organisations. The Greater London Council (GLC) and Metropolitan County Councils' abolition in 1986 removed this organisational nexus, leaving those organising in communities and those who remained in the state without the vocal political support, funds or networks they had earlier possessed.

The national Labour Party, meanwhile, remained ambivalent about anti-racism. As Paul Gilroy notes, journalistic and Conservative discourse often framed radical local councils as a threat to the nation's moral fabric, linking Black stridency to the destabilisation of the social order.[2] In this light, Darcus Howe read Neil Kinnock and Roy Hattersley's mobilisation against the expansion of Black Sections at the 1984 Labour Conference as an effort to soothe the minds of middle England, distancing the national party from the spectre of unrest after the 1981 riots and Ken Livingstone's proclamation of a 'rainbow coalition'.[3] While, as Camilla Schofield, Florence Sutcliffe-Braithwaite and Rob Waters note, urban anti-racism in the 1980s had always comprised more radical and moderate groupings, the stigmatisation of the former in journalistic and political discourse made it increasingly anathema for Kinnock's Labour. Many of the decade's more moderate figures and ideas, however, enjoyed enhanced influence in government from the mid-1990s.[4] Upon assuming office, New Labour presented diversity as a central feature of British public life; in 1997, for instance, Gordon Brown celebrated the existence of a 'multicultural, multi-ethnic and multinational Britain'.[5] New Labour accelerated the GLC's initiatives to increase Black and Asian representation in the workplace, expanding the pursuit of diversity to high public office and business.[6] Of particular interest to this chapter, Labour also identified *culture* as a key site through which to pursue their policies on race. Tony Blair created the Department for Culture, Media and Sport (DCMS), which established among its initial key goals 'excellence', 'access' for the previously marginalised and the development of new urban economies.[7] Cultural production – through theatre, music, art, film and literature – became an increasingly significant site of the connected pursuits of economic renewal, and the symbolic inclusion of the marginalised into the national community. We might see continuity here with the GLC's anti-racist cultural policies; indeed, Tony Banks, who had been chair of the GLC's Arts Committee, served as Sports Minister in the new DCMS.[8]

New Labour's embrace of the more moderate aspects of municipal anti-racism was accompanied by an antipathy toward its more radical variants, which sought economic transformation, or confrontations with racism's central place in imperial and postimperial British history.[9] Scholars have done much to trace the relationship between memory and race politics in this period. Georgie Wemyss notes that a focus on 'tolerance' served to emphasise the benevolence of the white majority and make minorities' presence conditional on that benevolence. Despite its liberal veneer, this silenced histories of colonialism and violence, and in doing so reproduced a 'hierarchy of belonging' in the present.[10] Paul Gilroy, meanwhile, argues that the ascent of a statistically insignificant number of Black people to the top of Britain's corporate structures obscured those structures' inherent exclusion and racism.[11] An emphasis on Britain's diversity and tolerance, then, produced first a political complacency, and second a hostility to those deemed anathema to these values. After the 2001 urban riots in Burnley, Bradford and Oldham, and the 11 September 2001 and 7 July 2005 attacks, New Labour increasingly turned against a Muslim population they perceived as illiberal, insular and violent.[12] Calls for these groups to assimilate to the values of liberal Britain drew on the same ideals of harmony and tolerance that had, a few years earlier, been central to celebrations of the multicultural nation.

In what follows I analyse these developments' influence on wider cultural debates about racism and history in 1990s and 2000s Britain by exploring one prominent site in these debates: east London. Through its port, the East End became, throughout the nineteenth and early twentieth centuries, a unique contact point between the industrial society of metropolitan Britain and the cargo, sailors and craft of the Empire and the wider world. In the late nineteenth century, the poverty of the workforce who powered the East End's industry led the area to become central to panics about the 'condition of England' and the racial 'fitness' of the imperial body. Throughout the postwar period, the area's status as a point of arrival for migrants made it one of the most vivid sites of British multiculture, and of electoral, violent and state-based racism. The area possessed among the highest levels of support for the National Front in the 1970s, and for the the British National Party who, in the 1993 local elections, averaged 13 per cent in Newham, won one council seat in Tower Hamlets and came close to winning several others.[13] Between 1991 and 1995, 589 incidents of racist abuse on the Isle of Dogs alone were reported to the Metropolitan Police, 179 of which were actual bodily harm.[14]

The area offers, then, a rich site to explore the intellectual genesis, life, and retreat of multiculturalism as it existed in 1990s and 2000s Britain. I characterise multiculturalism in this period as the process by which opposition to racism achieved the status of a broad cultural ideal – a form of common sense, central to the public life of the liberal new millennium – divorced from any notion of historical consciousness or contemporary struggle. This phenomenon was a legacy of the mixed fortunes of municipal anti-racism in the 1990s: specifically, of the wide cultural embrace of its moderate dimensions, and simultaneous political marginalisation of more radical variants and their attendant historical consciousness. The first part of the chapter explores debates surrounding a text published in 1990: popular historian Gilda O'Neill's oral history of Cockney women, *Pull No More Bines*. O'Neill's work reflected a growing anti-racist sentiment within British culture, as well as this sentiment's tendency to mischaracterise and misdiagnose racism's historical origins. The second part shows this multiculturalism's fragility in the early 2000s. It analyses author Michael Collins's *The Likes of Us*, to demonstrate that while the liberal left failed to grapple effectively with the formative place of race and empire in informing contemporary racism in London, the right celebratorily constructed a class identity in which whiteness and class were mutually constitutive. Collins's work received a level of respectability and critical acceptance, showing that racialised white identities retained real purchase in London's politics, belying the purported 'triumph' of multiculturalism. I conclude with Geoff Dench, Kate Gavron and Michael Young's *The New East End* (2006), exploring a moment when left-leaning sociological opinion actively disavowed the history of empire and postimperial racism to construct an image of the state as actively welcoming an entitled and insular Bengali community. This book's reception contributed to a broader resurgence in assimilationist politics in these years.

Through these debates, I explore the significance of memory to the history of multiculturalism in 1990s and 2000s Britain. Memories of race and empire were locked in a close, shifting and mutually constitutive relationship with developments in race politics. Anti-racism was reformulated after 1990 as a cultural ideal that celebrated interpersonal harmony and tolerance as British values, but marginalised radical activism or critical intellectual thought, producing a notion of racism as an aberration deriving from political neglect and economic alienation. This narrative often relied on the conscious disavowal of histories of race and empire. In turn, it generated a support for the racially excluded that was limited, conditional and – in the mid-2000s – summarily discarded.

Gilda O'Neill and the fate of anti-racist thought

Born in Bethnal Green in 1951, the popular historian and author Gilda O'Neill published five histories of and fifteen novels about the area in a prolific literary career between 1989 and 2010. Her childhood coincided with Bethnal Green's rise to prominence – following the publication of Michael Young and Peter Wilmott's *Family and Kinship in East London* (1957) – as perhaps *the* archetypal 'traditional working-class community'. These years were formative: much of O'Neill's work would, like that of Young and Wilmott, characterise the area according to its strong, supportive relationships between family and friends, upheld by intimate networks of terraced housing.[15] Like Wilmott and Young's, O'Neill's evocation of this world was also propelled by the inevitable sense of its loss, through successive waves of out-migration and urban redevelopment. Reflecting on O'Neill's life, one contemporary noted that her publicity events attracted large 'queues of people wanting her to sign books, responding to her warmth and generosity, wanting to share their own memories'.[16] This suggests the marked affective power that O'Neill's work had for many older and former East Enders whose lives had been profoundly reshaped by the urban, economic and social upheavals of the postwar period, an impression that is corroborated by the several hundred reader letters held at O'Neill's archive.[17] O'Neill's work showed a solidarity with the area's large migrant population. She thought at length about how to challenge the racist accounts of change she encountered among white correspondents and readers. One such moment arose around the research for her oral history of Cockney women's working holidays to pick hops in Kent, *Pull No More Bines* (1990).[18] The project used hop-picking as a means to explore East End women's sociability and community, and track later changes to community life. O'Neill assimilated racism, a priori, into her existing, class-based accounts of economic neglect and marginalisation through deindustrialisation and Thatcherite redevelopment. She conceptualised racism as the result of an alienation derived from these forces, and sought to counter it as such, reorienting local frustration away from support for the far right and toward community action against redevelopment. Yet letters to O'Neill suggested that racism was not an aberration, but had deeper roots in local culture and identity.

O'Neill's account of local racism centred the alienation produced by postwar redevelopment, which turned the East End's fabled 'close-knit communities' of terraced, largely pedestrianised streets into vast, alienating estates and concrete tower blocks.[19] Her subjects found themselves living in crumbling 'cardboard cities', using 'over-stretched social services, and an ailing National Health Service'.[20] O'Neill noted that it was in this context, 'of our discussion about change and loss of community', that racist comments 'were made'. 'The people they were blaming were being used as a target for their anger.'[21] O'Neill, then, conceived racism as emerging from the social upheaval, economic loss and anomie deriving from postwar redevelopment, suburbanisation and disinvestment in welfare. White Londoners' racism figured as a regrettable false consciousness, a misdirected resentment absolving the politicians and redevelopers responsible for the area's deindustrialisation and redevelopment. Here O'Neill sought, sincerely, to identify racism's origins, rooting her analysis in a sensitive and close reading of the experiences of the communities she worked with, and had herself grown up in.

O'Neill quoted a *Guardian* column by Simon Jenkins, reflecting on a recent opinion poll finding that a majority of Britons perceived the country to be in a state of moral decline:

> The idea of a country declining into immorality ... is stated as a fact by a majority of Britons. They feel threatened by some looming incoherence. They long for a golden age of yore. They read of yuppies on the rampage in the City, *of stabbings on the underground*, of lager louts battling police in market towns, of fare-dodging, vat fraud and insider dealing. They sense what Prince Philip has called 'an avalanche of lawlessness threatening to engulf our civilization'. *Beyond lie darker forebodings: that this decline may be due to precisely the sort of community that we are struggling to create, one founded on individualism, acquisitiveness and wealth.*[22]

O'Neill then continued in her own words:

> No matter that, for most of us, our experience is of a reasonably safe world, the tabloid press tells us that we are self-deluding fools. Our urban paranoia is inflamed, and we wait, knowing that the mugger is out there, waiting for us in the shadows ... People can, and some do, lay the blame for their helplessness on the alien 'other' who invades their landscape.[23]

O'Neill and Jenkins, then, echoed significant aspects of Gilroy and Stuart Hall's analyses of the relationship between discourses of national 'crisis' and racism. In Jenkins's account, cultural and political narratives of violence, anarchy and dissolute alcoholism combined to reify the city as a site of the corruption of the nation's values. This narrative, as Gilroy notes, implied the responsibility of racialised migrants for national disintegration by signalling tropes around Black criminality and violence.[24] O'Neill's more explicit approximation of the discursive constructions of the figure of the 'mugger', 'urban paranoia' and the invasion of 'alien other' similarly echoed Hall's classic argument that the 'mugging' moral panic served to construct a larger crisis of state authority and the dissolution of the white national community.[25] Crucially, for Hall and Gilroy, race was the animating force of these larger declinist discourses; the figure of the migrant underwrote all other concerns, embodying the deterioration of the built environment and the loss of urban community. But more, these cultural discourses – in Hall's account – actively compelled popular hostility to migrants: 'race', in Hall's crucial formulation, was 'the prism through which British people are called on to live through, to understand, and then to deal with the crisis conditions'.[26]

Yet O'Neill, and Jenkins, attributed this sense of national disintegration to an ascendant, rampant individualism that eroded social bonds and stimulated a paranoid anomie. For O'Neill, interviewees' racism was an aberration, a symptom of East Enders' and Britons' experience of deindustrialisation and alienating redevelopment. This was reflected in O'Neill's response to the racism that her interviewees expressed. When meeting East Enders putting forward racist accounts of change, O'Neill rejected 'any arguments that put unsupported blame on any group', asserting that the forces of deindustrialisation and comprehensive urban redevelopment were responsible for the area's deterioration.[27] This, O'Neill hoped, would direct residents' resentment toward neglectful councils and redevelopers, and away from migrants.

Letters to O'Neill from her readers suggest a vernacular participation in discourses similar to those identified by Hall and Gilroy, in which race functioned as a powerful force, animating and giving shape to wide conceptions of cities and the nation's decline. While O'Neill strikingly recognised many of this discourse's core tenets, she attributed racism solely to the economic exclusions of the late twentieth century. O'Neill's sincere and critical engagement with racism's core precepts marks the ascendancy of a broadly defined *liberal multiculturalism* as a central tenet of British public life, while her attribution of it purely to economic changes represents a reluctance to engage with it as a phenomenon with independent significance, historically present in local identities and itself shaping broader understandings of change. In this sense, O'Neill's anti-racism reflects the specific conditions of the early 1990s, when opposition to racism became a form of common sense, but the marginalisation of radical anti-racist thought and scholarship meant that its origins as a social phenomenon were often reduced to a by-product of other, economic, forces.

In an otherwise glowing letter, one reader responded directly to O'Neill's reflection on racism in *Pull No More Bines* as follows: 'personally I feel it's not your or my place *to* confront [older women's racism]; especially as most of these women *are* elderly ... obviously it *is* part and parcel of their lives, rightly or wrongly'.[28] This correspondent rejected O'Neill's attempts to challenge residents' racism, suggesting that such efforts were impractical, anachronistic and even intrusive, bringing to mind the longer histories of local white residents' identification with racial and national ideals. After the East End was particularly acutely affected during the Blitz, Cockneys embodied discourses of the popular sacrifice of the 'People's War'. The postwar ideal of the welfare state was framed as a reward for that sacrifice, signifying a close, reciprocal relationship with the state. Through this, Cockneys were central as a new mid-century nation was imagined, characterised at once by its trenchant social conservatism, economic egalitarianism and increasing affluence.[29] As John Davis recently noted, the 1950s marked a period of affluence and relative stability, especially in the East End's Docklands, marked by full employment and settled, ethnically homogeneous communities.[30] O'Neill's correspondents lamented the loss of this world, identifying strongly with conservative and racialised notions of the nation. Race emerged as an important component as they measured subsequent 'decline' against this ordered, prosperous, homogeneous mid-century moment.

The Second World War was foundational to these myths of the local community. One letter writer remembered the conflict in fairly representative terms: 'we were on the front line of the last war and I saw some terrible things with people dead in the street or as near as. When the bombing was on you just got on and made the tea as if nothing had happened.'[31] This pointed to residents' seemingly innate stoicism. Another letter writer presented the memory of wartime sacrifice in more explicitly racialised terms, recalling a recent trip to a museum in the East End where she had encountered a large group of local school pupils: 'I'm sure the little Black and Asian children I saw on my visit hadn't a clue who Mr. Hitler was!'.[32] This comment suggests two beliefs: first, in migrants' fundamental disregard of one of the central episodes of the nation's modern history, and second, that migrants had not contributed to the war effort. Instead, the war was conceptualised as a narrowly European conflict, in which Britain stood stoically alone against the march of fascism. Victory in the war was the zenith of the community's achievements and its history, while the dignity, stoicism and sacrifice that delivered it were conceptualised in narrowly national and racialised terms.

The war provided the yardstick against which subsequent change was measured. While one correspondent recognised the importance of the National Health Service, he believed its creation had 'created a group of hypochondriacs that are always a bit poorly, always adding to the load on the service and making it unsustainable'. Here were a people softened by the comfort of an expanded welfare state, which would protect them from want. This correspondent then proceeded to suggest that this weakening was also reflected in permissiveness and legal reform, where 'the laws of this country are making life slowly slide into anarchy. The police cannot operate because there is no law to back them up.' Reflecting that his father worked until 'nearly or just over 80', this correspondent also rejected contemporary concerns about unemployment: 'poverty in this country is a matter of choice'.[33] In contrast to the area's stoic, industrious and patriotic mid-century working-class, this correspondent narrated the arrival of a sickly, lazy population inhabiting lawless cities. If this suggested that national and urban decline had an almost racial dimension, brought on by the postwar settlement's softening of the population's innate character, it was in large part also the direct result of the arrival of migrants. This correspondent ended his letter by recalling London dockworkers' strike in support of Enoch Powell in May 1968, signalling his agreement with 'a lot of the things Our Mr Powell has preached'.[34] For this letter writer, then, migration figured as a particularly stark example of the broader corruption, since mid-century, of a national character marked by stoic sacrifice and industriousness.

Another letter, written jointly by a married couple, centred on their emigration from East London to New Zealand in 1965:

> We have only been back twice in thirty years. It all seemed even more crowded than before. Friends say 'England isn't for the English' anymore. So many coloured faces, and they are taking over the local businesses and public transport. I understand that Tesco's only employ ethnic people. My sister-in-law says that whenever someone moves out of their street a coloured person moves in. The white nationals feel in the minority. The streets were full of litter and the traffic fumes were hard to take. I feel that the East End as we knew it has certainly deteriorated.[35]

These correspondents linked pollution and litter to the arrival and apparent dominance of migrants. Again, London stood in for broader deteriorations in the dignified character and culture of 'England' itself, and of 'white nationals'. Migrants, in these accounts, seemed to embody broader processes of the *decline* of the area and the nation's stoic, dignified, conservative and homogeneous mid-century ideals. Rather than being an aberrant reaction to economic and social displacement, racism sat at the very centre of these longer life narratives, animating and giving shape to longer perceptions of the decline of the area's character and its connection to the conservative, dignified nation of mid-century. In this sense, letters to O'Neill point to the utility of contemporary critical scholarship on race and nation in understanding the racism she sought to address and combat. Yet her mischaracterisation of residents' testimonies revealed her assimilation of residents' racism into her a priori account of the area's economic neglect and, more broadly, the increasing marginalisation of critical discussions about racism's origins. In this sense, it suggests that anti-racist views' prominence in cultural production, divorced from more theoretical engagements with racism's origins, severely limited understandings of white identities and resentments from the early 1990s.

Michael Collins and the resurgence of whiteness

Yet if the left did not fully grapple with these racialised identities' persistence in the 1990s, they returned to prominence the following decade as a conspicuous fixture of cultural politics on the right. Michael Collins was born in Walworth in 1961, south of the Thames from O'Neill's Bethnal Green, but sharing many of the same social characteristics and mythologised histories. Collins left his comprehensive school at sixteen, training to become a tailor, before gaining employment writing for television documentaries about London's working class on Channel Four.[36] His account of the place of race in local identities directly contradicted O'Neill's. He published *The Likes of Us: A Biography of the White Working Class* (2004), a lament for the passing of a local white community for whom racial, national and class-based identities were mutually constitutive and firmly rooted in local cultures and identities. The book offered a history of Bermondsey between 1890 and 2000 with a close emphasis on Collins's family. Here, Collins constructed a self-conscious 'white working class' whose long presence and service entitled them to ownership of the area, but who had been marginalised and betrayed by mass migration, permissiveness and comprehensive urban redevelopment. The book's second part used this central narrative of racialised betrayal to launch a political attack on contemporary multiculturalism. Here, Collins positioned an identification with race and nation as enduring, historically formative influences on local identity: contemporary racism, he suggested, was a logical response to the government's betrayal of the 'white working class'.

Collins presented the racialised and imperial nation as central to Victorian and Edwardian working-class Londoners' identities. Cockneys, he remembered warmly, had given a rapturous reception to music hall acts offering racialised and exotic images of the Orient, including 'Indian Princess Zenobia'; 'Professor Desmonti and Nubar Hassan'; and 'Black Cookey', a performer who regularly appeared in blackface.[37] Furthermore, for Collins, Cockneys had also made significant – though overlooked – economic contributions to the Empire. Remaining in the late Victorian period, he invoked the Independent Labour Party politician Pete Curran to note that while London's 'white working class' had 'helped build England into the country on which the "sun never sets", they lived in slums in which "the sun had never risen"'.[38] Cockneys' economic exclusion was exacerbated by the phenomenon of late Victorian and Edwardian middle-class commentators travelling from the West End into east and south-east London to write voyeuristic literature on the 'slum', stigmatising and dehumanising working-class residents.[39] Following these sections on popular culture, labour and urban poverty, Collins offered a highly classed account of the First World War, in which incompetent officers harshly enforced rationing and conscription, condescending to and endangering patriotic local boys.[40] In these vignettes we see the fundamental duality of Collins's narrative emerge. London's 'white working class' figured as avatars of the late-nineteenth and early-twentieth-century imperial nation: giving their lives for it, providing the labour that built its wealth and patronising cultural outlets offering racialised representations of the colonies. Yet still, Britain neglected them: employers exploited their labour, slum landlords left them in squalor and commentators stigmatised them.

Collins traced further changes in the relationship of the 'white working class' with the state in the postwar period, presenting redevelopment, permissiveness and in-migration from the declining Empire as signifying governmental betrayal of the white majority. Between the late 1950s and early 1970s, successive councils oversaw Bermondsey's comprehensive redevelopment, replacing the intimate, familiar built environment with high-rise blocks that uprooted residents, eroded social bonds, introduced unfamiliar and antisocial tenants, and bred vice.[41] Collins spent one section rebuking claims that 'mugging' was a racialised moral panic, asserting that perpetrators of violent robbery were almost entirely Black.[42] On his estate, Collins recalled the installation of 'community murals' in one space where many attacks had occurred. 'The crimes continued', Collins remembered sardonically, 'but at least the victims got to bear witness to painted images of smiling multiracial faces for the duration of the attack'.[43] For Collins, the paintings themselves symbolised the contempt of a liberal housing authority, blithely embracing a multiculturalism that almost inevitably led to violence against whites.

Following these developments:

> Many of the urban white working-class saw themselves more as part of an ethnic group united by colour and culture, than as a class united by work. Those on the left, who argued that working-class culture had been threatened with extinction by American-style consumerism, were confronted with the fact that the white working class themselves believed that the greatest threat was the arrival, *en masse*, of black immigrants.[44]

In Collins's account, then, a (racial, imperial) nationalism had always been central to 'white working-class' identity. In the nineteenth and early twentieth centuries, London's 'white working class' had powered the Empire's industries, fought its wars and taken pride in it culturally, but had been neglected by British society. In the postwar period, Collins conceived Britain's eschewal of its earlier racial and imperial politics and its embrace of comprehensive redevelopment as analogous and mutually constitutive parts of the liberal state's betrayal of the true national community. If Collins's 'white working class' were indispensable to the earlier imperial state, they had – in recent decades – been 'colonised' by 'different races and nationalities as well as a new middle class'. The area was increasingly 'defined by Tate Moderns, lofts, lattes and multiculturalism'.[45] If O'Neill's work reveals a left-wing conceptualisation of racism as a temporary aberration deriving from alienation and neglect following social and economic change, Collins reveals a right-wing account of markedly similar communities' identities in which race, nation and empire were of foundational significance. Collins's 'white working class' figured as a sort of spurned *Volk*, first neglected by the imperial nation, which could not do without them, then betrayed by its liberal postwar successor and even 'colonised' themselves. In their limited historical consciousness, accounts such as O'Neill's were incapable of fully appreciating, or effectively engaging with, the long and complex place of race and empire in informing local identities, and right-wing politics.

Shortly after the book's publication, Paul Gilroy called Collins an 'intellectual outrider for the BNP'. Though partially a response to the party's growing success in the 2004 local and European elections, this still associated Collins with the political fringe.[46] But what seems remarkable about *The Likes of Us* is precisely its role in facilitating criticism of multiculturalism in respectable critical and journalistic circles. The book won the left-leaning Orwell Prize for political writing in 2005, and was widely endorsed in national newspapers for its attacks on a political 'elite' variously derided as 'upper class', 'metropolitan' and 'lily-livered liberals'.[47] *Times* journalist Mark Hodkinson ranked Collins's 'agenda-setting' book alongside E. P. Thompson's *The Making of the English Working Class* and Ellen Wilkinson's account of the Jarrow March, *The Town that Was Murdered*.[48] Several reviews of Collins's work used it as a platform to engage in their own attacks on multiculturalism. Also in *The Times*, Phil Baker commended the book for challenging the 'McCarthyite intensity of enforced "multiculturalism"' and the climate it created, in which 'the white working class is the only ethnic group it is ok ... to look down on'.[49] Bryan Appleyard described its central narrative as a 'passionate, human, brave and beautifully controlled' description of 'an appalling act of cultural genocide'.[50] Leo McKinstry in the *Telegraph* wrote that while 'Anti-racism has become the central theme of today's political culture', the 'white working class' were the 'one ethnic group that it is perfectly acceptable to insult and ignore', going on to frame the Macpherson Report as a liberal witch hunt.[51] The book's assertion of an embattled and persecuted white minority, then, received widespread critical support from journalists and critics across the right and portions of the liberal left. Many repeated Collins's framing of the 'working class' as necessarily white, and shared his conviction that contemporary multiculturalism had harmed this group and undermined their dignity.

The Likes of Us romanticised racialised white identities as historically embedded, closely held and uniquely persecuted. Moreover, the book was the catalyst for a larger, concentrated attack on the purported injustices of multiculturalism in the pages of the nation's leading newspapers. Journalists used *The Likes of Us* to engage in a defence of a politicised whiteness, rooted in a perception of the erosion of the cultural fabric of the nation through a liberal cultural policy. While an embrace of multiculturalism had become widespread within cultural production after the 1990s, O'Neill's work was suggestive of the disinclination of figures on the left to conceptualise racism as a force closely linked to British history, nationhood and culture. But it was precisely the erosion of the nation's historic, racial and cultural foundations that formed the basis of this wider political attack in the *Mail*, *The Times* and the *Telegraph*. Taken together, these moments offer insights into one root of the political fragility of the multiculturalism that characterised early-twenty-first century Britain. That is, its foundational marginalisation of critical thought about race and empire.

The New East End and the retreat of multiculturalism

This turn against multiculturalism accelerated following the publication by the Institute for Community Studies of *The New East End*, the published results of an investigation designed as a follow-up to Wilmott and Young's *Family and Kinship in East London*. While *Family and Kinship* was hugely influential in critiquing the alienation caused by postwar redevelopment, the East End had since gained prominence as a site of persistent popular racism. The widespread violence and the electoral success of the far right in the 1970s and 1990s suggested that efforts to understand the area's famed community might require new emphases and lines of enquiry. From the high point of New Labour's embrace of multiculturalism in the late 1990s and the early new millennium, the government and media, after the 11 September and 7 July bombings and the 2001 urban riots, increasingly cast British Muslims as a conservative, insular group, and a drain on a welfare state to which they had not contributed. This was the context in which the results of *The New East End* were published in 2006, following a decade of local research by Geoff Dench, Kate Gavron and Michael Young, before Young's death in 2002.

The authors foregrounded racial tensions from the outset, suggesting their sympathy to local white residents. While other scholars had 'either studiously avoided' the topic or 'simply put [tensions] down to white racism', they argued that 'dismissing white behaviour as merely irrational constituted a failure of analysis'.[52] They rooted London's contemporary diversity firmly within British imperial history, noting the significance of imperial trading networks to the construction of the docks, the flourishing of related industries and the arrival of early Bengali settlers following their service on British trading ships. In this sense, the book's authors showed that the Bengali community's arrival in London was closely tied both to imperial servitude and to the creation of London's industrial and commercial wealth.[53] Correspondingly, the authors' ethnographic interviews with local white residents led them to 'realise the importance of the Second World War. Many white respondents of all ages linked their complaints about draining the welfare state with remarks to the effect that Bangladeshis had not been here during the war, in a way which suggested this reduced their entitlement.'[54] (These assertions that the Bangladeshi presence did not have a longer history were incorrect.)[55] Since 1945, the authors claimed, the nature of welfare allocation itself had changed; while the state began this period by offering welfare as a reward for longest service, it had since moved to prioritise those in most severe need.[56] This had created a 'culture of entitlement', they wrote, which 'is now deeply entrenched in British society as a whole, and there can be no quick solution to the problem it creates'. Indeed, 'putting all this together', they surmised,

> What seems to have happened in Britain is that the compact between classes which made the late 1940s and early 1950s a golden age of aspirations and expectations has been undermined by the consequences of the unravelling of Britain's imperial history. When the welfare state was codified at the end of the Second World War, metropolitan Britain was still sealed off politically from the rest of the empire. So the extension of social democracy was a limited exercise, and gave rights to ordinary British people which they felt both to have been earned and to be valuable. With the subsequent dismantling of the empire, and the granting of residence and citizenship rights in Britain of a tiny proportion of the millions of former imperial subjects, this national legacy became shared out among a much larger group. In the eyes of some, the original post-war compact has been devalued as a result.[57]

The book's concluding chapter, 'Reclaiming Social Democracy', turned to offer policy recommendations. There, the authors wrote, Britain needed to end the 'culture of entitlement', abandoning the apparent prioritisation of the neediest to return to the principle of rewarding the longest and most substantial contributions. By this, they clarified, they meant the 'indigenous' white population.[58] Here was an uneven, contradictory conceptualisation of the area's imperial and postimperial history. Whereas Dench, Gavron and Young earlier made colonial entanglements central to the area's industrialisation, commercial wealth and diverse population, they abandoned this analysis later – at the crucial moment of offering policy prescriptions – to point to the primacy of white residents' entitlements and contributions. This selective account of the area's history entirely omitted the increasing restrictions placed on migrant citizenship between the 1960s and 1980s and the difficulties Bengali migrants faced in receiving support from the state.[59] This facilitated the text's notion of a 'national legacy' being shared among undeserving former colonial subjects, but obscured the reality that the colonies' contributions to Britain's wealth had increasingly been overlooked by the state. Young and the Institute for Community Studies had historically been, and remained, associated with the political left, seeking to contribute to progressive policy debates through social scientific research and thought.[60] Here, the authors' disavowal of their earlier emphasis on the close, significant relationships among Bengalis' presence, imperial history and postimperial racism served as a crucial intellectual foundation for policy proposals encouraging government to curtail the welfare granted to the descendants of migrants.

The book struck a chord with Trevor Phillips, then chair of the Commission for Racial Equality (CRE). In addition to his past chairmanship of the Runnymede Trust (1993–98), Phillips's major credentials included joint authorship of the triumphalist history *Windrush: The Irresistible Rise of Multi-Racial Britain* (1998), a text that reveals much of his conception of racism in Britain. The book suggested that the docking of the *Windrush* was the moment at which race became a significant factor within British history, going on to offer a triumphant story of a hesitant society coming to accept the permanent presence of a previously alien people initially invited to meet high labour demand in the postwar years. This was a narrative of Britain becoming liberal, culminating in a present marked by 'tolerance' and harmony.[61] Its appeal to the Labour Party spoke, more, to the centrality that a celebratory view of Britain's liberal values and culture had acquired within conceptions of multiculturalism by this period.

Phillips attended *The New East End*'s launch and penned an endorsement for the cover of the paperback edition, calling it 'one of the most important books I've read for a long time'.[62] In this, the chairman of the CRE found himself allied to surprising political voices. Reviewing *The New East End* in the *Daily Mail*, the director of Migration Watch, Andrew Green, championed the book's 'lessons for us all as we move on from naïve multiculturalism', arguing that the book disproved that there were real 'benefits of immigration'.[63] In *The Times*, meanwhile, Michael Collins suggested that the book vindicated one of the major arguments of *The Likes of Us*: that the needs and desires of the 'White working-class', a self-conscious 'ethnic' group who 'felt themselves united by colour', had been unjustly neglected.[64]

In the book's narrative and its reception, we see left-leaning social scientists and leaders of the state's anti-racism apparatus progressing from the contention that postwar Britain had benevolently granted migrants comfortable livelihoods to an assertion that the entitlement of migrants was threatening that success. Phillips was a prominent voice throughout the following decade in the assimilationist turn within British discourse on race, increasingly arguing that state multiculturalism could lead to *de facto* informal segregation, and that the welfare state's generosity to migrants was undermining its long-term sustainability.[65] In this, he was a leading figure as the highpoint of late 1990s multiculturalism, oversaw by New Labour, gave way to what scholars have termed the 'retreat of multiculturalism'.[66] *The New East End* was a prominent moment in this development, and one that revealed the innate contradictions and conditionality of this period's multiculturalism. Commentators and the state eschewed the historic consciousness that had animated much earlier anti-racism. In place of a critique of the place of race and empire at the centre of British history and politics, they moved toward a celebration of the increasingly liberal and benevolent character of the nation. *The New East End* and Phillips's *Windrush* suggest that this changing historical consciousness was a significant intellectual driver as sociological opinion and race-relations experts disavowed the persistence of contemporary discrimination against migrants and their descendants. This generated the paradoxical situation in which left-leaning think tanks and the government-appointed head of the CRE came to the same policy prescriptions as the chair of Migration Watch and a writer vocally criticising the betrayal of a politicised whiteness. In this sense, the marginalisation of critical analyses of the place of racism in British history and contemporary society, and its replacement by a historical consciousness emphasising 'tolerance' and 'harmony', were central to the genesis of this period's multiculturalism, its innate fragility, and its precipitous collapse and 'retreat'.

Conclusion

In the 1990s, the Blair government came to emphasise the significance of tolerance, diversity and multicultural harmony as central values of British public life and cultural production. This represented a significant continuity with more moderate aspects of the street-based and municipal anti-racism of the 1970s and 1980s. But it was accompanied by a rejection of more radical aspects of this earlier formation, including critical discussions about the historic place of race and empire within British politics. East London – a site that has long been central to both British multiculture and racism – offers a rich case study for understanding the impact of these policies on cultural debates about race, nation and empire in the 1990s and 2000s. Gilda O'Neill, a left-wing writer with anti-racist convictions, assimilated her accounts of local racism into an a priori analysis of white East Enders' economic neglect, despite the incongruence of this reading with the content of many letters sent to her by readers. This mischaracterisation of racism was particularly significant given the resurgence, the following decade, of a defiant, politicised 'white working class' identity. Michael Collins's *The Likes of Us* attacked contemporary multiculturalism and urban redevelopment as mutually constitutive symbols of the state's betrayal of the rightful national community, constructing a markedly similar racialised identity to those articulated by O'Neill's respondents. Finally, the following year, *The New East End* criticised the welfare state's indulgence of 'entitled' Bengalis, actively contradicting its earlier emphasis on the significance of empire to disavow migrants' longer service to the area and call for the prioritisation of white residents' needs. This marked a significant moment in the longer 'retreat' of multiculturalism, in which memories of the history of 'race' in Britain came to focus on the nation's benevolence and tolerance, denying the significance of contemporary discrimination against minorities.

Emphasising changing forms of memory politics is crucial, then, to understanding the genesis, inherent weakness and ultimate collapse of the multiculturalism that characterised British public life and culture in the 1990s and early 2000s. O'Neill's simultaneous repudiation of racism and misdiagnosis of its origins were symptomatic of the marginalisation of critical discussions of the relationship among race, nation and empire in Britain from earlier periods of anti-racism. *The Likes of Us*, however, suggested that identification with a (racialised and imperial) nationalism was widely felt, closely held and politically influential. The book's narrative was endorsed in many of the country's leading newspapers and among the judges of the Orwell Prize. If O'Neill sought to address racism by recentring economic displacement and reasserting the primacy of class identities, her readers' letters and Collins's work suggest that race was, in many cases, immanent to those identities. While the left failed effectively to confront racism's central place in local culture, the right celebrated that centrality as the basis of an attack on multiculturalism. Finally, *The New East End* and Phillips's *Windrush* offer vivid case studies into the active role that the disavowal of imperial histories played in the framing of Britain's historic 'tolerance' and 'benevolence', and the denial of contemporary racial inequity. They reveal the centrality of a limited, triumphant reading of British history in moving away from the perceived excesses of multiculturalism in the mid-2000s, and bringing left-leaning social scientists and the head of the CRE into political alignment with Collins and Migration Watch. In this sense, we can – through an attentiveness to the politics of memory – grasp the ways in which the multiculturalism of the 1990s and 2000s ultimately carried the seeds of its own destruction.

Notes

1 Adam Lent, 'The Labour Left, Local Authorities and New Social Movements in the Eighties', *Contemporary Politics*, 7:1 (2001), 7–25 (pp. 7–8).
2 Paul Gilroy, 'The End of Anti-Racism', *Journal of Ethnic and Migration Studies*, 17:1 (1990), 71–83 (pp. 71–4).
3 Darcus Howe, *Black Sections in the Labour Party* (London: Race Today, 1985), p. 7.
4 Camilla Schofield, Florence Sutcliffe-Braithwaite and Rob Waters, 'The Privatisation of the Struggle? Anti-Racism in the Age of Enterprise', in Florence Sutcliffe-Braithwaite, Ben Jackson and Aled Davies (eds), *The Neoliberal Age? Britain since the 1970s* (London: UCL Press, 2021), pp. 199–225 (p. 201).
5 Ibid.
6 Ibid., p. 203.
7 Jonathan Gross, 'The Birth of the Creative Industries Revisited: An Oral History of the 1998 DCMS Mapping Document' (2000), King's College London, www.kcl.ac.uk/cmci/assets/report.pdf (accessed 10 March 2023), pp. 5–6.
8 Hazel Atashroo, 'Beyond the "Campaign for a Popular Culture": Community Art, Activism and Cultural Democracy in 1980s London', PhD thesis (University of Southampton, 2017), p. 77.
9 On historical analyses of British racism within earlier forms of anti-racism, see Rob Waters, *Thinking Black: Britain 1964–1985* (Berkeley: University of California Press, 2019), pp. 93–124, 125–64.
10 Georgie Wemyss, *The Invisible Empire: White Discourse, Tolerance and Belonging* (London: Routledge, 2016).
11 Paul Gilroy, 'We Got to Get Over before We Go Under: Fragments for a History of Black Vernacular Neoliberalism', *New Formations*, 80 (2013), 23–38 (p. 25).
12 Nasar Meer and Tariq Modood, 'The Multicultural State We're In: Muslims, "Multiculture" and the "Civic Re-Balancing" of British Multiculturalism', *Political Studies*, 57 (2009), 473–97.
13 Nigel Copsey, *Contemporary British Fascism: The British National Party and the Quest for Legitimacy*, 2nd edn (London: Palgrave Macmillan, 2008), p. 59.
14 Janet Foster, *Docklands: Cultures in Conflict, Worlds in Collision* (London: UCL Press), p. 270.

15 Peter Wilmott and Michael Young, *Family and Kinship in East London* (London: Penguin, 1957).
16 Alison Joseph, 'Gilda O'Neill, 1951–2010', *History Workshop Journal*, 72:1 (2011), 335–7 (pp. 336–7).
17 Reader Letters and Other Communications, Archive of Gilda O'Neill, Bishopsgate Institute, London (AGO), O'NEILL/4.
18 Gilda O'Neill, *Pull No More Bines: Hop Picking – Memories of a Vanished Way of Life* (London: The Women's Press, 1990), p. 135.
19 *Ibid.*, pp. 126–8, quote at p. 126.
20 *Ibid.*, p. 155.
21 *Ibid.*, p. 134.
22 *Ibid.*, p. 156 (my emphasis).
23 *Ibid.*, p. 157.
24 Gilroy, 'The End of Anti-Racism', p. 73.
25 Stuart Hall, Chas Critcher, Tony Jefferson, John Clarke and Brian Roberts, *Policing the Crisis: Mugging, the State, and Law and Order* (London: Macmillan, 1978).
26 Stuart Hall, 'Race and "Moral Panics" in Postwar Britain', in Paul Gilroy and Ruth Wilson-Gilmore (eds), *Stuart Hall: Selected Writings on Race and Difference* (Durham, NH: Duke University Press, 2021), pp. 56–70 (p. 63).
27 O'Neill, *Pull No More Bines*, p. 135.
28 Reader Letters to Gilda O'Neill, AGO, O'NEILL/4 (original emphasis).
29 Gareth Stedman-Jones, 'The "Cockney" and the Nation, 1780–1988', in Gareth Stedman-Jones and David Feldman (eds), *Metropolis London: Histories and Representations since 1800* (London: Routledge, 1989), pp. 272–324 (p. 279).
30 John Davis, *Waterloo Sunrise: London from the Sixties to Thatcher* (Princeton: Princeton University Press, 2022), p. 217.
31 Reader Letters to Gilda O'Neill, AGO, O'NEILL/4.
32 *Ibid.*
33 *Ibid.*
34 *Ibid.*
35 *Ibid.*
36 Michael Collins, 'The Myth of Multiculturalism', *Guardian* (21 May 2007), www.theguardian.com/commentisfree/2007/may/21/inaseasonsimilarto (accessed 6 March 2023).
37 Michael Collins, *The Likes of Us: A Biography of the White Working Class*, 2nd edn (London: Granta, 2005), pp. 50–1.
38 *Ibid.*, p. 44.
39 *Ibid.*, pp. 35–6.
40 *Ibid.*, p. 98.
41 *Ibid.*, p. 137.
42 *Ibid.*, p. 192.
43 *Ibid.*, p. 206.
44 *Ibid.*, pp. 188–9.
45 *Ibid.*, p. 11.

46 Laurie Taylor, 'Low Blows of a Class Warrior', *Independent* (16 July 2004), www.independent.co.uk/arts-entertainment/books/reviews/the-likes-of-us-by-michael-collins-5544852.html (accessed 27 April 2023).
47 Other positive reviews include Hephizibah Anderson, 'Paperbacks', *Daily Mail* (10 June 2005), 51; Mark Simpson, 'To Their Manor Born', *Independent on Sunday* (25 July 2004), 43; Boyd Tonkin, 'The Week in Books', *Independent* (15 April 2005), 99; and Julie Burchill, 'My Choice', *The Times* (11 December 2004), 234.
48 Mark Hodkinson, 'Critic Chart', *The Times* (5 May 2007), 180.
49 Phil Baker, '*The Likes of Us: A Biography of the White Working Class* by Michael Collins', *Sunday Times* (19 June 2005), 302.
50 Bryan Appleyard, 'The Class that Time Forgot', *Sunday Times* (11 July 2004), 252–3.
51 Leo McKinstry, 'In Defence of the White Working Class', *Daily Telegraph* (15 November 2006). Published in February 1999, Sir William Macpherson's inquiry into the Metropolitan Police's investigation into the murder of Stephen Lawrence found that the force was 'institutionally racist'. This is often characterised as a significant moment in the history of policing in Britain, as well as in the history of state racism more broadly.
52 Geoff Dench, Kate Gavron and Michael Young, *The New East End: Kinship, Race and Conflict* (London: Polity, 2006), p. 2.
53 *Ibid.*, 'Introduction', pp. 1–10; Chapter 2, 'Settlement of the Bangladeshis', pp. 33–52.
54 *Ibid.*, p. 4.
55 See, for instance, Caroline Adams (ed.), *Across Seven Seas and Thirteen Rivers: Life Stories of Pioneer Sylheti Settlers in Britain* (London: THAP, 1987).
56 Dench et al., *The New East End*.
57 *Ibid.*, p. 6.
58 *Ibid.*, pp. 223–34.
59 On national immigration law infrastructure, see Nadine El-Enany, *Bordering Britain: Law, Race and Empire* (Manchester: Manchester University Press, 2020), pp. 73–6. On local histories, see Sarah Glynn, *Class, Ethnicity and Religion in the Bengali East End: A Political History* (Manchester: Manchester University Press, 2014), pp. 6–31.
60 Here, see Lise Butler, *Michael Young, Social Science, and the British Left, 1945–1970* (Oxford: Oxford University Press, 2020).
61 Trevor Phillips and Mike Phillips, *Windrush: The Irresistible Rise of Multi-Racial Britain* (London: HarperCollins, 1998).
62 On the book launch, see 'The Simmering Pot', review of *The New East End*, *The Economist*, 378:8465 (16 February 2006), www.economist.com/britain/2006/02/16/the-simmering-pot (accessed 9 June 2024). For Phillips's endorsement, see Gavron et al., *The New East End*, frontispiece.
63 Andrew Green, 'Betrayal of Brick Lane: An Important New Book, Analysing the Effect of Mass Immigration on London's East End, Finds Rage and Resentment

among ALL Communities and Asks Deeply Disturbing Questions', *Daily Mail* (4 March 2006).
64 Michael Collins, 'The White Flight to the Right', *The Times* (20 April 2006), 20.
65 Trevor Phillips, interviewed by Rob Berkeley on 7 April 2009, for *The Struggle for Race Equality: An Oral History of the Runnymede Trust, 1968–2008*, London, British Library Sound Archive.
66 Meer and Modood, 'The Multicultural State We're In'.

10

Tartan inclusivity or workers' internationalism? The St Andrew's Day Anti-Racism March and Rally in Scotland

Talat Ahmed

In October 2022, the Trades Union Congress (TUC) launched its anti-racism manifesto, stating 'Over the past two years, the TUC's Anti-Racism Task Force has scrutinised our movement, and found us wanting. We acknowledge that the trade union movement and individual unions still have some way to go to represent Black workers fully.'[1] The TUC has an Anti-Racism Action Plan adopted by Congress that resolves to 'refresh, renew and reboot the movement's campaigning, organising and bargaining work' to tackle racial inequalities in our workplaces and communities.[2] This represents a positive development, in that it forcefully acknowledges the problems of deep-seated racism within society and shows a determination to counter and challenge this. However, the manifesto also highlights the weaknesses and inadequacy of trade union campaigns historically in fully meeting this challenge.[3]

Trade unions in Britain and elsewhere have, however, long played a key role as a bulwark against fascism. In the 1970s, amid economic crisis and rising unemployment, the fascist National Front saw a rise in their electoral fortunes from barely 12,000 votes in the 1970 general election to 77,000 votes in the February 1974 general election and then to 114,000 votes in the October 1974 general election.[4] In response, the General Council at the TUC Annual Conference in 1974 declared that 'trade unions should actively oppose racialism within their own ranks' as well as the organised far right.[5] The role of the trade union movement in combating fascism and beginning the process of uniting its members in solidarity with each other has been a central pillar of anti-racism within trade unionism in the postwar period. Historic slogans such as 'An injury to one is an injury to all' and 'United we stand, divided we fall' have been the hallmarks of defining solidarity and a relationship of equals in the labour movement. Implicit in this is a belief that workers' associations are able to overcome racism as it is in the interest of unity for trade unionism.

One positive example of this work around interracial solidarity in recent decades is the St Andrew's Day Anti-Racism March and Rally event organised by the Scottish Trades Union Congress (STUC) every November since 1988. Each year for over three decades now, the STUC has organised and led groups of workers behind trade union banners in Glasgow to commemorate Scotland's patron saint's day as an anti-racist celebration. In this they are joined by members of Scotland's Black communities (primarily Asian but also African Caribbean and others), anti-racist activists and civic organisations, which include leading government ministers, councillors and members of the Scottish Parliament. Is this due to a modern Scottish 'exceptionalism' whereby 'tartan inclusivity' is inherently progressive? Or is this annual demonstration part of a longer tradition within the labour movement rooted in workers' internationalism from below? This chapter will investigate the origins of the St Andrew's Day anti-racism event and locate it within the broader history of modern Scotland. As such it seeks to interrogate traditions of anti-racism within the trade union movement in order to consider whether questions of Black and white unity are forged in paternalism bestowed from above or based in grassroots workplace and community activism. The chapter will probe the degree to which labour internationalism in Scotland has been consciously built from below, or whether the Scottish anti-racist tradition has been mythologised through liberal civic nationalism from above.

Finally, it aims to offer some lessons and insights for anti-racist work and campaigning in the twenty-first century. Today, there are debates around 'allyship' and solidarity, and the meaning and relevance of ideas of 'political Blackness'. The contemporary fashion for American phrases such as 'people of colour' seems to be attractive for a new generation of activists in Britain who see this as an inclusive category and are also concerned with demonstrating their 'allyship' with those experiencing racism. Though understandable, these conversations are often conspicuous by a lack of historical reference or understanding of past anti-racist struggles. Debates over political Blackness are ongoing and pertinent to contemporary anti-racist activism, which is why Saffron East's chapter in this volume is welcome. The political term 'Black' has its roots in the Black Power movement of the 1960s, where 'Black' was a term of pride to be used by all peoples of both African and Asian descent. This chapter will use Black in this political sense and will also demonstrate how the term Asian was used as a unifying framework to rally resistance to racism as opposed to the fragmentation of identity politics. It will also explore some of the tensions between ideas of 'allyship' and those of solidarity through an examination of how a very Scottish anti-racism event has its roots in not just the trade union movement but also the self-activity and self-organisation of Asian communities in Scotland.

Scotland, race and empire

The question of race and racism has long been characterised as essentially an 'English' problem that has no place or presence north of Gretna Green. Political rhetoric from the top of society signals a message of an open, 'welcoming' Scotland that celebrates diversity. This positivity is reinforced by a hospitable narrative around immigration that was epitomised in the 2014 independence referendum, whereby all those who had made Scotland their home, irrespective of birth place, nationality, religion, skin colour or language, were entitled to vote.[6] This marks a shift in official projections of Scottish identity predicated upon a rainbow nation. As Iain Macwhirter puts it, 'Historically, Scotland always regarded itself as a more egalitarian society: Jock Tamson's Bairns, Lad 'o' Pairts, A Man's a Man. The assumption has been that because we are not so class conscious, at least by comparison with our larger neighbour, then we must be more tolerant of racial minorities.'[7] However, language around migration is often framed in neoliberal terms around demographics and economics, with the notion that Scotland is more hospitable to outsiders unconsciously couched in the numbers game. 'Of course we have no racism in Scotland, we have fewer black people.' 'Scotland has an ageing population; Scotland needs immigration to shore up the economy.' Viewing immigrants as productive units of labour narrows migration policy to fit an agenda dictated by capitalist priorities relating to economic growth rather than genuine anti-racism based on the needs and priorities set by the oppressed without any conditionality.

It is true that Scotland is less ethnically diverse than the UK as a whole. Across the United Kingdom 13 per cent of people reported they were not white in the 2011 census. In Scotland only 4 per cent of people reported as such. The 2011 census figure records 140,678 Asians, 2.66 per cent of the population. This is almost double the figure from 2001, which stood at 71,317, 1.41 per cent. The population of Asian, African, Caribbean or Black, Mixed, or Other ethnic groups doubled to 4 per cent in that decade.[8] Figures from the 2022 census are not available at the time of writing, but a survey from 2018 has noted similar figures.[9] Nonetheless, a reductionist approach to migration that downplays the importance of contemporary Scotland's multicultural society and the levels of institutional and popular racism operates in tandem with historical amnesia over Scotland's role in slavery and empire. Here Scots were actively involved at all levels: as owners, investors, overseers, doctors and slaving crews. In the 1770s Edward Long suggested that 'very near one third of the [white] inhabitants of Jamaica' were either from Scotland or descended from Scots.[10] In 1796, Scotsmen owned nearly 30 per cent of the estates in Jamaica and, by 1817, a staggering 32 per cent of the enslaved people there.[11] While slavery was still legal on Scottish soil, adverts appeared in the papers for both the sale of enslaved people and rewards for the return of runaways.[12] Glasgow's wealth is built on the fruits of enslaved labour in the colonies in sugar, cotton and tobacco plantations. Familiar names such as the Scot Abram Lyle of Tate and Lyle built their fortune on sugar produced through chattel slavery.[13] James Ewing from Glasgow was the richest sugar producer in Jamaica.[14] Tobacco from the Americas arrived in Leith from slave plantations in the seventeenth century, and James Gillespie made a fortune selling Virginia tobacco and snuff.[15] The profits that enslaved people helped to create kick-started the industrial revolution in Scotland and brought its merchants and traders great wealth. Many Scottish enslavers were considered among the most brutal, with life expectancy on their plantations averaging a mere four years.[16]

The 1707 Anglo-Scottish Union created opportunities for more active Scottish involvement in the economic activities of the British Empire, particularly in the 'jewel of the crown', India. Many Scotsmen found employment in colonial government services, as missionaries, in commerce or in industry. Scotland's landed families gained access to the East India Company (EIC), and gradually became its dominant force, particularly when Henry Dundas both chaired and became president of the Board of Control of the EIC in 1784.[17] Under his leadership, as many as one-fifth of the company writers in Calcutta and Madras were of Scottish origin by the 1790s. Indian imperial Scottish merchant firms include many names still known today: Andrew Yule; Forbes, Forbes & Campbell; Balmer Lawrie. Dundas's Indian adventure was surpassed only by his role in the Caribbean by his brutal suppression of revolts by enslaved people in Grenada and Jamaica, where his troops were ordered to use dogs to hunt the Jamaican Maroons down.[18]

In colonial India at the political level, the first three governor-generals were Scots. By 1792, Scots made up one in nine EIC civil servants, six in eleven common soldiers and one in three officers. A still more prominent role was later played by Scots in the India military. Eight out of the thirty-eight Indian viceroys and governor-generals between 1774 and 1947 were of Scottish origin – the last being the Earl of Linlithgow. The riches of the East furnished a lavish lifestyle for Scottish elites, and George McGilvary estimates that between 1725 and 1833 around 3,500 Scotsmen worked in India, and were remitting from £500,000 to £750,000 per annum back home, 'a colossal stimulus to life in Scotland'.[19]

There is also a long record of racial attacks and violence in Scotland itself, connected to this imperial history. The 1919 race riots were not confined to London and ports in England and Wales. On 23 January that year Black sailors were set upon by white seafarers with knives, batons and guns in Broomielaw outside the offices of a mercantile marine depot in James Watt Street, Glasgow.[20] White sailors were resentful of Black labourers, whom they viewed as competitors for jobs, as they were offered and accepted lower wages. In fact, the first protests against Black sailors were organised by the British Seafarers' Union, led at the time by Emanuel Shinwell.[21] At the turn of the century, some trade unionists and labour organisers viewed immigrant labourers as economic competitors for scarce resources over jobs and housing. This hostility to fellow workers from racialised minorities has been termed 'white labourism' by Jonathan Hyslop, who contends that pre-First World War white workers identified as an imperial working class that was suspicious and resentful of outsiders.[22] This was an era when the Empire was at its height, and so perhaps it is not that surprising that white workers would identify with imperial ideologies that viewed 'non-white' peoples as inferior.

Failure to come to terms with the darker side of its history is mirrored in Scotland's 'postcolonial' present. Race and racism continue to be a critical issue in the contemporary landscape. Since the death of Sheku Bayoh in 2015 whilst in police custody, no police officer has yet been held to account. The family continue to seek justice in a case that has shocking parallels both to the death of Stephen Lawrence in 1993 in London and the murder of George Floyd in Minneapolis in the United States in 2020. The callous disregard for the life of a Black man and the refusal to see racism as the key factor underlines the extent to which institutionalised racism seeps into Scottish life. As Scotland's Chief Constable, Sir Iain Livingstone QPM, noted in May 2023, 'institutional racism, sexism, misogyny and discrimination exist. Police Scotland is institutionally racist and discriminatory.'[23]

The murders of Axmed Abuukar Sheekh in 1989, Surjit Singh Chhokar and Imran Khan in 1998, Firsat Dag in 2000, and Kunal Mohanty in 2009 point to this. In recent years, we have seen violent attacks on a Syrian refugee, Shabaz Ali, in 2018; assaults on Asian shopkeepers in 2020; and a spate of verbal and physical violence toward East Asians, which even Police Scotland record at 474 cases reported in 2020 – a 50 per cent increase on the previous year.[24] Racist harassment and bullying in schools has increased, with more than 2,200 racist incidents reported in the four years to 2021 – the majority directed against children with a Muslim background.[25]

To date, Scotland still has no systematic way of monitoring racist incidents, and as such the likelihood of 'race' being ignored or underplayed remains troubling across the criminal justice system. Additionally, overt racism remains stubborn and persistent in Scottish society – it exists alongside the everyday casual microaggressions that also impact racialised minority communities. Structural racism continues to operate in areas such as employment, housing and education, as well as the criminal justice system. The airbrushing of racism from Scotland's past and present needs to be acknowledged and actioned if we are to achieve an anti-racist future. That said, racism has not gone unchallenged in Scotland, and indeed there is a long historical tradition of working-class internationalism and anti-racism that helped pave the way for the St Andrew's Day Anti-Racism March and Rally. One might recall Robert Wedderburn, born in Jamaica to an enslaved African woman and a Scottish doctor and sugar planter but who became a key radical in the early British working-class movement in the early nineteenth century, or the internationalist spirit of John Maclean of 'Red Clydeside' fame who was imprisoned for opposing British imperialism during the First World War.[26] This anti-racist tradition can also be seen from the great reception the Black American singer and film star Paul Robeson, experienced among Scottish miners in Edinburgh in 1949, and when he led the Glasgow May Day march in 1960, as well as the role played by the Anti-Nazi League and others in the 1970s to ensure that the fascist National Front was smashed.[27]

The origins of the St Andrew's Day Anti-Racism March and Rally

Scotland's Black population is principally composed of South Asians who mostly settled in the UK during the 1960s and early 1970s. But as in England, there is an earlier presence and settlement of peoples from the Indian subcontinent in Scotland, which included various categories of 'Doms', better known as the 'Gypsies' in the court of King James IV in 1505.[28] Later arrivals included temporary stays of Indian aristocracy and students in the Scottish centres of tertiary education, such as the Universities of Glasgow, Edinburgh and St. Andrews. In the early nineteenth century, Indian seamen, or lascars, who had served on EIC ships and as servants of returning Scots from India, began to find a home initially in Glasgow but broadening out to other areas.[29] Anti-racist protests had been mounted by local Black communities in Scotland. The 1919 riots had seen protests by the African Races Association of Glasgow.[30] In 1927, colour bars were reported in clubs and restaurants in Edinburgh refusing entry to African, Chinese and Indian students, and members of the Edinburgh Indian Association, Edinburgh African Association and Edinburgh West Indian Association successfully challenged these.[31]

It was initiatives from the South Asian community based in Glasgow in the form of the Scottish Asian Action Committee (SAAC) that helped lead to the formation of the St Andrew's Day Anti-Racism March. The SAAC was a community organisation founded in 1981 as a secular campaigning and information service for the Asian community. According to one founding member, Hardial Singh Bhari, the organisation was 'the only secular organisation in the city; we don't discriminate against caste, creed or colour'.[32] It was set up as a non-party-political and non-sectarian organisation to make representations on behalf of the Asian communities throughout Scotland. This is evidenced by affiliated groups, which included the Ahmaddiya Muslim Association, the Asian Artists' Association, the Asian Christian Fellowship, the Bangladeshi Association, the Bangladesh Students' Association, the Bengali Cultural Association, the Bhatra Cultural Association, Central Gurdwara, Gryffe Women's Aid, Hindu Mandir Sabha, the Indian Association, the Indian Graduates' Association, the Indian Social and Cultural Association, the Indian Workers' Association (IWA), Kashatre Sahba, the Kashmiri Association, the Ramgharia Association, Shri Guru Ravi Dass Sabha, the Sikh Sabha Association, the Sri Lankan Association, and the Young British Pakistani Initiative Association.[33] This impressive list of affiliations demonstrates the degree to which the shared common experience of racism acted as a bonding unity for Scots Asians.

Committed to the principles of equal rights, they developed a reputation as an organisation that both offered individual support and promoted collective action. Some of the individuals involved included Gurdial Singh Soofi, who was involved with the IWA, which established a branch in Glasgow in 1971. In November that year IWA members formed the Scottish Immigrant Labour Council, which campaigned against the legislation of the Industrial Relations Act and the Immigration Bill. These were introduced by Edward Heath's Conservative government. The former was designed to curtail trade union power by outlawing unofficial industrial action. Unions had to accept legal restraints through registration with a government body. An unregistered body – whether a workers' committee or a union – would be subject to penalties if it called for action.[34] The Immigration Bill proposed to introduce the term 'patrial', granting a person with a British-born parent or grandparent the right to live in the UK, but not British passport holders from the Indian subcontinent and East Africa who did not have a British-born parent or grandparent at the time.[35] The Bill was aimed at granting white East Africans the right to live in the UK but not their Asian or African counterparts, so clearly a racist proposal. A characteristic feature of IWA activists was the coalescing of labour disputes with anti-racism.[36] So, the key motivating figure behind SAAC was Prasanta Kumar Bhawmik, a civil engineer who was a member of the Communist Party of Great Britain (CPGB) and a leading activist in the Glasgow IWA. Born in Eastern Bengal to a middle-class family who had been displaced by the partition of India, the young Bhawmik had been a political activist in the Communist Party of India and worked to protect communities from the communal violence that engulfed

Calcutta in the riots of 1947. According to Susan Bhawmik, his wife and an early member of SAAC, as an agitator Prasanta was forced into hiding as he was wanted by the police. His family made arrangements for him to be packed off to the UK, where he arrived in Glasgow and studied engineering at the Andersonian Institute, now the University of Strathclyde, in either 1953 or 1954.[37] Active in the Communist Students Society, Bhawmik graduated in civil engineering and became an active trade unionist in the National and Local Government Officers' Association (NALGO) as well as the CPGB.

The foundation of SAAC lay in the widespread community outrage at the racist and sexist remarks made during the mishandling by judge Sheriff Francis Middleton of an allegation of inappropriate sexual conduct involving a thirteen-year-old Vietnamese girl in Glasgow in 1981. In pronouncing judgment and giving just a £750 fine to the twenty-seven-year-old perpetrator, Sheriff Middleton called it an 'indiscretion' and blamed the teenage victim, stating: 'Girls mature much earlier in the East than they do here ... until very recently marriages were arranged at a very early age in the East. In the form of marriage which takes place there, intercourse occurs beforehand. This may have predisposed the girl to her actions.'[38] A mass meeting was called by Bhawmik in Nicksdale Road Gurdwara in Glasgow involving representatives of the entire local Asian community who were angry and fearful that young Asian girls would now be seen as 'fair game', and the meeting was publicised by mosques, temples, gurdwaras and community centre networks.[39] In June 1981 a report clearing Sheriff Middleton was described as a 'whitewash' by the local Labour MP in Glasgow, David Marshall, and questions were asked of the Scottish Secretary in Parliament.[40] For standing up for his local community, Bhawmik and his family received abuse and death threats, with phone calls to his home in the middle of the night 'threatening to burn his house down and murder his wife and child'. Yet as Bhawmik told the *Aberdeen Press and Journal*, SAAC had received strong support from the STUC and the Labour Party in Scotland.[41]

SAAC was funded by Urban Aid from 1983 until November 1990. In April 1990, SAAC applied to Strathclyde Regional Council for mainlined funding and was successful in this. From that year, its core funding came from the Social Work Department of the council, and also the Southside Project Grant, aided by the Scottish Office Industry Department. Its main surgeries were based in Pollokshields and Govanhill, thus reflecting the principal areas of settlement by Asians in Scotland.[42] SAAC supported the Anti-Apartheid Movement and joined calls for boycotts, disinvestment and sanctions on South Africa during the 1980s.[43] This demonstrates SAAC's political outlook and links to other forms of anti-racist solidarity activism.

In the late 1980s, the fascist British National Party (BNP), which had emerged as a splinter from the National Front in 1982, was beginning to raise its head in Scotland. The newly established Stirling Community Relations Council had reported a number of cases of discrimination against Asian people, and racist graffiti had appeared on bus shelters and toilet walls.[44] As well as postering walls, the BNP began to organise rallies on St Andrew's Day in Glasgow.[45] Stickers by the BNP exclaiming 'Put British People before Aliens!' appeared in Aberdeen and Inverness.[46] The senior Scottish officer for the Commission for Racial Equality (CRE) had stated that racial harassment was increasing in Scotland.[47] The BNP had begun mobilising on St Andrew's Day in Glasgow, and in response SAAC organised the first counter-demonstration against the BNP in November 1984.[48] SAAC did this for five years, and then in the run up to November 1989, SAAC approached the General Council of the STUC to help organise a Scottish Day of Action against Racism.[49] The General Council agreed to support SAAC and help publicise this.

The late 1980s was a time of decline for British manufacturing and heavy industry following the defeat of the miners' strike. On 10 November 1988 a historic by-election took place in Glasgow Govan, where Jim Sillars of the Scottish National Party (SNP) overturned a Labour majority of 19,000, a swing of 33 per cent to the SNP. The result pointed to a long-term crisis of working-class representation as the blue-collar base of Labour support in Scotland eroded amid a series of factory closures and redundancies.[50] There was also growing concern over the increasing fascist activity, and even attempts by the BNP and others to infiltrate the trade union movement. One such example was in the civil service, at the office of the Hither Green Department of Social Security in London, where Malcolm Skeggs, a known leading fascist BNP member, had a base. Skeggs had been sacked by Lewisham Council for surreptitiously photocopying a BNP leaflet. At the Hither Green office the Civil and Public Services Association (CPSA) of civil servants took strike action in April 1988, lasting over six weeks. The result was a partial victory; the fascist was removed from that office.

At that year's STUC Congress the motion on challenging racism had an amendment that noted the rise in openly Nazi activity and deplored 'the Government's refusal to confront the problem of racism'.[51] It went on to congratulate the civil servants in the CPSA who acted in London. It resolved to call on the STUC to 'draw up an appropriate educational programme and calls upon affiliates to prepare guidelines for stewards to advise them on how to deal with fascist or racist activities in the workplace and in the Movement'.[52] P. McGowan of North Ayrshire Trades Council moved the amendment, and it was seconded by delegate R. Squire of the National Union of Public Employees, supported by J. Grier of Edinburgh & District Trades Council, and unanimously carried. As McGowan stated of the London dispute, 'staff and clients didn't want benefits calculated by someone who belonged to a party which passes the German concentration camps off as a mere passage in history'. Squire stipulated that just as the Scottish Professional Footballers' Association had made clear that racist behaviour would not be tolerated, so the STUC should declare that membership of a fascist organisation 'is incompatible with being a Trade Unionist'.[53] This episode draws attention to the depth of anti-racist sentiment amongst a predominantly white trade union movement in the UK and points to their Scottish Federation actively taking a position to challenge racist behaviour within its own ranks and workplaces. This seems to reiterate both the essence and substance of solidarity with Black workers within the British trade union movement.

From the 1989 Congress onward the Scottish TUC agreed to establish a Race Relations Sub-Committee of the General Purposes Committee. The STUC took soundings from affiliated groups, and anti-racist, ethnic minority and community groups, and decided upon a structure comprising sixteen people composed of four General Council members and twelve trade unionists of ethnic minority backgrounds to be coopted by the General Council from nominations received from affiliates. It also agreed to have co-chairs: one to be a General Council member and the other from among the nominees. Its remit included a range of issues, from acting as a bridge and link between the STUC and ethnic minority communities in Scotland, to identifying and promoting initiatives to inform the work of the General Council and its committees. More broadly, the Race Relations Sub-Committee worked to ensure that the STUC and the labour movement in general were supportive of anti-racist struggles and of ethnic minority communities.[54] On 16 November 1991, the STUC organised a successful seminar on 'Trades Unions and Ethnic Minorities in Scotland' in Glasgow with the speakers Muff Sourani, Regional Officer of Manufacturing, Science and Finance (MSF) and member of the TUC Race Relations Committee, and Bill Speirs, Deputy General Secretary, chaired by Naren Sood, co-chair of the Race Equality Sub-Committee.[55] These commitments strongly suggest the extent to which the Scottish trade union movement put in place procedures to help embed anti-racism within its organisational operations and educate its members. It also signals how this was progressed in consultation with and informed by the experiences of Black communities in Scotland.

The success of SAAC in initiating, planning, organising and coalescing a range of supporting organisations for the St Andrew's Day anti-racism event suggests that SAAC and the local Asians who were leading this organisation were the prime motor for both challenging racism in the streets in Glasgow and ensuring that St Andrew's Day was marked up as a key date in the anti-racist calendar. With 1990 as Year of Culture in Scotland, the SAAC took responsibility for organising the first Glasgow Mela held in the Tramway, Glasgow, from 20 to 30 September. The Mela is an Asian festival of food, artistic events, cultural shows and performances. It was designed to showcase Scottish Asian life and contribution to the community. The 1990 event attracted about 70,000 visitors.[56] The STUC supported the event, indicating again close collaboration between Scotland's main trade union federation and the local Black community.[57]

Into the 1990s

As part of this now functioning renamed Race Equality Committee, it was reported that amongst various initiatives that year were the public exposure of BNP activity in Scotland and support for the SAAC in organising a Day of Action against Racism held in Glasgow on Saturday 24 November.[58] The rally was chaired by Kofi Tordzro of the STUC Race Equality Committee, and speakers were Usha Brown of the Scottish Low Pay Unit; Subash Pall, Director of the Alien Arts Theatre Company; and Henry McCubbin, member of the European Parliament for north-east Scotland.[59] Affiliated organisations in addition to the IWA included the Scottish Anti-Racist Movement (SARM), Community Relations Councils in Scotland, the Scottish International Labour Council and the Scottish Council for Civil Liberties. The full list comprised some forty-five names of trade unions, civic groups and voluntary organisations as well as the STUC, the Scottish Labour Party and the SNP.[60] SARM welcomed the previous year's resolution and suggested new ways to take anti-racism forward within the STUC: inclusion of practical measures to tackle racism on courses for trade unionists and holding a day seminar or conference on Black employment.[61]

All this suggests the degree of seriousness with which the STUC took its pivotal role in organising, mobilising and building the anti-racist movement in the late 1980s alongside groups such as SAAC. As well as the St Andrew's Day mobilisation in Glasgow, in Edinburgh on 3 June 1989, the Lothian Black Forum organised an anti-racist march that the STUC supported. In the late 1980s, and in the early days of the St Andrew's Day anti-racist mobilisations, it was clearly understood that far from the widely held view today that 'Scotland is not a racist Society', the STUC rejected any such assertion and argued quite forcefully that Scotland could not be complacent about racism, as it was very much apparent north of Gretna Green.[62] The first mention in reports of a STUC speaker at the St Andrew's Day March and Rally was in November 1992, when the Deputy General Secretary spoke on behalf of the Council.[63] Additionally, the Race Equality Committee met with the Scottish Professional Footballers' Association, who were very supportive of STUC initiatives such as issuing public statements against the racist chants of fans aimed at Black players from England.[64]

In 1993, the STUC noted with concern the 'massive increase in racism and fascism in Europe and the rise of political parties promoting such attitudes', including the growing electoral success of the Front National (FN) in France under the leadership of Jean-Marie Le Pen.[65] Scottish Asians also felt this acutely, as daily 'families and individuals are verbally and physically abused and harassed, threatened in their own homes, workplaces and on the streets'. SAAC noted with some alarm increased racism in Scotland as in Europe, with the rise of the far right in the form of increased support for Le Pen, and resolved its determination to ensure that this was 'a trend which must not be allowed to develop in Scotland'.[66] Alas, the growth of the far right was to bear fruit in the UK, as BNP member Derek Beackon won a council by-election in the Millwall ward of Tower Hamlets in September 1993. Winning by a mere seven votes in a bitterly contested election, Beackon declared 'The Asians are rubbish and that is what we are going to clear from the streets', and told one Asian 'I am going to repatriate all Asians.'[67] When asked how he saw his council duties, Beackon proceeded to announce that 'I am only going to represent white people ... They [Asians] have no right to be in my great country.'[68] Though Millwall is over 400 miles away from Scotland, there was great concern that such events could spread north of the border. These fears were not unfounded, as press reports quoted a BNP spokesperson boasting that their party was 'enjoying increasing support in Scotland', and that this was to be a 'prime recruiting ground to further their cause'.[69] The CRE regional briefing on Scotland for 1994 showed a 9 per cent increase in racial incidents reported to them.[70]

A sense of the degree of seriousness and willingness to stand up to increased openly racist and fascist activity after Beackon's election can be gleaned from the fact that the newly appointed Shadow Scottish Secretary, George Robertson, decided to forgo attendance at the usual St Andrew's Day event in Edinburgh in 1993 and instead attend the St Andrew's Day Anti-Racism March in Glasgow. As Robertson stated, 'as far as I am concerned, one of the biggest problems facing Europe today is the rise of racism, xenophobia and hostilities towards the ethnic minorities'.[71] That year's march on 27 November 1993 began at Blythswood Square with a rally at City Halls. SAAC papers for 1994 noted how that year represented Scotland's tenth annual march against racism and fascism, now organised by a steering committee comprising members from SAAC, the National Union of Students, the STUC and the Scottish Anti-Racist Alliance. The report states that attendance in 1993 exceeded 3,000 people, higher than previous years.[72] The STUC 'judged this year's march as the most successful of its kind in Scotland'.[73] The STUC also voted to support the actions of local council staff in east London in refusing to work with the fascist Councillor Beackon. Members of NALGO in local government had taken unofficial strike action and more than 350 council workers had walked out on 17 October 1993 after Beackon's election victory.[74] All this suggests that the winning of the first BNP council seat on the Isle of Dogs in east London and the increasing levels of both micro and macro forms of daily racism injected a sense of urgency amongst activists to show solidarity and stand as one against racism.

Such mobilisations and collaborative work would see dividends, as by 1994 the STUC could note some success through lobbying and petitioning alongside others, such as the relaunched Anti-Nazi League, successfully preventing a visit to Edinburgh by Jean-Marie Le Pen. Le Pen had been allowed to visit London but was met there with massive protests. The STUC ensured a Scottish presence at the TUC march and rally against racism on 19 March 1994 in London. This was called by the TUC but had to be fought for by anti-racist activists within unions.[75] The STUC were also concerned at how the creation of a single European Union (EU) was held to 'have an adverse effect on black people and other ethnic minorities living and working in the European Community'. The impact of this was believed to be the institutionalisation of 'European racism and continuing discrimination against black and migrant workers'.[76] Anxieties over the direction of EU policies were echoed by Scottish Asians. In 1994, the STUC pledged to continue supporting the St Andrew's Day March and Rally 'as a broadly-based demonstration against all forms of racism and fascism and in positive support of a multi-cultural Scotland'.[77] The success of this annual demonstration in Glasgow can in part be measured by the ripple effect that SAAC initiatives began to have elsewhere in Scotland. In 1991, Aberdeen hosted its first Day against Racism event in November. The march would see SAAC members attend and deliver speeches at the rally.[78] Aberdeen Trades Council also booked transport to bring activists to the Glasgow protest in 1994.[79] This suggests that anti-racists in other parts of Scotland were able to take inspiration from successive efforts established in Glasgow.

One gets a sense of the protests and demonstrations in this period from the STUC report of the St Andrew's Day March and Rally held on Saturday 30 November 1996. The report claimed that 'attendance at the event was over 1,000', the highest since 1993, and made a colourful impact on the public, assisted as it was by the GMB pipe band, the Black Star steel band and a drum band brought by Aberdeen Trades Council.[80] There was an impressive range of speakers, including Diane Abbott, MP; the Revd Dr Willibald Jacob, a prominent German anti-racist campaigner; Professor Denis Goldberg, a former prisoner of apartheid in South Africa; a representative from Glacier Rotating Plant Bearings, which was in dispute and whose staff were occupying its premises at the time; and the final speaker, Aamer Anwar, now Scotland's leading human rights lawyer, who had himself been a victim of racist violence. The theme of the march was 'an injury to one is an injury to all'.[81] At this time in 1996 another key organisational change was introduced when the STUC voted to replace the Race Equality Committee with an elected Black Workers' Committee. This included having two reserved places on the General Council for Black workers and establishing an annual Black workers' conference. All delegates would be Black trade union members but arrangements were to be made to allow non-Black members to attend as observers. This conference would elect the Black Workers' Committee, of whom ten members would be drawn from affiliated trade unions, one representative taken from affiliated trade union councils and two representatives nominated by the STUC General Council.[82] These positive developments do not imply that the STUC is immune to institutional racism. The case of Zaffir Hakim suggests otherwise.[83] But it does signal a direction of travel within the Scottish trade union body to strive consciously to address racism and to support Black trade unionists to organise and have representation as Black workers.

Through the 2000s, the BNP made a more concerted effort to turn to electoral politics under the leadership of Nick Griffin, downplaying their Nazi past. This led to a degree of worrying success, as they won two seats in the European Parliament in 2009. As Jim Murphy, a prominent Scottish Labour politician who would later become Scottish Labour leader, noted in 2009, the BNP won its seats in the European Parliament and had built its support base because of complacency:

> I worry that Scotland is still too complacent. We look at parts of England where the BNP has won and I fear that people think it could never happen here. Ten years ago, the number of people voting BNP in Scotland numbered just over 3,000. In June of this year, that increased tenfold to 29,000 people in Scotland who decided to put their cross in the BNP box. If this thought doesn't concern people, then the problem is only going to get worse.

Mr Murphy said it turned his stomach that the BNP would be on television, and urged politicians to take the threat from the party more seriously: 'They must not convince themselves the BNP are not a danger in Scotland. The threat is there and we need to act.'[84] Since 2010, thanks to serious work by anti-racists and anti-fascists, this has proved to be the highpoint of the BNP's electoral success, and the contemporary far right in Britain remain small and fragmented, a marked contrast to many of their European counterparts in places such as Hungary, Poland, Austria, France, Italy and Sweden.

Solidarity vs. allyship

The St Andrew's Day anti-racism event shines a light on contemporary questions of 'allyship'; solidarity; and the nature of support sought, provided and required for effective anti-racist activism. A conflation between 'allyship' and solidarity is sometimes made, and so some clarity of definitions and meaning is required. The Anti-Oppression Network defines allyship not as an identity, but rather as an ongoing process wherein privileged individuals offer support to marginalised individuals. Therefore, receiving recognition as an ally is granted through the trust of marginalised individuals.[85] In the wake of the Black Lives Matter movement following the death of George Floyd in 2020, this definition certainly seemed popular, as it is featured on several organisational sites from educational bodies, and government and corporate agencies. Many companies and brand names featured the black square and #BlackLivesMatter hashtag on Twitter as a means of showing their support for anti-racism. Whilst this can be viewed as worthy and positive in and of itself, it nevertheless has a number of deep flaws.

Such 'hashtag activism' entails minimal cost to the ally, as they are not required, and may not be prepared or willing, to participate in any other forms of advocacy on behalf of the cause, and do not necessarily speak up when people are affected by discrimination. Consequently, allyship as performance can be perceived as 'empty activism' from a 'position of privilege and motivated by a desire for increased social capital'.[86] Lisa B. Spanierman and Laura Smith persuasively argue that performative allies are driven by the need for validation and acceptance. They may intellectually understand the issues at hand, yet may not sacrifice their social or economic capital to challenge the systems they benefit from. This brand of allyship may be perceived as cosmetic, superficial and transitory, rather than as facilitating structural change.[87]

If allyship is prone to being performative and symbolic, solidarity on the other hand is defined by active participation and a willingness to 'to put yourself on the line' to challenge racial oppression. As the Fearless Futures website puts it, being an 'ally is a static state, whereas working in solidarity is active'.[88] The ally has ticked off their support and therefore 'acted'. While symbolic gestures can be powerful for visibilisation and fundraising, they are not enough on their own. Neither should solidarity with marginalised groups be conditional on their solidarity or alignment with another anti-oppressive cause or on any other contingency. Cureton describes solidarity as:

> a matter of a group of people being united or at one with regard to something (sympathies, interests, values, etc.), having genuine concern for each other's welfare, respecting others as group members, trusting one another not to intentionally undermine or free ride on the group, taking pride in the group as a whole, being ashamed of its failures and suffering loss or betrayal if members of the group do not live up to the requirements that the group places on itself, and perhaps having certain other affections for one's compatriot.[89]

This provides a more substantial definition to our understanding of what solidarity should look like, in that it moves beyond tokenism and self-congratulatory posturing.[90] If the St Andrew's Day Anti-Racism March and Rally had been conceived of by the STUC and merely entailed a one-day visible march, the Scottish trade union movement could so easily have fallen prey to a form of paternalism that the concept and practice of allyship is predicated upon. Instead, this chapter has shown how the agency and leadership of SAAC brought race and anti-racism into the heart of the trade union body. The STUC, in turn, initiated discussions with local community activists to help inform their practice and policies, leading to structural changes in how the Scottish trade union movement operates with anti-racism embedded into its organisational structures.

An even clearer sense of what active and effective solidarity looks like is provided by the great Trinidadian revolutionary socialist C. L. R. James in his epic history of the Haitian Revolution of 1791–1804, *The Black Jacobins*: 'The blacks will know as friends only those whites who are fighting in the ranks beside them. And whites will be there.'[91] In Scotland, when the local Black communities called upon the wider labour movement to support them in their hour of need against racial violence by the BNP, the predominantly white trade union movement rallied to their side. Drawing upon papers of SAAC and the STUC, as well as interviews with surviving SAAC members, this chapter about the history of the St Andrew's Day antracism mobilisations – which continue to this day – contributes to showing how anti-racism can be constructed as a genuine from of solidarity from below that is not centred upon liberal notions of paternalism and tokenism.

Conclusion

This chapter has set out to explain the history of one specific and key strand of anti-racism in Scotland. It purports not to represent the whole story of Scottish anti-racism but to highlight a much neglected, undervalued and overlooked annual procession organised by the chief trade union federation in Scotland. Today, the St Andrew's Day Anti-Racism March and Rally is celebrated as part of the Scottish calendar with participation by representatives of the Scottish government, the Labour Party and the SNP, as well as leading figures from civil society. This is a positive development, but as the chapter has demonstrated, the momentum and drive to build St Andrew's Day as an anti-racist event emerged outside institutional structures of government and power. Its roots lie instead in the self-activity of local Asian communities, principally in Glasgow, through SAAC. Their annual reports from the early 1990s comment with pride about SAAC's role in taking the initiative in countering the BNP on St Andrew's Day, and note how as a result of their efforts 'the march has become an annual event, usually organised on the Saturday nearest to St. Andrew's Day with the theme Scotland for all people living in Scotland irrespective of race, class, sex, colour or creed'.[92]

Many SAAC members were also trade unionists, and the fact that they saw the labour movement as the critical vehicle through which to challenge the racist activity of the BNP and wider racism attests to a firm belief in the trade unions as collective combinations based on solidarity, equality and justice. This shows the power of constructing an anti-racist tradition from below as opposed to one crafted by liberal political elites. This tradition from below is one characterised by democratic forms of grassroots political activity and agency of non-elite actors in forging and shaping an anti-racist agenda. As such, the chapter has challenged the notion of Scottish exceptionalism and 'race-blindness' that has dominated the Scottish landscape, one that has viewed racism as a peculiarly English disease. The notion of 'tartan inclusivity' is cerebrally superficial, intellectually impoverished and one not grounded in empirical evidence or historic accuracy. The history of the St Andrew's Day anti-racism event demonstrates how an anti-racist tradition has had to be actively campaigned for and vigilantly defended to make it a living reality and tradition in Scottish life.

In the contemporary era of toxic racism emanating from the top of society on the part of the political establishment, it is important to remember and celebrate effective, united and broad anti-racist movements and politics. As Hakim Adi rightly notes, the history of anti-racism in Britain is as old as racism itself.[93] So anti-racism is fundamental to a democratic and pluralist culture that is part of a living tradition of struggles from below, and we need such struggles and movements more than ever today.

Notes

1 *A Manifesto to Build an Anti-Racist Trade Union Movement 2022–27* (London: Trades Union Congress House, College Hill Press, 2022), p. 2.
2 *Ibid.*, p. 2.
3 For more on race and class in British labour history, see S. Virdee, *Racism, Class and the Racialized Outsider* (Basingstoke: Palgrave Macmillan, 2014).
4 S. Taylor, 'The National Front', in R. Miles and A. Phizacklea (eds.), *Racism and Political Action in Britain* (London: Routledge Kegan Paul, 1979), pp. 124–46 (p. 134).
5 Miles and Phizacklea, *Racism and Political Action in Britain*, p. 199.
6 Martin Currie, 'Q&A: Voting in the Scottish Independence Referendum', BBC News (8 January 2014), www.bbc.co.uk/news/uk-scotland-scotland-politics-25420827 (accessed 2 June 2024).

7 *The Herald* (7 June 2020). In Scotland, it is common to hear the phrase 'We're all Jock Tamson's Bairns', which translates as 'We're all the same.' 'Lad 'o' Pairts' translates as 'Man of many parts', a clever or talented person; 'A Man's a Man' is Robert Burns's 1795 poem endorsing equality of peoples, opposition to social injustice and democratic republican ideals.
8 www.scotlandscensus.gov.uk/census-results/at-a-glance/ethnicity/ (accessed 2 June 2024).
9 www.statista.com/statistics/367842/scotland-ethnicity-of-population/ (accessed 2 June 2024).
10 Edward Long, *The History of Jamaica*, II (London: T. Lowndes, 1774), p. 287.
11 Black History Month (BHM), 'Scotland and Slavery' (19 August 2015), www.blackhistorymonth.org.uk/article/section/history-of-slavery/scotland-and-slavery/ (accessed 2 June 2024). For more on Scotland and slavery, see Michael Morris, *Scotland and the Caribbean c. 1740–1833: Atlantic Archipelagos* (New York: Routledge, 2015); and T. M. Devine (ed.), *Recovering Scotland's Slavery Past: The Caribbean Connection* (Edinburgh: Edinburgh University Press, 2015).
12 See advert from the *Edinburgh Evening Courant* (13 February 1727).
13 Philippe Chalmin, *The Making of a Sugar Giant: Tate and Lyle 1859–1989* (London: Harwood, 1990).
14 Anthony Cooke, 'An Elite Revisited: Glasgow West India Merchants, 1783–1877', *Journal of Scottish Historical Studies*, 32:2 (2012), 127–65.
15 Darren McCullins, 'Charting Edinburgh's Slave Trade History', BBC News (31 October 2018), www.bbc.co.uk/news/uk-scotland-edinburgh-east-fife-46030606 (accessed 20 March 2021).
16 BHM, 'Scotland and Slavery'.
17 H. V. Bowen, *The Business of Empire: The East India Company and Imperial Britain 1756–1833* (Cambridge: Cambridge University Press, 2005).
18 Melanie Newton, 'Henry Dundas, Empire and Genocide', *Open Democracy* (30 July 2020).
19 George K. McGilvary, 'The Scottish Connection with India, 1725–1833', *Etudes écossaises*, 14 (2011), 13–31 (pp. 26–7).
20 Jody Harrison, 'Dark History of the Red Clydeside Race Riot', *The Herald* (23 January 2019). See also Virdee, *Racism, Class and the Racialized Outsider*, pp. 81–5.
21 See Paul Griffin, 'Labour Struggles and the Formation of Demands: The Spatial Politics of Red Clydeside', *Geoforum*, 62 (2015), 121–30.
22 Jonathan Hyslop, 'The Imperial Working Class Makes Itself "White": White Labourism in Britain, Australia, and South Africa before the First World War', *Journal of Historical Sociology*, 12:4 (1999), 398–421 (p. 399).
23 See 'Chief Constable Statement on Institutional Discrimination', www.scotland.police.uk/what-s-happening/news/2023/may/chief-constable-statement-on-institutional-discrimination/ (accessed 2 June 2024).
24 Christina Ong and Debbie Jackson, 'Covid in Scotland: People are Treating Us like the Disease', BBC News (15 March 2021), www.bbc.co.uk/news/uk-scotland-edinburgh-east-fife-56113045 (accessed 2 June 2024).

25 David Bol, 'Thousands of Racist Incidents Reported in Scottish Schools', *The Herald* (6 January 2021).
26 Virdee, *Racism, Class and the Racialized Outsider*, pp. 19–20; Michael Morris, 'Robert Wedderburn: Race, Religion and Revolution', *International Socialism*, 132 (2011), https://isj.org.uk/robert-wedderburn-race-religion-and-revolution/ (accessed 2 June 2024); Dave Sherry, *John Maclean: Red Clydesider* (London: Bookmarks, 2014), pp. 40–4, 66–71.
27 Colin Reilly, 'Paul Robeson's Scottish Connections', *History Scotland* (28 October 2020), www.historyscotland.com/history/paul-robesons-scottish-connections/ (accessed 2 June 2024); on the Anti-Nazi League, see Virdee, *Racism, Class and the Racialized Outsider*, pp. 135–44.
28 Bashir Mann, *The New Scots: The Story of Asians in Scotland* (Edinburgh: John Donald, 1992), p. 62.
29 *Ibid.*, pp. 62–4.
30 J. Jenkinson, 'Black Sailors on Red Clydeside: Rioting, Reactionary Trade Unionism and Conflicting Notions of Britishness Following the First World War', *Twentieth Century British History*, 19:1 (2008), 29–60.
31 See *Edinburgh Evening News* (21 and 25 May 1927).
32 Author's interview with Hardilal Bhari, Glasgow, 7 February 2023.
33 *Ibid.* Also see SAAC, *Newsletter*, 1 (Spring 1994).
34 See S. C. Ghosh, 'The British Trade Unions and the Labour Law: The Case of the Industrial Relations Act 1971', *Relations Industrielles/Industrial Relations*, 35:2 (1980), 251–78.
35 The National Archives, Kew (TNA), FCO 53/269, 'Amendment of British Nationality Act 1948 by the Immigration Act 1971' (1972).
36 For more on the Scottish Immigrant Labour Council, see University of Warwick, Modern Records Centre, MSS.126, Transport and General Workers' Union International Workers' Branch (1/1647): papers of Alvaro de Miranda, 1972–81, 'Anti-Racism and Race Relations: Conference Papers and Other Documentation, 1972–1975'.
37 Author's interview with Susan Bhawmik, 12 April 2023.
38 *Daily Mirror* (22 April 1981), p. 13. See also *Daily Record* (22 April 1981).
39 Author's interview with Susan Bhawmik, 12 April 2023.
40 *Aberdeen Press and Journal* (18 June 1981). See also 6 Parl. Deb., HC (16 June 1981), cols 315W–316W, https://api.parliament.uk/historic-hansard/written-answers/1981/jun/16/sheriff-francis-middleton#column_315w (accessed 2 June 2024).
41 *Aberdeen Press and Journal* (6 July 1981); interview with Susan Bhawmik, 12 April 2023.
42 SAAC, *Newsletter*, 1 (Spring 1994).
43 See advert 'Scotland Condemns Apartheid', *Daily Record* (16 June 1986), 15.
44 *Stirling Observer* (27 May 1988), p. 20.
45 *Aberdeen Press and Journal* (18 November 1988), p. 2.
46 *Aberdeen Press and Journal* (5 December 1991), p. 10.
47 *Ibid.*

48 SAAC, Annual Report, 1994 (Glasgow: SAAC, 1994), p. 1. See also A. Dunlop, 'A United Front? Anti-Racist Political Mobilisation in Scotland', *Scottish Affairs*, 3 (1993), 94–5 (p. 99).
49 Glasgow Caledonian University Archive Centre, Records of the Scottish Trades Union Congress (GCUAC), STUC General Council, 92nd Annual Report, Aberdeen (17 April 1989), p. 184.
50 *Ibid.*, p. 185.
51 *Ibid.*, p. 230.
52 *Ibid.*
53 *Ibid.*, pp. 230–1.
54 GCUAC, STUC General Council, 93rd Annual Report, Glasgow (16 April 1990), pp. 167–8.
55 GCUAC, STUC General Council, 95th Annual Report, Perth (20 April 1992), p. 171.
56 SAAC, Annual Report, 1991–92 (Glasgow: SAAC, 1992), p. 3.
57 GCUAC, STUC General Council, 96th Annual Report, Glasgow (19 April 1993), p. 163.
58 GCUAC, STUC General Council, 94th Annual Report, Dundee (15 April 1991), p. 218.
59 SAAC, Annual Report, 1989–90 (Glasgow: SAAC, 1990), p. 14.
60 See full list of affiliates at *ibid.*, p. 14.
61 STUC General Council, 93rd Annual Report, p. 167.
62 *Ibid.*, p. 168.
63 STUC General Council, 96th Annual Report, p. 163.
64 *Ibid.*
65 *Ibid.*
66 SAAC, *Annual Report 1991–92*, p. 4. In the 1988 French presidential elections, Le Pen's FN polled 14.4 per cent, doubling the vote from 1984.
67 *Daily Record* (18 September 1993), p. 2.
68 *Ibid.*
69 *Ibid.*
70 Quoted in SAAC, *Newsletter*, 2 (Autumn 1994).
71 Quoted in *Daily Record* (2 November 1993), p. 4.
72 SAAC, Annual Report, 1994, p. 1.
73 GCUAC, STUC General Council, 97th Annual Report, Dundee (18 April 1994), p. 165.
74 GCUAC, STUC General Council, 98th Annual Report, Perth (17 April 1995), p. 173.
75 STUC General Council, 97th Annual Report, p. 165.
76 STUC General Council, 96th Annual Report, p. 163.
77 STUC General Council, 98th Annual Report, p. 174.
78 *Aberdeen Press and Journal* (1 November 1991), p. 3.
79 See report in *Aberdeen Evening Express* (25 November 1994), p. 11.
80 STUC General Council, *Centenary Annual General Council Report* (Glasgow: STUC, 1997), p. 34.

81 *Ibid.*.
82 GCUAC, STUC General Council, 99th Annual Report, Edinburgh (15 April 1996), p. 35. This was part of a wider national development toward forming Black Workers' Committees in trade unions. See Virdee, *Racism, Class and the Racialized Outsider*, pp. 155–61.
83 Zaffir Hakim won an employment tribunal against the STUC for racial discrimination in 2016; www.equalityhumanrights.com/sites/default/files/the_scottish_trades_union_congress_v_mr_zaffir_hakim_-_summary.pdf (accessed 2 June 2024).
84 Quoted in *The Scotsman* (21 October 2009).
85 https://theantioppressionnetwork.com/allyship/ (accessed 2 June 2024).
86 S. E. Erskine and D. Bilimoria, 'White Allyship of Afro-Diasporic Women in the Workplace: A Transformative Strategy for Organizational Change', *Journal of Leadership & Organizational Studies*, 26:3 (2019), 319–38 (p. 329).
87 See Lisa B. Spanierman and Laura Smith, 'Roles and Responsibilities of White Allies: Implications for Research, Teaching, and Practice', *The Counselling Psychologist*, 45 (2017), 606–17.
88 www.fearlessfutures.org/moving-from-allyship-to-solidarity/ (accessed 2 June 2024).
89 A. Cureton, 'Solidarity and Social Moral Rules', *Ethical Theory and Moral Practice*, 15 (2012), 691–706 (p. 696).
90 For more on theorising solidarity, see David Featherstone, *Solidarity: Hidden Histories and Geographies of Internationalism* (London: Zed Books, 2012); and Zeina Maasri, Cathy Bergin and Francesca Burke (eds), *Transnational Solidarity: Anticolonialism in the Global Sixties* (Manchester: Manchester University Press, 2022).
91 C. L. R. James, *The Black Jacobins: Toussaint Louverture and the San Domingo Revolution* (London: Secker and Warburg, 1938), p. 315.
92 SAAC, *Annual Report 1991–92*, p. 9.
93 See lecture delivered by Hakim Adi, 'Anti-Racism: A British Tradition' (10 November 2021), https://www.youtube.com/watch?v=VQnME2wUwQc (accessed 2 June 2024).

11

'Martin Luther King fought for a colour-blind society': African American civil rights in UK political discourse

Megan Hunt

Calls for closer public attention to Britain's histories of empire, migration and racism are not new, but have received unprecedented coverage and support in the wake of local, national and international Black Lives Matter protests in 2020. While UK protesters were outraged by the murder of George Floyd in Minneapolis and the entrenched white supremacy evident in the systems and practices of US law enforcement, many were concurrently incensed by a domestic political culture that continued to mark race as an American problem. This latter sentiment was often communicated via placards at protests and posts on social media that read 'The UK is not innocent.' However, such protesters met a considerable opponent in white British racial amnesia, defined by Stuart Hall in 1978 as 'a decisive mental repression – which has overtaken the British people about race and Empire since the 1950s', and works to 'wipe out and efface every trace of the colonial and imperial past'.[1]

Protests in 2020 therefore revealed a new chapter in a longstanding history of transatlantic solidarity, which, in recent decades, and as the result of neoliberal anti-statism, is often frustrated by what Remi Joseph-Salisbury defines as ' "post-racial" white supremacy'. Under such white hegemony, which erases the very context that enables it to endure, race rarely figures in official, governmental interpretations of equality and opportunity. However, in the United Kingdom, demands for more diverse histories in schools, for example, particularly in relation to slavery, empire and migration, have further exposed an 'American-centric' understanding of Black history, which prioritises narratives of another place and another time, and fails to explore 'the links between Britain as Empire and Britain as Nation'.[2] Evident in historical curricula, such attitudes, as I have argued elsewhere, deny students the opportunity to assess legacies of race and racism in their own nation and communities, further entrenching Hall's lament that race, as understood in the modern United Kingdom, has 'nothing intrinsically to do with the [national] condition'.[3] Therefore, while British students may be able to determine the origins of racialised violence and ongoing protest movements in the United States, they are not generally taught to ask similar questions of the United Kingdom.

In the wake of the solidarities that evolved through the 2020 protests and government efforts to arrest these developments, this chapter reassesses why the place of US civil rights histories in UK political culture still matters. This includes an assessment of the language of 'colorblindness,' which has obstructed efforts toward meaningful racial equality in the United States since the 1970s, and which continues to punctuate British political discourse at vital moments of potential racial reckoning, from the murder of Stephen Lawrence in the 1990s to the treatment of Meghan Markle in the present day. Tracing transatlantic continuities of colorblind rhetoric, as well as important distinctions between the two political cultures, this chapter documents the performative assumption of British racial and cultural 'tolerance' that continues to equate national identity with whiteness and imply that serious racial anxieties are a uniquely American phenomenon.[4] In doing so, it pays particular attention to the role of immigration in British thinking on race, and identifies 'tolerant' multiculturalism as the dominant rhetorical kin to the US ideology of colorblindness, which, according to Justin Gomer, 'prohibit[s] the discussion, analysis, study, or legislation of matters of racial inequality'.[5]

In his position as the leading figure of the African American civil rights movement, Martin Luther King, Jr is central to the US myth of colorblindness, but can be found at the centre of simplistic, one-dimensional historical narratives of racial progress on both sides of the Atlantic. Such narratives empower conscious and unconscious defenders of Britain's racial hierarchies, who cite King when side-stepping accusations of racism at both the personal and structural level. Even before the 2020 protests, Black British author Reni Eddo-Lodge, most famous for her 2017 bestseller *Why I'm No Longer Talking to White People about Race*, wrote of white critics who centred King's words in their rejection of her work. Informing Eddo-Lodge that the slain civil rights leader would not approve of her book, nor her wider advocacy of safe spaces for marginalised communities, Eddo-Lodge's critics 'lectured [her] about segregation'.[6] More recently, both the 'alt-right' celebrity Laurence Fox and the Conservative MP Ben Bradley have used King's dream of a colorblind society to attack those who spotlight racial and gender privilege in modern Britain.[7] In doing so they exhibit a disingenuous adoption of anti-racist language, often couched as concern for 'all people,' rather than minority groups, which reinforces a triumphal concept of British multicultural 'tolerance'. This chapter observes and analyses such moments and argues that US-focused critiques of colorblind ideology offer a toolkit for undermining celebratory narratives of Britain as 'a beacon to the rest of Europe and the world'.[8] By better understanding the uses and misuses of 'American-centric' racial histories in Britain, including efforts to excommunicate race from public discourse in pursuit of the false panacea of colorblindness and tolerance, this chapter traces trajectories and continuities between the emergence of American neoconservative values, such as those articulated by Ronald Reagan during the 1980s, and the British alt-right of the early twenty-first century.

'American-style' racial dramas

King is necessary to any telling of modern US history, but his British allies and counterparts, not to mention his own visits to and critiques of Britain, are seldom considered part of 'our island story'.[9] Indeed, King's centrality within a popular global understanding of anti-racism implies that there are no equivalent histories in the UK, either during the 1950s and 1960s when King's career was at its peak, or broadly. This is despite obvious examples of British activists adopting methods of protest and persuasion most famously associated with King, such as the organisation of the Bristol bus boycott in 1963, and the development of a non-violent civil rights movement amongst Catholics in Northern Ireland.

King's place in UK schools therefore offers considerable avenues for teachers and students invested in exploring the local, national and global fights for racial equality, and can serve as a vital gateway to discussion of international solidarity and global patterns of white supremacy. Historically, though, UK curricula and popular representations have spotlighted the USA's racial tensions in complete isolation from the UK or Europe, foregrounding a national US culture overburdened by the entrenched impact of slavery and racial segregation. Against a backdrop of white supremacist violence and frequent, high-profile killings of Black men and boys in particular, the concept of a racially divided, politically polarised America is universally accepted in Britain, where divisions within political and cultural life are assumed to be less extreme. Indeed, the recent public debate regarding Meghan Markle's treatment at the hands of the British royal family and the UK press has inspired a new wave of defensiveness about race in modern Britain, with Markle's critics accusing her of transplanting 'American-style' racial dramas to a comparatively tolerant, multicultural United Kingdom. Such accusations have a long history in the British press, with African American advocates of racial progress often cited as irrelevant to and ignorant of the UK racial context. E. James West, for example, has documented this adversarial attitude in the context of the US civil rights leader the Revd Al Sharpton's UK visit in 1991, following the racist murder of London teenager Rolan Adams. According to *Newsweek*, the British press treated

Sharpton's arrival 'as a graver threat to public order than if the [Spanish] armada had reappeared off the coast'. Efforts to prevent Sharpton's entry into the UK echoed earlier campaigns against Stokely Carmichael (later Kwame Ture), who was prevented from re-entering the UK following eleven days of speaking engagements in July 1967.[10]

In more recent years, Meghan Markle has emerged in the UK press as the latest in a long line of African American troublemakers. Indeed, her very presence within the British royal family has forced a national debate on race, albeit one that fails to acknowledge the structural concerns that impact the daily lives and opportunities of Black and ethnic-minority people. Rather, this debate is limited to the personal, in which racism is reduced to 'skirmishes expressed in the language of hurt feelings and symbolic gestures', as Markle and her husband Prince Harry lament the extent to which 'a status based on bloodline superiority was not distributed equally to them'.[11] Resulting attempts to proceed beyond Markle's specific complaints to a broader assessment of racism in Britain have been met with defensiveness and hostility. When Rachel Boyle, an audience member on the BBC's *Question Time*, described Markle's treatment as a product of 'racism' in January 2020, panellist Laurence Fox responded 'It's not racism. We're the most tolerant, lovely country in Europe.' Boyle, whose ancestors were enslaved in Barbados, then invited Fox to consider his own status as 'a white privileged male', to which Fox responded that such an observation was in itself racist. The following day, Fox used his Twitter account to imply further that being forced to confront his white male privilege contradicted Martin Luther King, Jr's dream of colorblindness, which the civil rights leader articulated at the August 1963 March on Washington for Jobs and Freedom. Posting an image of King alongside a short quotation from the civil rights leader's famous 'I have a dream' speech, Fox wrote that King's words, in which he hoped that his four children would 'one day live in a nation where they will not be judged by the color of their skin, but by the content of their character', represented the position that Fox himself adopted on *Question Time* as well as in his wider life. 'If you can improve on it, I'm all ears', Fox wrote, 'Or you can keep screeching "Racist!" at me and I can carry on having a jolly good giggle at your expense. The tide is turning.'[12]

While Markle has been accused of bringing an 'American-style race row' to Britain's shores, Fox's use of a decontextualised soundbite from King's most famous speech demonstrated a far more tangible influence of American rhetoric on race. Indeed, in adopting such a specific extract of King's speech, Fox consciously or unconsciously repeated a mantra central to decades of American neoliberal politics that has repositioned and repurposed King as a national, consensus hero rather than a radical critic of US capitalism, white supremacy and imperialism. Scholarship on the Martin Luther King US national holiday celebrated every January since 1986, alongside work discussing the monument to King unveiled in Washington, DC, in 2011, has concluded that the slain civil rights leader's image has been dramatically reshaped by cross-party efforts to solidify King within a national story of racial progress, rather than acknowledge the unfulfilled promise of the 1960s and the continued reality of racial and economic inequality in the United States.[13] As a result, King is no longer the figure that most white Americans rejected and resented during the 1960s, but is frozen at a particular moment during his famous 1963 speech, the very moment that Fox referenced to evade consideration of his own white male privilege. Disjointed from his wider worldview, writings, speeches and even the rest of the 'I have a dream' speech itself, this King apparently advocated for the complete disavowal of race as a frame of analysis, a convenient interpretation that, far beyond the ramblings of an alt-right British celebrity, has enabled the legal dismantling of some of the civil rights movement's most significant victories, from voting rights to affirmative action. Fox's frequent use of this soundbite, like that of countless American politicians, celebrities, businesses and commentators, reflects a profound misinterpretation of King's message that, where unchallenged, continues to hinder anything resembling an anti-racist awakening or movement.[14]

King and the colorblind myth in the USA and UK

Ronald Reagan, the most prominent architect of King's redevelopment into a colorblind prophet, personally maligned the civil rights movement along with other social movements during the 1960s while he was governor of California. His election to the presidency in 1980 saw him win just 14 per cent of the Black vote, at the time the lowest proportion of the African American vote secured by a Republican president in US history. By Reagan's re-election in 1984, this had dwindled to 9 per cent.[15] Faced with an unfavourable record on civil rights, Reagan signed the Martin Luther King holiday into law in 1983, and increasingly aligned himself with King's legacy, helping to popularise what Gomer calls an 'ideology of colorblindness' that 'cherry-picks and co-opts language from the civil rights era', notably King's 'I have a dream' speech.[16] Taking King's words out of context, Reagan implied that King's desire for a colorblind United States mandated a removal of race from all political discourse, and a refusal to acknowledge or address race as a category of identity or analysis. In doing so, Reagan and his allies failed to address the fact that King's dream of colorblindness was articulated in 1963, in a United States that literally segregated its citizens by race in most public spaces and upheld a segregated public school system declared unconstitutional almost a decade earlier.[17] While segregation was, in practical terms, a largely southern phenomenon by the early 1960s, it was unchallenged and often reinforced by the federal system, which turned a blind eye to the brutality inflicted on Black communities and activists across the country. It is thus unsurprising that King felt that a colorblind society was something he could only dream about.

A cursory glance at King's wider career highlights the hypocrisy of citing his colorblind dream as a rationale for dismantling affirmative action and court-ordered busing to desegregate US schools. But campaigns to end both programmes in the 1970s helped to develop what Gomer deems 'civil rights compliant language' that worked against the aims of the original movement and advocated 'an individualistic approach to analyzing racism' within a decade of King's assassination. Such rhetoric, which Reagan then perfected from the White House, prevents governmental intervention on behalf of civil rights, and thus justifies the dismantling of the civil rights victories that King fought so hard for.[18] Through its emphasis on interpersonal relationships, the ideology of colorblindness reinforces a triumphal narrative of racial progress, celebrating the formal demise of racial segregation, but refusing to acknowledge the lingering realities of white supremacy and centuries of inequality. Like the debates over Meghan Markle's treatment in the UK, the parameters of discussion are limited to the individual rather than the structural: the royal family rather than the Home Office, the press coverage of one woman rather than its constant degradation of 'migrants, Muslims and other minorities'.[19] By spotlighting such comparisons, it is easy to see how colorblind politics undermines anti-racist action in modern Britain, just as it does in the United States.

For example, when the 1999 Macpherson Report cited failings and institutional racism at the heart of London's Metropolitan Police following the racist murder of Black teenager Stephen Lawrence in April 1993, it constituted an important moment in modern British history and political culture, 'where racism was named not merely as an act related to individual prejudice but as something that was linked to the structuration of the state'.[20] However, critics including the then journalist Michael Gove dismissed both the Macpherson Report and the subsequent recommendations from the Commission for Multi-Ethnic Britain (CMEB) as 'a forced march down one path, paved with good intentions, towards a massive and illiberal extension of state power'. Writing in *The Times*, Gove argued that the CMEB recommended 'huge interference in the autonomy of individuals and corporations' and that it would 'institutionalise racial discrimination'. Citing Martin Luther King, who 'fought for a "colour-blind society"', Gove contended that the CMEB 'is arguing for employment policies based on colour, a stance once the sole preserve of apartheid's apologists'.[21]

By contrast, Gove wrote appreciatively of a Civitas report, *Racist Murder and Pressure Group Politics*, which questioned the intellectual and legal integrity of the Macpherson Report and offered its own interpretation of British race relations through the lens of African American history, concluding that Doreen and Neville Lawrence transitioned from an 'integrationist and self-help mutual aid model of Frederick Douglass and Booker T. Washington' following their son's murder, ultimately choosing 'the Malcolm X and Stokely Carmichael model of victimhood, confrontation, and separation.' Somewhat ironically, the Civitas report had previously criticised Macpherson for citing 'works that not only have no connection with the Lawrence case, but works that do not deal with this country at all', including assessments of the Rodney King case in Los Angeles and works by Stokely Carmichael, who popularised the term 'Black Power' in 1966. According to the authors of the Civitas report, Carmichael 'had no special qualifications' and should therefore not be taken as an authoritative voice on institutional racism, the very concept of which Macpherson attributed to him. In particular, the Civitas authors cited Carmichael's eventual opposition to King's integrationist stance as further evidence of Carmichael's unreliability as a source on anti-racism, whereby they consciously or unconsciously cited King as the authority on matters of anti-racist protest and strategy.[22] In doing so, they tangled themselves in a revealing double bind, embracing an image of King readily available via the American right, which paradoxically undermined their overarching argument that African American political movements have no relevance to or bearing on UK racial issues. Such arguments seek to extinguish transatlantic solidarity and the apparent import of 'American-style racial dramas', as evidenced by hyperbolic media responses to planned visits from African American civil rights leaders, but simultaneously cite King as the only acceptable example of anti-racist work.

Here, the Civitas authors, like Michael Gove, parroted the 'colorblind' rhetoric of the American right, claiming King as an acceptable oracle on tolerance, all the while dismissing African American racial thought as irrelevant in the British context. Meanwhile, the UK Labour government's commitment to multiculturalism promptly wavered in the aftermath of racially motivated riots in Burnley, Bradford and Oldham in 2001, which pitted white residents against their South Asian, mostly Muslim neighbours. Scrambling for an explanation, politicians and commentators cited a lack of social cohesion stemming from 'self-segregating' South Asian communities who failed 'to adhere to the dominant values of British society'. Meanwhile, focus on contingents of far-right activists and sympathisers amongst white rioters prevented meaningful acknowledgement of 'systematic forms of racism and racial exclusion', such as segregationist housing policies that endured into the 1990s, and the vital context that it was white Britons who, in 2001, were overwhelmingly likely to live in racially exclusive areas.[23] Nevertheless, as the rhetoric of 'self-segregating minorities' endured, it further spotlighted Britain's own 'colorblind' myth: that normative British identity is something anyone can integrate into.

The 'host/immigrant binary': Race and immigration in modern Britain

In the wake of the 2001 riots, rhetoric around 'self-segregating' minority communities prompted anxieties about radicalisation, national security and a lack of social cohesion as the United Kingdom joined the United States in its War on Terror. Just as the 'pathology of the single-parent African-Caribbean family' dominated political and journalistic attempts to explain urban unrest in the 1980s, 'notions of South Asian family dissolution from within' assumed ethnic, generational and gendered dysfunction, here testament to the evident failures of multiculturalism, as a younger generation of British Muslim men 'struggled to deal with an apparent disjuncture' between their upbringing by immigrant parents and their British citizenship. Rather than 'an assertion of belonging, [or] a demand for full acceptance free from racist exclusion', the actions of British South Asian males during the riots were considered 'a rejection of citizenship'. In later years, the government would make similarly prejudiced appeals to British Muslim women, urging them to discard the *niqab* and other face and head coverings, which, according to then Home Secretary, Jack Straw, constituted 'a visible statement of separation and of difference'.[24]

Sociologist James Rhodes's exploration of the extent to which 'colour blind racism' hindered governmental responses to race riots in the early twenty-first century suggests that a dominant political rhetoric of 'cultural differences' prevented meaningful engagement with the hardships and inequalities facing ethnic minority communities in Britain. As Eduardo Bonilla-Silva has argued in relation to the United States, 'abstract liberalism' rejects the idea of intervention to alleviate racial inequality, which it renders as an encroachment on individual rights. However, in the aftermath of the 2001 race riots, British politicians adopted 'a discourse of cultural pathology and inherent cultural differences that lie primarily between white and "non-white" groups', which limits the concept of racism to 'extreme actions such as police brutality or forms of racial violence'. As in the United States, such concepts have emerged as a cross-party consensus in modern Britain, assuming a 'commonsense' logic rooted in a shared logic of neoliberalism.[25]

As Rhodes concludes, British discussions of citizenship constitute an important distinction between otherwise remarkably similar concepts of colorblind ideology in the UK and USA. While plurality is considered integral to American exceptionalism, where birth right citizenship is also constitutionally defined, British discussions of race and culture are rooted in a 'host/immigrant binary', whereby white Britishness constitutes a normative, assumedly indigenous identity. Though 'others' are theoretically welcomed, reflecting a paternalistic conceptualisation of equality and civil rights as granted from above, non-white British citizens continue to be thought of as immigrants for generations, including those born in Britain or its former colonies.[26] This is painfully clear in the recent *Windrush* scandal, in which citizens with familial or personal origins in the Caribbean faced deportation, including those who arrived in Britain as children and thus lacked official documentation, or whose landing cards were destroyed by the Home Office. Similarly, the UK Supreme Court's decision to remove Shamima Begum's British citizenship because of her links to Islamic State militants in Syria further reinforced the idea that citizenship for non-white Britons is contingent on behaviour and at the mercy of the government. Rejecting Begum's appeal in February 2023, the Special Immigration Appeals Commission ruled that the UK Home Secretary's power to strip Begum of her citizenship was not limited by the 'credible suspicion' that Begum was a victim of child sex trafficking when she travelled from Britain to Syria aged fifteen, or that the decision leaves London-born Begum *de facto* stateless.[27] In these cases, as in so many others, national identity is often cited as a commitment to 'British values', which obscures the extent to which it is racially exclusive. The development of 'citizenship tests', which emerged in the aftermath of the 2001 riots, redefined UK citizenship as something rooted in national loyalty and fluency in the English language, and thus implied that all claims to British identity were rooted in a sense of integration and acceptance by the dominant group. This shift marked the evolution of a particularly British myth of colorblindness: a myth of tolerance, acceptance and cohesion, in which the burden of integration is limited to non-white minorities, whose status in the United Kingdom remains contingent regardless of British imperial patterns or their place of birth. 'It is not that racialised others cannot belong', Rhodes argues, paraphrasing this governmental logic, 'but that they choose not to'.[28]

Laurence Fox appealed to this same narrative when he refused to accept that racism may have impacted Meghan Markle's treatment at the hands of the UK press. Citing the UK as 'the most lovely, tolerant country in Europe', Fox demonstrated the defensiveness that meets accusations of both everyday and structural racisms in modern Britain, rooted in what Les Back et al. define as a 'postcolonial paradox'. Here, 'the remnants of racially exclusive nationalism and the phantoms of imperial greatness' coexist with commitments to diversity, as politicians scramble to 'placate racism and xenophobia within [an] increasingly disenchanted electorate'.[29] Since New Labour's landslide election in 1997, government rhetoric on immigration evolved from the Conservatives' open hostility; to a tolerance rooted in economic necessity; to Theresa May's 'Hostile Environment', Brexit, the *Windrush* scandal; and, most recently, Rishi Sunak's proposed 'Stop the Boats' legislation, which would grant British authorities considerable powers to immediately deport someone entering the UK without official asylum or visa status, as well as imposing a lifetime ban on the migrant in question. Sunak's proposal, deemed illegal by the United Nations, bears strong resemblance to Australian policies that have seen those seeking asylum in Australia held on remote Pacific islands for the last two decades.[30] However, it is also a natural manifestation of hostile political and public attitudes toward immigration and asylum seekers in Britain that have normalised language of 'careful management' and potent distinctions between 'desirable' and 'dependent' migrants. As a result, 'current legislation on migration and on race relations in Britain assumes that good race relations depend on ever more strict immigration controls' that ensure that those entering Britain are committed to integration and contribution.[31] Herein lies a distinctly British manifestation of the colorblind ideology, which implies that the United Kingdom is open to all those who ascribe to its values, but has the right to reject people at will.

'A bad habit with a long history': Comparing racial politics in Britain and the United States

Commitment to a British concept of colorblindness, rooted in an assumed white national identity that underpins a tolerant, cohesive society, is evident in defensiveness toward accusations of everyday and structural forms of racism. But the looming spectre of the United States, which through gun violence and extreme political polarisation appears ever more racially explosive, encourages British complacency. With the United States as a frequent reference point, British politicians, voters and commentators suffer from what Barnor Hesse famously described as 'racism's conceptual double bind', in which the presence of 'extremism or exceptionalism' prevents our ability to fully comprehend the 'conventional and mainstream'.[32] While Hesse's original argument centred on the distinction between the white nationalist extremes within all western societies and the seemingly mundane ways in which governmental structures prioritise and sustain white supremacy, it can also be argued that Hesse's double bind is further entrenched in Britain because of a tendency to cite the USA as a reference point. Indeed, as the historian David Olusoga writes, 'downplaying British racism with comparisons to the US is a bad habit with a long history', often serving as a 'distraction'. Focusing on police brutality rather than 'the racism that inspired it' implies that the USA is 'beyond meaningful comparison', Olusoga writes, reminding readers that George Floyd was a victim not of gun violence, but rather of excessive physical force from police officers, and that Black men in Britain are nine times more likely to be stopped and searched than white men.[33] Olusoga might have drawn further comparison with Mark Duggan, a twenty-nine-year-old Black Londoner fatally shot by police in 2011, and whom Black Lives Matter protesters have argued should be considered Britain's George Floyd.

Despite evidence of the disproportionate monitoring and criminalisation of Black communities in Britain, Rhodes argues that a scholarly emphasis on the British New Right's development of a 'racially exclusive conception of national identity' has obscured from public discourse all but the most extreme forms of racism and/or far-right mobilisation. As such, failure to recognise 'the naturalization of racial inequalities' that uphold white hegemony has exacerbated existing imbalances in political, cultural and social opportunities.[34] Unlike the United States, where the publication of Michelle Alexander's 2010 book *The New Jim Crow: Mass Incarceration in the Age of Colorblindness* brought national and international attention to the disproportionate rate at which Black and Brown Americans are incarcerated, there has been no equivalent attention to the UK's incarceration figures, particularly a 2008 Ministry of Justice report that stated that 15 per cent of the UK prison population were Black despite Black people making up just 2.2 per cent of the UK population. Though the United States incarcerates considerably more of its population, meaning that a Black person is still more likely to be imprisoned in the USA than in the UK, the disproportionate number of Black prisoners in the UK criminal justice system compared to the country's overall Black population actually exceeds the comparable figures from the USA.[35] Therefore, though Black Britons are less likely than Black Americans to be shot dead by police or incarcerated, they nevertheless face potentially lethal force through disproportionate interactions with the criminal justice system. Indeed, no police officer has been convicted of involvement in the death of a Black person in Britain since 1969, when two officers were found guilty of assaulting David Oluwale in Leeds, the first recorded case of a Black person dying in police custody in the United Kingdom.[36]

'We're equal. Now you want to define people by their physical characteristics?' British politicians and the language of colorblindness

While this chapter has emphasised the importance of understanding British colorblindness on its own terms, as well as in comparison with that of the

United States, it remains apparent that Martin Luther King, Jr, remains a powerful point of reference. As suggested, this reachability is rooted in neoliberal manipulation of King's image and legacy in the decades since his assassination. Performative social media solidarity, such as that advocated by politicians, celebrities and multinational companies on Martin Luther King Day or during the prominent Black Lives Matter protests have alerted a new generation of British commentators, politicians and everyday social media users to the apparent malleability of King's image, even in the hands of government agencies that wiretapped his phones, attempted to undermine his marriage and urged him to commit suicide during his own lifetime.

One can only hope that the experiences of Ben Bradley, Conservative MP for Mansfield, will make British adherents of colorblindness think twice before appropriating King again. On 23 November 2020, after a summer of anti-racist protests and debates in the United States, Britain and beyond, Bradley cited disembodied lines from King's 'I have a dream' speech in a hastily deleted tweet just days after his speech in the House of Commons in celebration of International Men's Day: ' "I have a dream … will one day live in a nation where they will not be judged by the colour [*sic*] of their skin, but by the content of their character." [King's] point was than [*sic*] skin colour doesn't matter. We're equal. Now you want to define people by their physical characteristics?'.[37]

In his speech to the Commons on 19 November 2020, Bradley argued that 'the constant drive for equality and diversity seeks to drag others down rather than lift everyone up', and lamented 'the impact of equalities legislation, which sometimes seems to provide additional help for everyone except men and boys'. While the exact purpose of his tweet about King remains unclear, Bradley was likely responding to critics of his speech on International Men's Day, in which he argued that successful efforts to support women and girls in education constituted 'misuse of our equalities law to exacerbate gender inequality, rather than fixing it, with countless programmes to support girls into HE [higher education] and none for boys'. Referring to figures that demonstrated girls now outperforming boys across UK schools, Bradley argued 'that selecting who to help based on physical characteristics alone is the very definition of discrimination; that the need for this help should be evidenced if it is to comply with the law; and that boys need help too'.[38]

With this context, Bradley outlined efforts to support a group historically marginalised in UK education as discriminatory. In supporting women and girls, UK authorities were excluding men and boys, particularly those from the white working class. Bradley's use of King's speech in this moment, when encouraged to consider wider practices and manifestations of white male privilege, echoed Laurence Fox's defensiveness in the aftermath of his *Question Time* appearance earlier in 2020, and further evidenced the power of colorblind rhetoric in British political culture. Like the 'All Lives Matter' response to Black Lives Matter, Bradley's attention to men and boys in the wake of female educational success engendered an apparently humanistic concern for all, albeit one that he articulated specifically in support of white working-class men and boys. Arguing that women and girls no longer required support toward educational attainment, Bradley minimised the continued impact of sexism and misogyny in modern Britain and argued that it was in fact white working-class boys that now required 'special treatment'. Despite raising general concerns about the difficulties faced by men more generally, Bradley's particular emphasis on white working-class males was not unintentional. As such, his citation of King's hope for a colorblind society was intended to undermine the current use of the Equality Act 2010, just as generations of conservative and neoliberal politicians have argued that US civil rights legislation secured in the 1960s is no longer necessary, and in some cases serves to bolster minority advancement at the expense of white Americans. Such arguments have been most prevalent in debates over affirmative action, school integration via bussing, and voting rights protections.

Psychologists argue that colorblind rhetoric is most common amongst those who seek to avoid accusations of bias and prejudice, and that while many people claim to be colorblind, race remains a quick and often automatic means of identification.[39] Such observations align with historical assessments of Ronald Reagan's adoption of colorblind rhetoric while dismantling the hard-fought victories of the civil rights era, and could help to explain Bradley's defensiveness when discussing what he perceived as a 'general discourse that so often seems to pervade our society that talks of male privilege, of toxic masculinity, and of men as oppressors rather than positive contributors or role models'.[40] Though Bradley had considerable, legitimate concerns for white working-class men and boys, he knew that to discuss dismantling programmes supporting women and girls would invite accusations of sexism. In leaning on the distorted memory of Martin Luther King, Bradley adopted the strategy of his American peers, who have done so since the 1970s. However, testament to the power of social media, the highest-profile response to Bradley's tweet came from King's own daughter, Bernice King, who promptly schooled Bradley on her father's message and true legacy: 'My father's point and central to his beliefs, teachings and activism (per his speeches/books) was this: We cannot condone racism, but must eradicate it as one of the pervasive, systemic, overt and destructive Triple Evils, with militarism and poverty being the other two.' In a follow-up tweet, Bernice King further entrenched the significance of her father's message to contemporary issues, in a direct challenge to those, like Bradley, who implied that King's work has been done. Her father's words, Bernice King argued, should 'stop the type of suppression of Black votes that's being attempted in Georgia, Pennsylvania, and Michigan right now. And to end health, policing and housing disparities driven by racism. Eradicate racism.'[41]

To truly apply Martin Luther King's message to the realities of racism in modern Britain would require politicians to acknowledge his understanding of global capitalism, in which goods, money and white supremacy can travel with ease, but people cannot. Racialised borders of all kinds, at the local and national level, keep people apart, denying them recognition, solidarity and, therefore, resistance. In recent years, as both the UK and USA have surged to the right politically, liberal commentators have lamented each nation's apparent loss of moral standing. They therefore imply that there was once a time when the United States and the United Kingdom projected better values than those crystalised in President Donald Trump's 'Build the Wall' rhetoric, or the consistently anti-immigration stances adopted by British politicians and journalists. The implication that such a period ever existed, as Michael B. McCormack and Althea Legal-Miller have argued, is a fiction that King undermined decades ago when he acknowledged that both nations 'were deeply implicated in global manifestations of white supremacy'. In 1964, while in London en route to Oslo to collect his Nobel Peace Prize, King drew attention to 'thousands and thousands of colored people' arriving in Britain 'from the West Indies, from Pakistan, from India, from Africa', arguing that these migrants 'have the just right to come to this great land, and they have the just right to expect justice and democracy in this land'. Citing Steven W. Thrasher, McCormack and Legal-Miller argue that the Black Lives Matter movement advocates a borderless message similar to King's, rooted in transnational solidarities and united struggles against white supremacy and settler colonialism.[42] This advocation has proven crucial to the recent politicisation of many in Britain, where racism has often been sidelined by the media, politicians and education as an American issue. Furthermore, as Thrasher continues, Black Lives Matter has compromised the concept of 'respectability politics', and therefore the argument that 'if black people are just upstanding enough they won't experience racism', or that 'the only black lives worth saving are those of idealized, sanitized saints'.[43]

Conclusion

Despite King's explicit assertion 'that racism is a world problem', and despite his acknowledgement of the rights of Britain's migrant communities, racism's long history and powerful presence in Britain remain 'starved of oxygen' in our national story. Meanwhile, as Reni Eddo-Lodge continues, 'the US struggle against racism is globalised as *the* story against racism that we should look to for inspiration' (emphasis mine). Historical assessment of the African American civil rights movement of the 1950s and 1960s therefore encourages British students to recognise the USA's racial history and present as singularly important, often from a young age, 'eclipsing the black British story so much that we convince ourselves that Britain has never had a problem with race'.[44] Seldom do UK curricula and textbooks attempt to link the US movement to concurrent events in the UK during a pivotal period in the development of modern Britain that shaped its racial present. For many British students, whether at schools or universities, American history modules or classes often constitute the first formal educational setting in which the histories of race and racism are discussed, a reality that the overwhelmingly white UK American studies community is increasingly forced to reflect upon.[45]

As this chapter has demonstrated, those citing King as inspiration in the decades since his assassination are not confined to anti-racists or even the left. Rather, as in the United States, the depoliticised King is used to challenge any number of activist demands in modern Britain, from those of Stephen Lawrence's parents to the more recent Black Lives Matter protests. Even those asking commentators simply to consider their racial and gender privilege have been met with combative assertions of King's apparent colorblind dream, further evidencing King's unique position within the neoliberal imagination. However, and as noted, it is important to be sensitive to the unique contours of British colorblind rhetoric, which is centred in relation to immigration rather than plurality, and which continues to assume an apparently indigenous 'host' culture that remains exclusively white. All others are to be tolerated, within reason, and national rhetoric strongly implies that those welcomed in the United Kingdom, including those born here or otherwise entitled to citizenship, enjoy great privilege compared to the racial realities of the contemporary United States. But if the USA suffers from more explicit political and racial discord, especially that which plays out through gun violence, the United Kingdom remains largely indifferent to its histories of empire, colonialism and exclusion, as well as their contemporary manifestations. Baroness Casey's 2023 report into the practices of the Metropolitan Police records little progress on challenging racism, misogyny and homophobia in the force since the Macpherson Report a quarter of a century earlier.[46] If, as King wrote, 'injustice anywhere is a threat to justice everywhere', activists, scholars and allies must recognise and challenge the UK's own myth of colorblindness, its assumed white normativity, and its manipulation of King's image and message to justify a lack of meaningful action.[47]

Notes

1 Stuart Hall, 'Racism and Reaction', in *Five Views of Multiracial Britain: Talks on Race Relations Broadcast by the BBC* (London: Commission for Racial Equality and BBC, 1978), pp. 23–35 (p. 26).
2 Remi Joseph-Salisbury, '"Does anybody really care what a racist says?" Anti-Racism in "Post-Racial" Times', *Sociological Review*, 67:1 (2019), 63–78 (pp. 64–5).
3 Megan Hunt, Benjamin Houston, Brian Ward and Nick Megoran, '"He was shot because America will not give up on racism": Martin Luther King, Jr. and the African American Civil Rights Movement in British Schools', *Journal of American Studies*, 55:2 (2021), 387–417; Hall, 'Racism and Reaction', p. 26.
4 This chapter explores the British adoption of the US term 'colorblindness', and will therefore maintain the US spelling of the concept, except where quoting British sources.
5 Justin Gomer, *White Balance: How Hollywood Shaped Colorblind Ideology and Undermined Civil Rights* (Chapel Hill: University of North Carolina Press, 2020), p. 4.
6 Reni Eddo-Lodge, *Why I'm No Longer Talking to White People about Race* (London: Bloomsbury, 2018), pp. 28, 1, 100–1.
7 'Alt-right' is a loosely defined collective label for a range of groups and individuals that specialise in right-wing provocation, usually on social media and other internet forums. The term 'alt-right' therefore encompasses a blurred organisational structure, which includes figures indistinguishable from neo-Nazi far-right groups, such as Richard Spencer of the US-based National Policy Institute, and those who use social media as a tool for political provocation, the spreading of conspiracy theories and/or financial gain.
8 Tony Sewell, 'Foreword from the Chair', *Commission on Race and Ethnic Disparities: The Report* (March 2021), https://assets.publishing.service.gov.uk/media/6062ddb1d3bf7f5ce1060aa4/20210331_-_CRED_Report_-_FINAL_-_Web_Accessible.pdf, p. 8 (accessed 4 June 2024).
9 Hunt et al., 'He was shot because America will not give up on racism', p. 399. For one account of King in the UK, see Brian Ward, *Martin Luther King in Newcastle: The African American Freedom Struggle and Race Relations in the North East of England* (Newcastle upon Tyne: Tyne Bridge, 2017).
10 E. James West, 'Roil Britannia! Al Sharpton, the British Press, and the 1991 Murder of Rolan Adams', *Immigrants and Minorities*, 37:3 (2019), 184–210 (pp. 185–6). For the campaigns against Stokely Carmichael, see Rosie Wild, '"Black Was the Colour of Our Fight": The Transnational Roots of British Black Power', in Robin D. G. Kelley and Stephen Tuck (eds), *The Other Special Relationship: Race, Rights, and Riots in Britain and the United States* (New York: Palgrave Macmillan, 2015), pp. 24–46 (pp. 39–40); and Clive Webb, 'Enoch Powell's America/America's Enoch Powell', in Daniel Geary, Camilla Schofield and Jennifer Sutton (eds), *Global White Nationalism: From*

Apartheid to Trump (Manchester: Manchester University Press, 2020), 105–30 (pp. 108–9).

11 Nesrine Malik, 'Why the Woes of Harry and Meghan Tell Us Little about British Racism', *Guardian* (19 December 2022), www.theguardian.com/commentisfree/2022/dec/19/harry-and-meghan-racism-britain-netflix-documentary? (accessed 20 March 2023).

12 Bethany Minelle, 'Laurence Fox Slams Black and Working Class Actors for "Only Complaining after Becoming Famous"', *Sky News* (20 January 2020), https://news.sky.com/story/laurence-fox-slams-black-and-working-class-actors-for-only-complaining-after-becoming-famous-11912649 (accessed 20 March 2023); Jamie Doward, 'Lecturer Says She Faced Online Abuse after Question Time Clash with Laurence Fox', *Guardian* (18 January 2020), www.theguardian.com/tv-and-radio/2020/jan/18/question-time-clash-lecturer-tells-of-hate-mail (accessed 20 March 2023).

13 For debates about King's legacy and memory, see Daniel T. Fleming, *Living the Dream: The Contested History of Martin Luther King, Jr. Day* (Chapel Hill: University of North Carolina Press, 2022); E. James West, 'A Hero to Be Remembered: *Ebony* Magazine, Critical Memory and the "Real Meaning" of the King Holiday', *Journal of American Studies*, 52:2 (2018), 503–27; Patrick Hagopian, 'The Martin Luther King, Jr. Memorial and the Politics of Post-Racialism', *History and Memory*, 32:2 (2020), 36–77; Kevin Bruyneel, 'The King's Body: The Martin Luther King Jr. Memorial and the Politics of Collective Memory', *History & Memory*, 26:1 (2014), 75–108.

14 For further examples of Fox citing King, see https://twitter.com/thereclaimparty/status/1543978064492765184 and https://twitter.com/LozzaFox/status/1608035736179146752 (both accessed 4 June 2024).

15 Lilia Fernandez, 'Ronald Reagan, Race, Civil Rights, and Immigration', in Andrew L. Johns (ed.), *A Companion to Ronald Reagan* (Hoboken, NJ: John Wiley & Sons, 2015), pp. 184–203 (p. 185); Roper Center, Cornell University, 'How Groups Voted in 1980', https://ropercenter.cornell.edu/how-groups-voted-1980 (accessed 20 March 2023); Roper Center, Cornell University, 'How Groups Voted in 1984', https://ropercenter.cornell.edu/how-groups-voted-1984 (accessed 20 March 2023).

16 Gomer, *White Balance*, p. 2.

17 *Brown v. Board of Education of Topeka*, 347 US 483 (1954).

18 Gomer, *White Balance*, pp. 2–3.

19 Malik, 'Why the Woes of Harry and Meghan Tell Us Little about British Racism'.

20 Nisha Kapoor, 'The Advancement of Racial Neoliberalism in Britain', *Ethnic and Racial Studies*, 36:6 (2013), 1028–46 (p. 1033).

21 Michael Gove, 'Be Politically Astute, Not Politically Correct', *The Times* (10 October 2000), 20.

22 Norman Dennis, George Erdos and Ahmed Al-Shahi, *Racist Murder and Pressure Group Politics*, Institute for the Study of Civil Society, London (September 2000), www.civitas.org.uk/content/files/cs05.pdf, pp. 147–8, 34–5,

96 (accessed 20 March 2023). The authors also cited Carmichael's criticisms of Zionism and Israeli policies toward Palestinians as evidence of antisemitism, which, in their view, further undermined Carmichael's status as an anti-racist campaigner and thinker.
23 Oldham's local authority was found guilty of operating a segregationist housing policy in 1993. The average white person in Britain in 2001, studies suggested, lived in a ward that was more than 90 per cent white. For Pakistani groups in Britain, residential areas had an average Pakistani population of 17 per cent. See Kapoor, 'The Advancement of Racial Neoliberalism', pp. 1035–6; Nissa Finley and Ludi Simpson, *'Sleepwalking to Segregation'? Challenging Myths about Race and Migration* (Bristol: Policy Press, 2009), p. 124.
24 James Rhodes, 'Revisiting the 2001 Riots: New Labour and the Rise of "Colour Blind Racism"', *Sociological Research Online*, 14:5 (2009), n.p. For discussion of the British media's coverage of race and riots in the 1980s, see Simon Peplow, *Race and Riots in Thatcher's Britain* (Manchester: Manchester University Press, 2019); and Kieran Connell, *Black Handsworth: Race in 1980s Britain* (Berkeley: University of California Press, 2019).
25 Rhodes, 'Revisiting the 2001 Riots'; Eduardo Bonilla-Silva, *Racism without Racists: Color-Blind Racism and the Persistence of Racial Inequality in the United States* (Washington, DC: Rowman & Littlefield, 2006). In fact, a 'convergence between Labour and the Conservatives on migration' emerged as early as 1964, when the Labour government of the time issued a White Paper advocating tighter controls on immigration. See Liza Schuster and John Solomos, 'Race, Immigration and Asylum: New Labour's Agenda and Its Consequences', *Ethnicities*, 4:2 (2004), 267–300 (p. 268).
26 Rhodes, 'Revisiting the 2001 Riots'.
27 Yasmin Ahmed, 'Shamima Begum Ruling a Dark Stain on the UK Justice System', *Human Rights Watch* (23 February 2023), www.hrw.org/news/2023/02/23/shamima-begum-ruling-dark-stain-uk-justice-system (accessed 20 March 2023).
28 Rhodes, 'Revisiting the 2001 Riots'.
29 Les Back, Michael Keith, Azra Khan, Kalbir Shukra and John Solomos, 'New Labour's White Heart: Politics, Multiculturalism and the Return of Assimilation', *Political Quarterly*, 3:4 (2002), 445–54 (p. 452).
30 Ben Doherty, '"Stop the Boats": Sunak's Anti-Asylum Slogan Echoes Australia's Harsh Policy', *Guardian* (8 March 2023), www.theguardian.com/uk-news/2023/mar/08/stop-the-boats-sunaks-anti-asylum-slogan-echoes-australia-harsh-policy (accessed 19 March 2023).
31 Schuster and Solomos, 'Race, Immigration and Asylum', pp. 278–9, 284.
32 Barnor Hesse, 'Im/Plausible Deniability: Racism's Conceptual Double Bind', *Social Identities*, 10:1 (2004), 9–29 (p. 14).
33 David Olusoga, 'Britain Is Not America. But We Too Are Disfigured by Deep and Pervasive Racism', *Guardian* (7 June 2020), www.theguardian.com/commentisfree/2020/jun/07/britain-is-not-america-but-we-too-are-disfigured-bydeep-and-pervasive-racism (accessed 1 March 2023).

34 Rhodes, 'Revisiting the 2001 Riots'.
35 Randeep Ramesh, 'More Black People Jailed in England and Wales Proportionally than in US', *Guardian* (11 October 2010), www.theguardian.com/society/2010/oct/11/black-prison-population-increase-england (accessed 20 March 2023); Michael B. McCormack and Althea Legal-Miller, 'All Over the World like a Fever: Martin Luther King Jr.'s World House and the Movement for Black Lives in the United States and the United Kingdom', in Vicki L. Crawford and Lewis V. Baldwin (eds), *Reclaiming the Great World House: The Global Vision of Martin Luther King Jr.* (Athens: University of Georgia Press, 2019), pp. 254–82 (p. 262).
36 Siana Bangura, 'We Need To Talk about Police Brutality in the U.K.', *Fader* (29 March 2016), www.thefader.com/2016/03/29/police-brutality-uk-essay (accessed 20 March 2023).
37 Isobel Frodsham, 'Martin Luther King Jr's Daughter Criticises Tory MP Ben Bradley for Appropriating Father's Words', *Independent* (24 November 2020), www.independent.co.uk/news/uk/politics/martin-luther-king-jr-daughter-ben-bradley-b1761110.html (accessed 20 March 2023).
38 Ben Bradley, speech to the House of Commons, International Men's Day, 684 Parl. Deb., HC (19 November 2024), https://hansard.parliament.uk/commons/2020-11-19/debates/FF3FD025-D6F1-4872-84A1-09FBFDA4E4A0/InternationalMen%E2%80%99Sday (accessed 20 March 2023).
39 Evan P. Apfelbaum, Samuel R. Sommers and Michael I. Norton, 'Seeing Race and Seeming Racist? Evaluating Strategic Colorblindness in Social Interaction', *Journal of Personality and Social Psychology*, 95:4 (2008), 918–32.
40 684 Parl. Deb., HC (19 November 2024).
41 Frodsham, 'Martin Luther King Jr's Daughter'.
42 McCormack and Legal-Miller, 'All Over the World like a Fever', pp. 254–5.
43 Steven W. Thrasher, 'Black Lives Matter Has Showed Us: The Oppression of Black People Is Borderless', *Guardian* (9 August 2015), www.theguardian.com/commentisfree/2015/aug/09/black-lives-matter-movement-taught-black-oppression-borderless-michael-brown (accessed 20 March 2023).
44 Martin Luther King, Jr, quoted in Stephen Tuck, *The Night Malcolm X Spoke at the Oxford Union: A Transatlantic Story of Antiracist Protest* (Berkeley: University of California Press, 2014), 175. Eddo-Lodge, *Why I'm No Longer Talking to White People*, pp. 54–5.
45 Kate Dossett, Annette K. Joseph-Gabriel, Hasan Kwame Jeffries et al., 'Exchange: Teaching African American Studies in the US and the UK', *Journal of American Studies*, 52:2 (2018), 528–54 (p. 535); see also Hunt et al., 'He was shot because America will not give up on racism'.
46 Baroness Casey of Blackstock, 'An Independent Review into the Standards of Behaviour and Internal Culture of the Metropolitan Police Service' (March 2023), www.met.police.uk/SysSiteAssets/media/downloads/met/about-us/baroness-casey-review/update-march-2023/baroness-casey-review-march-2023.pdf (accessed 22 March 2023).
47 Martin Luther King, Jr, *Letter from a Birmingham Jail* (April 1963), www.africa.upenn.edu/Articles_Gen/Letter_Birmingham.html (accessed 20 March 2023).

Afterword

Priyamvada Gopal

In a newspaper photograph from 11 May 1958, the veteran British politician and Labour MP for Eton and Slough, Fenner Brockway, stands in a curiously jaunty pose, one foot on the front steps of his house, pipe in mouth, hands striking what may be a matchbox. Though fully dressed in a suit and tie, a bespectacled Brockway appears to be wearing comfortable house slippers as he looks at the camera with a slight smile. When our eye zooms away from him, the full implications of the paint-splashed scene sink in. At his feet there is a huge swastika daubed in starkly white paint, the arms of another swastika can be seen behind him, a third yet to the pillar on his left, and three more on the front door of his house. 'KEEP BRITAIN WHITE', screams graffiti on the steps leading to the front door, and again on the walls. On the floor of the patio, a more personal instruction: 'BROCKWAY GET OUT.' Faintly discernible above him are the words 'NO RACE MIXING LAW' (or perhaps it is 'MIXTURE').[1]

Brockway's crime in the eyes of the British far right was to have brought to Parliament the previous day a Private Member's Bill – in all he would do so no less than eight times starting in 1957 – that would legally prohibit racial discrimination, or the infamous 'colour bar' that enabled the denial of goods and services to non-white people in Britain. The experienced parliamentarian Brockway fronted these legislative campaigns, but they derived from his long history of friendships, work and alliances with anti-racist campaigners, including the cricketer and parliamentarian Learie Constantine, and the journalist and Communist activist Claudia Jones, all of whom challenged the discrimination that they and their fellow people of colour were subjected to. In their opening to *Anti-Racism in Britain*, Saffron East, Grace Redhead and Theo Williams note that the history of anti-racism in Britain 'is characterised at one end of the spectrum by paternalism and at the other end by solidarity' and observe correctly that 'movements of solidarity and abolition often found themselves uncomfortably sharing rhetorical and organisational space with paternalist actors'. Over his long and rich life, Brockway had himself travelled from the somewhat patrician liberalism of his youth to developing robust anti-racist and anti-colonial commitments; key to this political journey were his travels to British India and parts of Africa under colonial rule, and critical engagement with Black and Asian anti-colonial and anti-racist movements and actors. By the time he took charge of the Movement for Colonial Freedom, established in 1954 and later renamed Liberation, Brockway had become an indefatigable voice for liberation from racism and colonialism at the heart of the British political establishment, though its political inflections sometimes moved between the liberal and the radical, the pragmatic and the oppositional, the patrician and the vernacular. Something of these tensions can also be seen in George Orwell's attitudes to colonialism, as Theo Williams's chapter here demonstrates.

The question of solidarity, the difficult work of which is undoubtedly exemplified by Brockway's long and committed career raising challenges to racism and colonialism along with his allies, is at the heart of this richly textured collection. Between them, its chapters offer a detailed mapping of the multiple trajectories and tensions of anti-racism in Britain over the long twentieth century into the present, and also ask how the 'usable pasts' of anti-racism might bear upon the specific challenges of the present. Contrary to the claims of ubiquitous commentary in the British media, no sudden onset pandemic of 'wokeness' distinguishes our post-Brexit, pandemic-scarred present conjuncture; anti-racist resistance is of much longer duration. As the contributions in this valuable compendium make comprehensively clear in adding to the scholarship, those affected by it directly have always contested and organised against racial oppression, if in a range of ways, some moderate and others more directly oppositional. From 1880 to the present, activists, campaigners, writers, students, politicians, journalists, trade unionists, community organisations, mutual aid associations and religious institutions have been involved in a range of ways and across communities in challenging racial discrimination and creating more egalitarian structures and policy frameworks. Then, as now, moral panics around demographic change, cultural integration, and national identity were stoked by actors on left and right, if differently. Almost all who fought for an end to racial oppression were subjected to different forms of pushback and hostility, Brockway being no exception in this regard.

To read the chapters in this volume together is, on the one hand, to see continuities both in forms of racialised oppression and in the range of resistance offered to it. At the same time the arc (or multiple trajectories) from the 1880s to the 2020s prompts us to identify what shifts have in fact taken place and what specific challenges these have generated for our present. Two obvious points of change are the achievement of juridical racial equality (always under pressure and never to be taken for granted) and the dissolution of the British Empire, leaving behind what is now a significantly diminished former world player in the North Atlantic. If we add Britain's departure from the European Union (Brexit) to that mix – curiously not given much attention in this collection despite its marked impact on discourses of migration and race in recent times – then we start to see both the continuities and the shifts from an earlier moment in which anti-racism and anti-colonialism were closely tied together. More salient now are attacks on economic globalisation from both left and right that can take the form of anti-migrant discourse, as was salient during the lead up to Brexit and in the election of Donald Trump to the United States Presidency in 2016. In both cases, valid material questions about the condition of late capitalism and its multiple modalities were transformed, quite deliberately, into anti-migrant and xenophobic discourse.

Another important feature of the present is the emergence of a significant number of Black and Asian political actors with a consequential role in shaping public discourse on race and racism. In the current Parliament alone, we have had no fewer than three home secretaries and a prime minister of Asian immigrant background, and several Black senior ministers, including a chancellor (albeit one who served a particularly truncated term). The Conservatives, not known for a starring role in historical anti-racist campaigns, have taken a predictable pleasure in pointing to the undoubted and unprecedented diversity of recent cabinets. It hardly needs to be said that this is a diversity that has been wielded against minorities and immigrants, including, and in particular, refugees, with some of the most virulent and racist commentary coming from Black and Asian figures such as former Home Secretary Suella Braverman and Prime Minister Rishi Sunak himself. While token figures of colour have long been positioned within both colonial and racialised structures to give them legitimacy, the increased numbers and political clout of the current formation require our attention. What does it mean when the legatees and beneficiaries of anti-racist campaigns, now occupying positions of power and consequence, are deployed against the larger unfinished project of racial equality?

Similar tactics were used historically to suggest that Britain had no need of anti-racist legislation, as we see in Joseph Finlay's illuminating chapter on the role of a 'desire to protect Britain's Jewish community from fascist verbal and printed attacks' in ensuring the passage of the 1965 Race Relations Act. This chapter shows how both opponents and proponents of racial equality legislation made Britain's Jews central to their arguments even as representative Jewish community organisations did not make the case for Jews as a 'racial' (rather than religious) minority who needed to be included in a 'Race Relations Act'. There is still a tendency on the part of some MPs and the British state to emphasise the rights of some minorities over others, even more consciously weaponised now in twenty-first-century iterations of 'divide-and-rule'. What is under attack is the principle of anti-racism as indivisible and applicable to all who are vulnerable to racialised discrimination: Islamophobia and antisemitism would both be treated equally, for instance, as part of the apparatus of exclusion and discrimination. The fact that racism is always 'historically specific', as Felix Lösing reminds us via Stuart Hall in his chapter, and the fact that putative advocates of universal principles do not always hold to them, does not change the fact that anti-racism is universal and indivisible – or it is nothing. As Edward Said reminds us, the task, particularly for intellectuals, 'is explicitly to universalise … to give greater human scope to what a particular race or nation suffered, to associate that experience with the sufferings of others'; this does not automatically entail 'a loss in historical specificity'.[2] In the present, racism can now take the form precisely of *not* universalising, such that the sufferings of Ukraine under Russian invasion can be presented as altogether different in degree and kind – and more worthy of solidarity – than the even more catastrophic invasion and violence inflicted by the Israeli state upon Gaza in Palestine since October 2023. That catastrophe has made abundantly clear that the international order remains profoundly racialised and frankly racist – it is not possible to mince words on this – and that some lives, Palestinian in this case, are clearly deemed to matter considerably less than others, indeed not at all. As I write this in late February 2024, the United States has vetoed in the United Nations an end to the killing in Gaza for the third time while calling for more aid for Ukraine. The problem of the twenty-first century remains the problem of the colour line.

The dialectic of the specific and the universal(able) is also raised in Saffron East's chapter on the concept of 'political Blackness' in relation to the question of solidarity. An umbrella term that is now largely abandoned in anti-racist discourse, political Blackness's history in relation to British South Asian communities raises questions of what, despite their clear limitations, such conjoined identities did make possible. East shows how, in the case of some established organisations, political Blackness served to bring together different second-generation South Asian communities as opposed to the anti-racist unity with Black communities of African and Caribbean heritage that it had spelled for an earlier generation. Subcontinental fractures along religious and national lines presented – as they still do – a particular challenge for anti-racist British South Asians to which political Blackness provided a way out (of sorts), aligning their resistance with a wider socialism and anti-racism in Britain. The present conjuncture does not just confront us with the vitiation of any political umbrella behind which to unite politically divided South Asians – with each other and other minority communities. Anti-racist action within South Asian communities has also to reckon with the impoverishment and hardening of religious and ethnic identities that has taken place under both state-sponsored multiculturalism and the rise of ethnonationalism in India, Pakistan and elsewhere. East rightly considers political Blackness in terms of a 'usable past' for thinking about anti-racist solidarities while noting that it has been replaced by new vocabularies. What do we do, however, about the reality of fissures that have been actively embraced beyond the forms that give us a dizzying plethora of options: British Indian, British Pakistani, British Bangladeshi, British Muslim, British Hindu, British Buddhist and so on? Never mind political Blackness, we might say, whatever happened even to 'British Asian' as an umbrella? The case gets more complicated when we look not only at the Asian anti-Blackness that East acknowledges but also consider the question of caste (acknowledged by the Equality Act of 2010 as 'an aspect of race') and the undoubted realities of caste discrimination in the Indian diaspora.[3] These raise the question of whether and how anti-racist unities can challenge majoritarian racism while simultaneously paying attention to and addressing discrimination, oppression and inequalities within and between minoritised communities.

If political Blackness now sits in the realm of a usable past that we may yet draw on, one significant challenge of our times might well be described as 'political whiteness'. It takes the form of deploying a not insubstantial number of Black and Asian actors to shore up majoritarian norms, driving home the assertion that Britain is tolerant, welcoming and unimpeded by racism while simultaneously articulating aggressive anti-migrant discourse. It is no small irony that this phenomenon was facilitated by the development of what Finn Gleeson describes as New Labour's emphasis on 'diversity as a central feature of British life', which drew, however, on a stigmatisation of 'radical' anti-racism in media and politics combined with increased influence for 'moderate' representatives for Black, Asian and Minority Ethic (BAME, in the language of the state) communities. This bifurcation has been consequential, enabling the rise of a not always necessarily statistically insignificant number, indeed class, of BAME figures who can at once serve ostensibly to embody the tolerant and equal-opportunity nature of the British polity while undermining the kind of 'radical' equality work that actually forced those opportunities open. What I am pointing to here is not just the obscuring of racist structures but an active BAME participation in producing and consolidating them. One notable instance of this was the controversial 2021 *Report of the Commission on Race and Ethnic Disparities*, which was set up in the wake of Black Lives Matter protests in 2020. The Commission was chaired by a Black education consultant and now peer, Tony Sewell, and populated by other BAME figures such as the prime ministerial advisor Munira Mirza, both known already to be hostile to the concepts of institutional and structural racism.[4] The report predictably concluded that the term 'institutional racism' was overused, though there might be some anecdotal instances of overt prejudice, and that more emphasis should be put on individuals, their families and communities over 'invisible external forces'. In stressing agency in this fashion, the report suggested – to understandable outrage – that 'the Caribbean experience' of enslavement should not just be 'about profit and suffering' but also positive cultural transformation 'into a remodelled African/Britain' (sic). The report was overt in its advocacy of what it called 'the decent centre ground' in Britain, charging what it called 'well-organised single-issue identity lobby groups' with proliferating 'pessimistic narratives'. It was not subtle, either, in reproducing a familiar 'political whiteness' talking point, discussed also in Gleeson's analysis of Michael Collins's *The Likes of Us* – that an undue emphasis on racial diversity had, in fact, resulted in actual racial harm to an entity called 'the white working class'. Both Brexit and the election of Trump relied on an incantatory invocation of the putative needs and desires of this entity, harmed, it would be claimed repeatedly, by a focus on race. It is a quick step from talking about the 'white working class' in this incantatory fashion to assuming or suggesting that the working class itself is necessarily white.

The transformation of class into a matter of political whiteness has had the desired effect of at once centralising whiteness as the racial category most in need of reparative policy-making and marginalising class itself as a structural issue. Thus, even as whiteness is repeatedly foregrounded as the site of vulnerability to which attention must be paid, 'colour-blindness' is advocated as the 'real' solution to racial inequalities. This is a point forcefully drawn out by Megan Hunt's chapter, which tracks the repurposing of Martin Luther King into an advocate for 'not seeing' race by virtue of the famous dream in which his children would 'one day live in a nation where they will not be judged by the color of their skin'. As Hunt points out, even as much discourse on racism in Britain insists on the unique nature of Britain's benevolence and tolerance and the inapplicability of the United States as an analytical model for race in Britain, the rhetoric of colorblindness is itself imported from the United States and Ronald Reagan's misappropriation of King to enjoin 'a removal of race from all political discourse'. In the context of the aggravated 'culture wars' stoked by the political right in Britain, such importations have only increased in frequency and force. One example is the attacks on 'wokeness' and 'critical race theory', both fomented by Republicans in the United States in the first instance and reproduced in British political discourse by Tory ministers, particularly by two women of colour, Kemi Badenoch and Suella Braverman.[5] The latter has claimed that multiculturalism has 'failed' in the UK despite her own meteoric rise – and position as race mascot – being clearly attributable to its workings.

Braverman, Badenoch and other votaries of political whiteness have also targeted the calls that have echoed over the last decade to 'decolonise' British history and institutions. Decolonisation in this sense calls for an active engagement with Britain's colonial and racial history while looking forward to a horizon of liberation and equality for all. It is manifestly not about 'inherited racial guilt', which Badenoch reduces it to, but offers all Britons a way to understand themselves in history and society, a history that does not write out the biggest empire the world has ever known and its continued influence on the present. This volume has done a wonderful job of outlining the multiple trajectories of anti-racism that are constitutive of that history and elucidated the vital connections among ideas, episodes and actors within it. The work of decolonising British history is demanding, not reducible to the childish soundbites to which its detractors have reduced it. In this regard, we in the present, like the many historical actors discussed here, must keep on, as they, doing the work.

Notes

1 The photograph can be viewed at www.gettyimages.com.au/detail/news-photo/british-politician-fenner-brockway-the-labour-mp-for-eton-news-photo/886650150 (accessed 10 February 2024).
2 Edward W. Said, 'Lecture 2: Holding Nations and Traditions at Bay', in *REITH LECTURES 1993: Representations of an Intellectual*, http://downloads.bbc.co.uk/rmhttp/radio4/transcripts/1993_reith2.pdf, p. 8 (accessed 20 February 2024).
3 'Asian Caste Discrimination Rife in UK, Says Report', *Guardian* (11 November 2009), www.theguardian.com/society/2009/nov/11/caste-discrimination-uk-report (accessed 19 February 2024).
4 Commission on Race and Ethnic Disparities, *The Report of the Commission on Race and Ethnic Disparities* (March 2021), www.gov.uk/government/publications/the-report-of-the-commission-on-race-and-ethnic-disparities (accessed 14 February 2024).
5 'Kemi Badenoch Woos Tory Members with Culture War Attacks on Labour', *Politico* (2 October 2023), www.politico.eu/article/kemi-badenoch-uk-conservative-labour-culture-war/ (accessed 21 February 2024).

Index

43 Group 126

Abbott, Diane 219
Aberdeen Press and Journal 214
Aberdeen Trades Council 219
abolition 2
Aborigines 90
   aboriginal land, nuclear testing on 172, 177–8, 191
   citizenship status 91–2
   human rights 93–4
   political activism 80, 83
   society and anthropology 90
Aborigenes' Protection Society (APS) 31–2
Achebe, Chinua 65
ACSHO *see* African-Caribbean Self-Help Organisation
Adams, Rolan 230
Adelphi 64, 65
African Friendship Society 103, 105, 106, 107
African Races Association of Glasgow 212
African Society, the 37–8
African Times and Oriental Review (ATOR) 37
African Union Society 35
Africana 115
African-Caribbean Self-Help Organisation (ACSHO) 167
Ahmaddiya Muslim Association 213
Ali, Dusé Mohamed 37, 38
Ali, Shabaz 211
Alien Arts Theatre Company 217
Aliens Act 1905 25, 36
All-Colonial Peoples' (or Subject Peoples') Conference, 1945 116

allyship 13, 208, 220–2
Anderson, Tony 172
Anglo-Scottish Union 1707 210
Anthropological Institute of London 26
Anti-Apartheid Movement 214
Anti-Caste see Impey, Catherine
anti-fascism 64, 66, 73, 74, 124, 125, 139, 220
anti-imperialism 7, 8, 9, 15, 64, 66, 68, 69, 71, 73, 74, 104, 112, 153
Anti-Lynching Committee 32
Anti-Nazi League 125, 212
Anti-Raids Network (ARN) 177
antisemitism 25, 31, 107, 124, 125–6, 127–9, 131, 134–5, 138, 139, 250
Anti-Slavery and Aborigenes' Protection Society (ASAPS) 37
Anti-Slavery Society (ASS) 31–2, 83, 84–5, 86, 87, 88, 92
Anwar, Aamer 219
Appleyard, Bryan 197
APS *see* Aborigines' Protection Society
ARN *see* Anti-Raids Network
ASAPS *see* Anti-Slavery and Aborigenes' Protection Society
Asha refuge 173
Asian Artists' Association 213
Asian Christian Fellowship 213
Asian Women Community Workers Group 173
ASS *see* Anti-Slavery Society
ATOR see African Times and Oriental Review
austerity 179
Awaz 165, 167, 168, 172–4, 175, 178

Index

Badenoch, Kemi 253
Baden-Powell, Robert 27
Ballard, Arthur 66
Balmer Lawrie 210
Bambatha Rebellion 28
Bangladesh Students' Association 213
Bangladeshi Association 213
Barnes, Isaac Edmestone 36
Battle of Adwa 27
Battle of Tsushima 27
Bayoh, Sheku 211
BBC *see* British Broadcasting Corporation
Bean, Gerlin 167
Begum, Shamima 236
Bell, Ronald 126-7
Benenson, Peter 129
Bengali Cultural Association 213
Bennett, Mary Montgomerie 84
Berlin, Isaiah 130
Bhari, Hardial Singh 213
Bhatra Cultural Association 213
Bhawmik, Prasanta Kumar 214
BHM *see* Black History Month
Biko, Steve 175
Bindman, Geoffrey 124, 132
Black History Month (BHM) 155, 156
Black House 169
Black Liberation Front (BLF) 166, 167
Black Lives Matter 1, 8, 176, 221, 228, 238, 239, 241, 242
Black Panther Party 148, 167
Black People's Alliance (BPA) 16, 144-5, 147-50, 158, 159
Black People's Information Centre 167
Black Power 134, 143, 144, 165, 166, 167, 169, 208
Black Unity and Freedom Party (BUFP) 166, 167
Black Voice 167
Blair, Tony 188, 201
Blaize, R. B. 37
BLF *see* Black Liberation Front
Blyden, E. W. 34, 37
BNP *see* British National Party
Board of Deputies 124, 126, 127, 130-1, 133-4, 135-6
Bond of Brotherhood 31
Bonham-Carter, Mark 132
Bourne, Henry Fox 14, 31
Boxer Rebellion 27, 33

Boyle, Rachel 231
BPA *see* Black People's Alliance
Bradley, Ben 229, 239-40
Braine, Bernard 131
Braverman, Suella 249, 253
Brexit 237, 249, 252
Bristol 1, 8
Bristol Solidarity Defendant Group 177
British Broadcasting Corporation (BBC) 73, 108, 231
British Council 113
British Movement 136
British National Party (BNP) 189, 214-15, 217, 218, 219, 220, 223
British royal family 231
British Sailors Society 9, 111
British Seafarers' Union 211
Britishness 68-71
Brixton Black Women's Centre 153
Brixton Black Women's Group 167, 174
Broadwater Farm Youth Association (BWFYA) 172
Brockway, Fenner 66, 68, 92, 126, 127-8, 136, 247, 248
Brooke, Henry 132
Brown, George 136-7
Brown, Gordon 188
Brown, Usha 217
Bryan, Beverley 143
Buck, Anthony 131
BUFP *see* Black Unity and Freedom Party
BWFYA *see* Broadwater Farm Youth Association

Callaghan, James 134
Cameron, Verney Lovett 48
Campaign against Racial Discrimination (CARD) 129, 132, 148
CAR *see* Council for Aboriginal Rights
CARD *see* Campaign against Racial Discrimination
Carmichael, Stokely 149, 166, 231, 234
Casement, Roger 14, 46, 51, 53, 54
Central Gurdwara 213
Channel Four 195
Chhokar, Surjit Singh 211
Christian Evidence Society 30

Christianity 1, 25, 27, 29, 38, 51, 112, 128
  Anglican Church 4
  Brotherhood Church 29
  Christian cooperative movement 86
  Christian socialism 82
  missionaries 8, 49–50
  Quakers 14, 29–30
citizenship 3, 6–7, 15, 37, 69, 71, 83, 103, 144, 199–200, 235–6, 242
Civil and Public Services Association (CPSA) 215
Civil Rights Act 1964 (USA) 132
CMEB *see* Commission for Multi-Ethnic Britain
Cole, Irene 110, 115
Collins, Michael 189, 195–8, 202–3
Collins, Sidney 116
Colonial Defence Association 166
Colonial House, North Shields 105, 112, 113
Colonial Office 6, 35, 37, 109, 110, 111–12, 115, 117
colonial rebellion 26
Colonial Students' Club 105, 107, 110, 111
colourblindness/colorblindness 14, 229–30, 231, 232–3, 236, 237, 238–9
Coloured Seamen's Association 111
Colston, Edward 1, 8, 176
Commission for Multi-Ethnic Britain (CMEB) 233
Commission for Racial Equality (CRE) 137, 138, 200, 201, 218
Commonwealth Immigrants Act 1962 124
Commonwealth of Nations 91
Communism 65–6
Communist Party 67, 89, 90, 94
  Communist Party of Great Britain (CPGB) 213
  Communist Party of India (CPI) 213
Community Relations Councils 217
Congo Reform Movement 9, 12, 14, 44, 46–7, 53, 57–8
Conrad, Joseph 46, 54, 65
Conservative Party 155
Constantine, Learie 132, 247
Cooper, Anna J. 33

Council for Aboriginal Rights (CAR) 83
COVID-19 pandemic 13, 16, 175–6, 178
CPGB *see* Communist Party of Great Britain
CPI *see* Communist Party of India
CPSA *see* Civil and Public Services Association
CRE *see* Commission for Racial Equality
cricket 70
Crummell, Alexander 32

Dadzie, Stella 143
Daily Mail 198
Dashiki 167
Davies, Charles Columbus 26
Davis, Angela 175
DCMS *see* Department for Culture, Media and Sport
Defamation Act 1952 126
Department for Culture, Media and Sport (DCMS) 188
Dhingra, Madan Lal 36
Dilke, Charles 45
Douglass, Frederick 26, 234
Doyle, Arthur Conan 46, 51
Du Bois, W. E. B. 34, 37
Duggan, Mark 238
Dundas, Henry 210

East India Company (EIC) 210, 212
Eddo-Lodge, Reni 229
Edinburgh & District Trades Council 215
Edinburgh African Association 212
Edinburgh Indian Association (EIA) 212
Edinburgh West Indian Association 212
Edwards, Brother Herman 167, 168–70
Edwards, Celestine 14, 30–1, 32, 39
Edwards, Shona 168
EIA *see* East Indian Association
EIC *see* East India Company
Elbow (activist group) 167
Elkin, A. P. 90
Empire Day 27
Equal Rights (activist group) 134
Equality Act 2010 240, 251
Ethiopian Association 35

Ethiopian Progressive Association 35
Ethiopian Review 35
EU *see* European Union
European Parliament 220
European Union (EU) 219, 249
Evening News 25, 35
Ewing, James 210

Family and Kinship in East London (Michael Young and Peter Wilmott) 190, 198
Fanon, Frantz 149
fascism 2, 124, 125, 126, 127, 131–2, 133, 137–9
FCAA *see* Federal Council for Aboriginal Advancement
Federal Council for Aboriginal Advancement (FCAA) 86
First World War 6, 196, 211–12
Fitzpatrick, Brian 91
Five Continents Club 37
Floyd, George 176, 211, 221, 228, 238
FN *see* Front National
Foot, Dingle 131
Forbes, Forbes & Campbell 210
Foreign Office 46
Fox, Laurence 229, 231–2, 236
Fraternity 30, 31
Free University for Black Studies 167
Freedom News 167
Freeson, Reg 129
Front National 218
Froudacity: West Indian Fables Explained (J. J. Thomas) 70
Futters industrial dispute 174

Galton, Francis 36
Garnett, Charles 36
Garvey, Amy Ashwood 67
Garvey, Marcus 37
gendered violence 12
George Jackson Trust 167
George Padmore School 166
Gillespie, James 210
GLC *see* Greater London Council
Gluckman, Max 88
GMB union 219
Goldberg, Denis 219
Gove, Michael 233–4

Grassroots 167
Greater London Council (GLC) 187, 188
Griffiths, Peter 132
Grunwick industrial dispute 11, 174
Gryffe Women's Aid 213
Guardian 155, 191
Guinness, Henry G. 45

Haddon, Alfred 89
Hakim, Zaffir 220
Hall, Stuart 146
Hampton, Fred 167
Harambee 16, 165, 167, 168–70, 175, 178
Hardie, Keir 31
Haringey Labour Movement 172
Harris, Alice 46
Harris, John 14, 31, 46
Harry, Prince, duke of Sussex 231
Hattersley, Roy 187
Heath, Edward 213
Hedge, John 25, 28
Hindu Mandir Sabha 213
Hinduism 136
  British Hindu communities 153
Hines, Vince 167
Hobsbawm, E. J. E. 89
Hodkinson, Mark 197
Hogg, Quintin 134, 137
How the West Indian Child Is Being Made Educationally Subnormal in the British School System (Bernard Coard) 171
Howe, Darcus 187
Human Rights Commission 84
humanitarianism 2, 9, 25, 29, 31, 44–7, 49, 50–1, 53, 54–5, 56–7, 74
Huxley, Julian 89

IASB *see* International African Service Bureau
ICMAA *see* International Coloured Mutual Aid Association
Ighodaro, Samuel 115
ILP *see* Independent Labour Party
Immigration Act 1971 213
Impey, Catherine 26, 29–30, 32
Independent Labour Party (ILP) 65–8, 73, 196

Indian Association 213
Indian Graduates' Association 213
Indian National Congress 73
Indian rebellion of 1857 26
Indian Social and Cultural
　　Association 213
Indian Workers' Associations (IWA)
　　144, 149, 174, 213
　Indian Workers Association
　　Glasgow 213
　Indian Workers' Association Southall
　　(IWA Southall) 150
Industrial Relations Act 1971 213
Institute for Community Studies 200
Institute of Race Relations 4
International African Service Bureau
　　(IASB) 66–7, 70–2
International Coloured Mutual
　　Aid Association (ICMAA)
　　105, 112–14
International Convention on the
　　Elimination of All Forms of
　　Racial Discrimination 45
International Friendship League 107
International Men's Day 239
International Peace Campaign 81
International Seamen Union 110
Islam 136
　British Muslim communities
　　153, 155
Islamophobia 188, 198, 211, 234
IWA *see* Indian Workers' Associations

Jacob, Willibald 219
James, C. L. R. 15, 67, 68,
　　69, 222
Janner, Barnett 126, 131
Janner, Greville 137
Jenkins, Roy 135, 136
Jenkins, Simon 191–2
Jewish Chronicle 131, 136
John, Gus 167
Johnston, Harry 46, 53
Jones, Chris 67
Jones, Claudia 247
Joseph, H. Mason 32, 36
Jowell, Jeffrey 124, 129

Kashatre Sahba 213
Kashmiri Association 213

Kenmure Street protests 177
Kenyatta, Jomo 67
Keskidee 167
Kiffin, Dolly 172
King, Bernice 240
King, Martin Luther 17, 229, 230,
　　231–3, 234, 239–41, 242, 252
King, Rodney 234
Kinloch, Alice 14, 32, 39
Kinnock, Neil 187
Kipling, Rudyard 47
Kropotkin, Peter 164
Kwame Nkrumah School 166

Labour Party 128, 187–8, 214,
　　215, 247
Langton, Bernard 125, 132
Larbi, Koi Obuadabang 108,
　　111–12, 116–17
Lawrence, Doreen 234
Lawrence, Neville 234
Lawrence, Stephen 211, 229, 242
LCP *see* League of Coloured Peoples
Le Pen, Jean-Marie 218, 219
League of Coloured Peoples (LCP) 83,
　　104, 109, 110, 111
League of Universal Brotherhood
　　and Native Races Association
　　(LUBNRA) 36
Léopold II 46, 48–50, 51, 57, 94
Lester, Anthony 124, 129, 134,
　　135–6, 137
liberalism 2, 3, 14, 80, 132, 235, 248
Lincoln, Fredman Ashe 129
Likes of Us, The (Michael Collins) 189,
　　195–8, 202–3, 252
Livingstone, Iain 211
Livingstone, Ken 187
Locke, Alain 35
Long, Edward 209
Lothian Black Forum 217
LUBNRA *see* League of Universal
　　Brotherhood and Native Races
　　Association
Lux 30
Lyle, Abram 210

Maclean. John 212
Macpherson Report 1999 233–4
Makonnen, T. Ras 67, 70

Malcolm X Montessori Programme 166
Malinowski, Bronisław 88
Mangena, Alfred 35
Marcus Garvey School 166
Markle, Meghan 229, 230, 231, 233, 236
Marriages Act 1949 138
Marxism 149
Mau Mau uprising in Kenya (1952–1960) 89
Mayo, Isabella 30
McCubbin, Henry 217
McKinstry, Leo 197
McLeod, Don 86, 87
Merriman-Labor, A. B. C. 26
Middleton, Francis 214
Migration Watch 201, 203
Miller, Maurice 129, 136
miners' strikes (1984–85) 11
Minto, Charles Udor 112–13, 116–17
Mirza, Munira 251
Mohanty, Kunal 211
Monday Club 126
Montgomerie, Mary Bennett 92
Moody, Harold 110
Morant Bay Rebellion 26
Morel, Edmund D. 14, 38, 45, 52, 54, 55
Morris, Olive 167
Mosley, Oswald 127
multiculturalism 2, 9, 16, 135, 175, 188–9, 192, 195, 196–8, 200–3, 229, 230, 234, 235, 251, 253
Murphy, Jim 220
mutual aid 9, 13, 16, 103, 111, 112, 114, 117, 118, 179, 234, 248

Naoroji, Dadabhai 30
NALGO *see* National and Local Government Officers' Association
National and Local Government Officers' Association (NALGO) 214, 218
National Council of Women 128
National Front 136, 139, 189, 212
National Health Service (NHS) 191, 193
National Peace Council 81
National Socialist Movement Trafalgar Square Meeting 1962 128
National Society for the Protection of the Dark Races 35
National Union of Public Employees 215
National Union of Students (NUS) 218
nationalism 3, 11
Natives Land Act, 1913 32
Negro Welfare Association 166
neoliberalism 165, 179, 235
New Beacon Books 167
New East End, The (Geoffrey Dench et al.) 202
New Leader 66, 67
Newcastle International Club 106, 107
Nigerian Civil Service 114
North East Coast Exhibition, 1929 106
Northern riots 2001 234
Nunoo, Titus Henry 107
NUS *see* National Union of Students

Odulate, Albert 110, 115
Odulate, Folake 115
Oluwale, David 238
Omoniye, Bandele 39
O'Neill, Gilda 190–5, 202
Orbach, Maurice 129, 134
Organisation of Women of African and Asian Descent (OWAAD) 153, 165, 167, 172, 174
Orwell, George 15, 64–6, 68–9, 71–4
Orwell Prize 197
Osamor, Martha 170, 171, 172, 179
OWAAD *see* Organisation of Women of African and Asian Descent
Oyenuga, Victor 103, 107

Padmore, George 15, 67–72, 73–4
Pall, Subash 217
Pan African Association 32–3
Pan-African Conference, 1900 31, 33–4, 35
Pan-African Federation 116
pan-Africanism 1, 15, 37, 66, 67, 68–9, 70, 104, 110, 112, 115, 116, 117, 118
Partido Obrero de Unificación Marxista 66
paternalism 2, 4–5, 7, 13, 55, 58, 67, 68, 73, 104, 169, 173, 208, 222, 236, 247

260 Index

Philip, Prince, Duke of Edinburgh 191
Phillips, Trevor 200–1
Pindan cooperative 86, 87, 91
Plaatje, Sol 29, 31, 36
Pleasant Sunday Afternoon movement 29
Plummer, Leslie 126
Police, Crime, Sentencing and Courts Act 2022 177
political Blackness 10, 12, 13, 16, 146, 148, 150, 154–9, 208, 250–1
Porter Report on Defamation 1948 126
Powell, Enoch 136, 194
Protocols of the Elders of Zion 126
Public Order Act 1936 125
Public Order Act 1963 132
Public Order Act 1986 137
Pull No More Bines (Gilda O'Neill) 190

Quinlan, John 35
Quit India Movement 73

RAAS *see* Radical Action Adjustment Society
Race Relations Acts 9, 15–16, 139
  Race Relations Act 1965 124, 130, 138, 249
  Race Relations Act 1968 135
  Race Relations Act 1976 137
Race Relations Board 15–16
race riots of 1919 166, 212
racialisation 138
Radical Action Adjustment Society (RAAS) 166, 167, 169
Ramdin, Ron 143
Ramgharia Association 213
Reagan, Ronald 230, 232, 252
Red Cross 113
Report of the Commission on Race and Ethnic Disparities 2021 251–2
Robeson, Eslanda 83
Robeson, Paul 83, 212
Robinson, Cedric 71
Rose, Fred 88, 89–91
Rose, Jim 129
Rose, Paul 129, 136
Royal Anthropological Institute 83
Rubusana, W. B. 37
Runnymede Trust 134, 200

SAAC *see* Scottish Asian Action Committee
SARM *see* Scottish Anti-Racist Movement
SBS *see* Southall Black Sisters
Scafe, Suzanne 143
Scarman Report 174
Scholes, Theophilus 26, 35, 39
scientific racism 25, 26
Scoles, Theophilus 14
Scott, Michael 83
Scott, Stafford 172
Scottish Anti-Racist Alliance 218
Scottish Anti-Racist Movement (SARM) 217
Scottish Asian Action Committee (SAAC) 212–13, 214, 215, 218, 219, 222–3
Scottish Council for Civil Liberties 217
Scottish Immigrant Labour Council 213
Scottish International Labour Council 217
Scottish Labour Party 217, 220
Scottish Low Pay Unit 217
Scottish National Party (SNP) 215, 217
Scottish Parliament 208
Scottish Professional Footballers' Association 216
Scottish Trades Union Congress (STUC) 208, 214, 215, 218–20, 222
Seale, Bobby 148
Second Boer War 33
Second World War 6, 71–4, 79–80, 107, 111–14, 124, 193, 199
Seme, Isaac Pixley 35
September 11 2001 attack 188, 198
Sewell, Tony 251
Sharpton, Al 230
Sheekh, Axmed Abuukar 211
Shinwell, Emanuel 211
Shri Guru Ravi Dass Sabha 213
Sikh Sabha Association 213
Sikhism 136
  British Sikh communities 152–3
Sivanandan, Ambalavaner 143, 146, 165
Smith, Dudley 134
SNP *see* Scottish National Party
socialism 1, 31, 143–4, 145, 146–7, 148, 150, 151, 154, 157

Socialist League 31
Society for the Cultural Advancement
    of Africa 105, 107, 108, 115
Society for the Recognition of
    the Brotherhood of Man
    (SRBM) 30, 32
Society of Labour Lawyers 129
solidarity 1, 3–4, 8, 10–14, 16, 17, 44,
    55, 58, 67, 72, 74, 79, 104,
    110–11, 116, 132, 144, 147, 148,
    149, 151, 153–4, 155, 156–9,
    164, 168, 176, 177, 190, 207–8,
    216, 219, 220–2, 228, 230, 239,
    241, 247, 248, 250
Soofi, Gurdial Singh 213
Soskice, Frank 130, 131, 132
South African Native National
    Congress 31
South Wales Association of the Welfare
    of Coloured People 166
Southall Black Sisters (SBS) 16, 143,
    144–5, 149–51, 152–4, 158,
    159, 173
Southall Youth Movement (SYM) 16,
    143, 144–5, 149–52, 158, 159
South-East London Summer School 166
Sowande, Fela 108
Spade, Dean 168
Spanish Civil War 66
Spender, Harold 14, 47, 51
SRBM see Society for the Recognition
    of the Brotherhood of Man
Sri Lankan Association 213
St Andrew's Day Anti-Racism March
    and Rally 207–8, 212, 216, 217,
    218, 219, 220, 222–3
Stanley, Henry M. 48, 49, 50, 52
Stead, W. T. 34, 52
Straw, Jack 235
Street, Jessie 15, 79–82, 83–4, 85–6,
    87–9, 90–5
Streit, Clarence 64, 73
Sunak, Rishi 237, 249
SUS Law 171, 179
Sylvain, Benito 33
SYM see Southall Youth Movement

Tate and Lyle 210
Tate Modern 197
Taylor, Samuel Coleridge 39

Telegraph 197, 198
terrorist attacks
    11 September 2001 188, 198
    7 July 2005 378, 397
Thomas, J. J. 70
Thompson, E. P. 89, 197
Thompson, Thomas J. 32
Times, The 197, 198, 233
Tobias, David E. 14
Tordzro, Kofi 217
trade unions 11, 31, 39, 82, 125,
    207, 211
Trades Advisory Council 134
Trades Union Congress (TUC) 207
Trinidad Guardian 69
Trump, Donald 241, 249, 252
TUC see Trades Union Congress
Twain, Mark 94

UBWAG see United Black Women's
    Action Group
UCPA see Universal Coloured People's
    Association
UN see United Nations
UNIA see Universal Negro
    Improvement Association
Union Movement 127
United African Association 35
United Black Women's Action Group
    (UBWAG) 16, 165, 167, 168,
    170–2, 175, 178, 179
United Nations 45, 82, 83, 84–5, 92,
    93, 128, 250
Unity Bookshop 167
Universal Coloured People's Association
    (UCPA) 148, 166
Universal Negro Improvement
    Association (UNIA) 37
Universal Races Congress, 1911 36–7
Urban Programme 169–70, 174, 214

Vagrancy Act 1824 171

Wallace-Johnson, I. T. A. 67
Walters, Alexander 33
Washington, Booker T. 234
WASU see West African Students'
    Association
Wedderburn, Robert 212
welfare state 6, 193, 194, 199, 202

Wellesley Cole, Robert 107, 108, 113–14
Wells, Ida B. 14, 30
West African Society, the 105, 110, 114–16
West African Students' Union (WASU) 104, 106, 107, 111
West African Union of Great Britain 108
West African Women's Association 105, 115
West Indian Student Centre 10
West Indies Sailors House 105, 111–12
Wilkinson, Ellen 197
Williams, Henry Sylvester 14, 32, 33, 36, 39
Wilson, Amrit 172–3
Windrush scandal 236–7
Windrush: The Irresistible Rise of Multi-Racial Britain (Trevor Phillips) 200, 202
Women's International League for Peace and Freedom 82, 84
Wood, Wilfred 168
Workers' Educational Association 107
World Jewish Congress 130
World Peace Council 82, 84
Worsley, Peter 88, 89, 90, 91

X, Malcolm 149, 166, 234

Young British Pakistani Initiative Association 213
Yule, Andrew 210

Zander, Michael 129

www.ingramcontent.com/pod-product-compliance
Ingram Content Group UK Ltd.
Pitfield, Milton Keynes, MK11 3LW, UK
UKHW022039050325
4871UKWH00004B/76